Adolph Sutro

Adolph Sutro

*King of the Comstock Lode
and Mayor of San Francisco*

William R. Huber

Forewords by
Patrick Neylan *and*
Charles A. Fracchia

McFarland & Company, Inc., Publishers
Jefferson, North Carolina

LIBRARY OF CONGRESS CATALOGUING-IN-PUBLICATION DATA

Names: Huber, William R., 1941– author. | Neylan, Patrick, writer of foreword. | Fracchia, Charles A., writer of foreword.
Title: Adolph Sutro : king of the Comstock Lode and mayor of San Francisco / William R. Huber ; forewords by Patrick Neylan and Charles A. Fracchia.
Other titles: Adolph Sutro, king of the Comstock Lode and mayor of San Francisco
Description: Jefferson, North Carolina : McFarland & Company, Inc., Publishers, 2020 | Includes bibliographical references and index.
Identifiers: LCCN 2020008064 | ISBN 9781476680392 (paperback) ∞
ISBN 9781476638409 (ebook)
Subjects: LCSH: Sutro, Adolph, 1830–1898. | Mayors—California—San Francisco—Biography. | Mining engineers—Nevada—Biography. | Comstock Lode (Nev.)—Biography. | Sutro Tunnel (Nev.) | Real estate developers—California—San Francisco—Biography. | German-Americans—Biography. | San Francisco (Calif.)—Biography.
Classification: LCC F869.S353 S88 2020 | DDC 979.4/6104092 [B]—dc23
LC record available at https://lccn.loc.gov/2020008064

BRITISH LIBRARY CATALOGUING DATA ARE AVAILABLE

**ISBN (print) 978-1-4766-8039-2
ISBN (ebook) 978-1-4766-3840-9**

© 2020 William R. Huber. All rights reserved

No part of this book may be reproduced or transmitted in any form or by any means, electronic or mechanical, including photocopying or recording, or by any information storage and retrieval system, without permission in writing from the publisher.

On the cover: Lithograph of the Sutro Baths, and image of Adolph Sutro courtesy of Sutro Library, California State Library

---

Printed in the United States of America

*McFarland & Company, Inc., Publishers
Box 611, Jefferson, North Carolina 28640
www.mcfarlandpub.com*

*To the memory of my father,
the first engineer I knew.*

Contents

Acknowledgments   ix
Foreword—Nevada Chapters
    by Patrick Neylan   1
Foreword—San Francisco Chapters
    by Charles A. Fracchia   3
Preface   5
Introduction   9

1. The End   11
2. Roots and Uprooted   13
3. Some That Glitters   16
4. The Country Reacts   23
5. Go West, Young Man   30
6. Sutro, the Shop Owner   37
7. Mr. Sutro Goes to Washoe   44
8. All the News   54
9. Mining in Hell   58
10. From Riches to Rags   65
11. William Ralston—Boat Captain to Financial Captain   68
12. Rehabilitation   74
13. Homework   79
14. Endorsement   83
15. Rejection   88
16. Starting Over   92
17. Workin' on the Railroad   99
18. Mines, Mills and Money   103

19. Start Digging!	107
20. Mr. Sutro Goes to Washington	118
21. That Sounds French	126
22. Sutro Builds Sutro	131
23. Water, Water	136
24. The King Is Dead; Long Live the Kings	138
25. A Hole in the Ground to Pour Money Into	146
26. The Devil Is in the Details	156
27. A Family Man?	159
28. Return to San Francisco	164
29. Sutro Heights	167
30. Clara and Leah	176
31. The Cliff House—Before Sutro	179
32. The Cliff House—With Sutro	184
33. Gingerbread Palace	191
34. Glass Houses	196
35. The Philobiblist	206
36. His Honor, the Mayor	211
37. Decline, Demise, Disputes	216
38. Epilogue—Nevada	223
39. Epilogue—San Francisco	234
Chapter Notes	249
Bibliography	265
Index	277

Acknowledgments

Writing a book is not an individual effort. Images of Stephen King sitting alone in a cabin in the snow-covered Maine woods are not realistic, at least not for a nonfiction book such as this. An author must have help and lots of it. Much research can come from previous publications and the internet, but personal contact is essential to discover little-known but relevant information.

My help started and continues with my wife, Angie, who encouraged me to write, and who read and critiqued every draft and finished chapter. A nonfiction writing course by Lisa Adams taught me the basics of writing for a general audience, which is far different from the technical writing I had been doing for the previous thirty years.

In Nevada, where Adolph Sutro fought for 20 years to achieve his vision, new friends made my search far easier than Sutro's. Foremost was Patrick Neylan, curator of two museums, the St. Mary in the Mountain's Museum in Virginia City, Nevada, and the Dayton, Nevada, Museum. In addition to his knowledge of Sutro and the treasures contained in his museums, Pat knows everyone in the area and enlisted their aid in finding vintage photos and obscure information. In addition, he acted as a personal guide of the entire Comstock region.

Among those whom Pat introduced me to were Steven Saylor, executive director of the Comstock Foundation, and Don Bergstrom, historian of the Foundation. Steven and Don guided me on a tour of the restored Donovan Mill, answered my questions about milling ore, and corrected numerous errors in my initial text. Other friends of Pat Neylan who contributed information and photos are Stony and Laura Tennant, Greg Hess, and Tim Roth.

My other significant source of information on the Comstock was the Nevada Bureau of Mines and Geology (NBMG) in Reno. Charlotte Stock and Jack Hursh patiently answered my questions and provided unique illustrations.

In San Francisco, the name that recurs when discussing the area at Lands End where Sutro accomplished so much is John Martini. John is a retired National Park Ranger, author of several books about San Francisco, and historical lecturer. I was fortunate to meet John and take his tour of the Sutro Baths area. His knowledge is deep and accurate, and he was willing to share it with me by answering countless questions.

A tour of Sutro Heights by Gene Golfus of the San Francisco City Guides program provided more information about Sutro and his home by the ocean. Gene's insight helped me to understand the history and current status of the area.

Libraries and librarians are the unsung heroes of most books. For me, the Sutro Library within the J. Paul Leonard Library at San Francisco State University was an obvious and essential destination. There Dvorah Lewis, Mattie Taormina, and Diana Kohnke provided tireless and insightful help in finding and providing countless documents. Christina Moretta, at the San Francisco History Center of the San Francisco Public Library, searched for obscure photos that I had vague clues were in the collection, and was able to locate them. Kimberly J. Roberts, at the Special Collections Department of the University of Nevada–Reno, searched for and found several key photos to illustrate the Comstock narrative. Heather Fordham, at the Society of California Pioneers, located high-quality images of the theodolite at the mouth of the Sutro Tunnel, thus confirming how Sutro was able to hit a small target four miles away. Karalea Clough, at the Nevada Historical Society, searched their archives to find a photo of Leah Harris Sutro and another of the Comstock miners cooling off from the heat of the mines. Kami Ingersoll and Tiffani Prentice, of the Nevada Department of Transportation, located a unique photo showing the mill and Sutro Mansion together, the only such photo I have ever seen. For the University of San Francisco Library, which I was unable to visit in person, Jacquie Proctor went for me and spent countless hours searching boxes and taking pictures. Thanks to her and to the librarian, John Hawk.

Reviewers of some or all of my initial drafts include Pat Neylan, Joe Tingley of the Nevada Bureau of Mines and Geology (retired); old friends Ken Owen, Carl Lewis Wagner, Bob Ray, Virgil Koning, Carol Cherne, Pat Hite, and Bill Reed; and new friends Jacquie Proctor, Christine Miller, and noted San Francisco historian, Charles Fracchia. I thank them for their insight, patience, and comments, both kind and critical. The clever program, Grammarly, checked and rechecked my writing for spelling, verb tense, word choice, and other details that often escape me. Of course, as every author says, all errors are mine alone.

Many others provided photos and essential bits of information. Foremost among these are Gary Stark and Dennis O'Rorke of the Cliff House Project, and Rich Blaisdell. Rich is the son of the late Marilyn Blaisdell, who ran the Cliff House Gift Shop and collected thousands of photos of the Cliff House, Sutro Baths, and the surrounding area. In captions, I have noted names or organizations responsible for photos.

Whatever success this book achieves rests on the shoulders of these contributors. Thank you!

Foreword—Nevada Chapters
by Patrick Neylan

Dr. Huber, through careful and extensive research, has woven together threads of every major social, economic, and political event of the late 19th century. With Adolph Sutro and his challenging vision as the central focus, he tells the compelling stories of the foundational players who came together to change the history of Nevada and the West.

For most items in life, the cost of acquisition or creating is simply measured in dollars, but for Adolph Sutro, the cost of fulfilling his dream and creating his monumental tunnel far exceeded just the few million dollars it cost to build. For Mr. Sutro, the price included his family life, his personal life, and even his reputation and integrity. His wife, Leah Sutro, and their children had a high price to pay also.

The discovery and development of the famous Comstock Lode is one of the most significant mining stories in the history of the West. Mining laws, technology, and equipment utilized 150 years ago are still on the books or form the foundation for mining today. In this context, reading the story of the Sutro Tunnel is akin to reading a murder mystery when you already know "the butler did it." As with the mystery, you might know the ending—the tunnel certainly did get built—but you still can't put the book down until you learn how it happened.

The book is a fascinating refresher for the past student of Mr. Sutro, and also a fabulous introduction for a new historian who just stumbled onto the existence of one of the major engineering and construction marvels of the 19th century. What will delight all readers is a look at what has taken place at the tunnel and townsite in the decades since their glory days. The Sutro Tunnel and the town of Sutro still evoke magic and mystery in the hearts of Nevadans.

Patrick Neylan is a Sutro expert and 25-year member of the Historical Society of Dayton (Nevada) Valley and the Nevada Historical Society. He has served as curator of St. Mary in the Mountain's Museum in Virginia City, Nevada, since 2012; and as curator of the Dayton, Nevada, Museum since 2014. He helped develop the 2016 and 2017 tours of the Sutro Tunnel. Mr. Neylan is an avid collector of vintage Cadillacs and resides in Dayton, Nevada.

Foreword—San Francisco Chapters
by Charles A. Fracchia

Adolph Sutro was a protean figure in the history of the West; and William Huber's *Adolph Sutro—King of the Comstock Lode and Mayor of San Francisco* chronicles the decades and personal characteristics that made him so.

Sutro can take his place among the moguls and titans of 19th-century America, by building a diverse financial empire, constructed against all odds. And he accomplished this feat largely without the machinations of a Jay Gould, the violence of a Henry Clay Frick, or the stock manipulation of a James Fiske.

In addition to his innovative engineering genius—which ties him to today's technology titans—Sutro was one of the 19th century's principal book and art collectors, albeit without the discrimination of a Morgan, a Flick, or a Widener.

His personality had much to do with his successes—and his failures. His intransigence caused the Sutro Tunnel to be built. His bumptious inability to compromise put numerous difficulties in the way of his road to successes. His tangled family relationships helped to destroy his legacy.

The intricacies of 19th-century business and financial practices are well laid out by Dr. Huber, who does an excellent job of placing Sutro in the broad context of this maze. Sutro stands out for his nonconventional approach to his empire building. Rather than a mega-mansion on Nob Hill, he opted for a modest home on the western edge of San Francisco, overlooking the Pacific Ocean. Instead of intricate financial operations, the Sutro Tunnel, his principal asset burden, was the result of his creative, inventive genius. And, in opposition to the reactive views and protestations of his fellow financiers, he developed an abiding concern for the working classes.

Sutro's benefactions to the public—Sutro Baths, Sutro Heights, his railroad to the Baths, and his various political attempts to serve the working classes of San Francisco—were doomed, the result of a corrupt age and of his physical and mental deterioration. Even the statues he bequeathed to the public were vandalized and destroyed.

Sutro's perspicuity continues to astonish me. He was one of the only of his contemporary businessmen to appreciate the values of San Francisco real estate, eventually buying one-twelfth of the city.

It is fascinating that all of Sutro's achievements had this approach: the Comstock Tunnel had a very limited use and became obsolete, his remaining book collection exists as a remnant of the once-splendid collection, his art collection and antiquarian holdings are scattered ... the list goes on. And, yet, Sutro's name is one of most prominent of the city's historical figures: Sutro Baths, although gone, is still referenced; Sutro Forest; Sutro Tower. There is probably not another name that remains as prominently and known as his.

Dr. Huber's superb biography records the man and his work in a satisfying manner.

Charles Fracchia, a renowned San Francisco historian, founded the San Francisco Historical Society in 1988. He has taught at City College of San Francisco and the University of San Francisco, lectures extensively throughout the Bay Area, and has been an investment banker for more than 30 years.[1] He is the author of several books describing the history of San Francisco, and the publisher and editor-in-chief of The Argonaut, *the journal of the San Francisco Historical Society.*

Preface

Inspiration

When talking with people about writing this book, the first question they ask, especially if they grew up east of the Rockies, is "Who was Adolph Sutro?" If they are not glassy-eyed after my answer, they invariably ask, "Why on earth did you decide to write about him?" In 1982 I was on a business trip to San Francisco when a colleague recommended eating at the Cliff House. I had never heard of the place but agreed to try it. Nearing the entrance, I noticed what looked like the foundation for a massive building far below on the shore of the Pacific Ocean. I later learned that the foundation was all that remained of the Sutro Baths, once the largest indoor swimming facility in the world with a capacity of over 1,000 swimmers and 24,000 spectators.

On a later trip, I learned that Adolph Sutro, who designed and built the Sutro Baths, had been the mayor of San Francisco and also had something to do with a tunnel on the Comstock Lode. Sutro sounded like a fascinating guy, and I wrote to one of my favorite authors suggesting that he write a biography of Sutro. Fortunately, he never did, and the idea of writing one myself simmered in the background for many years.

After my first career as an integrated circuit designer and manager ended, I became an expert witness in patent litigation cases. Several of my cases took me back to San Francisco, and whenever possible, I visited the Cliff House. The Musee Mecanique (Mechanical Museum), which was then housed in the basement of the Cliff House, held a special fascination for me as an electrical engineer.

In 2017 I moved on to my third career, as an author. The long-delayed biography of Adolph Sutro became my first project, and he turned out to be even more fascinating than I had imagined. Who do you know who built a four-mile-long tunnel in the Nevada desert, the largest enclosed swimming facility in the world, and collected over two hundred thousand items for his private library? The *Jeopardy!* response is, "Who was Adolph Sutro?"

Iconic lithograph of Sutro Baths, circa 1896 (courtesy Sutro Library, California State Library).

Scope

The period from 1848 to 1870 was pivotal in the formation and development of the western United States. The first portion of the book describes the impact of the important milestones of that era on the life of Adolph Sutro.

The discovery of gold in Mexican Alta California, on January 24, 1848, triggered a mass migration of people from all over the world to Yerba Buena, a tiny settlement on the west coast of North America. Just nine days later, a treaty ended the Mexican-American War, resulting in over 500,000 square miles of territory, comprising all or part of what would later form seven western states, becoming part of the United States. Of course, the treaty also resulted in the riches from the California gold flowing to the citizens and government of the United States. California became a state on September 9, 1850. Yerba Buena grew from under 1,000 people in 1847 to become San Francisco, the dominant city in the western United States in 1900, with a population of 343,000 people.

In 1859, gold and then silver were discovered near Virginia City, Nevada Territory. With a total value of over $400 million at the time of production, the Comstock Lode was comparable in value to the California gold mines. Almost all of the Comstock riches flowed to San Francisco, facilitating the growth of that city.

The Pony Express, from April 1860 to October 1861, aided communication with the isolated west, carrying news of the Comstock Lode to the rest of the country. But the completion of a transcontinental telegraph line in October 1861 immediately made the Pony Express obsolete.

The American Civil War (1861–1865) had minimal impact on the west, but, along with the value of the Comstock, contributed to early statehood for Nevada in 1864.

Construction of the transcontinental railroad started in 1863 and culminated with the driving of the golden spike in 1869. The 1,912-mile route connected the existing eastern rail network near Council Bluffs, Iowa, to Sacramento, California.

The later part of Sutro's life, from 1870 to 1898, saw the addition of Washington, Montana, North Dakota, and South Dakota as states in 1889; Wyoming and Idaho in 1890, and Utah in 1896. While this growth and consolidation were completing the map of the nation, Sutro built his tunnel in Nevada and then moved on to San Francisco to acquire 1/12 of that city's land and build his new empire.

Organization

Adolph Sutro's adult life was a dichotomy. From age 30 to 49, he was laser-focused on a single immense project, planning and executing the Sutro Tunnel on the Comstock Lode in Nevada. From age 50 until his death at age 68, Sutro's life was a frenetic rush to plan and build a multitude of projects, including his hilltop estate called Sutro Heights, an eight-story Victorian Cliff House, the aforementioned massive natatorium called Sutro Baths, two short railroads, and one of the largest private libraries in the United States.

The organization of this biography is similarly split. The first portion, from Sutro's birth in Prussia to the completion of his Sutro Tunnel, is chronological, with a few diversions to provide a broader context to Sutro's activities. The second portion, Sutro's San Francisco years, explores each of his projects in dedicated chapters. It is amazing that Sutro was able to keep so many large balls in the air, and we can best understand what he did by focusing on each project separately.

In keeping with the split nature of Sutro's life, this biography even has two Forewords and two Epilogues, one each for the Nevada and California locations where Sutro lived his life. But the story is firmly linked together by the man who persevered against all odds.

Research Methodology

The advent of the internet has transformed the task of researching a book. The authors of the first complete biography of Adolph Sutro (published in 1962 and cleverly titled *Adolph Sutro—A Biography*[1]) spent 10 years researching and writing their book. They had the advantage of living in California with easy access to the Bancroft Library in Berkeley but had none of the computerized search and recovery tools we enjoy today. In addition to extensive use of the internet, I read or consulted all of the available books about the Comstock Lode and its characters, including Mark Twain, William Ralston, William Sharon, and the Bonanza Kings, John Mackay, James Fair, James Flood, and William O'Brien. But by far the most important and informative research consisted of visits to Carson City, Dayton, and Virginia City, Nevada; and San Francisco. In addition to seeing Sutro's locales, I met true experts on the Comstock Lode and Lands End, the area of San Francisco where Sutro lived and worked. I was able to visit the San Francisco Public Library and the Sutro Library, the founding of which is described in detail in the book.

I have long believed that the best way to learn a subject is to teach it. Now I know that an even more effective way is to write a book about it.

A Note about Money

This book deals with the time period 1830 to 1900, and often specifies an amount of money. That amount is always stated in historic terms, e.g., dollars in 1870. Readers always want to know how much that represents in current dollars. In some instances, I will do a conversion using actual inflation rates from the historic date to the current time, but often I will not. A very simple and reasonably accurate conversion can be made by simply multiplying the historic amount by 20 (double it and add a zero). So $50,000 in 1870 corresponds to about $1 million today.

Introduction

A biography of one born in 1830 is sure to end with the death of the subject, and the opening chapter describes that inevitable outcome. Then we start at the beginning, with the Sutro family in Prussia in the 1820s. The Sutros were wealthy Jews, allowed to reside in Prussia and serve in the military, but not allowed to be full citizens. Given their wealth, the Sutros were less persecuted than their poorer compatriots, but the prejudice affected all Jews. Without letters of "protection" from the government, Jews were prohibited from most trades and professions. To marry, a Jew had to purchase a *matrikel*, or registration certificate, costing 1,000 guldens (about $720 U.S. dollars in 1850, or $14,000 today). As a result, over 250,000 Jews emigrated from Prussia or Germany to the United States between 1840 and the beginning of World War I in 1914.[1,2] Most of the Sutro family joined that flow of Jewish immigrants to America.

Chapter 1

The End

I hate biographies; they always end badly.
—William Huber

Less than two years earlier, in January 1897, Adolph Sutro had been mayor of San Francisco, but today he did not know where he was. Sutro was dying, and his favorite child, Emma Sutro Merritt, had defied her siblings by removing him from his beloved Sutro Heights estate to her apartment. Emma and her husband were both physicians, and Emma had been named Adolph's guardian by the court. But she provided no rational explanation for the move, and it accelerated a rift with her five siblings that would grow wide upon Sutro's death.

On August 8, 1898, at the age of 68, Adolph Sutro died. A simple Hebrew funeral followed on August 10, and Sutro took his last trip, in a hearse, to the crematory at Odd Fellows' Cemetery.

The only will left by Adolph Sutro was written in 1882, after he was legally separated from his wife, Leah, who died on December 9, 1893. Sutro's children gathered to hear his will read on August 11, 1898, the day after the funeral.[1] In the will, Sutro named numerous relatives, including his brothers, sisters, nieces, and nephews, as beneficiaries of up to $30,000 each. Politicians and judges who helped Sutro in his various legal fights also received from $2,000 to $10,000. Sutro's will endowed two scholarships totaling $10,000 at Vassar College in Poughkeepsie, New York. Daughter Emma received "all the books, papers, scrapbooks, manuscripts and pictures contained in my library; also all private papers, letters,

Adolph Sutro with his muttonchop sideburns ca. 1870s.

accounts and account books, and all other written papers, whether contained in my desk, safes or safe deposit vault or elsewhere."

But the largest and most controversial bequest read as follows:

> Unto Miss Hattie Trundle of Washington D.C., heretofore known as Mrs. George Allen, the sum of fifty thousand dollars ($50,000) as a reparation, as far as it may be possible, for the injury done her by a scandalous charge, falsely and maliciously, at Virginia City, State of Nevada, in the month of July, 1879, then and there brought against her.

Sutro's children were left to wonder, "Who the hell is Hattie Trundle, and why is our father compensating her for a scandalous charge?"

Chapter 2

Roots and Uprooted

Happy are those who dream dreams and are ready to pay the price to make them come true.
—Cardinal Leo Joseph Suenens

Charlemagne, or Charles the Great, reigned as king of the Franks from 768 to 814 AD and united most of Europe.[1] He named Aachen, Prussia (*Aix-la-Chapelle* in French) as his preferred Imperial residence and capital of his empire.[2]

Located on the western border of Prussia near present-day Belgium and the Netherlands, Aachen was later the residence of Emanuel Sutro and his wife. Emanuel and his elder brother, Simon, had married sisters, Rosa and Helena Warendorff. The brothers, sons of Samuel Abraham Sutro and Ester Baruch, founded and operated a woolen cloth factory known as "S. and E. Sutro." Emanuel and Rosa Sutro were prosperous and lived in a 20-room mansion at Bergdriesch 48.[3]

Over a span of 18 years, they filled the house with 11 overactive children, seven boys and four girls[4]:

1. Emanuel (nicknamed "Sali") Sutro (January 14, 1827–October 2, 1908)[5]
2. Juliana Sutro (March 2, 1828–September 26, 1904)[6]
3. Adolph Heinrich Joseph Sutro (April 29, 1830–August 8, 1898)[7]
4. Emil Sutro (February 16, 1832–October 27, 1906)[8]
5. Otto Sutro (February 24, 1833–January 19, 1896)[9]
6. Hugo Aron Sutro (August 9, 1837–May 10, 1906)[10]
7. Laura Sutro (1838–August 5, 1869)[11]
8. Ludwig Sutro (April 8, 1839–March 17, 1920)[12]

Map showing Aachen, Germany, then in Prussia (courtesy Mapswire.com).

9. Elise Sutro (August 4, 1840–September 28, 1899)[13]
10. Emma Bertha Sutro (September 21, 1841–August 8, 1926)[14]
11. Theodore Sutro (March 14, 1845–August 28, 1927)[15]

In the large family, Adolph in particular tried the patience of his parents. He once jumped from a second-floor window to escape punishment for violating family rules. His small chemical laboratory yielded satisfying explosions, and a broken clock tested his mechanical skills.

Of all Adolph's interests, his favorites were books and machinery. At age seven he started to buy books at local sales, usually far exceeding the allowance provided by his parents. Adolph learned at a young age how to spend money on the things he wanted. The large complex machines at his father's woolen factory fascinated and educated young Adolph. The employees there happily taught him the intricacies of their craft, especially how to detect defects in the cloth. Adolph became an expert in wool cloth and how to manufacture it.

Adolph's father, Emanuel, died December 8, 1847, at the age of 55 from injuries suffered in a carriage accident. Adolph, age 17, reluctantly dropped out of school to work with his older brother, Sali, in managing his father's cloth business. But the violent German Revolutions of 1848–1849[16] destroyed their market, and the boys closed the mill.[17] Sali, lured by reports from relatives who had emigrated to the United States and now lived in Birmingham, Alabama, left for the United States himself to become a salesman.

Meanwhile, Mr. O.G. Kaapche, a rich industrialist from Memel, East Prussia, visited Aachen to inspect and purchase surplus equipment from the shuttered Sutro woolen mill. His goal was to establish a cloth mill in a vacant public bathhouse in Memel that he had purchased for that purpose. Impressed with Adolph's knowledge (Adolph spoke German, French, and English) and abilities, Kaapche recruited him to remodel the bathhouse, establish the factory, hire workers, and manage the mill. Adolph could live rent-free in a suite of rooms inside the factory.[18] With the blessing of his mother, Rosa, Adolph accepted the offer.

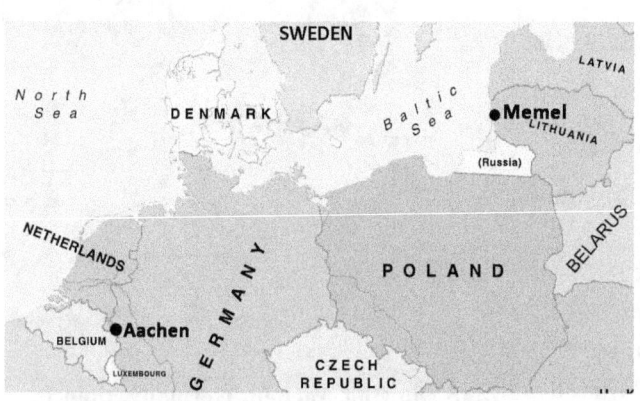

Map showing Aachen and Memel on a modern map. Memel, East Prussia, is now Klaipėda, Lithuania (courtesy Mapswire.com).

Memel was on the eastern shore of the Baltic Sea, 1,100 miles from Aachen; and Adolph traveled there by train, steamship, and coach. The trip was a revelation to an 18-year-old who had never been far outside of Aachen.

Mr. Kaapche had considered all possible problems regarding a cloth mill except one: water. Clear, soft water was necessary for rinsing the wool to make it soft and white. While roaming the country buying wool, Adolph reported to his mother, "I found near the factory a brook, clear as crystal, which has very soft water and is of great value for the factory."[19] Adolph arranged to have a pipe installed from the stream to the factory and agreed to pay $12 per year to the government for the water. Water, either too little or too much, would be the focus of Adolph's entire life.

Adolph missed his family, especially his recently deceased father and his loving mother. Each Sunday he wrote long letters to his family, pleading that they would write back to him, praising the beauty of Memel, commenting on the progress in establishing the cloth factory, and offering guidance to his mother and siblings. But brother Sali, newly situated in the United States, also provided advice. Adolph wanted brother Emil to stay in agricultural school, and Otto to continue his musical education. Sali countered that the whole family should come to Baltimore to work in the retail store that Sali would establish there.

In one letter Adolph told his mother that he had built an iron forge as part of the cloth factory. He wrote, "…the forge is working day and night, because we make all the iron we need for doors and windows ourselves. In the same way Mr. Kaapche is making everything for his ships in the forge. You cannot imagine how convenient it is to have a forge in the factory."[20]

By the end of 1849, Rosa had decided to stay in Aachen. The Memel cloth factory was now operating and had produced 12 large sections of cloth. Mr. Kaapche awarded Adolph a raise in salary to about $467 per year,[21] plus one-fourth of the profits from the mill.[22]

By February 1850, Mr. Kaapche had another offer for Adolph. He proposed to sell the newly completed mill to Adolph and would loan him money and help him secure bank credit to facilitate the purchase.[23] But again, war was imminent. Bitter rivals Prussia and Austria were equipping their armies. Adolph was reluctant to buy the mill with this hostility in the air, so Mr. Kaapche decided to close it and Adolph was suddenly unemployed.

With Adolph out of work, three of her sons likely to be drafted, and Sali beckoning, Rosa made the momentous decision: she would take her family to the United States. She instructed Adolph to return home by way of Antwerp, where he should buy steamship passage to the United States in August 1850 for the whole family except Otto and Emil, who would continue their educations as Adolph had suggested earlier. Then Adolph was to buy supplies for Sali's new store in Baltimore. At the age of 20, Adolph was no longer a woolen mill manager and part owner; he was again a son following his mother's orders.[24]

Rosa Sutro and eight of her children, ages four to 21, departed from Antwerp for New York in August 1850 aboard the ship *Peter Hattrick* with John E. Rockwell, master. Sali Sutro, of course, was already in the United States; Otto and Emil remained in Aachen to continue their studies. The *Hattrick* carried 219 passengers in steerage; the Sutros were nine of just 14 fortunate passengers berthed in cabins. They carried with them 38 crates of clothing, bedding, and furniture, much of it intended for Sali's Baltimore store.[25]

The Atlantic crossing took about six weeks, and speculation about the discovery of gold at a place called Sutter's Mill in California filled every waking moment.

Chapter 3

Some That Glitters

Gold—what can it not do, and undo?
—William Shakespeare

In late January 1848, John Sutter considered the alternatives: Would the discovery of gold at his mill lead to incalculable wealth, or would the chaos of thousands of starry-eyed prospectors destroy his property and life?

Born February 15, 1803, in Kandern, Germany, Johann Sutter was educated in Switzerland and married Anna Dubeld, the daughter of a wealthy widow, on October 24, 1826. But his profligate spending habits soon depleted his wife's resources, and he faced legal action. Rather than risk jail, Sutter left his wife of 7½ years and four children and sailed on the ship *Sully* in May 1834, bound for New York City. It would take 18 years for the family to be reunited.

Now known as John Augustus Sutter, he traveled extensively, first to the St. Louis area, then to Santa Fe, New Mexico (then a province of Mexico). From there he moved north and west to Westport in the Oregon Territory. In 1838 he joined a group of missionaries and journeyed via the Oregon Trail to Fort Vancouver, Oregon Territory. Still seeking adventure, and also easy money, Sutter crossed the sea again, this time on the British ship *Columbia*, bound for Hawaii. He arrived in Honolulu on December 9, 1838. Ever the self-promoter, Sutter made friends among the politicians and merchants of Hawaii for the next four months. Then on April 20, 1839, he hired the brig *Clementine* to sail to New Archangel (now Sitka, Alaska), capital of the Russian-American Company colonies. Always on the lookout for influential friends, Sutter joined several balls hosted by Russian governor Kupreyanov. Finally, Sutter sailed on the *Clementine* to Alta California, then a Mexican province, arriving on July 1, 1839, at Yerba Buena (now San Francisco). In total, Sutter traveled over 10,000 miles by land and sea in the five years after he arrived in New York City.

To obtain permission to settle in the Mexican territory, Sutter had to visit the governor, Juan Bautista Alvarado, in Monterey, Alta California. The governor granted permission to settle and purchase land provided Sutter reside in the territory for one year and become a Mexican citizen. By mid–1841 Sutter had fulfilled his residency requirement, completed a fortified settlement, which he called New Helvetia (New Switzerland),

and received title to almost 49,000 acres on the Sacramento River. The site of New Helvetia, commonly called Sutter's Fort, is now part of the California state capital of Sacramento.[1,2,3] The 48 survivors of the tragic and infamous Donner Party were taken to Sutter's Fort in early 1847 to recuperate.[4,5]

As more settlers entered California, Sutter conceived other projects that could become moneymakers. One of these was a sawmill in the foothills of the Sierra Nevada to provide lumber for constructing a flour mill for Sutter as well as buildings and fences in the small village of Yerba Buena. Various Indian and Mexican skirmishes delayed the search for a suitable site for the sawmill, but by June 1847 a drifter from New Jersey named James W. Marshall met Sutter and proposed a partnership. If Sutter outfitted him, Marshall would locate an appropriate site and build the sawmill, the output of which would then be shared by Sutter and Marshall.[6]

In about a month, Marshall returned with news of a suitable site on the South Fork of the American River at Coloma, California. But several factors, among them lack of money, scarcity of trustworthy laborers, and hostile Indians, delayed the beginning of construction.

By luck or divine providence, the enlistment period of the Mormon Battalion ended in July 1847. The Mormon Battalion, the only religiously based unit in United States military history, had been formed of about 550 volunteers to support the United States in the Mexican-American War of 1846–1848. The battalion had marched almost 2,000 miles from Council Bluffs, Iowa, to San Diego, California. The men were discharged on July 16, 1847, in Los Angeles.[7,8,9]

On August 26, 1847, remnants of the Mormon Battalion arrived and camped on

Route of the Mormon battalion (adapted from Briancole at English Wikipedia).

the American River, about two miles from Sutter's Fort at New Helvetia. Among the Mormon party were carpenters, blacksmiths, wheelwrights, millwrights, farmers, and common laborers. They were seeking employment so they could buy horses, cattle, and supplies for traveling east the next summer to rejoin their families in the Salt Lake Valley. To Sutter's delight, they were willing to accept livestock and supplies as part of the payment for their work.

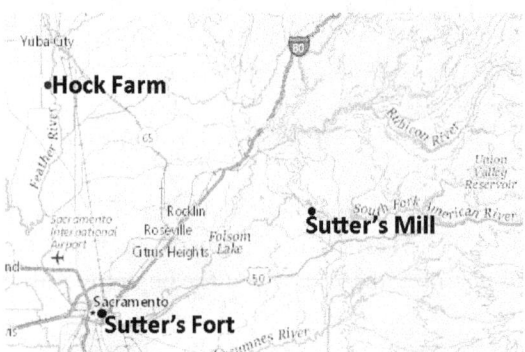

Sutter's Mill was about 40 miles northeast of Sutter's Fort and present-day Sacramento.

By early September 1847, a group of about 50 Mormons had been hired by Sutter and traveled with Marshall from Sutter's Fort to the site proposed for the sawmill.[10]

In early January 1848, construction of the mill was complete, and water was diverted to start it up. But the ditch or millrace that was to carry water away from the wheel was not wide or deep enough. Therefore, the water backed up and kept the wheel from turning. Marshall decided to fully open the gates above the wheel and allow the full volume of the American River to run through the race overnight, thus scouring out the race and making it wider and deeper.

Marshall's plan worked. On the morning of January 24, 1848, he shut the gates above the wheel and examined the race. The rushing current had dug away the sides and bottom and deposited a great mass of sand and gravel at the end of the ditch. Among the gravel, under about six inches of water, Marshall noticed several shiny, yellow flakes. He picked out one flake and examined it. He knew of just two minerals with this appearance: sulphuret of iron (iron pyrites, or "fool's gold"), which is bright and brittle; and gold, which is bright, heavy, and malleable. Marshall worked the sample between two stones and found he could hammer it into various shapes without breaking it. It must be gold![11]

Sutter's Mill as it appeared at the time of the discovery of gold.

Henry W. Bigler, one of the two mill workers who kept a diary, wrote, "This day some kind of mettle was found in the tail race that looks like goald."[12]

As soon as he could

ready himself, Marshall traveled to New Helvetia with two or three ounces of samples to meet his partner. Sutter, who by now had bestowed the rank of captain before his name, recalled the meeting.[13]

> I was sitting one afternoon, ... when I was interrupted by Mr. [James] Marshall, a gentleman with whom I had frequent business transactions—bursting hurriedly into the room. From the unusual agitation in his manner, I imagined that something serious had occurred, and, as we involuntarily do in this part of the world, I at once glanced to see if my rifle was in its proper place. You should know that the mere appearance of Mr. Marshall at that moment at the Fort, was quite enough to surprise me, as he had but two days before left the place to make some alterations in a mill for sawing pine planks, which he had just run up for me, some miles higher up the Americanos [American River]. When he had recovered himself a little, he told me that, however great my surprise might be at his unexpected reappearance, it would be much greater when I heard the intelligence he had come to bring me. "Intelligence," he added, "which if properly profited by, would put both of us in possession of unheard-of-wealth—millions and millions of dollars, in fact." I frankly own, [words missing in typescript] when I heard this that I thought something had touched Marshall's brain when suddenly all my misgivings were put at an end to by his flinging on the table a handful of scales of pure virgin gold. I was fairly thunderstruck and asked him to explain what all this meant, when he went on to say, that according to my instructions, he had thrown the mill-wheel out of gear, to let the whole body of water in the dam find a passage through the tail race, which was previously too narrow to allow the water to run off in sufficient quantity, whereby the wheel was prevented from efficiently performing its work. By this alteration, the narrow channel was considerably enlarged, and a mass of sand and gravel carried off by the force of the torrent. Early in the morning after this took place, Mr. Marshall was walking along the left Bank of the stream when he perceived something which he at first took for a piece of opal, a dark transparent stone, very common here—glittering on one of the spots laid bare by the sud-

Site of Sutter's Mill, on the South Fork of the American River (photo by author).

denly crumbling away of the bank. He paid no attention to this, but while he was giving directions to the workmen, having observed several similar glittering fragments, his curiosity was so far excited, that he stooped down and picked one of them up. "Do you know," said Mr. Marshall to me, "I positively debated within myself two or three times whether I should take the trouble to bend my back to pick up one of the pieces and had decided on not doing so when farther on, another glittering morsel caught my eye—the largest of the pieces now before you. I condescended to pick it up, and to my astonishment found that it was a thin scale of what appears to be pure gold." He then gathered some twenty or thirty pieces which on examination convinced him that his suppositions were correct. His first impression was that this gold had been lost or buried there, by some early Indian tribe—perhaps some of those mysterious inhabitations of the west, of whom we have no account, but who dwelt on this continent centuries ago, and built those cities and temples, the ruins of which are scattered about these solitary wilds. On proceeding, however, to examine the neighboring soil, he discovered that it was more or less auriferous. This at once decided him. He mounted his horse and rode down to me as fast as it could carry him with the news.

At the conclusion of Mr. Marshall's account, and when I had convinced myself, from the specimens he had brought with him that it was not exaggerated, I felt as much excited as himself. I eagerly inquired if he had shown the gold to the workpeople at the mill and was glad to hear that he had not spoken to a single person about it. We agreed not to mention the circumstances to anyone and arranged to set off early the next day for the mill. On our arrival, just before sundown, we poked the sand about in various places, and before long succeeded in collecting between us more than an ounce of gold, mixed up with a good deal of sand. I stayed at Mr. Marshall's that night, and the next day we proceeded some little distance up the South Fork and found that gold existed along the whole course, not only in the bed of the main stream, where the water had subsided but in every little dried-up creek and ravine. Indeed, I think it is more plentiful in these latter places, for I myself, with nothing more than a small knife, picked out from a dry gorge, a little way up the mountain, a solid lump of gold which weighted nearly an ounce and a half.

Notwithstanding our precaution not to be observed, as soon as we came back to the mill we noticed by the excitement of the working people that we had been dogged about, and to complete our disappointment, one of the Indians who had worked at the gold mine in the neighborhood of La Paz cried out in showing us some specimens picked up by himself,—Oro!—Oro—Oro!!! [Gold—Gold—Gold!!!]

Sutter's Hock Farm—first white settlement in Sutter County. On the banks of the Feather River. Established 1844. General John A. Sutter retired to this farm in 1850. Partrially destroyed by debris from mines in flood (Historical Landmark No. 346, Department of Public Works, Division of Highways).

Now the secret was out, and Sutter knew his life would change forever. What he did not know was the direction or magnitude of that change.

On June 12, 1848, an official delegation led by Colonel Richard Barnes Mason and Lieutenant William Tecumseh Sherman commenced a trip to investigate the size and importance of the gold discovery. They were to report their findings to the brigadier-general, R. Jones, adjutant-general in Washington, D.C. They reached Sutter's Fort at New Helvetia on July 2, and said, "Along the whole route mills were lying idle, fields of wheat were open to cattle and horses, houses vacant, and farms going to waste."[14] Sutter's Fort had much more activity. Carts transferred cargo from riverboats to the fort; several

3. Some That Glitters

Lititz, Pennsylvania, home of General John A. Sutter, now the General Sutter Inn (photo by author).

stores and a hotel were crowded; merchants paid monthly rents of $100 for a single-room shop; a two-story house was rented as a hotel for $500 a month.

Despite the booming business at Sutter's Fort, Colonel Sutter (now General Sutter; he had promoted himself again) was in trouble. Sutter wrote,

> So soon as the secret was out my laborers began to leave me, in small parties first, but then all left, from the clerk to the cook, and I was in great distress.... What a great misfortune was this sudden gold discovery for me! It has just broken up and ruined my hard, restless, and industrious labors, connected with many dangers of life, as I had many narrow escapes before I became properly established.
>
> From my mill buildings I reaped no benefit whatever, the mill stones even have been stolen and sold.
>
> My tannery, which was then in a flourishing condition, and was carried on very profitably, was deserted, a large quantity of leather was left unfinished in the vats; and a great quantity of raw hides became valueless as they could not be sold; nobody wanted to be bothered with such trash, as it was called. So it was in all the other mechanical trades which I had carried on; all was abandoned, and work commenced or nearly finished was all left, to an immense loss for me.
>
> By this sudden discovery of the gold, all my great plans were destroyed. Had I succeeded for a few years before the gold was discovered, I would have been the richest citizen on the Pacific shore; but it had to be different. Instead of being rich, I am ruined.[15]

Sutter left New Helvetia and initially moved to another site on the south fork of the American River, about 10 miles above the gold fields. Soon that area also became overrun with prospectors and drinking and gambling establishments. So Sutter returned to New Helvetia, where he retrieved what assets he could and left for his Hock Farm (see map on page 18).

In addition to establishing Sutter's Fort (New Helvetia) on his 49,000-acre grant from Mexico, Sutter built Hock Farm, the first large-scale agricultural settlement in Northern California, cultivating grain, orchards, vineyards, and cattle. The farm was

Tombstone of John and Anna (Dubeld) Sutter (photo by author).

intended by Sutter to be a retirement location for his family.[16,17] To escape the chaos of the gold fields, Sutter retreated to Hock Farm in 1850, and brought his wife and children from Switzerland in 1852, 18 years after he had left them there.

By 1865, the situation at Hock Farm became untenable. Able-bodied men had all deserted to search for gold, and Sutter's financial situation deteriorated. The final insult occurred on June 21, 1865, when a vagrant ex-soldier, whom Sutter allowed to loaf around the farm, started a fire to retaliate against Sutter for having him bound and whipped after being caught stealing. The blaze destroyed the house and all of Sutter's personal records, as well as works of art and priceless relics except for a few treasured medals and portraits that Sutter was able to save.[18]

At the end of 1865, Sutter and his wife left California for good and moved to Washington, D.C., where he petitioned the government for reimbursement of losses associated with the gold rush. He was ultimately awarded a pension of $250 per month.

Finally, in 1871, Sutter and his wife, Anna, moved to Lititz, Pennsylvania, to take advantage of the healing springs and fine Moravian schools where three of his grandchildren could be educated. The Sutters built their new home across from the Lititz Springs Hotel. That home survives today as the General Sutter Inn.

John A. Sutter died on June 18, 1880, at the age of 77, far from his beloved New Helvetia and far from being a rich man. His wife, Anna, died seven months later, on January 19, 1881. He and his wife are buried together in the Moravian Cemetery, God's Acre, in Lititz, Pennsylvania.[19]

Chapter 4

The Country Reacts

Gold conjures up a mist about a man, more destructive of all his old senses and lulling to his feelings than the fumes of charcoal.
—Charles Dickens in *Nicholas Nickleby*

Gold was discovered near Sutter's Mill in the Mexican territory of Alta California on January 24, 1848. In historically bad timing for Mexico, the Treaty of Guadalupe Hidalgo, ending the Mexican-American War, was signed just nine days later, on February 2, 1848.

Under the terms of the treaty, Mexico ceded to the United States all of Upper California, the entire future states of Nevada and Utah, and parts of the future states of Wyoming, Colorado, Arizona and New Mexico. Mexico also relinquished all claims to Texas and recognized the Rio Grande as the southern boundary of the United States. The United States paid Mexico $15 million "in consideration of the extension acquired by the boundaries of the United States."[1] In total, Mexico ceded 525,000 square miles of territory to the United States in return for the $15 million.

The resulting price of four and a half cents per acre was an incredible bargain, comparable to the three cents per acre paid for the Louisiana Purchase in 1803 and the two cents per acre for the Alaska Purchase in 1867.[2] Of course, Mexico also relinquished the riches from the just-discovered gold at Sutter's Mill. Estimates of the value of gold extracted during the gold rush period range from $500M to $2B in 1850 dollars.[3,4] The bulk of that money would now flow to the citizens and government of the United States instead of Mexico.

The treaty of Guadalupe Hidalgo was negotiated under bizarre circumstances by Nicholas Phillip Trist, husband of Thomas Jefferson's granddaughter and chief clerk to Secretary of State James Buchanan. Wallace Ohrt told the story in detail in his 1997 book.[5] Scott Bomboy capsulized the highlights[6]:

> In April 1847, Buchanan (Secretary of State James Buchanan) ordered Trist to go to Mexico when the American victory became apparent. When Mexico City fell to United States troops in September 1847, Trist began peace talks with three Mexican negotiators from that nation's troubled government.
>
> However, Polk (President James K. Polk) wanted the talks to take place in Washington, and he sent orders to Mexico recalling Trist as the treaty negotiator. During the six weeks it took for Polk's orders to make their way to Trist, the diplomat realized he had a brief period to negotiate a treaty with the unstable government in Mexico.
>
> So Trist ignored the recall order and negotiated terms that allowed the United States to buy Cali-

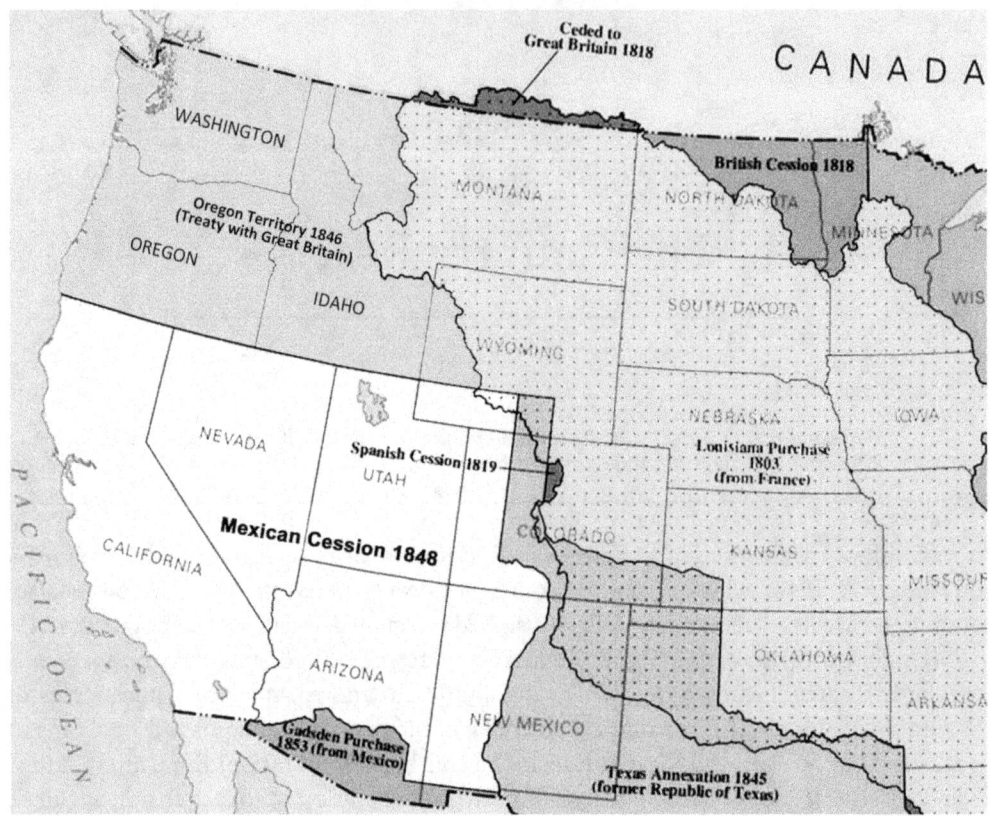

Area colored white was ceded by Mexico under the Treaty of Guadalupe Hidalgo (National Atlas.gov).

fornia (north of the Baja Peninsula), as well as what amounted to half of Mexico's territory for $15 million.

On Trist's return to Washington, he was promptly fired by Polk and denied any salary payments earned during treaty negotiations. He died on February 11, 1874, as a forgotten figure in one of the most significant moments in American history.

It's interesting to contemplate what would have happened if Trist had not ignored Polk's recall order and the resulting delay in completing the treaty had allowed Mexico to find out about the discovery of gold. The treaty with Mexico has had an enormous impact on the development of the United States and Mexico. How might knowledge of the gold discovery have affected the negotiations?

Both news of the discovery of gold and acceptance of that news were slow. A chronology of events after the gold strike reveals initial disbelief followed by increasing excitement and finally hysteria.[7]

- **March 15, 1848:** The *Californian* reported the discovery of gold along the American River at a sawmill owned by Capt. John A. Sutter. San Franciscans remained skeptical.
- **March 25, 1848:** A news item in the *California Star* about the discovery of gold had little impact in San Francisco.

4. The Country Reacts

- **May 12, 1848:** Sam Brannan set off gold fever in San Francisco when he ran through the streets waving a bottle of gold dust and shouting, "Gold! Gold! Gold on the American River!" He had received the gold as payment for goods he sold in his store at Sutter's Fort in New Helvetia.

Sam Brannan's enthusiasm was calculated and self-serving. His arrival in California and subsequent activities are the subjects of several books, many highly critical.[8,9,10,11] Brannan was so instrumental in publicizing the discovery of gold that he deserves our attention. The following discussion is adapted from *Voyage of the "Brooklyn"* by Joan Hamblin.[12]

Seventy men, 68 women, and 100 children, 238 in all, sailed from New York City on February 4, 1846. All but 12 of the passengers were Mormons.[13] They did not have enough money to travel overland as so many other Mormons were doing, so 26-year-old Brother Samuel Brannan had been appointed to lead them on what turned out to be a 24,000-mile voyage to Yerba Buena (now San Francisco) by way of Hawaii. Brannan lived lavishly in the ship's officers' quarters, but that was far from the case for the rest of the passengers. The trip was beyond perilous, with severe overcrowding, tropical and arctic storms, 12 deaths, and two births. Six months later, on July 31, 1846, the exhausted travelers arrived to find that the United States had claimed Yerba Buena in the Mexican-American War.

In San Francisco, Brannan used the printing press he had brought with him on the *Brooklyn* to establish the *California Star* as the first newspaper in San Francisco. The *Star* released its first formal issue on January 9, 1847.

Mormon President Brigham Young would finally arrive in the Salt Lake Valley with the bulk of the Mormon flock on July 24, 1847, a full year after Brannan and his fellow *Brooklyn* passengers arrived in San Francisco. Meanwhile, many of the Saints from the *Brooklyn* enjoyed the California climate and opportunities so much they decided to remain there. In time, only about one-third of the oceangoing pioneers joined the main body of the Church in Utah.

Brother Samuel Brannan met with Brigham Young in the Salt Lake Valley and tried to convince him to bring the Saints to California. Failing in this effort, the disappointed Brannan returned to California.

As the only Church leader in the region, Brannan continued to receive

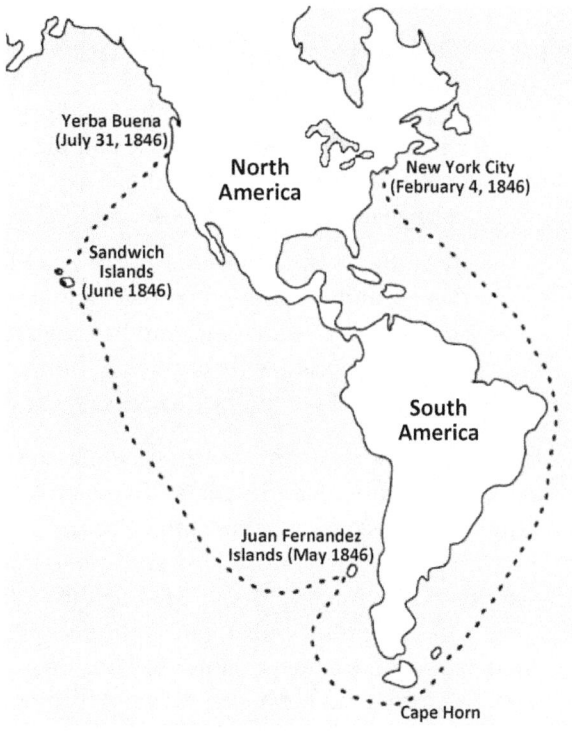

Route of the *Brooklyn*, 1846.

tithes of the Church members, but no records have been found showing Brannan forwarded those tithes to the leaders of the Church in Utah.[14]

Brannan moved to New Helvetia, where he opened a store at John Sutter's Fort. When gold was discovered, Brannan owned the only store between San Francisco and the gold fields—a fact he capitalized on by buying up all the mining supplies he could find, and then running up and down the streets of San Francisco, shouting, "Gold! Gold on the American River!" He paid 20 cents each for prospecting pans, then sold them for $15 apiece. In nine weeks, he made $36,000.

In the summer of 1848, with Sutter away from the fort, Brannan convinced Sutter's son to lay out a new town on the banks of the Sacramento River. Later, he persuaded the Sutters to give him 200 lots in the new town, called Sacramento City, as payment to keep his store there. By the mid–1850s, Brannan was rich, dabbling in banks, railroads, and telegraphs as well as land.

But alcoholism led to some disastrous business decisions, and an expensive divorce bankrupted him. By the time of his death, in San Diego County in 1889, Brannan was reduced to sleeping in the back rooms of saloons. California's first millionaire was a forgotten failure.[15]

After Sam Brannan launched gold fever with his announcement on May 12, 1848, hysteria took hold.[16]

- **May 27, 1848:** Crewmen on ships in San Francisco deserted and rushed to the gold fields. Some coastal cities saw a significant drop in population as the citizens rushed to the Sierra foothills.

- **May 29, 1848:** The *Californian* complained: "The whole country from San Francisco to Los Angeles, and from the seashore to the base of the Sierra Nevada's, resounds with the sordid cry of gold, GOLD, GOLD! while the field is left half-planted, the house half built, and everything neglected but the manufacture of shovels and pickaxes." The *Californian* also announced the suspension of publication because of staff leaving for the diggings.

- **June 10, 1848:** The *California Star* wrote, "Every seaport as far south as San Diego, and every interior town, and nearly every rancho from the base of the mountains in which the gold has been found, to the Mission of San Luis, south, has become suddenly drained of human beings."[17] Four days later, the *California Star* ceased publication because the staff had rushed to the gold fields.

But there was other excitement in the summer of 1848. With the Mexican-American War ended, the issue of slavery was once again in focus and was a pivotal issue in the upcoming presidential election.

The Whig Party chose Zachary Taylor, not because he espoused Whig principles, but because he was popular for leading the war effort against Mexico. Millard Fillmore, New York State comptroller, ran as the vice presidential candidate with Taylor. Incumbent president, Democrat James K. Polk, declined to run for reelection, so the Democrats nominated Michigan senator (and former governor) Lewis Cass. In doing so, they alienated former President Martin Van Buren. Van Buren broke from the Democrats and ran as a third-party candidate under the banner of the Free-Soil Party.

4. The Country Reacts

Upper, left to right: **Lewis Cass (Democrat), ca. 1860; Zachary Taylor (Whig), ca. 1850.**
Lower, left to right: **James K. Polk, 1849; Martin Van Buren (Free-Soil), ca. 1855–58.**

The Free-Soil Party opposed the expansion of slavery into the western territories, especially those recently obtained from Mexico.

For the first time, the election was held on the same day in every state, on November 7, 1848. Zachary Taylor won both the popular vote and the electoral vote over Lewis Cass. The popular vote was split among the three candidates as follows: Taylor 47.3 percent; Cass 42.5 percent; and Van Buren 10.1 percent.

Meanwhile, excitement about gold spread east and prospectors traveled west by every means possible.

- **July 11, 1848:** Military governor of California, General Richard Barnes Mason, visited gold fields to gather information for a report to the U.S. Government.[18] His aide, Captain William T. Sherman, accompanied him.
- **August 19, 1848:** The *New York Herald* printed an item about the discovery of gold in California.
- **September 27, 1848:** The Royal Mail steamship *Europa* sailed from New York carrying news of gold discoveries in California and arrived in London on October 10. But news of cholera at home, turmoil following the recent French Revolution, the outbreak of war between Austria and Hungary, and combat among the separate kingdoms of Italy that had forced the pope to flee the Vatican for his life pushed any news of gold to page four of the *London Times*.
- **November 28, 1848:** The U.S.S. *Lexington* departed San Francisco with $500,000 in gold destined for the U.S. Mint in the East.
- **December 5, 1848:** In a message to Congress, President Polk confirmed the discovery of gold in California. His message was based on reports from General Mason, the governor of California. In his 1848 State of the Union address to Congress, the president said, "The accounts of abundance of gold are of such an extraordinary character as would scarcely command belief were they not corroborated by the authentic reports of officers in the public service. The explorations already made warrant the belief that the supply is very large and that gold is found at various places in an extensive district of the country."[19]

  The California Natural Resources Agency stated, "Thus began one of the largest human migrations in history as a half-million people from around the world descended upon California in search of instant wealth."[20]
- **February 28, 1849:** The arrival of the Pacific Mail's steamer *California* inaugurated the first regular steamboat service to California. Businessman Thomas O. Larkin and Captain William T. Sherman went into the bay by small boat to greet the vessel.
- **April 19, 1849:** Friends of a Rail-Road to San Francisco held a public meeting at the U.S. Hotel in Boston to present P.P.F. Degrand's plan for the construction of a railroad to California.
- **May 18, 1849:** The sailing ship *Grey Eagle* arrived in San Francisco with 34 passengers from the East in 113 days, a record.
- **June 4, 1849:** The *Panama* arrived in San Francisco Bay. There were already about 200 deserted ships in the harbor because the crews had abandoned them for the gold fields. Dr. Stephen R. Harris arrived on the *Panama*. He later was elected to the posts of mayor, controller, and coroner.

With President Polk's December 1848 message to Congress, regular steamboat service to California, and the planned construction of a railroad across the country, the rush was on. A New Yorker commented, "Any person strolling along our docks cannot help being struck with the quantity of merchandise of all kinds, which is marked for shipping to the new El Dorado. Nearly a million dollars' worth of supplies have been shipped from this port alone, of which not less than $400,000 have been sent within the last thirty days."[21]

Into this unbounded enthusiasm would soon come a 20-year-old Jewish immigrant from Prussia named Adolph Sutro.

Chapter 5

Go West, Young Man

Go west, young man, and grow up with the country.
—Incorrectly attributed to Horace Greeley,
probably originated by John B.L. Soule

The ship *Peter Hattrick*, carrying the Sutro family, arrived in New York Harbor on September 30, 1850. The scene at the harbor was chaos, with supplies bound for San Francisco piled high everywhere. Adolph was mesmerized by the activity. Almost immediately he decided to travel on to California in any way possible. He convinced his mother that the crates of supplies intended for Sali's Baltimore store would bring far more money if sold in California. Reluctantly she agreed to allow Adolph to take the clothing and bedding with him on his journey.

Rosa Sutro and her other seven children, including three under ten years of age, would travel to Baltimore where eldest child, Sali, was waiting for them.

Traveling from New York to San Francisco was no small venture. People were talking about a transcontinental railroad, but it would be 19 more years before that link would become a reality. Numerous overland routes started from St. Joseph, Missouri; Independence, Missouri; or Council Bluffs, Iowa. From any one of those Midwestern starting points, the trip to California would take four to six months, but one had to embark between early April and early July to avoid harsh winter weather.

An all-water route around Cape Horn through the perilous Strait of Magellan could take six to eight months and featured rough storms, seasickness, and a lack of fresh water, fruits, and vegetables. Diseases such as scurvy and cholera were common. Despite these hazards, in 1849 more than 15,000 people traveled in over 500 ships from New York to California around the Horn.

The fastest route was by way of Panama, with ship travel at both ends of the isthmus crossing. The Panama Canal did not open until August 1914, 64 years too late for Sutro. But hardy travelers still chose the route via Panama because it was the shortest and fastest. Depending on the availability of ships from Panama City on the Pacific side, the Panama route to California could take just one month. Multiple hazards included bandits, swarming insects, poisonous snakes, malaria, yellow fever, and cholera.

Adolph Sutro had three alternatives to choose from, and he was anxious to get started making his fortune. But he was no gold hunter; he planned to carry merchandise to sell to the thousands of prospectors. Sutro was an impatient young man who wanted to join the excitement of California now. To travel the overland route would require him to get to a Midwestern city, wait until spring, and then ride behind mules or oxen for at least five months. Traveling by ship around Cape Horn would take anywhere from six to eight months. There was only one choice for Adolph: the Panama route. In just one month, the 20-year-old Sutro could be in San Francisco.

The route from New York to California via Panama had been authorized by the U.S. Congress on March 3, 1847, to transport mail. The Secretary of the Navy issued contracts for four steamships suitable for use both as warships and mail carriers. In addition, two contracts to operate steamship companies, one from New York to Chagres, Panama, and one from Panama City to California, were issued. The U.S. Mail Steamship Company, headed by George Law, ultimately received the contract for the Eastern portion. After much controversy and a lawsuit, the Pacific Mail Steamship Company, headed by William H. Aspinwall, emerged as the contractor for the Western portion.[1] By mid–1849, a tenuous mail link between the East and California had been established.

Neither steamship company initially provided any means to transport mail across the isthmus. For an additional fee from the government, the Pacific Mail Steamship Company agreed to handle that portion of the trip. But their service was very poor, and the responsibility eventually fell to the Panama Railroad in 1852. But the railroad itself was not completed until January 1855.[2]

Because of the mail-carrying steamships, the Panama route to California was the

Left: **George Law, ca. 1855–1865.** *Right:* **William H. Aspinwall, portrait by Daniel Huntington, 1871.**

shortest and fastest. But in 1850, it was by no means easy. The first leg was by steamship from New York City to the primitive port of Chagres in Panama. Next was a hazardous voyage by canoe 40 miles up the Chagres River to Cruces. The Panama portion finished with a 20-mile overland trek by mule or donkey to the town of Panama City on the Pacific side. Finally, the traveler had to fight for passage on another steamship to San Francisco.

Not knowing of the travails ahead, Adolph Sutro booked passage for Panama on the first available ship, the *Cherokee*, a 210-foot-long by 35-foot-wide wooden hull steamship with side paddlewheels, initially launched in 1848.[3]

1850 newspaper ad for steamship fares to California and Oregon.

Sutro undoubtedly saw an ad like the one at left, which appeared in the October 8, 1850, edition of the *Baltimore Sun*.[4]

The *Cherokee* was to depart at 3:00 p.m. on Saturday, October 12, which was just 12 days after Adolph arrived in New York City. The cost for a Saloon State Room to Chagres was $100 in 1850, or about $3,000 in 2018 dollars.

Among the passengers on the *Cherokee* were the first senator from the new state of California, John C. Frémont, and his family. In addition to being a famous explorer and controversial military leader, Frémont owned land in California where gold had recently been discovered. If Sutro met Frémont, they would certainly have discussed the excitement of the gold rush.

Continuing a practice he had started while in Memel, East Prussia, Adolph wrote long, highly descriptive letters to his mother and siblings. His first letter is dated October 30th, and he mailed it from Chagres, Panama, where the ship had arrived on October 21st. Adolph wrote first of his ultimate destination, California:

> Already I know California fairly well, as I have talked with thousands, returning from this land of promise, hungry and miserable. The mines are extraordinarily rich, overrun by 100,000 persons. Among 100 miners, five make a fortune, 50 earn the necessities of life, the rest barely live or perish of hunger. Miners return like robbers, hair and beard uncut for years, clothes in rags. Many squander their money in gambling houses. Merchants from the east do a large business with California. If an article becomes scarce, the merchants order large quantities, causing overstocks. Safe business is difficult, but with foresight and judgment, much money is to be made.[5]

Sutro went on to describe the voyage on a mirror-smooth ocean. The *Cherokee* passed Brooklyn, Staten Island, and Sandy Hook. Cape Hatteras came in sight on October 14th, and Florida the next day. They crossed the Tropic of Cancer on October 16th and sighted Haiti on the 18th. By October 20th, they approached the hazardous port of Chagres. The next morning, because the harbor was too shallow for the *Cherokee*, the passengers went ashore in small boats. Sutro described tropical trees and birds with brilliantly colored plumage: "All this makes the place very romantic and interesting." But then he saw the town of Chagres, with its miserable bamboo huts on one side of the river and better huts with large signs proclaiming *Washington Hotel* and *Astor House*. "But what hotels? Pigs, chickens, etc., were running amid the humans, and for food, there was only fruit."[6] The comfortable part of the trip was over.

Adolph describes the native inhabitants of Chagres in unflattering terms:

> They are very lazy and passionately fond of smoking, especially the women. Nearly every girl has a cigar in her mouth or sticks it behind her ear like a pen. Men and women are clad from the hips down or not at all, and have no shame. Some women are dressed in fine light-colored materials, with coal-black hair, decked in pearls and gold.

He also described the unhealthy conditions in Chagres, the pale, miserable, emaciated whites who look like,

> ... reflections of yellow fever. The white men last only a few years; the chief cause of the unhealthiness is the thick fog, laden with moisture and malaria, which rises every night from the ground. A single night's exposure may ruin one's health forever. Four nights were spent in this suffocating fog. We were saved from the fever only by the regular dose of quinine given us by the ship's doctor.

Sutro and three other travelers hired native canoe operators to take them up the Chagres River to Cruces for $100:

> We packed all our goods in the canoe and started at 1 p.m. The river is rapid, with strong eddies, dangerous in a dugout. Luxurious tropical vegetation with coconut trees, palms, bananas, oranges, citrus, wild fig, mangoes, guavas, and other often colossal trees. Thick green bamboos, sugar cane, tule, house-high grasses, cactuses, and leaves as long as a man and several feet in width. Then the climbers and parasites which grow to the top and grow down, intertwining in a thousand ways, making an impenetrable smothering foliage.
> There are thousands of parrots, always in pairs, pelicans, wild ducks, hundreds of hummingbirds, eagles, and vultures. In the grass, you see large lizards, chameleons, iguanas, and in the air fly large colorful butterflies. In the river are the much-dreaded alligators. The river makes many sharp, unexpected turns. By 7 p.m. we had covered about 8 miles and stopped at a native village, Catten. So far, we were delighted and excited, and had feasted on provisions from the ship.

In Catten, slogging through the mud, there was no place to sleep. A few hammocks were used by the ladies, but 200 to 300 people gradually arrived, sleeping on the ground or in canoes. Adolph chose to stay in the canoe to guard his baggage. To avoid sickness, he feasted on crackers and some yellow river water. The gambling tables were the main occupation of the boatmen, who made good money but invariably lost it all. Adolph spent the night in the boat, besieged by a horde of mosquitoes and drenched by rain.[7]

The next day (Wednesday, October 23rd), the canoe journey continued. At noon, a "disgusting" lunch was served, covered with flies, little worms, and ants. Then a terrible drenching thunderstorm occurred before the next station, which was furnished with two huts. About 60 people arrived, and Adolph again slept in the boat. There was nothing to eat but guava preserves. Hordes of fireflies appeared, and mosquitoes filled the air.

On Thursday, October 24th, travel on the Chagres continued,

> ... often barely avoiding logs and capsizing. Four Frenchmen were upset today, but all were saved. Last week fourteen Americans were drowned.
> Next day, Thursday the 24th, at 3 o'clock, we reached Gorgona, where we finally had some warm food. The road from here to Panama City is virtually impassable because of the mud. We finally persuaded

our boatman to go on to Cruces, seven miles further, the worst part of the river. This (part of the trip) was really dangerous in the dark, and we were thankful for the boatman's skill. We had imagined this was a real town, with good places to sleep, but we were again disappointed. At the United States Hotel, 300 people were crowded in. Supper of coffee, bread, and already tainted meat cost one dollar. I was glad to be in the closed house after 4½ days on the river. The large sleeping room had about 150 cots, crowded and stacked, with no bedding at all. But I had a good night's rest anyhow.

In the morning of Friday, October 25th, the challenge was finding a way to get to the town of Panama City on the Pacific coast. After hard bargaining, Adolph rented a mule to ride and three pack mules for his baggage.

It is impossible to describe the journey from Cruces to Panama City. At every step, you are in danger of being thrown. Many seasoned travelers, who have crossed the Cordilleras and the Alps, told me that this was the worst trail in the world. Ten minutes after we started, the mules sank down to their bellies in the mud. I thought I would never get out again. The path cut through roots and was often so narrow that the mules barely scraped through and were unable to find their feet. We crossed creeks and swamps and got covered totally with mud. Then there was the dread of robbers. The night before we left, a young man was murdered and robbed of $9,000.

Finally, by evening, we reached a native hut to spend the night. I shall never forget this night. At dark, my traveling companions left me, and I stayed to guard my baggage, alone with the muleteers who spoke only Spanish. I was armed but quite frightened. At the nearby open hut were about 150 men returning from California, who looked like highwaymen. I had had no food all day, then found a man who sold me a piece of bread for a shilling. It had rained all day, and I was again totally soaked with no possible clothing change. At last I lay on the ground among these ruffians, but sleep was impossible.

Next morning there was nothing to eat. The baggage was loaded, but Sutro's riding mule had been stolen during the night. Adolph was forced to go on foot, potentially for seven miles.

In a half hour I was so exhausted I could hardly move a step. The heat was insufferable. Finally, a man let me ride his mule for a few dollars. By 9 a.m. I was overjoyed to see my first sight of Panama City and the Pacific.

At the American Hotel, the rate was $2 a day. In the mirror, Adolph was shocked by his appearance. His pants were tucked into his boots and mud covered everything. He wore an immense straw hat and a leather belt in which a pistol was stuck. His face was covered in mud, his hair unkempt and disheveled. Clean clothes and a bath seemed like a rebirth after the five-day ordeal.

The old Spanish town of Panama City was mostly in ruins.

I eat scarcely anything but bread and a cup of tea; the meats all smell. In my room are six beds; some have fifty, stacked three or four high. You won't believe the terrible inconvenience; in all Panama City, there is no water closet. Everyone must go on the walls of the city, even if you are unwell in the night. The natives live on yams, bananas, and coconuts. There is no agriculture and no vegetables. The natives are all Catholics, so there are lots of priests and church bells. The soldiers are truly ridiculous, black, white and yellow all mixed up, none with shoes. I shall be delighted to get on the steamer tomorrow.[8]

After six steamy, disagreeable days in Panama, on Friday, November 1, 1850, Adolph boarded the steamship *California* bound for San Francisco. The fare from Panama City to San Francisco was $300 for a cabin or $150 in steerage (about $9,000 for the cabin or $4,500 in steerage in today's money)![9] Sutro chose the cabin. It must have seemed like heaven to leave the desolation of Panama for a modern ship. Among the passen-

U.S. Pacific mail ship *California*.

gers on the *California* was John C. Frémont,[10] whom Sutro had met both during their voyage from New York to Chagres on the *Cherokee* and on their terrifying crossing of Panama.

The *California* was built by William H. Webb and was the first of the Pacific Mail steamers to depart from its point of construction in New York. A young man named John Mackay was an apprentice in Webb's shipyard while the *California* was being built. We shall meet Mr. Mackay later in Virginia City, Nevada.

The 1,050-ton ship was to sail around Cape Horn and take its position in the Pacific for its impending mail service. She left New York City bound for San Francisco on October 6, 1848. It was to be a difficult voyage. Major mechanical problems plagued the ship. To make matters worse, less than one month into the voyage, Captain Forbes fell ill with a pulmonary hemorrhage and transferred command of the ship to Mate Duryee. En route to Rio de Janeiro, Duryee made a navigational error that forced the ship to backtrack, thus extending its long and painful journey.

The *California* finally arrived at San Francisco Bay on February 28, 1849, having traveled 1,400 miles in 144 days. She was the first steamship to enter the Golden Gate. Within one day of landing on the California shore, most of the crew, including the captain, deserted the ship in search of gold.[11]

By the time Sutro and his traveling companions boarded the *California* on November 1, 1850, she was a well-seasoned vessel captained by Lieutenant Budd. She left Panama City filled with gold-seekers. Her first stop after leaving Panama City with Sutro aboard was Acapulco, and Adolph went ashore in a canoe to visit the town and old Spanish fort. At dusk, he took a refreshing swim in the bay and was later horrified to learn of the man-eating sharks he had luckily escaped.

The next stop was at Mazatlan, a beautiful town with 15,000 inhabitants. Sutro had quickly forgotten his experience in Acapulco:

> The ocean looked very inviting, the water was shallow, and I decided to take a dip. I thought it was too shallow for sharks. Just before I stepped in, a dark-skinned girl ran up, and warned of nearby sharks. Now I discovered these greedy monsters, at least 10–15 of them, less than 20 steps away. My hair stood on end, and I was thankful that this black angel had saved me. That was the end of my desire for ocean dips.

Stops at San Diego, Santa Barbara, and Monterey followed before reaching San Francisco on Friday, November 21. Sutro wrote of his destination:

> The climate is said to be good, but I doubt it. The nights are cold and it rains almost daily. I wear woolen underdrawers and woolen undershirts. No city in the world has ever been built so rapidly. Most streets have very clean wooden pavements. On one square alone there are 10–12 magnificent gambling places, always filled. Almost every night a gambler is shot or stabbed. Rents are $500–$600 a month for a tiny store, interest rates are 5%–10% a month.[12]

Welcome to California, Adolph Sutro!

Chapter 6

Sutro, the Shop Owner

Success is taken by the man who has made himself ready for its arrival.
—Chris Murray

Adolph Sutro, age 20, had made it to San Francisco. Despite the travails of Panama, he had salvaged most of the goods that were originally intended to stock brother Sali's shop in Baltimore, and now comprised all of Adolph's worldly possessions. But he needed a place for himself and his trunks. He also had one more important item, a letter of introduction to August Helbing, a fellow countryman and family friend who had fled Prussia in 1844 and arrived in San Francisco in October 1850, just one month before Adolph. Helbing had established a dry-goods company, Meyer, Helbing, Strauss & Co. August Helbing also founded the Eureka Benevolent Society,[1] to "afford aid and relief to indigent, sick, and infirm Jews; to bury the dead; and in general to relieve and aid co-religionists who might be in poverty or distress."[2] Adolph located Helbing's store at California and Sansome Streets and was relieved to find a place to sleep.

Meyer, Helbing were importers of crockery, glass, and china. The store had no fire watcher, essentially a night watchman, and Adolph's job was to watch for fires in the shop or the adjoining buildings. If a fire occurred, he was responsible for saving the goods from burning or looting. Despite depressed conditions and a half-dozen ships a day delivering full cargoes of supplies, Adolph sold his goods for a profit and even started buying sample goods, which he bought at wholesale and resold for a 5 percent to 10 percent commission.[3] At night he continued his practice of writing letters, including one to his cousin, Bernard Frankenheimer, who lived in Stockton, a town on the San Joaquin River 83 miles east of San Francisco.[4]

Frankenheimer, born in Germany in 1826 and an aspiring clothing merchant,[5] was among 200 to 300 Jews who moved to Stockton in 1850. Stockton was the shipping point for goods for the recently discovered gold mines of California, and therefore an attractive location for shopkeepers.[6]

Bernard invited Adolph to join him in Stockton, where together they opened a small store selling clothing, boots, shoes, and cloth. In March 1851 they moved to a larger location, which Adolph described as "about the finest store on the levee." Stockton was a bustling town because it was the eastern terminus for oceangoing ships as well as scheduled steamships from San Francisco. But because the buildings were either wooden or canvas tents, fire was a constant danger. On May 6, 1851, soon after Sutro and his cousin moved to their larger location, fire struck the town. Sutro's store survived undamaged, and business improved because their competition was not as fortunate. Much of their business involved selling goods to the stores at Sutter's Fort.

Adolph and Bernard were prosperous enough that Adolph wrote to his family in Baltimore suggesting that the males (Sali, Emil, Otto, Hugo, and Ludwig) come to California, where he could get them well-paying jobs. Three of his brothers took Adolph up on his offer. Emil and Otto, who had recently emigrated to Baltimore from Prussia, arrived in San Francisco in 1851, and Hugo in 1853. Emil became a salesman for Hamberger Brothers at 93 California Street in San Francisco, and musician Otto played the organ at several churches. Hugo worked at a jewelry store, Dubor's Brothers at 129 Montgomery Street. Despite their success in San Francisco, ties to their mother and siblings were strong, and all three brothers eventually returned to Baltimore.

Lawless San Francisco

In late August, 1851, Adolph Sutro was visiting San Francisco and sleeping at Helbing's store when he witnessed one of the horrifying aspects of life in the near-lawless city. The bell of the Monumental Fire Company awoke him at 2 a.m., but it was not to announce a feared fire, but rather a hanging.[7]

Lacking adequate police protection and in reaction to rampant crime, San Francisco citizens established a vigilante group, the Vigilance Committee, on June 9, 1851, to provide quick punishment for lawbreakers. The Committee engaged in policing and punishing offenders, investigating disreputable boardinghouses and vessels, deporting immigrants, and parading its militia.[8] One of the founders of the Vigilance Committee was Samuel Brannan, the Mormon leader who in 1848 had proclaimed the discovery of gold at Sutter's Mill. Largely because of his work with the Committee, Brannan was disfellowshipped from the LDS church.[9]

A group of criminals, known as the Sydney Ducks, had come from the British penal colonies in Australia to pursue illicit gain in the boomtown of San Francisco.[10] Two of the Ducks, Samuel Whittaker and Robert McKenzie, became targets of the Vigilance Committee when they were identified by a companion, James Stuart, in a vain attempt to save his own life after he was accused of murder. Whittaker and McKenzie were convicted not so much for any individual crime as for their lengthy careers of robbery, often violent—for "diverse offences, whereby the safety of lives and property have been endangered" (as read the executive report on Whittaker) that rendered each "a hardened offender, and dangerous to this community ... it would be unsafe to hand him over to the Authorities or mete out to him a less Penalty than Death" (as read the report on McKenzie).

After the Vigilance Committee captured Whittaker and McKenzie, California Governor John McDougall intervened and arranged for their transfer to the county jail. Frustrated by this interference by legal authority with their vengeance, 36 members of the Vigilance Committee stormed the jail on Sunday, August 24, 1851, when the prisoners were attending chapel services. They seized Whittaker and McKenzie, and the newspaper *Steamer Alta California* reported the subsequent happenings in its September 1, 1851, editorial:

> Through every street, in all directions, the hurrying crowd of humanity rushed with the utmost precipitation—no one knew whither, no one knew for what. The bell of the Vigilance Committee had sounded its alarum note—and instantly the streets were living, swaying masses of human beings—uncertainty and conflicting fears and hopes ruled the hour ... with a sweep like the rushing of a torrent of lava they bend their course towards the Rooms of the Vigilance Committee. Almost instantly California street, Battery street, and all their approaches, are filled with one dense mass of human beings. From lip to lip the news flies that the two criminals, Mackenzie and Whittaker, have been taken by force from the jail, by an armed posse of the Vigilance Committee. On the eager and excited multitude press toward the Rooms. On, on, on—the crowd becomes denser and broader. Wonder is stamped on every face—a solemn, almost awful silence pervades the thousands who are anxiously gazing up at the building, when quickly the doors are opened—a moment of preparation—and the numberless multitude holds its breath as the two malefactors are seen suspended by the neck—a struggle or two, a spasmodic heaving of the chest—and each spectator feels a thrill of terror coursing his veins as he involuntarily utters—dead, dead, dead!

The hangings took place at Vigilance Committee headquarters on Battery Street between California and Pine Streets, just one block from where Adolph Sutro was staying in August Helbing's store.[11]

Sutro wrote of witnessing the hangings of Whittaker and McKenzie in a letter to his family, in which he credited the Vigilance Committee with bringing order to lawless and corrupt San Francisco.[12]

Return from Stockton[13]

Despite the potential for violence in San Francisco, in November 1851, Sutro left his cousin Bernard and their store in Stockton and returned to the growing city, where the action was. He established a store on Long Wharf, where he sold everything from turpentine to lager beer. By 1854, he had expanded to two stores. At 103 Clay Street, he sold imported cigars and tobacco. The store at 110 Sacramento Street handled imported variety goods, which he shipped to the southern gold mines via Stockton and to the northern mines via Sacramento.

Adolph continued to expand his commercial presence. We don't know what happened to his stores on Clay and Sacramento Streets, but he soon had three more stores. The first was at 116 Montgomery Street and sold cigars, Meerschaum pipes, and tobacco. To draw attention, Adolph installed a five-foot-high smoking automaton in front of the store. The figure held a large tobacco pipe in its lips and sucked and puffed under the control of a weight tied to a string.

His second store was in the Armory Hall Building on Montgomery Street. This store was a wholesale and retail importing business, also focused on cigars, pipes, and tobacco. Adolph's third store at this time also sold smoking products and was located on Washington Street.

Adolph's cousins, Gustav (1827–1897) and Charles (1829–1901), helped to run these stores. Gustav and Charles were brothers and were born in Aachen, Prussia, as was

Adolph. We have no record of why or when Gustav and Charles arrived in California, but it is likely that Adolph wrote to them, as he wrote to his own brothers, about the opportunities in the growing city.

In 1855, Adolph again encountered the violence of the city. Mr. A.J. King had lost a package of scrip in the 116 Montgomery Street store. Charles Sutro found the package and returned it after a delay of two or three days. King, angered by the delay, attacked Charles with a knife, seriously cutting his lower lip. Later that day, King confronted Adolph when they met by chance at the entrance to City Hall. Adolph later said,

> Mr. King passed me and then sprang around and said, "You call me a scoundrel?" He then cut me with a knife a ghastly wound from the ear down to the mouth. There were fifty persons standing about, but it was done so suddenly that I doubt if any person witnessed it.[14]

As a result, Adolph grew flowing side whiskers, called mutton chops, to hide the wound, and wore them for the rest of his life.

Leah Harris Sutro, ca. 1869 (courtesy Nevada Historical Society).

Change in Status

Major changes in the life of Adolph Sutro came in 1855–56. First, he married Leah Harris, who was born in London, England, on August 6, 1832. Their 1855[15] wedding ceremony followed Hebrew traditions, as Leah was far more religious than Adolph.

Second, a daughter, Emma Laura Sutro, was born to the couple on December 15, 1855.[16] Emma would become Adolph's favorite child, and she would lovingly care for him during his final days.

Finally, Adolph became a United States citizen. Adolph exercised his new citizenship by voting for John C. Frémont in the 1856 presidential election. The two had met during the challenging trip across Panama, and also on the ship *California* on the final leg of their trip to San Francisco. Frémont lost the election.

Gold Bug Bites

Adolph had resisted the call of the Sutter's Mill gold, but in 1858 there was a gold discovery near the village of Yale on the Fraser River in the non-sovereign territory of Britain called New Caledonia. To handle the massive rush of foreign prospectors, Britain quickly established the colony of British Columbia.

At least 30,000 gold-seekers flooded the area.[17] As a result of the influx of prospectors,

6. Sutro, the Shop Owner 41

Sign advertising Sutro tobacco products (courtesy Sutro Library, California State Library).

a real estate boom was underway in nearby Victoria. In June 1858, Adolph and his cousin Gustav Sutro went there to establish a cigar store. There was some gold, but not nearly enough to satisfy the thousands of prospectors. Most found only meager or no gold, disillusionment, hardships, or death. Virtually all of the gold was gone by 1860.[18] Adolph and Gustav returned with lighter wallets and a vacant lot of little value in downtown Victoria.

In what would become typical of the Sutros, Adolph was away more than he was home. He was in Victoria, British Columbia, when Leah gave birth to their second child, Rosa Victoria, on July 1, 1858.[19]

Gold and Silver

Traces of gold had been found in 1849 near Dayton, Nevada, by Abner Blackburn, a guide for Mormons crossing the Washoe Mountains. Then in May 1850, a Mormon party passing through on the way to California stopped to feed and water their animals. One of the group, William Prouse, started to pan for gold beside a small stream. Prouse discovered a few flakes in his pan and encouraged some friends to join him farther up the stream. They passed through a mountain gulch, which they christened Gold Canyon. About a mile farther upstream, Prouse and his companion, Nicholas Kelly, found some gold nuggets in a rock fissure. Prouse and his group moved on, but news of their find attracted other prospectors.[20]

No substantial ore deposits were found until the fall of 1857. Then two brothers, Ethan Allen and Hosea Ballou Grosh, sons of a Pennsylvania minister and veterans of the California goldfields, found significant deposits. Unlike most of the prospectors, the Grosh brothers knew how to assay ore and kept an assay kit and a small oven in their cabin. They took ore samples from their strike and analyzed them that evening. To their surprise, they found not only gold but also silver of greater value. However, before they could work or file the claim, both died tragically. Hosea Grosh ran a pick through his foot, which eventually resulted in lockjaw (septicemia), and he died on September 2, 1857. His brother, Allen, while traveling to Last Chance, California, in November 1857, got caught in a snowstorm and suffered severely from exposure. Though he was found before his death and taken to Last Chance, his legs were completely frostbitten, and he died on December 19, 1857. Their secret of silver in the ore died with them, at least for a while.

Also working in the area was a Canadian named Henry Tompkins Paige Comstock, known as "Old Pancake." This same Henry Comstock was on the ship *California* with Adolph Sutro on their journey to San Francisco. Comstock had befriended the Grosh brothers, but they had not shared the location of their find or its silver content with him. In the spring of 1858, when Comstock heard of Allen Grosh's death, he took possession of their cabin and went in search of their claim.

In the spring of 1859, two miners named Peter O'Riley and Patrick McLaughlin began to work the area around the head of Six-Mile Canyon. By June, they had hit "pay-dirt," but when Henry Comstock learned of the find, he told the men they were working on land he and Manny Penrod had already claimed for "grazing purposes." With little in the way of grass or even sagebrush, it was unclear what kind of animals Comstock planned to raise, but the crazed look on his face scared the prospectors. Comstock threatened that he would take the claim, but the miners finally agreed to give him an interest in the gold find. From this small claim developed the Ophir mine, one of the six richest bonanzas in what would be called the Comstock Lode.

Another man who did little but whose name became famous was Virginian James Fennimore. Fennimore had killed a man in California, so he moved to Utah and changed his name to Finney. Now he was in Nevada and went by the name

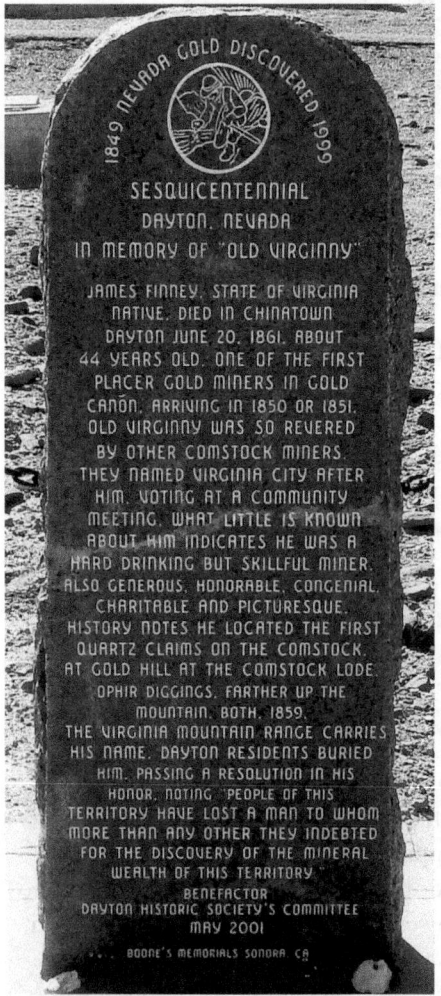

Memorial to James "Old Virginny" Finney (photo by author).

James "Old Virginny" Finney. According to a story told by "Old Pancake" Comstock, Finney was out drinking one night when he fell and broke his whiskey bottle. As he struggled to his feet, he proclaimed, "I baptize this ground Virginia." With the undeserved addition "City," the settlement sitting on top of the Comstock Lode's richest deposits became forever known as Virginia City.[21]

Having few resources to develop these claims and unsure of the size of the strikes, all of the original discoverers sold out without ever making the huge fortunes that would come later for men such as William Chapman Ralston, William Sharon, and several others. Henry Comstock left the area broke in 1862 and went to Oregon, where he continued to prospect. From there, he traveled to Montana, where, on September 27, 1870, he killed himself. Though Comstock died poor and obviously unhappy, the rich lode that he had an early part of was named for him.[22] A survey made in 1876, 17 years after the Ophir discovery, showed that half of the prospectors from 1859 were dead, most of the rest were living in "reduced circumstances," and none were rich.[23]

The small-time miners who initially worked their claims complained of "annoying blue stuff" that clogged the equipment used to wash soil to retrieve gold. This blue stuff was the same ore that the Grosh brothers had found to contain silver in 1857, but they did not live to benefit from their discovery. On June 27, 1859, Melville Atwood, an assayer from the California gold fields, analyzed a sample of the "blue stuff" and determined that one ton of the material would yield $876 in gold and nearly $3,000 in silver. The blue stuff miners had discarded for almost two years was actually a rich concentrate of silver sulfide. Within days, the West experienced yet another rush.[24]

Although news of the Comstock strike reached San Francisco in July 1859, it made little impression because of the recent Fraser River disappointment and also because the site was so remote. But in the fall of 1859, glowing stories of the potential riches piqued interest. By then, however, winter storms prevented travel to the Washoe Mountains. In early spring, one of the first people to travel to see the gold and silver strike was Adolph Sutro. What he found would consume him for the next 19 years, and drastically impact the futures of both Nevada and San Francisco.[25]

Chapter 7

Mr. Sutro Goes to Washoe

The mountains are calling and I must go.
—John Muir

Adolph Sutro was determined to visit the Washoe area to see for himself what the San Francisco newspapers were reporting—the possibility of riches beyond belief at the Comstock Lode. But the trip from San Francisco was not a simple one. It took about five days to get to Virginia City,[1] the largest settlement in the Washoe area. The first leg was by boat from San Francisco to Sacramento. From there, a railroad took passengers to Folsom, and a stagecoach and mule ride completed the trip to Virginia City.

Adolph started his journey on March 18, 1860. The boat trip on the Sacramento River took under eight hours and included a large and sumptuous dinner. Many steamers departed San Francisco daily at 4:00 p.m., including the *Chrysopolis* and the *Cornelia*, which were advertised as shown below.[2]

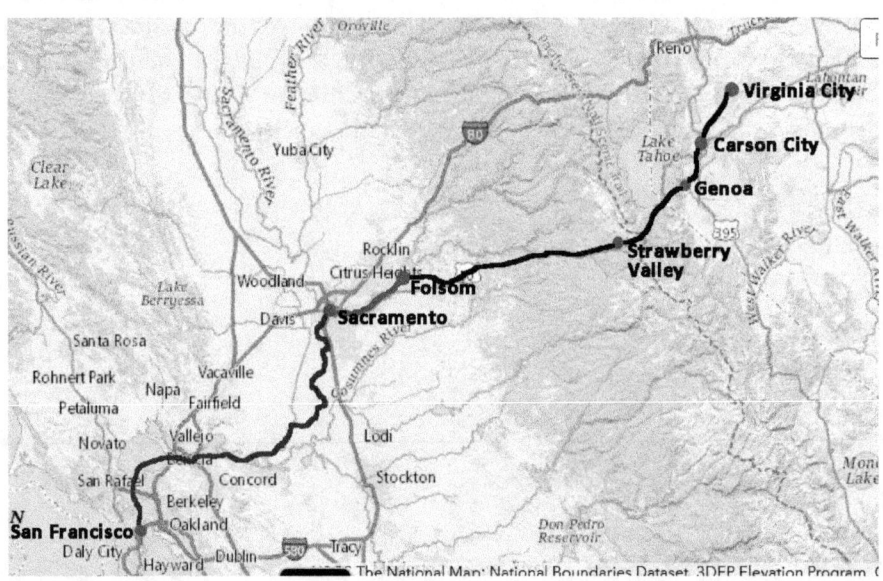

Route from San Francisco to Virginia City, overlaid on current map.

The Sacramento Valley Railroad provided transportation from Sacramento to Folsom, 22 miles away. William Tecumseh Sherman, who had accompanied Colonel Richard Mason on the official evaluation of the California gold fields in 1848, was the vice president of the SVRR. The chief engineer for the SVRR was Theodore Judah, born in Bridgeport, Connecticut, in 1826.[3] Judah, educated at Rensselaer Institute in Troy, New York, had been associate engineer for the Niagara Gorge Railroad before being recruited for the SVRR. In 1854, he and his wife, Anna Pierce Judah, traveled to California via Nicaragua, on a route previously established by Commodore Vanderbilt.[4]

The SVRR was the first steam railroad in California and commenced service in 1856. While not as luxurious as the steamships, the ride on the rails was reasonably comfortable.

Such comfort was not available for the final leg of Sutro's trip. The 150-mile journey over the Sierra Nevadas started with a horse-drawn stagecoach. The coaches were first produced in 1827 by the Abbot-Downing Company of Concord, New Hampshire. Called the Concord Coach from its place of origin, versions of these vehicles appear in every Western movie. The ones used in the west weighed about 2,500 pounds and required six or eight paired horses to pull them. Eight or nine passengers occupied seats inside the coach, with "steerage" passengers sitting on roof seats. When used on smooth dirt or gravel roads, the coach rode smoothly on twin leather straps laced between the axles.

Such comfort disappeared when traversing the rutted, rocky mountain trails on the way to Strawberry Valley. Sutro described the arrival at Strawberry Valley and the subsequent trip to Virginia City in an article later published in the *Daily Alta California*:

> After being crammed in the stage all day, jostled and thrown about, we arrived at Strawberry at six p.m., almost worn out. Strawberry Valley contains one house, kept by Berry & Crosby, who try to

1854 ad for steamer from San Francisco to Sacramento.

Abbot-Downing Concord Coach (courtesy Owls Head Transportation Museum, Owls Head, Maine).

> make travelers as comfortable as circumstances will admit. They set an excellent table and have good beds; but the house is usually so crowded that it is difficult to get a place to sit down. The main room contains an immense fireplace, where they put on pieces of wood five feet long and sometimes two feet thick; and the fire throws out such heat that a person cannot come within ten feet of it.
> After a good night's rest we got up on our mules, which are furnished by the stage company, and continued our journey. From Strawberry to the Summit the distance is nine miles, and there is a gradual rise until the highest point is reached. The snow all along here was from two to ten feet in depth, but the road at the same time was in excellent condition, the night before having been cold and the ground all frozen. On reaching the Summit the descent commences into Lake Valley, following round the side of a very steep mountain, which point is the only dangerous one on the whole route, on account of the snow-slides which take place here very frequently, and which carry with them many tons of rocks; and should an unfortunate traveler be caught by one, it will carry him and his animal down a dizzy height and crush him to atoms. After descending about half a mile, Lake Bigler (Tahoe) comes in view to the northward, a beautiful sheet of water, some thirty-six miles long and fifteen miles broad. The highest point, or the summit, is 7,500 feet above the level of the sea. Lake Bigler is nearly 6,000.

The travelers arrived at a roadhouse called "Woodfords," at the head of the Carson Valley. Sutro continues:

> We left Woodford's at six o'clock next morning, for Genoa, a distance of 18 miles. The road follows the side of the hills of Carson Valley, through an apparently fruitful country. Every acre seems to be taken up, to judge from the substantial fences which line the road. Genoa is a small town, formerly a Mormon settlement; it lies under a steep hill covered with pine trees, and the spot is rather prepossessing in appearance. Fourteen miles further along Carson Valley brought us to Carson City.

> This place is to be the metropolis of the new territory. Carson City contains at present about seventy-five houses, which are mostly used for hotels and restaurants, very few stores being here as yet, on account of the difficulty of bringing merchandise across the mountains.
>
> That morning we left in the stage for Virginia City and the great mining district. Two miles out of Carson, the smell of sulphur, caused by some boiling hot springs not far from the road, attracted our attention. The next place we came to is called "Nick's," where the hills rise again, and we enter the mining district.
>
> The hills here are all barren and rocky, covered with sage brush; not a tree, except some dwarf pines is to be seen. Soon we entered a canyon, following up which to the northward, brought us to the first settlement called Silver City. Another two miles in the northward brought us to the Gold Hill district, where the celebrated Gold Hill claims and many other rich claims are located; from here we had to leave the stage and walk up a high hill, from which we soon reached Virginia City.
>
> Virginia City is located on the eastern slope of a range of hills, which run from north to south, and which contains the far-famed Comstock Lode. The streets run parallel with the Lode, and there are three of them laid out, A, B, and C Streets; lots running from street to street, being one hundred feet in depth. No cross-streets are provided for.
>
> The uppermost street is called the "Exchange," for the "honest miners," and the "speculators," and the "sharpers," and everybody else meet there to trade in claims, swap them off for others, "bull and bear" mining stock, take in some greenhorns, and, after all, transact considerable *bona fide* business. Some days, the trade consummated on the Exchange would compare with the transactions on Front Street (in San Francisco); but where there is such a mixed crowd of people, there must naturally be a good deal of humbug.
>
> The living is somewhat of the '49 style in California. There are very fair eating houses, where everything that the market affords is provided. I am sorry to say that the market affords but very little; beef, pork, beans, and rice are the staples, but most of them have given out by this time. The water is bad, it looks milky and contains alkali and copper; yet people drink it, and eat what they can get with more relish than they would the greatest delicacies in the cities; the fresh, invigorating air giving a glorious appetite.[5]

As Sutro reported, Virginia City is on the eastern slope of a range of hills. It sits one mile east of Mount Davidson, the highest peak in the region; and two miles west of another mountain, Flowery Peak. The respective elevations are Mount Davidson—7,864 feet; Flowery Peak—6,581 feet; and Virginia City—6,150 feet.

At the age of 29, Adolph Sutro had developed into a sturdy five-foot, 10-inch-tall man weighing 225 pounds. Although physically strong and resilient, he had no desire to seek wealth by prospecting for gold or silver. And he never planned to work underground with a miner's pick. He was a problem-solver at heart, dating to his time in Prussia exploring his father's woolen mill and later building a woolen mill for Mr. Kaapche in Memel. Sutro found many problems both in Virginia City and at the Comstock mines. Some of these, such as poor mine drainage and the lack of an efficient refining process for the silver ore, he could attack. Others, such as native Indians understandably upset by the incursions of hundreds of white men, were well beyond his capabilities.

As Sutro explored Virginia City, which had about 2,300 people, he asked questions on every possible topic of everyone he encountered. The town comprised just three streets with no cross-streets and had a half dozen stone structures, 25 wooden houses, and hundreds of tents. During his 10-day visit, Sutro gained great insight into the present conditions as well as future potential of both the town and the mineral resources on which it depended. He later wrote of his impressions of the mining operations in Virginia City in the *Daily Alta California*:

Virginia City, 1861.

WORKING THE MINES

The mine-working is done without any system as yet. Most of the companies commence without an eye to future success; instead of running a tunnel low down on the bed, and thus sinking a shaft to meet it, which at once insures drainage, ventilation and facilitates the work, by going upwards, the claims are mostly entered from above, large openings made which require considerable timbering, and which expose the mine to wind and weather.

A RAILROAD

A railroad from Virginia City to Carson River, some seven miles distant, could be built at a very small expense, the country sloping gently down towards it. The cars loaded with ore could be made to pull up the empty train, and the ore, once at the river, can be easily worked. Smelting furnaces, quartz crushers, and all machinery required for the successful working of the ore, should be erected, and an inexhaustible supply of wood furnished, by floating timber down Carson River from any point some distance above, where there is an abundance of it.[6]

These two passages reveal that Sutro was a visionary. After just a brief visit, he saw the advantages of a tunnel to drain and ventilate the mines, even before significant underground water had been encountered. Nineteen years later, in 1879, his Sutro Tunnel would accomplish those objectives. The tunnel project would show that, in addition to being a visionary, he also was willing to do the hard work to make his visions come true. Sutro's vision for a railroad would also be realized by the Virginia and Truckee Railroad, which was completed in 1869. To his chagrin, Sutro had no part in building that railroad.

Sutro was especially impressed and concerned by the speculative market in mining shares. Because it was early in the development of the mines, some claims had verified value; others in close proximity were unproven but likely to be valuable; and claims further away could be bonanzas or busts. Virginia City residents, whether miners, mine owners, or merchants, spent their spare time speculating on and investing in the various claims. The modern focus on gambling as a major industry in Nevada has its roots in this speculation in mining stocks.

On April 3, 1860, Sutro was anxious to return to San Francisco. He and seven companions left behind the primitive accommodations, poor food, and smelly water of Virginia City and boarded a stagecoach for the trip over the mountains. The weather was spring-like, and snow had melted from all but the hilltops and deep ravines. After a sound night's sleep, probably at Carson City, the party mounted mules for the next leg. Within an hour, the former sunny weather transformed into a gale. Sutro would later write, "The storm grew fiercer and fiercer as we went on; the flakes of snow and hail were blowing into our faces with such power that they stung like needles, and nearly blinded us. The lofty pine trees swung to and fro, and the noise of the wind breaking through their branches, creaking and howling, was truly fearful."[7] Finally, at 3 p.m., the party reached Strawberry Valley House, where they found refuge from the storm and beds for the night. Strawberry Valley House had been built four years earlier and had just been established as a Remount Station for the Pony Express. As Sutro's party arrived, they saw the first-ever eastbound Pony Express rider as he carried his precious cargo of mail. Sutro wrote, "On the very summit, we met a lonely rider dashing along at a tremendous rate. We wondered what could possibly induce him to go on through that gale and thought it must be some very important business. It was the Pony Express."[8] The first eastbound Pony Express rider departed Sacramento on April 3, 1860,[9] and encountered Sutro's party late the next day.

After rest and food, Sutro's party headed west again. But conditions were even worse. The snow of the previous day had accumulated both on the ground and on the branches of the pine trees. The slightest wind shook the trees and brought down cascades of snow. They were now riding in a coach, but even with the men pushing to assist the horses, the coach got stuck in the snow and had to be abandoned. The driver unhitched the horses, and everyone either rode bareback or walked to the next shelter, a roadhouse called "Perrin's."

Other travelers had abandoned their coaches and wagons because of the snow, and the many horses and mules soon consumed all available feed. These animals were available to carry Sutro and his friends down the mountain, "some seated on broad pack saddles, compelled to have their knees on a horizontal line, some with no saddle at all. Everybody who could get away was fleeing out of the mountains, and soon our caravan numbered at least one-hundred animals."[10] The rutted, muddy roads were now covered with two to four feet of snow, which Sutro said, "could not possibly be in any worse condition." "Every step the animal would take, it would go down to the very bottom, and sometimes sink in, in such a way that only with the greatest effort it would extricate itself. In the efforts to get out, the animal would flounder and kick about, and we poor riders go head over heels into the snow."[11]

It was with great relief that Sutro and his fellow travelers reached Folsom and civilized transportation by train and steamboat back to San Francisco.

Adolph learned of a whole new world of opportunity on his trip to Washoe, and he would never again be content to be a tobacco merchant. He was ready to solve the problems confronting the Comstock Lode.

Back in San Francisco

The family of Adolph and Leah Sutro was growing. Their third child and first son, Gussie Emanuel, had been born in the fall of 1859. To help support the family, the Sutros rented and then sublet two lodging houses. One, which they called the Government House, on the corner of Sansome and Washington Streets, cost them $500 per month. The second, called the Sutro House, was on the corner of Montgomery and California Streets and cost them $400 per month. Leah managed the houses while Adolph liquidated his tobacco businesses and made another trip to Washoe in May 1860.[12]

While Sutro had no interest in mining gold or silver ore himself, he saw a great need for mills to process the ore. As he had learned on his trips to Washoe, it would be totally impractical to transport massive quantities of ore from Virginia City across the mountains for processing in Sacramento or another western town. It made much more sense to extract the valuable gold and silver from the ore at a location adjacent to the mines, and then transport the far smaller weight of bullion. The many claims in the Comstock Lode were each too small to afford the expense of building a mill, but together their ore output would more than justify such a facility.

Extracting silver and gold from ore is not a simple process. Different methods evolved, both due to different ore compositions and experimentation. All significant milling methods start by crushing the rock containing the ore into small particles.

In the patio process, dating to Mexico in the mid-1500s, the ore-bearing rocks were placed on the ground in a shallow circular "patio" of flat stones. An arm mounted on top of a post in the center of the patio carried heavy stones attached by ropes. Horses pulled the arm and stones over the ore, crushing it. Then water and chemicals such as salt, copper sulfate, and mercury (commonly called quicksilver) were added to the crushed ore and the mixture agitated by horses drawing paddles through it. After weeks of mixing and soaking in the sun, a complex reaction resulted in silver (or gold) amalgamated with the mercury.[13] The mercury was then boiled off, leaving silver (or gold). Because it took weeks to process ore, and because of the much lower temperatures on the Comstock, the patio process proved to be impractical for extracting metal from the ore mined there.[14,15]

Sutro wanted to develop a more efficient process to extract gold and silver from the quartz ore found at the Comstock and build a mill to implement that process. He contacted John Randohr, a German chemist he had met on the ship *California* on their voyage from Panama City to San Francisco in 1850. Together they established a small metallurgical works in San Francisco to perform chemical studies and experiments for the treatment of the Comstock ores. In 1861 the work was advanced enough to convince other parties to join Sutro in the establishment of a mill and amalgamating works at Dayton, about seven miles from Virginia City. In the spring of 1862, the Sutro Metallurgical Works was enlarged and then enlarged again in 1863. At its peak, the facility consisted of eight stamping machines ("stamps"), two roasting furnaces each twelve feet in diameter and capable of roasting one ton of pulverized ore at a time, twenty amalgamating pans, and an assay office. Wood from the Sierra Nevadas, ferried on the nearby Carson River, fueled furnaces that produced steam to drive the machinery. A contract with the Gould and Curry Co., operators of one of the large mines, gave the mill $75 per ton for the better-yielding ores. At a capacity of six tons per day, the mill showed a profit of $10,000 a month, a satisfying result for a facility that had cost less than $30,000 to build.

Adolph brought his brother Hugo from Baltimore to run the mill. Hugo's presence freed Adolph to negotiate ore contracts and think more about his idea for a tunnel to drain and ventilate the mines. However, in 1864 the mill burned down, and a man sleeping there perished. The mill was heavily insured, and rumors spread that the owner might have arranged the fire. But Sutro was never a violent man, and he had always maintained excellent relations with his workers. It is highly unlikely that he would have endangered an employee. Furthermore, the insurance went to pay for expenses incurred in operating the mill, leaving Sutro almost broke.[16,17]

The loss of the Sutro Metallurgical Works barely interrupted the processing of ore in the Comstock. By the end of 1861, the region boasted 76 mills, with a total of over 1,000 stamps to crush the ore. Initially, there was not enough ore to fill those mills, and by the spring of 1862, just 23 of the 76 mills were operating.[18]

Self-taught mining engineer Almarin Paul arrived in California by way of Panama in November 1849 and was a member of the Vigilance Committee in San Francisco.[19] At about the same time that Sutro was working on his extraction process, Paul invented the Washoe Pan Process that became the standard for extracting metal from the Comstock ore. Again, the initial step is crushing the ore-bearing rocks. But horses were replaced by steam-driven rotating shafts. As a horizontal drive shaft rotated, cams forced vertical shafts

Bank of five stamps at Donovan Mill. Ore was pulverized into sand-sized pieces. Structure is about 18 feet tall (photo by author).

Circular iron tank at Donovan Mill (photo by author).

to rise slowly and fall rapidly, thus crushing ore-bearing rocks fed to bins at the bottom of the vertical shafts.

Twelve hundred to 1,500 pounds of ore particles were then placed in large iron tanks (called "pans") and heated by steam with other materials, such as one-half to three pounds of common salt, which converted silver sulfide to silver chloride. Water and scrap iron were then added to the mix, along with 60 to 70 pounds of mercury and a like amount of copper sulfate (bluestone). A circular iron plate called a muller was lowered into the tank and rotated to provide both agitation and additional grinding. Steam pipes heated the tanks.[20] The slurry was agitated by rotating iron paddles. The iron captured the chlorine from the silver chloride, yielding pure silver. More mercury was then added and formed an amalgam with the silver or gold present.

As with the patio process, the mercury was boiled off, but this time in a retort, a closed container connected to a condenser. The retort vaporized and then condensed the mercury for reuse instead of allowing it to escape into the atmosphere. Paul's Washoe Pan Process was fast and efficient for extracting precious metals from ore, especially for gold. But even with the improvements of the Washoe Pan Process, much silver remained behind in the residue (called "tailings") and was washed away.[21,22]

Unfortunately, the Washoe Pan Process also left behind an ugly environmental legacy. The whole process is dirty, noisy, and polluting of the water and ground. Large amounts of mercury used in the process escaped and washed downstream in the Carson River with the mill tailings. Over the mining lifetime of the Comstock Lode, about 15 million pounds (7,500 tons) of poisonous mercury were lost in extracting silver and gold from the ore.[23] Today the Comstock mill sites are contaminated with mercury levels 26 times higher than federally established limits.[24] Both the mill areas and the Carson River are EPA Superfund sites. The Nevada State Health Division advisories recommend limited or no consumption of fish and ducks from the Carson River due to high levels of mercury.[25]

After fire destroyed the Sutro Metallurgical Works, Sutro had no funds of his own, but he continued to plan for his tunnel. The ore deposits near the surface had long since been picked clean, and ore extraction now required deeper and deeper vertical shafts and horizontal drifts. More depth brought more problems and more expense. The miners took more time to reach the bottom of the shafts to work; ore had to be lifted greater distances to reach the surface; getting fresh air to the miners became harder; and worst of all, water, although scarce on the surface, flooded the deeper shafts. Adolph Sutro was convinced that his tunnel would solve all of these problems.

Chapter 8

All the News

Clothes make the man. Naked people have little or no influence on society.
—Mark Twain

Another unknown but soon-to-be-famous young man came to the Nevada Territory in the early 1860s. Samuel Clemens was born in Florida, Missouri, on November 30, 1835. Clemens's family moved to Hannibal, Missouri, in 1840, where he gained the background and inspiration to later write *The Adventures of Tom Sawyer* and *The Adventures of Huckleberry Finn*. Samuel left Hannibal at 18 and worked as a printer in New York, Philadelphia, Cincinnati, and St. Louis. Around 1857, Clemens apprenticed as a cub pilot on a Mississippi River steamboat and eventually received his pilot's license. While still training, Samuel convinced his younger brother, Henry, to join him. Samuel was forever haunted when Henry was killed in the explosion of the steamboat *Pennsylvania* below Memphis on June 13, 1858, because Samuel had foreseen the explosion in a dream one month earlier.

After a brief stint in a local Confederate unit at the start of the Civil War, Clemens found he disliked military life and resigned. When his older brother, Orion, was nominated in March 1861 by President Abraham Lincoln to be secretary to James W. Nye, governor of the Nevada Territory, Orion asked Samuel to become his private secretary. The pair left from St. Joseph, Missouri, via stagecoach on July 18, 1861, for the 19-day trip to Carson City, Nevada Territory.

Samuel quickly tired of working for his brother. The lure of easy money from the Comstock Lode proved too strong, and he prospected for gold and silver near the mining camps of Humboldt and Esmeralda. By then, most of the surface deposits had been scooped up, and little was left for Samuel to find.

In February 1862, Clemens started sending often-satirical letters to the *Virginia City Daily Territorial Enterprise*, the major newspaper in the Nevada Territory. He usually signed those letters with his pen name, Josh, and that is the origin of the phrase, "I was just Joshing you." By the fall of 1862, the owner of the *Enterprise*, Joseph Goodman, offered Clemens the job of city editor of the paper at the princely salary of $25 per week. Despite his concerns that he was too inexperienced for such a responsible position, Clemens accepted. By December he was covering the territorial legislature and courts in Carson City.

Carson City House, where Orion Clemens lived (photo by author).

When Samuel Clemens arrived at the *Territorial Enterprise*, he met a reporter named William Wright. Wright had also tried and failed as a precious metal prospector, and the two became close friends and roommates. He wrote under a pen name, Dan DeQuille. In Wright's case, the pen name virtually replaced his real name. DeQuille later wrote a folksy history of the Comstock called *The Big Bonanza*. It is now apparent that he was one of the Old West's most accomplished authors, ranking just behind Twain, Ambrose Bierce, and Bret Harte.[1]

On February 3, 1863, Clemens sent another of his satirical letters to the *Territorial Enterprise*, complaining of a lavish party that had kept him awake for 48 hours. He signed the letter Mark Twain, and a legend was born. The origin of Twain's pseudonym is controversial. Although the phrase "mark twain" was the call designating the two-fathom point on a ship's anchor chain (two fathoms, or twelve feet being the safe-water depth for steamboat operation), at least two other writers had claimed that name before Samuel Clemens took it. Whether Clemens knew of the previous Mark Twains is uncertain, but he made the name famous throughout the world.

Samuel Clemens and Adolph Sutro were both active on the Comstock from 1862 until Clemens left for San Francisco in 1864, Clemens with the *Territorial Enterprise* and Sutro with his ill-fated Metallurgical Works. At some point, they met and became friends. The Missouri-born Clemens and Prussian-born Sutro seemed an unlikely pair, but both were independent free spirits who admired inventiveness and fresh ideas.

Mark Twain later told of his time in Nevada in his book, *Roughing It*. Twain and Sutro corresponded, mainly by telegram, in 1870 and 1871, and met on occasion. One series of exchanges in August 1871 occurred during the writing of *Roughing It*[2]:

To Adolph H. Sutro
19 August 1871 * Hartford, Conn.

149 Asylum St.
Hartford, Aug. 19

Friend Sutro,
 Got your letter to-day. When do you sail? Can't you run up here for one day? I'm awful busy on my new book on Nevada & California. And by the way you might tell me something about the tunnel that would make an interesting page, perhaps. It was about another matter that I wanted to see you principally & very particularly, but one might as well kill various birds with one stone.
 Riley is in England—London.

Yrs.
Sam'. L. Clemens

To Adolph H. Sutro
Per Telegraph Operator
4 August 1871 * Hartford, Conn.

 When do you sail? How long shall you remain in NY when leave & whither

Saml L Clemens
155 Asylum St

To Adolph H. Sutro
Per Telegraph Operator
25 August 1871 * Hartford, Conn.

 All right will see you in New York before you sail

S L Clemens

To Adolph H. Sutro
Per Telegraph Operator
29 August 1871 * Hartford, Conn.

 How long will tunnel be when finished find Riley at American Minister give me your London address

Saml L Clemens
149 Asylum St

In a footnote after Chapter LII of *Roughing It*, Twain includes a comment that resulted from this discussion with Adolph Sutro:

The Sutro Tunnel is to plow through the Comstock lode from end to end, at a depth of two thousand feet, and then mining will be easy and comparatively inex-

Mark Twain, photo by A. F. Bradley, New York, 1907.

pensive; and the momentous matters of drainage, and hoisting and hauling of ore will cease to be burdensome. This vast work will absorb many years, and millions of dollars, in its completion; but it will early yield money, for that desirable epoch will begin as soon as it strikes the first end of the vein. The tunnel will be some eight miles long, and will develop astonishing riches. Cars will carry the ore through the tunnel and dump it in the mills and thus do away with the present costly system of double handling and transportation by mule teams. The water from the tunnel will furnish the motive power for the mills. Mr. Sutro, the originator of this prodigious enterprise, is one of the few men in the world who is gifted with the pluck and perseverance necessary to follow up and hound such an undertaking to its completion. He has converted several obstinate Congresses to a deserved friendliness toward his important work, and has gone up and down and to and fro in Europe until he has enlisted a great moneyed interest in it there.[3]

It is always fascinating to see how historical figures and events intersect. Twain went on to great success as a writer and lecturer but suffered many disasters both financial and personal. He died April 21, 1910, in Redding, Connecticut.

Chapter 9

Mining in Hell

You load sixteen tons, what do you get? Another day older and deeper in debt.
—Merle Travis and Tennessee Ernie Ford

The hydraulic pump had stopped working, and without its constant pumping, water levels in the Chollar-Hale & Norcross-Savage mineshaft would rise quickly and prevent mining. Thomas Veale, a car man working at the 2,400-foot level, climbed aboard the elevator cage to go to the surface for tools and parts to repair the pump. After traveling up just four feet, Veale signaled the hoist operator to stop the ascent. Feeling faint from the heat, Veale fell through the open side of the cage and plunged 280 feet into the scalding water at the bottom of the shaft. Several fellow miners descended to the bottom and worked with grappling hooks for hours before they were able to retrieve Veale's body from the water. Injuries and death were normal occurrences at the Comstock mines. Between 1863 and 1880, almost 300 miners died and 600 more were injured in various mine-related accidents.[1]

Underground mining is a dirty, difficult, and dangerous occupation; mining at the Comstock was hell. T.H. Watkins, the western historian and biographer of Secretary of Interior Harold L. Ickes, described it as, "A catalog of horrors to challenge Dante's tour through the inferno. Besides falling down a mineshaft, miners could be torn to shreds by premature explosions of blasting materials, roasted in underground fires, hit by falling equipment, or crushed by a runaway ore car."[2]

All underground mines risk cave-ins, and the Comstock mines were no exception. The soil in the Comstock region was so friable that even a small hole could not be dug without the sides collapsing. So a tunnel or stope[3] would have been impossible without supporting the walls and ceiling.

Mining engineer Philip Deidesheimer was born in Germany in 1832 and started work in the California gold fields in 1852. By 1860 the problems of supporting the mine workings in the Ophir Mine, a major mine in the Comstock Lode, demanded a solution. W.F. Babcock, a trustee of the mine, met with Deidesheimer in San Francisco in early November 1860. Babcock asked if Deidesheimer had ever seen or worked a quartz lode over 60 feet wide. Deidesheimer declined to offer any advice until he had seen the mine, which he did one week later. After about three weeks spent studying the problem, he devised a method of building square sets of timbers on top of each other. The mine carpenters implemented his system in a chamber (stope), in the Ophir Mine about 215 feet below the surface. By building and extending his "square sets," the carpenters successfully stoped the chamber from wall to wall, some 65 feet wide, and from floor to ceiling.

By February 1861, Deidesheimer had installed enough square-set timbering so the concept could be readily understood by mining men or men of other professions. Dan DeQuille of the *Territorial Enterprise*, wrote, "All who examined the system at once acknowledged that it was the only true way of stoping out and timbering up ore bodies of great width."[4] The system, comparable to honeycombs, virtually eliminated the danger of cave-ins in the Comstock mines.

Deidesheimer declined to patent this critical and widely used invention but later became rich as part owner of the Young America Mine in Sierra City, California.[5] His fictionalized story was told in Episode 8 of Season 1 of the popular TV series *Bonanza*.[6] *Bonanza*, set on the fictitious Ponderosa Ranch near Virginia City, ran on NBC for 14 years, from 1959 to 1973. The Deidesheimer episode and most others are available online.

Philip Deidesheimer's square set timbering as used in the Comstock mines to support a stope.

Many mines have fetid or explosive gasses. The Comstock mines had foul-smelling air but also had scalding hot water that sometimes gushed from cuts made in the mine walls. Massive and noisy pumps worked full-time to pump out the water. Blowers on the surface, linked to fresh-air tubes, attempted to provide fresh air to the miners. Supplies of cold water and ice cooled overheated miners during frequent breaks at cooling stations. All of these measures were required to make it barely tolerable to work in the deep mines of the Comstock.

Why Were the Comstock Mines So Hot?

There were many theories as to the source of the heat in the Comstock mines. An early (1878) study was conducted by John A. Church, professor of mining at The Ohio

State University in Columbus, Ohio.[7] Professor Church opened his report with the following introduction:

> One of the most striking phenomena connected with the mines on the Comstock lode is the extreme heat encountered in the lower levels. This heat is not due to the burning of candles, heat of the men, and decomposition of timbers, all intensified by bad ventilation, as was the case nearer the surface. It proceeds from the rock, which maintains constantly a temperature very much higher than the average of the atmosphere in Nevada. The heat of these mines is a matter of more than usual interest, for they are the only hot ones now worked in the United States, and both in the present temperature encountered and in the increase which is to be expected as greater depths are reached, they appear to surpass any foreign mines of which we have a record.

Professor Church continues:

> The rock in the lower levels of the Comstock mines appears to have a pretty uniform temperature of 130° Fahrenheit.
> These readings were obtained by placing a thermometer in a drill-hole immediately after the hole was finished, and leaving it there for periods varying from ten minutes to half an hour.

Professor Church next reports on the temperature of the air in the drifts[8]:

> ... the average temperature of those drifts which are considered to be distinctively "hot," is usually not above 108° to 112° F, though rising to 116° F, when they are very long."

Finally, he addresses the water temperature:

> But the water varies in temperature in different parts of the lode, like the rock and the air. In the East crosscut 2,000-foot level of the Crown Point Mine, which is noted for its extreme heat, the water, after flowing for nearly one hundred and fifty feet over the bottom of the drift, was found to have a temperature of 157° Fahrenheit. On the contrary, in other places the water is much less hot, but I believe it is as a rule always hotter than the air, and in many cases it appears to be hotter than the rock is found to be, except in especially hot spots.

After examining possible sources for the excessive heat, Professor Church postulated a zone of feldspar rock below 1,000 feet in depth. He claimed that this rock was decomposing into clay by chemical reaction with water that had seeped through crevices from the surface. This supposed exothermic reaction generated enough heat to convert the water into steam, which then traveled through those same or other rock fissures toward the surface. As the steam rose, it heated the surrounding rocks. Here is how Professor Church stated his case:

> To recapitulate briefly the facts here given, this explanation of the heat phenomena connected with these remarkable mines therefore supposes the existence of a cold, and what may be called a burnt out, layer of rocks, extending for a thousand feet below the surface, a zone of hot rock still in active decomposition, which has been found to exist for a depth of about fifteen hundred feet more, and no doubt extends thousands of feet further, and, finally, a mass of cold rock at a great depth, which has not yet begun to decompose. This hypothesis will be found to satisfy all of the observed facts.
> All the known facts strengthen the supposition which is advanced in this report, that the heat in the mines is subject to a steady and moderate increase as their depth is increased, this comparatively regular progression being broken by the passage through belts of rock heated above the average of the "country."

Based on the data he gathered, Professor Church concluded that, beyond the 1,000-foot depth, the temperature in the Comstock mines increased about 2.2° F for every 100 feet in depth.

Thirty-four years after Church's original study, in 1912, Augustus Locke submitted his ideas for the source of heat in the Comstock Lode.[9] Despite the additional years of information, Locke's results seem no more conclusive or useful than those of Professor Church.

Speculation

As a believer in the Law of Parsimony, also known as Occam's Razor or the KISS (Keep It Simple, Stupid) Principle, I believe there is a much simpler explanation for the high temperatures in the Comstock mines. The Law of Parsimony is the problem-solving principle that, when presented with competing hypothetical answers to a problem, one should select the answer that makes the fewest assumptions.[10]

Consider these facts:

- Taking Professor Church's conclusion, the temperature in the Comstock mines increased about 2.2° F for every 100 feet in depth. This fact alone clearly points to a heat source farther down in the earth, below the lowest level of the mines.
- A 2009 publication of the Nevada Bureau of Mines and Geology states, regarding a tour of the Comstock region, "Almost all the rocks we see today will be volcanic in origin...." This volcanic activity started about 18 million years ago with some activity continuing to just 1 million years ago.[11]
- A 2003 study of geothermal activity around Steamboat Springs, Nevada, just six miles ("crow-flight" distance) from Virginia City, concludes, "The geochemical indicators that have been developed for geothermal systems across the Great Basin, coupled with the position of Steamboat Springs..., provide compelling evidence that the deep Steamboat system is driven by magmatism that is not evident at the surface."[12] In other words, the likely source of heat powering the hot springs at Steamboat Springs is magmatism, which is the formation and motion of magma under the surface of the earth's crust.

In summary, the Comstock exhibits a deeply submerged heat source in a region formed by volcanic activity and is just six miles from a geothermal feature likely fueled by magma that is not evident on the surface. Therefore, I speculate that the cause of the hot air, hot rocks, and hot water in the Comstock mines is submerged magma from the long-dormant volcano that created the mountains of the Comstock region.

Effect on Miners

Whatever the source of the heat, it forced miners to consume tremendous quantities of water and ice. Three gallons of water and 95 pounds of ice were allotted every day for each miner. In such intense heat, miners could work only 15 minutes before they needed a half-hour rest break. However, the visit to the cooling-off station could be an irritation of its own. According to the *Territorial Enterprise*:

Comstock miners at a cooling station. Lithograph from *Frank Leslie's Illustrated Newspaper* of March 23, 1878 (courtesy Nevada Historical Society).

> In a place where the temperature is ninety, the man will feel so cold as to shiver. Often at the cooling off station, where the temperature is 100 degrees, the perspiration will cease, and the man will begin to feel very uncomfortable. On leaving and going back to where the temperature is from 115° to 120°, as the perspiration begins to start, there is for a minute or two an intolerable itching over the whole body.[13]

Water, Water Everywhere

Incredibly long diamond drills were used to explore the unexcavated portion of the drift for water pockets. The *Territorial Enterprise* for June 2, 1882, reported:

> The great use of the diamond drill is now acknowledged to be not in hunting for ore, but in guarding against water. When the drill has been run ahead and the ground to be passed probed for a distance of 150 to 250 feet, the miners feel perfectly safe in banging right along on a drift.

Tragically, the diamond drill released a fine spray of silica dust that would lodge in the miner's lungs and, over time, led to death from silicosis. The later practice of flooding the drill bit with water suppressed the dust and reduced the danger.

If a miner's pick punctured the wall around porous rock filled with hot water, that water under high pressure could pour out and fill the drift to many feet deep.

As depths increased, so did the danger from water pockets. "Bodies of water are liable to be reached that stand under such pressure that the whole face of the drift may be forced in and a torrent of scalding water poured out," the *Territorial Enterprise* wrote. "In the event of such an accident occurring the men could only run for their lives to the nearest shaft or winze. In not a few situations loss of life would be almost inevitable."[14]

Eliot Lord, in his classic work, *Comstock Mining and Miners*, discussed the water problem in detail. The following information is adapted from his 1883 book.[15]

Water in the mines became a problem as soon as mineshafts replaced open pits. For the first few years, buckets of excess water were hoisted to the surface. As the shafts got deeper, adits[16] were cut ranging from 700 to 3,300 feet in length, which intercepted shafts and provided drainage for the water. By 1862, twelve small pumps had been installed in the principal shafts on the lode.

Miners had learned to avoid cutting away particular types of deposits, especially clay, which often served as walls for underground reservoirs. One experience in the Ophir Mine served as an unforgettable lesson. On January 18, 1863, a miner working in a tunnel 313 feet below the surface drove his pick through a clay seam. The stream of hot water flowing from the hole forced the miners to drop their picks and run for their lives. One miner was badly scalded; another died.[17]

Fifty hours later, the water had formed a 21-foot-deep lake measuring 30 feet by 100 feet. Pumps working at full capacity could not stay ahead of the rising water. Additional pumps and the use of a bailing tank in the adjacent Mexican Mine, which lifted over 50,000 gallons of water per day, finally kept the water from rising further. Five months later, in July 1863, the stream still flowed, and an adjoining shaft 100 feet deeper than the tunnel had to be abandoned.

The Ophir Mine suffered another flood on Christmas Day 1864 when a massive underground reservoir was tapped at a point 25 feet above the bottom of the shaft. Water rushed in with such force that the men in the shaft narrowly escaped death by drowning. By the following day, water stood at 160 feet deep in the shaft.

Although the Ophir Mine was the most flood-prone, other mines also fought the water. Water in the main shaft of the Belcher Mine was 30 feet deep, and work had been suspended for some time before the company finally installed a new 12-inch bore pump on April 26, 1864. Although the new pump discharged over 1 million gallons a day, work on the 520-foot level of the mine remained stopped for nearly three more months.

On June 10, 1864, the Crown Point Company gave up the attempt to remove the water in their shaft, because the pump could lower the water level by just two feet, leaving some 80 feet still in the shaft.

The Overman Mining Company suspended operations during the same month, as water flowed into their shaft so rapidly that they were unable to continue work until they installed a new pump.

In the Yellow Jacket Mine on July 6, 1864, a miner tapped a hidden reservoir at 317 feet below the surface. Water entered the shaft as a stream 2½ inches in diameter, filling it to a depth of 20 feet, and forcing the company to install a pump immediately.

In September 1864, the San Francisco–based owners of the Gould and Curry Mine ordered the installation of a massive 50-horsepower engine and pump, manufactured by the Vulcan Iron Works of San Francisco.

Inside a 42-by-22-foot cavern 200 feet down, workers constructed a stone foundation 22 feet long, 8 feet wide, and 16 feet deep and attached the machinery with iron bolts. When the great day arrived, mine managers and San Francisco officials, many in black suits and top hats, descended into the mine to witness the pump at work. The engine started to rotate; the pump turned, slowly at first. Soon the water level receded, and everyone celebrated with chilled champagne and Russian caviar. The water had been defeated.

Eight months later, rapidly rising water tore the great machine from its foundation, thus halting mining operations again.[18]

The owners were disappointed but not defeated. They ordered a much-larger 120-horsepower engine and pump to remove the 100 feet of water that stood in the 725-foot-deep main shaft of the Gould and Curry. It took over a year to build and install the new equipment.

The high cost of pumping, the frequent shutdowns, and the constant refilling of the mineshafts by new underground springs made deep-mining the Comstock unprofitable.[19] Mine owners began to wonder if they should have ever invested in the Comstock Lode.[20] But Adolph Sutro knew that his tunnel would completely change the economics of deep-shaft mining on the Comstock.

Chapter 10

From Riches to Rags

There are two times in a man's life when he should not speculate: when he can't afford it, and when he can.
—Mark Twain

The chance to get rich quick always has an irresistible allure. Californians succumbed by investing millions of dollars in hoisting machinery, hydraulic pumps, processing mills, and all other equipment involved in retrieving wealth from the earth. Trading in Comstock mining shares had become an obsession for many San Francisco residents. The volume of transactions on these stocks was so large that it was the primary stimulus for organizing the San Francisco Stock and Exchange Board on September 11, 1862. All the Comstock stocks were listed there, and orders to buy and sell streamed in from California, and indeed, all the civilized world.

Everyone seemed to believe that the resources of the Comstock were unlimited and invested accordingly. Some investors accumulated massive fortunes. Others received incomes of thousands of dollars per month. Comstock Fever infected even the most conservative investors. Men, women, and even older children played the market, usually with little or no understanding of the underlying factors involved in successful mining.

Shares in the mines themselves were initially sold "by the foot," and a given claim might be 1,500 feet long. This method of valuation meant that buying or selling feet of a mine required a cumbersome and expensive series of real estate conveyances.[1] Prices were highly volatile. Gould and Curry mining stock was quoted at $6,300 per foot on July 1, 1863. On April 1, 1864, it was down to $4,550 per foot; and just four months later, on July 30, 1864, it had fallen to $900 per foot.[2] Because the mines were in Nevada and stock sales were mostly in San Francisco, "stock-jobbers" were able to manipulate share prices and consequently make money through rumors of new strikes or floods in the mines.

Eventually, entrepreneurs formed corporations that owned the assets of the mines and sold certificates, or shares, which represented abstract slices of ownership. By issuing a large number of shares, the cost per share could be set in reach of even small investors. Having a large number of owners suited the mining companies. Based on provisions of California and Nevada laws, corporate owners were allowed to levy assessments on shareholders for unexpected expenses such as litigation fees. Most Comstock investors either had Silver Fever or were ignorant of how silver mining operated and thus did not question such assessments. Abuse of assessments was common, as evidenced by the Yellow Jacket and Imperial Empire mines, which closed operations having levied more in assessments than they paid out in dividends. Only six mines—Consolidated Virginia, California, Belcher, Crown Point, Gould & Curry, and Kentuck—paid more in dividends than they collected in assessments. Several mines never paid any dividends.[3]

In late 1864, the two-year-old San Francisco Stock and Exchange Board was in chaos. Three mining stocks dominated trading. The Overman and Uncle Sam mines were trading above $1,000 per foot because they adjoined the North America mine, and the North America was said to be in bonanza. Bonanza denoted a situation that creates a sudden increase in wealth or profits; while the opposite, borrasca, denoted a mine that was not producing profitably. The three mines were in litigation to resolve overlapping claims, and investors believed that the North America would eventually gain control of the other two mines.

William Sharon shared that belief and resolved to buy as much North America as he could, regardless of the cost.

Sharon was born in Smithfield, Ohio, on January 9, 1821. Although sickly, he traveled by wagon train and on horseback from St. Louis to Sacramento, where he and his friend, John D. Fry, established a mercantile business. Their business prospered until January 8, 1850, when torrential rains caused the Sacramento and American Rivers to flood and swept away their merchandise. Sharon and Fry moved west to San Francisco. Fry was appointed a special agent of the U.S. Post Office, where he remained until 1860.

William Sharon.

Sharon went into real estate, first with others, and then in 1852, he formed his own real-estate business. Sharon quickly became active in politics and was elected assistant alderman on the first city board in May 1850.

In August 1850, Sharon and seven others, including future San Francisco mayor John Geary and future U.S. senator David Broderick, established an organization to help the flood of migrants who were arriving from the East. The next month, on September 9, 1850, California became a state. As building in San Francisco boomed to accommodate all of the new residents, Sharon and his real-estate business prospered. Between 1850 and 1864, Sharon bought and sold land and accumulated a small fortune totaling $150,000. Now in late 1864, he was ready to multiply that amount by buying stock in the North America mine, of which he already owned 1,000 shares. Sharon and Fry were both associates of the San Francisco Stock and Exchange Board, so they knew well the mechanics of buying and selling mining stock.

When trading on the Exchange opened at 11 a.m., the Ophir mine was called for trading first. After the Ophir furor died down, North America was called, and Sharon responded. E.P. Peckman, president of the Exchange, recalls what happened:

> Well, when the list was called I offered 100 shares of North America at $290. "Take it," said Sharon. One hundred more was offered. "Take it," said Sharon; "but haven't you got any more?" "Here's 500," I replied. "I'll take 500 more if you have it." "Here's 500 more." "Take it," he said. "Here's 500 more if you want it." "Take it," he said and left the room.[4]

In just a few minutes, Sharon had bought 1,700 North America shares at $290 per share, a massive total of $493,000! Of course, he did not have that much cash on hand, and he would have to raise it before the stock settlement meeting at 2 p.m. that day. He would liquidate his property, including his home on Stockton Street. But even with what he had saved over the last 14 years, he would not have enough. He would have to borrow the balance from the recently formed Bank of California. It would all be worth it, as Sharon, with the 1,000 shares he held before that day's action and the 1,700 shares acquired that day, would control the vast riches of the North America mine.

Shortly after 2 p.m., John Fry was with Sharon in his office in the Plume Building on Montgomery Street when Peckman entered. The atmosphere was not triumphant as Peckman had expected, and he knew something was wrong. Sharon said, "Peck, I have an idea that there has been a job put up to rob me in this stock sale. I don't believe you had anything to do with it, of course. Let us look at those certificates. If there is a red mark in red ink in the letter O in North America, it is my stock that I put into the pool." The men examined the stock certificates that Peckman had brought. Sharon's heart sank as they discovered that 1,000 of the 1,700 shares bore the red mark that Sharon had previously placed there.[5] He had rebought his own stock at a price much higher than he paid for it in the first place. He was the victim of a swindler, then called a stock-jobber, who, instead of holding Sharon's stock certificates for safekeeping, had put them up for sale. Rather than paying $290 per share to buy 1,700 shares, Sharon had in effect paid over $700 per share to obtain 700 additional shares.

In the primitive, rough-and-tumble world of the San Francisco Stock and Exchange Board, Sharon had no recourse. In less than an hour, he had lost much more than it had taken him 14 years to accumulate. Despite his shrewdness, Sharon had allowed greed to overcome common sense. His speculation cost him everything he had, not just his financial assets but also his reputation. But his integrity was intact. Rather than declare bankruptcy, he would somehow pay his debts. His first step would be to approach his friend, John Fry, who had connections at the Bank of California.

CHAPTER 11

William Ralston—Boat Captain to Financial Captain

Everything comes to him who hustles while he waits.
—Thomas Edison

William Ralston was the sugar daddy of San Francisco. No one did more to promote, finance, and build the boomtown, starting with the formation of Ralston's Bank of California in 1864 to its spectacular flameout in 1875.

William "Billy" Chapman Ralston was born January 12, 1826, on a farm near Plymouth, in north-central Ohio. The family soon moved to Wellsville, Ohio, on a bend in the Ohio River. Ralston's maternal grandfather, William Chapman, operated a river ferry at Chapman's Landing on the Ohio River, and the river became young Billy's playground. He learned to swim and dive and was fearless at retrieving coins from the river bottom.

When his father built a boat, the *Dominion*, Billy became clerk to Captain Sam Tyler. Billy learned not only how to maneuver a riverboat in the strong currents but also how to conduct himself among adults. He gained confidence and self-reliance, even in the face of disaster. One night a storm combined with an overloaded boat and a submerged rock led to the sinking of the *Dominion*. Billy first helped to save most of the cargo and then saved himself.

In 1842, when Billy was 16, he became the clerk on a much larger vessel, the *Constitution*, a Mississippi River floating palace. But bad luck followed Billy, and the *Constitution* was destroyed by fire while in port at Memphis. Undaunted, he moved next to become clerk on the *Convoy*, another floating palace, which was captained by Cornelius K. Garrison. Garrison was aggressive, fearless, and courageous—traits that Billy admired and learned quickly. Billy's engaging manner, natural charisma, and willingness to tackle any task won many friends both among the passengers and the crew. Captain Garrison introduced Billy to other river men such as J.C. Ainsworth, a packet boat captain who would go on to start the Oregon Steam Navigation Company in 1860. Young Billy also met Ralph S. Fretz, captain of the riverboat *Memphis*. Garrison and Fretz would team with Billy a few years later in Panama.

Meanwhile, Billy Ralston was enjoying life. The wide-open river towns of St. Louis,

11. William Ralston—Boat Captain to Financial Captain

Memphis, Vicksburg, Natchez, and New Orleans revealed a new world for the farm boy from Ohio. Because he was so personable, people invited Billy to the theater, the opera, to horse races, and to luxurious private parties where he learned to appreciate fine crystal, silver, marble statues, and French tapestries. New Orleans in particular fascinated Billy. The passionate French, Spanish, and Creole descendants reveled in entertainment of all kinds, from theater to bullfights to gambling halls to dancing. Billy learned and savored them all. He also learned to dress in style, to stand tall, to swagger with his cane, and to swing his fists when necessary.

By May 1848, Billy was a popular 22-year-old adult, and he and his friends talked of nothing but the discovery of gold in California. As soon as they had heard the news, Captains Garrison and Fretz took off for the gold fields. Billy continued to enjoy his fun-filled life but missed his friends and soon heeded the same golden call. After borrowing $300 from his friend Adam Sproule of Louisville, Billy boarded the ship *Madonna* and sailed downriver to the Caribbean and on to Panama.

Panama was in chaos. As the fastest route to California, the isthmus drew thousands of gold-hungry travelers, but there was no established way to cross to the Pacific side. Billy Ralston arrived in Aspinwall (now called Colon, but originally named for William H. Aspinwall, owner of the Pacific Mail Steamship Company) in 1849 and soon met Captains Garrison and Fretz, his old river friends. They had found enormous traffic and financial issues when they arrived in Panama, so they started a banking and shipping business to address the problems. They were making money too fast to count it but couldn't find honest help to transport a freight shipment to the Pacific side. Would Billy help them? Never one to turn down a friend, Billy agreed to supervise the shipment. The goods arrived safely, and a partnership was formed. Billy Ralston continued to work with Cornelius Garrison and Ralph Fretz, and they all continued to prosper.

In late August 1851, the steamship *New Orleans* arrived at Panama City from San Francisco. The ship was in trouble, with the dual issues of a balky engine and a captain too sick for the return trip. Garrison and Fretz had booked 200 anxious gold-seekers on the ship, and there were no sea captains available on the isthmus. They pleaded with Ralston to take the *New Orleans* and her passengers to California. Billy agreed, and after the engine repairs were completed, the *New Orleans* set sail. Although he had experience navigating the Mississippi, captaining a steamship on the Pacific Ocean was quite different from clerking on the river. His skill at detecting submerged rocks based on the color of the water, combined with constant vigilance and a great deal of luck, was sufficient to bring the *New Orleans* within sight of the entrance to San Francisco Bay. On September 20, 1851, just 18 days after departing Panama, Ralston observed the chaotic, mist-covered city. After docking, the passengers and cargo were unloaded; passengers returning East embarked, and Ralston cast off for the return trip to Panama City. He was now a successful sea captain!

On his return, Garrison and Fretz congratulated Billy and reorganized their company as "Garrison, Fretz & Co." Billy Ralston was now recognized as "& Co." Although the business of transporting people and goods was still very profitable, conditions on the isthmus were changing. Crossing the isthmus remained the bottleneck for travel from East to West and back, and a better solution was in the works.[1]

The Panama Railroad

William H. Aspinwall, who owned the Pacific Mail Steamship Company, connecting Panama City to California, formed the Panama Railroad Company with his partners, John L. Stephens and Henry M. Chauncey. The company signed a contract with the government of New Granada (as Panama was called then) to build a railroad across the isthmus. The Panama Railroad Company retained the right to operate the road for 49 years from the date of completion, and the construction was to take no more than six years. Construction of the railroad started in May 1850. The initial estimates were six months for construction and a cost of $1 million. Like the Panama Canal 58 years later, bottomless swamps, swarming insects, poisonous snakes, impenetrable mangrove jungles, cholera, yellow fever, and malaria conspired to make the initial estimates laughable. The 47 miles of the railroad were finally completed on January 27, 1855, 55 months after beginning.[2] The total cost was $7.4 million. But almost one-third of the cost was paid by fares charged for passengers and freight carried during construction on whatever portion of the railroad was complete at the time. Gold-seekers were willing to pay for transportation even if it ended in the middle of the Panamanian jungle! After completion, fares were set at arbitrarily high levels: $25 for first-class passage; $10 for second-class; personal baggage at 5¢ per pound; and express service at $1.80 per cubic foot. No one complained, and these exorbitant rates continued for 20 years.[3]

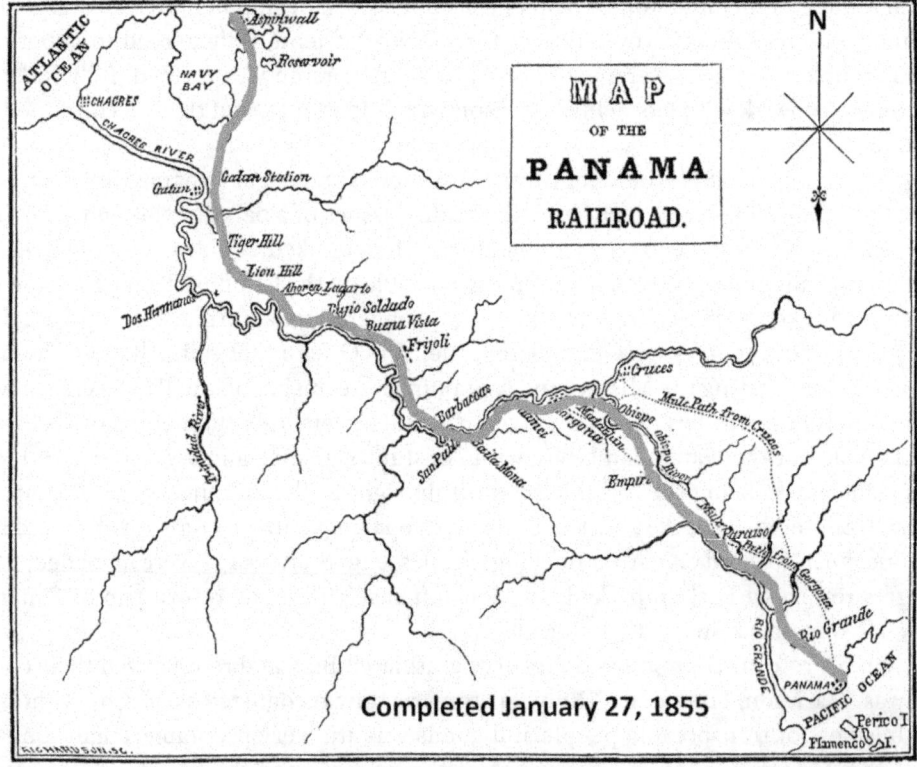

Map showing route of the Panama Railroad.

Nicaragua Transit Company

With the railroad imminent, Garrison, Fretz & Co. joined forces with Commodore Cornelius Vanderbilt to form a competitor, the Nicaragua Transit Company. The purpose of the company was to provide safe passage between the East Coast of the United States and California. The planned route was to travel by ship south from the United States to San Juan del Norte (Greytown), on the Caribbean coast of Nicaragua. There, passengers would transfer to another steamship and sail 120 miles up the San Juan River to Lake Nicaragua. After navigating across the lake, passengers would disembark at the lake port of Virgin Bay in the Rivas Isthmus. Finally, a short 20-mile stagecoach ride would get them to San Juan del Sur on the Pacific Ocean. From there, they would board a third ship and travel north to California.

The trip was a profitable operation for Vanderbilt. With a ticket price of $200 per person and up to 3,000 passengers a month to transport, it brought in about $7 million a year in revenue. The Transit Company operated several steamships, stagecoaches, and oceangoing vessels. The company created a booming economy in Greytown on the Caribbean coast and San Juan del Sur on the Pacific Ocean.[4,5]

Vanderbilt offered Garrison $60,000 per year to manage the California operation of the Nicaragua Transit Company, and he of course accepted. On March 20, 1854, Ralston followed his boss to San Francisco, where he took over as manager of the Garrison, Fretz & Co. office on Sacramento Street.

Tragedy of the Yankee Blade

In his new job, Ralston managed several fine ships, including the *Uncle Sam* and the *Yankee Blade*. The *Yankee Blade*, launched June 1, 1854, was built for speed. To demonstrate that speed, on September 30, she departed the Jackson Street Wharf in San Francisco at 4:30 p.m., bound for Panama. Ralston had instructed Captain Henry Randall to try for a speed record with an estimated 1,200 passengers and $153,000 of California gold on board. Several ships departed together, with bets as large as $5,000 that the *Yankee Blade* would be the first to arrive in Panama. She immediately pulled ahead of her competition and disappeared into the fog of the bay. Rather than head out to sea for a safer route, the Yankee Blade hugged the coastline to cut the distance.

In the early morning of Monday, October 2, a messenger aroused the sleeping Ralston at his Stockton Street home. At 3:30 p.m. on Sunday, October 1, the *Yankee Blade* had hit the hidden, fog-shrouded reefs of Point Arguello and sunk. Three hundred passengers and all the gold were gone.[6] Survivors arrived aboard the ship *Brother Jonathan* and marched in protest to Ralston's office. Police had to be called to disperse the crowd. Ralston was devastated, and never forgot the *Yankee Blade* tragedy. Soon after, Garrison, Fretz & Co. exited the shipping business.

Banking Is Safer, or Is It?

For the new year of 1856, Ralston moved in a new direction. On January 1, he and his associates launched the banking firm of Garrison, Morgan, Fretz and Ralston with

THE BANK OF CALIFORNIA.
INCORPORATED UNDER THE LAWS OF THE STATE.

Capital Stock, (*Paid up in Gold Coin,*) **$2,000,000.**
WITH THE PRIVILEGE OF INCREASING TO
$5,000,000.

STOCKHOLDERS.
SAN FRANCISCO.

D. O. MILLS,	THOS. BELL,	HERMAN MICHELS,	A. B. McCREARY,
WM. C. RALSTON,	JNO. O. EARL,	FREDERICK BILLINGS,	R. M. JESSUP,
R. S. FRETZ,	WM. NORRIS,	GEORGE H. HOWARD,	SAMUEL KNIGHT,
J. B. THOMAS,	J. WHITNEY, Jr.,	H. F. TESCHEMACHER,	A. C. HENRY,
LOUIS McLANE,	O. F. GIFFIN,	A. HAYWARD,	J. C. WILMERDING,
ASA T. LAWTON,	A. J. POPE,	MOSES ELLIS,	WM. ALVORD.
WM. E. BARRON,			

PORTLAND, OREGON.
JACOB KAMM.

D. O. MILLS, President.   WM. C. RALSTON, Cashier.
Correspondents in New York, LEES & WALLER, No. 33 Pine Street.
in London, BANK OF LONDON.

The undersigned give notice that the above named corporation has been organized for the purpose of carrying on the Banking and Exchange Business, in all its branches, in this City and with the interior of this State, the neighboring State and Territories, and with Mexico; also with the Atlantic Cities, Europe, China, and the East Indies; for which they are provided with ample facilities, and in conformity with articles of association will commence operations on the 5th day of July next, at the Banking House now occupied by DONOHOE, RALSTON & Co., Corner of Washington and Battery Streets.

With the view of giving to the business of the corporation all the efficiency and promptitude of a private banking firm, together with that confidential seclusion of private business matters so generally desired, the immediate management of its affairs is committed exclusively to D. O. MILLS and WM. C. RALSTON, as President and Cashier respectively, to whom, or either of them, the customers of the Bank will apply in all business matters. The regular meetings of the Board of Trustees will take place monthly.

The undersigned deem it advisable to call particular attention to the following peculiarities of their organization, which are positively binding on all its members:

First.—Sales of its Capital Stock can be effected only after due appraisement by Stockholders selected for that special purpose; and the Trustees of the corporation have, in all cases, the right to become purchasers of the Stock appraised at the appraisement, for the benefit of the remaining Stockholders. This restriction is printed upon each Certificate of Stock.

Second.—Loans cannot be made to Stockholders, except upon collaterals other than their Shares in the Capital Stock of this Bank.

D. O. MILLS,	HERMAN MICHELS,	A. J. POPE,	⎫
LOUIS McLANE,	W. C. RALSTON,	O. F. GIFFIN,	⎬ TRUSTEES.
WM. NORRIS,	J. B. THOMAS,	JAS. WHITNEY, Jr.	⎭
JNO. O. EARL,	THOS. BELL,		

SAN FRANCISCO, June, 18th, 1864.

Organization paper, Bank of California, 1864.

a capitalization of $700,000. By July 1857, Garrison disagreed with Ralston over the San Francisco Vigilance Committee of 1856[7]; and Charles Morgan was focused on his newly formed Southern Steamship Company.[8] Two new partners, Joseph Donohoe and Eugene Kelly, joined and formed Donohoe, Ralston & Co. in San Francisco and Eugene Kelly & Co. in New York.

Ralston was the constant presence in all the firms, and his charm, industriousness, and connections, along with the general economic prosperity, led to great financial success.

The 1857[9] discovery of gold and subsequently silver at the Comstock Lode in Nevada fascinated Ralston, and he was the first to appreciate its possible importance to San Francisco and to his bank. He viewed the mines and associated industries as excellent investments and advised all who asked to invest their money there. He had loaned much of the bank's money to support Comstock mines and their related enterprises. San Francisco and the Comstock Lode became symbiotic; Californians invested their money to support the Lode, and bullion flowed from the Lode to finance the development of commerce, construction, and multiple industries in San Francisco.

Ralston's banking partners were less than enthusiastic about his loans to the Comstock mines and mills, and other businesses outside of California. Their chief concern was the lack of security for the loans; Ralston was being too speculative. Ralston countered that Kelly and Donohoe were too conservative for the fast-growing West. He secretly planned to break away and form a new company where overcautious partners would not hamper his progressive views. He convinced Darius Ogden (D.O.) Mills, the most respected financier on the West Coast, to act as head of the new bank, although Ralston would actually run the bank under the unassuming title of cashier. On July 4, 1864, before either Kelly or Donohoe knew what was coming, Ralston formed the Bank of California and captured some of the most important accounts, including all of those associated with the Comstock Lode. Of course, Donohoe and Kelly were both amazed and angry with Ralston's secret maneuvering.

Ralston was rightly viewed as the prime mover behind the success of the former Donohoe, Ralston & Co., so investors flocked to his new venture. Ralston used those funds to buy the usual bank instruments such as bonds but invested most of the bank's $3 million capitalization in Comstock Lode mines, mills, and foundries.[10]

Chapter 12

Rehabilitation

A leader takes people where they want to go. A great leader takes people where they don't necessarily want to go, but ought to be.
—Rosalynn Carter

The decision to avoid bankruptcy brought William Sharon's thoughts to Billy Ralston at the Bank of California. Sharon's friend, John Fry, was the foster father of Ralston's wife. Ralston was known as a compassionate man, a man who was always ready to lend a helping hand. Perhaps Ralston would buy what was left of Sharon's real estate or at least loan him money on it. Fry and Charles Wakelee, another friend of Sharon's, went to visit Ralston at the Bank of California.[1,2]

Ralston had his own problems. All was not well in Nevada. From 1861 through 1863, gross production from the Comstock had doubled each year. But by 1864, production had dropped to a paltry $16 million. All the easily obtained surface ore had been picked clean, and a sizable investment would be required to continue exploring any deeper deposits. And the deep mines that existed, such as the Gould and Curry and the Ophir, reported vast amounts of water flooding them. The rumor mill shifted into full gear: it was the end of the Comstock; no pumps could handle such large quantities of water. The stock market, overheated by previous good news, crashed. Stock in the Gould and Curry mine dropped from $6,300 per share to $2,400 and then to $900. Ophir fell from $1,580 to $300. The normally sanguine Ralston was greatly alarmed.

When Fry and Wakelee arrived to plead William Sharon's case, Ralston set aside his problems with the Comstock and welcomed them warmly. After hearing of the financial disaster that had befallen Sharon, Ralston was all sympathy. He hated underhanded dealing, especially when it involved his beloved Comstock stocks. He agreed to see what he could do to help Sharon.

A few days later, the Bank of California directors voted to take over Sharon's remaining real estate and loan him enough money to pay for his stock purchases. Shortly after that, Ralston advanced the penniless and disgraced Sharon $250 per month from his own funds.[3,4]

Ralston now had to deal with even more bad news from the Comstock. Without warning, the Virginia City bank headed by J.W. Stateler and N.O. Arrington, but secured by Ralston's San Francisco Bank of California, failed. Viewed as "conceited and unscrupulous" by a fellow banker, Stateler dominated his alcoholic partner.[5] Stateler and Arrington's primary client was the Gould and Curry Company, whose treasurer was none other than William Ralston and whose directors included George Hearst, father of William Randolph Hearst.

Gould and Curry required vast amounts of gold coin to meet payroll at the beginning of each month. Stateler and Arrington had been permitted to supply this money, but Stateler abused the privilege. Stateler had cashed a large draft and soon tried to cash another. Ralston saw something was wrong and refused to honor the second draft. Stateler promptly closed the bank, defaulting on $20,000 owed Wells Fargo and Company and $30,000 owed the Bank of California. Ralston and his bank needed to recover their debt from the remaining assets of Stateler and Arrington. And beyond the money, the reputation of the fledgling Bank of California was at risk.

Ralston considered what to do, and he resolved to send a direct employee of the Bank to clean up the mess in Virginia City. He chose his trusted receiving teller, Edney S. Tibbey, for the job. Tibbey, who was familiar with all aspects of the bank and its mining loans, agreed to go, and the other bank directors agreed. They seldom disagreed with Ralston. As Tibbey was preparing to depart, John Fry and Charles Wakelee again appeared in Ralston's office to propose Sharon for the Virginia City assignment. Ralston hesitated. Sharon had recently fallen for a stock swindle and knew nothing about either mining or banking. Fry and Wakelee were insistent, and Ralston wanted to please his friends (and the foster father of his wife). He reluctantly agreed to send Sharon to Virginia City.

A few days later Sharon visited Ralston to discuss the assignment. Ralston stressed the importance of the Comstock to the Bank of California and the future of San Francisco. Did Sharon think he could handle the situation? But Sharon's thoughts were more on retribution and the restoration of his reputation. "I'll get even with the Comstock yet," he swore as he left Ralston's office to head for Virginia City.[6]

Ralston and Sharon were a study in contrasts. Ralston was a stocky, handsome man. His focus to the point of compulsion was the well-being of his beloved city of San Francisco. He favored any enterprise that would cause the city to grow, with the ultimate goal of making San Francisco the commercial center of the western United States. At his bank office, he met inventors, promoters, and ordinary citizens to hear their ideas. He bought patents and loaned money to establish the first California vineyards, a California wool industry, and San Francisco's California Theater. Not only his business

William Ralston, ca. 1865.

associates but his employees and even casual acquaintances regarded Ralston as a generous friend. He visited the businesses in which he had invested and talked with the employees. They felt that he knew, cared about, and respected them.[7]

William Sharon weighed but 135 pounds, and his eyes, depending on the observer, were searching and projecting intelligence to his friends; or black and beady, sly and devious to his detractors. He could be generous, but his underlying motive always seemed to be self-interest. He laughed but rarely smiled. Sharon favored black broadcloth suits, which gave him the appearance of a cleric. Although Sharon managed and invested heavily in the Comstock mines, he almost never descended into them. He was aloof and distant.

Sharon's first job in Virginia City was to select from deeds, promissory notes, and mortgages held by the closed Stateler and Arrington bank. By selecting the best of the remaining assets, he recovered nearly all the Bank of California claims.[8,9] While evaluating the assets, Sharon quickly decided that a branch of the Bank of California could prosper in Virginia City. And of course, who better to manage that branch than William Sharon! He observed that the headlong growth of the Comstock had resulted in gross inefficiencies that an on-site presence could correct and prevent. Mining, milling, transportation, and lumbering were all viewed as separate enterprises, while an organized approach could weave them together into a single money-generating operation.[10]

Sharon did not trust the people providing critical information to him. In particular, he routinely checked the ore assayers by sending the same samples to several assayers. He later encouraged his nephew, G.H. Sharon, to study assaying and then brought him to Virginia City as his primary assayer.

Although 1864 was a down year for the Comstock, Sharon firmly believed there was still great wealth underground. Sharon wrote to Ralston to propose that a real bank (the Bank of California) in the Comstock region would be profitable. Ralston agreed to meet to discuss the idea.

When they met in mid–1864, Sharon argued that a local presence could better monitor and optimize the entire process from mining to bullion production. He also proposed himself as the manager of the new branch. The bank directors objected to both recommendations. Placing a branch in Virginia City when the current outlook was so bleak was too much of a risk. And Sharon was recently wiped out financially, hardly a man with whom to trust bank money. But Ralston liked the idea of a branch in Virginia City, so he would have eyes on what was by far the bank's most important investment. As far as whom would manage the branch, it again came down to Sharon versus Tibbey. At the age of 29, Tibbey was far more familiar with bank operations than was Sharon. But Sharon had much more business experience. And when faced with financial ruin, Sharon had refused the easy way out, bankruptcy, and had vowed to repay his debts in full. Possibly the deciding factor was Sharon's acknowledged skill at poker! Sharon possessed the traits important for winning at poker, and possibly at other endeavors: discipline, a strong desire to win, knowledge of probability, an analytical mind, the ability to judge others, a steadfast demeanor, and controlled emotions. A friend warned Ralston that Sharon was a dedicated poker player. Ralston asked if Sharon won or lost. When the friend said that Sharon almost always won, Ralston replied, "He sounds like the very man I want."[11] As usual, Ralston overrode his bank directors. The Bank of California would open a branch in Virginia City, and William Sharon would manage it. But Ralston hedged his bets. He sent his brother, James Ralston, to be the cashier at the new Virginia City branch.

At the end of October 1864, Comstock newspapers announced the opening of the Bank of California branch in Virginia City. On October 31, President Abraham Lincoln proclaimed Nevada a state. On November 17, a newspaper announced that the Virginia City branch, at the southwest corner of C and Taylor streets, was accepting deposits of coin or bullion. Sharon moved in upstairs.

In the wild atmosphere of the Comstock, Sharon was an oddity. He was older than most residents and had much more formal education. He was industrious during the day, but, with his family back in San Francisco, his evenings were free for his favorite entertainment, high-stakes poker. He hosted games in his rooms above the bank and, of course, won more than he lost. Other hobbies included fiddling, at which he was an expert; cockfighting; and attendance at Virginia City's newly completed theater, the Opera House, where he reserved a stage box for opening nights. One other thing set Sharon apart—he had a full-time valet. Ah Ki, a Chinese immigrant of the same small stature as Sharon, was polite, affable, and loyal. He had come to America 10 years earlier and remained Sharon's valet for 23 years, until Sharon's death in 1885.

The other Virginia City banks had formed an association in August 1863. In the absence of antitrust and usury laws, the association established the interest rate on loans at the incredible rate of 5 percent per month.[12] Given the previous boom times and the lack of an alternative, the capital-intensive mines and mills had to accept loans at that rate. Sharon, as the new kid in town, changed the game. The Bank of California would charge only 2 percent interest per month (24 percent per year, still exorbitantly high by today's standards). The cash-hungry mine and mill owners flocked to Sharon's bank, and he was seen as a savior. He loaned up to one-sixth the value of the property, but the end game should have been clear to anyone. If lean times continued, the indebted owners could not pay back their loans, they would be in default, and the Bank of California would foreclose. That sequence of events is exactly what happened.

The year 1865 was no better than the down year of 1864. Then on April 9, 1865, Confederate General Robert E. Lee surrendered at Appomattox Court House, Virginia, thus effectively ending the American Civil War. That news encouraged all Union states (of which Nevada was one) about their future. That boost to morale was quickly quenched six days later when reports of Lincoln's assassination at Ford's Theater on April 15 reached Virginia City.

Although bullion production in 1865 almost matched that of 1864, thousands of people left Virginia City, thinking that the boom was over. Charles Carroll Goodwin, prominent Nevada judge and later journalist, said, "In '63 and '64 the first rich deposits were pretty well dug out all along the Comstock, and in '65 the impression got out that the old lead was about worked.... I do not know what might have happened had not Mr. Sharon kept his nerve and kept work going."[13]

On May 1, 1865, the Bank of California foreclosed on the Swansea mill in nearby Gold Canyon. By May 1867, the bank had foreclosed on and now owned seven mills. Sharon was beginning to look more like the devil than a savior.

The ever-conservative directors of the Bank of California were not impressed.

Darius Ogden (D.O.) Mills, the prominent and respected banker whom Ralston had recruited to lend credibility to the new Bank of California, was the bank president. He and other directors insisted that Sharon and Ralston account for the $700,000 advanced in loans to Comstock companies. At a meeting, most likely held in Virginia City, Mills expressed shock at the use of bank funds in such risky ventures. He demanded that the Virginia City branch close. Sharon argued that closing the branch would further depress Virginia City and damage the entire Bank of California. Ralston recognized the symbiotic relationship between the Comstock riches and the bank's finances. Furthermore, the industries he had financed in San Francisco depended on the flow of Comstock capital. Sharon continued, explaining that wasteful mining and milling practices had consumed much of the loans and that more effective management would reduce costs. He brought mining superintendents into the meeting to support his arguments. Rather than pull out, he proposed that the bank take control of the most promising mines and mills. D.O. Mills insisted the bank was in the banking business, not the mining business, and could not take such a risk.

Sharon broke the impasse by proposing to take the mills personally for what they cost the bank. These mills would later form the basis for the Union Mill and Mining Company. Ralston declared that he would take responsibility for any losses the bank might incur. As there would be no jeopardy for himself or the bank, Mills consented, and the rest of the directors concurred. The agreement reinforced the strong bond between Ralston and Sharon that would endure for the next ten years, and it also cemented the relationship between the Bank of California and the Comstock.

Chapter 13

Homework

Spectacular achievement is always preceded by unspectacular preparation.
—Robert H. Schuller

On Adolph Sutro's first visit to the Comstock in 1860, he dreamed of a tunnel to drain water from the mineshafts. For over four years the idea had percolated in his mind, and the tunnel details had become more specific. He now envisioned a 4-mile-long tunnel starting near the Carson River, at an elevation of about 4,400 feet, and proceeding northwest to intersect the Comstock mines 1,800 feet under Virginia City. This tunnel would not only drain the mineshafts of hot, smelly water; it would offer many other benefits:

- Provide a path for efficient air circulation within the mines;
- Allow easy transport of timbers to implement Philip Deidesheimer's square set timbering;
- Convey miners to and from the mines more effectively;
- Permit easier escape for miners in the event of fire or mine collapse; and
- Carry ore from the mines to the mills on railroad cars, thus eliminating the slow, expensive hoisting operations and wagon transport to the mills.

Sutro had been busy laying the groundwork for his tunnel. Nevada approved a constitution in September 1864 and was admitted as the 36th state of the United States on October 31, 1864. Soon afterward, Sutro approached the first Nevada legislature to request a franchise to build his tunnel. In his later testimony before the Committee on Mines and Mining of the U.S. House of Representatives, Sutro recalled,

> A few thinking men in the Legislature were struck at once with the idea, and they investigated the matter, although the majority of them said I must be hopelessly insane to propose any thing of the kind, and would waste my time for nothing, for the project could never be carried out—the majority of them, I say, ridiculed it. But they granted the franchise by a unanimous vote nevertheless.[1]

On February 4, 1865, the Nevada Legislature unanimously granted Sutro a franchise and right-of-way for a tunnel to the Comstock Lode.

At Sutro's request, Baron Ferdinand Richthofen,[2] a famous German geographer and geologist, studied the future of the Comstock and the feasibility of building a tunnel to drain the mines. In a lengthy letter to Sutro dated February 16, 1865, Richthofen wrote first about the prospects of finding rich deposits at deep depths.

> My experience on the Comstock vein is based on close and repeated examinations of nearly all the mines on its course. I believe, to concur with almost everybody, who has equal experience about them, in the opinion, that it is a true fissure vein, of extraordinary length, and extending downward much farther than any mining works will ever be able to be carried on. It would be too lengthy to enumerate the various reasons which lead most positively to this conclusion. It is now assumed almost universally as a fact, and the number of those who consider it as a gash vein, or a system of gash veins, is fast diminishing.
>
> As to the downward continuance of the ore-bearing character, every instance goes to show that the average yield in precious metals remains about equal at every depth. Some mines had accumulations of ore near the surface (Ophir, Mexican, Gold Hill); in others, they commenced very near under the surface (Gould & Curry, Potosi, Yellow Jacket, Belcher); at others, again, considerable work had to be done before bodies of ore of any amount were struck (Chollar, the southern part of Gold Hill, Uncle Sam, and others), and some which had no ore heretofore, appear to have good prospects to find it soon. The fact that some rich bodies of ore, which were found near the surface, gave out at the depth of a few hundred feet, induced the common belief that the Comstock vein was becoming poorer in its lower parts. But the explorations of the last months have entirely defeated this opinion. On the contrary, the enormous amount of bullion, which is being produced by the mines at present, may almost appear to prove that the vein is improving in depth. But this conclusion is probably equally fallacious, as it must be borne in mind that many mines have been developed at different levels, and ore is being extracted from several of those. Hoisting works, and the mode of extracting the ore, have also been improved, and, of course, help to increase the daily production. This average equality of the produce of the vein at every different level is not only true for the amount of ore extracted, but also for its yield. The rich body of ore in the Ophir and Mexican mines forms the only exception to this rule, as none of equal average percentage in silver and gold has been found again. Even the relative proportion of gold and silver in the ore has not undergone any material change, though the bullion, on account of the more imperfect processes of reduction, contained at first proportionally more gold than at present. The ore found in the Uncle Sam mine, at the depth of 414 feet, is as rich in gold as any found in other parts within 100 feet from the surface. There is no reason to doubt that this equality of average produce and yield throughout the entire length of the vein, will continue downward to any depth.[3]

Richthofen then addressed the practicality of a tunnel.

> The second subject about which you requested me to state my views, is the practical feasibility of your project. The best starting point of the drain tunnel will, of course, be at such a place, where the greatest possible depth on the vein can be reached by the shortest possible route. Besides, it has to be taken into consideration, which qualities of rock the tunnel would have to run through, and which are the facilities for sinking air shafts. I will try to argue these different points, as my numerous geological examinations and rambles over the country of Washoe have made me pretty familiar with its physical outlines and its geological structure.
>
> As to the starting point of the drain tunnel, you have, with remarkable sagacity, selected a place which so far supersedes any other, as to be indeed the only feasible one in the country. South of Webber Canon, the range of hills which slope into Carson Valley, recedes in the shape of an amphitheater and allows the almost level bottom of the desert to approach the Comstock vein within less than four miles. The level of the Carson River at Dayton is about 1900 feet lower than the croppings of the Comstock vein at the Gould & Curry office. If the tunnel starts 100 feet above the river, at the foot of the hills, it will strike the Comstock vein 1800 feet below those croppings. Making no allowance for the Eastern dip of the vein, its length would be about 19,000 feet; thus making the proportion of depth to length, as 1 to 10.55.
>
> There is no place more suitable along the banks of Carson River.
>
> The facilities of excavating the tunnel will mainly depend upon the quality of the rocks through which it will pass. It is a remarkably fortunate incidence that the route selected by you promises, also, in this respect, to be the most advantageous.

> The first 6000 or 7000 feet will be run through trachyte and trachytic breccia which in a broad semicircular belt of prominent hills, swing from Dayton by the Sugarloaf to Washoe Valley. Trachytic breccia can easily be worked by the pick, yet is ordinarily solid and dry enough to require no timbering.
>
> The next 2,500 feet will, to all probability, exhibit a great variety of rock, some of which will be rather hard. This applies chiefly to certain volcanic rocks of dark color (andesite), which flank the trachytic range to the west; but as they occur in dykes parallel to the same, they will retard work but slightly.
>
> The following 10,000 feet, which bring you to the vein, will most likely consist of the same material as is traversed by the numerous tunnels which lead at present to the Comstock vein. This rock (trachytic greenstone) would offer serious obstacles if it were in an undecomposed state. But from the general nature of its decomposition, which, evidently, was performed from below, by ascending steam and vapors, during a time of volcanic action, I believe to be justified in the conclusion that you will find it for the entire length of 10,000 feet of the same rotten nature, as in the shallow tunnels at present in existence. It varies in them constantly, some varieties being easily worked by the pick, while others, occurring in streaks parallel to the vein, are less decomposed, and have to be blasted. Timbering would probably be required but to a limited degree in a small tunnel; but if you make it of sufficient size for a double track, you may have to timber almost all of the 10,000 feet.

Baron Ferdinand Richthofen, 1879.

Next, Richthofen emphasized the desirability of air shafts placed along the line of the tunnel.

> A third requirement, though not absolutely necessary with the present accomplishments of tunneling, will be the sinking of air-shafts. Also, in regard to these, your tunnel offers greater facilities than any other route. It passes first under a high range of hills, which is accompanied on either side by deep ravines. Each of them will be a suitable starting place for an air-shaft; the depth of the latter would be about 500 and 750 feet. The first of the two would be about 3,000 feet distant from the mouth of the tunnel, the second about 3,600 feet from the first. Approaching the Comstock vein, there are two more places suitable for air-shafts, the distance from the second to the third being 2,500 feet, that of the third to the fourth, 4,000 feet, thus leaving about 6,000 feet distance from the fourth shaft to a point vertically under the Gould and Curry croppings. The two last shafts would have a depth of 1,200 and 1,300 feet. One of them will, no doubt, be sufficient.

Regarding the importance of a tunnel to the future of the Comstock, Richthofen stated the following:

> The future of Washoe, indeed, depends entirely on the execution of this magnificent enterprise. It is of vital importance for the State of Nevada and will have great influence on the neighboring California, which chiefly derives the benefits of the mines of Washoe. The numerous advantages will only be fully understood when the work will be completed.

Richthofen concluded:

Allow me to congratulate you to have been the first to have taken an enterprise of such vast importance firmly in your hand. With the sincere wish, that you may overcome the difficulties which you will no doubt meet in carrying out a work of such magnitude,

> I remain yours very sincerely,
> FR. RICHTHOFEN.[4]

At the end of the booklet containing Baron Richthofen's letter, Sutro included a brief but strong statement of support signed by 68 mine superintendents, mine owners, bankers, mining engineers, Nevada Supreme Court justices, district judges, state government officials, and Nevada state senators. Following is the statement they endorsed:

OPINION OF MINING SUPERINTENDENTS—AND OTHERS

The undersigned, fully aware of the importance and urgent necessity of providing means for draining the Comstock ledge by means of a deep drain tunnel, and foreseeing the difficulties which must present themselves, before long, in removing the water from these mines; and being satisfied that the best interests, of not only the owners of the Comstock ledge, but the people at large of this State, would be seriously affected by neglecting this matter; we would most earnestly recommend the immediate construction of such a work, and ask the co-operation of all parties interested, in order that this important undertaking may speedily be carried out.

Virginia, February 15th, 1865.[5]

With a franchise and right-of-way from the state of Nevada, the endorsement of the expert geologist Baron Ferdinand Richthofen, and the strong support of Comstock mining superintendents and other notable Nevada citizens, Adolph Sutro had done his homework and was ready to seek money to finance his dream. Who better than Billy Ralston to bless the project?

Chapter 14

Endorsement

Do not follow where the path may lead. Go instead where there is no path and leave a trail.
—Ralph Waldo Emerson

Adolph Sutro had to have approval and ideally financial support from William Ralston and the Bank of California for his crazy tunnel idea to become a reality; Ralston had to find a solution to the water inundating the mines of the Comstock. At the end of February 1865, Adolph Sutro appeared in Ralston's office with the answer to Ralston's water problem—a massive tunnel. After hearing the details of what would be "the greatest mining enterprise that has ever been undertaken in this country,"[1] Ralston was sold. He could see the benefits of Sutro's proposal, and he always liked to be associated with ambitious projects that would benefit his beloved city of San Francisco. Ralston promised to do everything in his power to help Sutro, and he issued a strong endorsement of the project on March 1, 1865:

PROPOSITION TO MINING COMPANIES

The undersigned convinced of the necessity of constructing a deep drain Tunnel to the Comstock ledge, and desirous of seeing this great work speedily carried out, begs leave to lay the following proposition before the different Companies of the Comstock ledge, and is of the opinion that its acceptance will ensure the carrying out of this important enterprise.

The proposition would be about as follows:

No wonder that the enterprising American people, particularly the adventurous portion of Californians, became excited over visions of great wealth and pictures of the immense amounts of precious metals produced by the Spanish-American mines for the last three centuries. The natural consequence was a great influx of people to these newly discovered regions, and a vigorous prosecution of work, which shortly established the fact that the great Comstock ledge not only contains ores of great value, but that the same extends for miles in length, and promised to be of enduring depth.

The Companies will by these means secure to the Tunnel Company a small interest on the capital invested. *They have to pay out nothing until they derive benefit from the drainage of their mines, and then pay nothing, should they have no ore.* Should they have ore, the amount to be paid to the Tunnel Company is so small compared to the advantages they will derive, that they will save the amount to be paid per ton, *alone in the advantages they would enjoy in extracting the ore from the mines.*

If the following pages are studied carefully, it will be found that the cost of erecting the necessary pumping machinery, and the cost of maintaining the steam engines, is so immense, that the advantages offered by the tunnel company, must strike the mining companies to be of vital importance to their own interests.

The Tunnel Company will have to take all the risk as to the future yield of these mines. They have to embark in an undertaking which involves the outlay of millions for a number of years, before any benefit can be derived from it, and after they complete the work, they only ask a low interest on the capital invested, from those parties who can afford to pay, by being enabled, through their agency, to extract ores from their veins. It may as well be stated here, that some parties are fearful of getting into litigation, by having an outside company construct this tunnel, and striking the Comstock at this great depth; on this point we would state, that the objects of this Tunnel Company being for the purpose of draining these mines, they would not be in competition for extracting ore from the Comstock ledge.

To the people at large of the Pacific states, by securing the permanent working of the Comstock ledge, which in our opinion would be accomplished by constructing a deep drain tunnel, we most cheerfully endorse Mr. Sutro's proposition to the Companies, and shall do all in our power to assist him in carrying out his project.

San Francisco, March 1, 1865.
JOHN PARROTT, LOUIS McLANE, W.C. RALSTON.[2]

Significantly, however, Ralston realized that neither he nor the Bank of California had funds available to provide the $3 million loan needed to finance the tunnel.

Sutro next made it official by incorporating the company in Nevada. On July 24, 1865, he formed the Sutro Tunnel Company. The first trustees included William Stewart, a leading attorney and the first U.S. senator from the state, who served as the president of the new company.

Now that the Sutro Tunnel Company was a reality, and with Ralston's endorsement in hand, Sutro was ready to approach the Comstock mine owners and superintendents. They had already expressed their support of the tunnel project in principle, but now it was time to define the exact financial terms. Agreeing to an idea and agreeing what to pay to achieve that idea are two distinct questions, and Sutro had to negotiate a financial contract with over 20 separate mining companies. The talks dragged on for nine months,

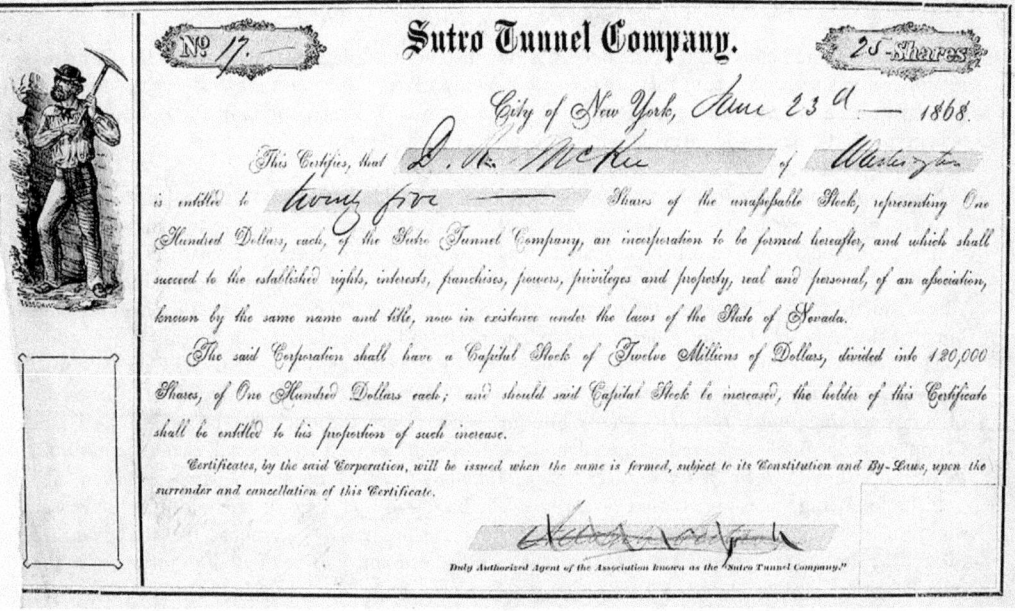

Early stock certificate from the Sutro Tunnel Company, 1868.

but by April 1866, 23 of the mining companies, representing 95 percent of the market value of all the mines on the Comstock, signed binding articles of agreement. The articles specified that, once the extension of the tunnel and its lateral drifts reached designated points within their boundaries, each company would pay in perpetuity the amount of $2 per ton of ore extracted from their respective mines. This basic fee covered the services of water drainage and mine ventilation. To place this vital clause of the agreement in perspective, the average value of a ton of ore extracted on the Comstock through June 1880 was $43.86.[3] So the $2 per ton royalty was less than 5 percent of the average ore value.

In addition, the mining companies could elect to use the tunnel to transport ore from the mines to the mills (or timber or other materials from the mouth of the tunnel to the mines) for a fee of 25¢ per mile per ton. Miners could ride through the tunnel to or from the mineshafts for a fee of 25¢ each way. The tunnel was to be at least seven feet in height and eight feet in width, with a grade of not less than 1 inch per 100 feet. To guarantee the completion of this drain way within a reasonable term of years, the Sutro Tunnel Company contracted to secure subscriptions amounting to $3 million before August 1, 1867, and to expend at least $400,000 annually in completing the work.[4,5]

Because Ralston could not commit either his own or Bank of California funds to the tunnel project, Sutro asked him for a letter of introduction to the Oriental Bank Corporation of London. Ralston complied, writing on Bank of California letterhead,

THE BANK OF CALIFORNIA

D.O. Mills
President

W.C. Ralston
Cashier

San Francisco, May 4, 1866

To the Oriental Bank Corporation, London.

Dear Sirs:

This letter will be presented to you by Mr. A. Sutro, of this city, who visits England with the view of laying before capitalists there a very important enterprise, projected by himself, and known as "the Sutro Tunnel," in the State of Nevada. This tunnel is designed to cut the great Comstock Lode or ledge, upon which our richest silver mines are located, at a depth of two thousand feet from the surface, to drain it of water, render it easily accessible at that point, and thus increase the facilities and diminish the expenses of the progressive development of these mines.

Too much cannot be said of the great importance of this work, if practicable upon any remunerative basis. We learn that the scheme has been very carefully examined by scientific men, and that they unhesitatingly pronounced in its favor on all points—practicability, profit, and great public utility. Mr. Sutro, we presume, is furnished with the necessary documents to make this apparent; and our object in this letter is simply to gain for him, through your kindness, such an introduction as will enable him to present his enterprise to the public fairly and upon its merits.

Commending Mr. Sutro to your courteous attention, we remain, dear sirs, very truly,

W.C. Ralston
Cashier[6]

Senator William Stewart, the president of the Sutro Tunnel Company, wrote letters of introduction to leading New York figures, including Collis P. Huntington of the Central Pacific Railroad, and James Gordon Bennett, editor of the *New York Herald* newspaper.[7]

The tunnel would be on public lands reserved to the United States (as were all the mines on the Comstock), so the Tunnel Company sought one more level of governmental approval. The Company requested an act by the U.S. Congress granting to Adolph Sutro the right to construct a mining, draining, and exploring tunnel to and through the Comstock Lode. Congress passed the Tunnel Act on July 26, 1866. In addition to granting Sutro (significantly, not the Sutro Tunnel Company, but "Sutro, his heirs and assigns") the right to build his tunnel, the Act also provided:

- The right to sink air shafts along the tunnel;
- The right to purchase up to two sections (total of 1280 acres) of public land near the mouth of the tunnel for $1.25 per acre;
- The right to purchase mineral veins and lodes (other than the Comstock Lode) within 2,000 feet on each side of the tunnel for $5 per acre;
- All mines on the Lode must pay to the Sutro Tunnel Company the amount agreed to by the owners representing a majority of the estimated value of the Lode.[8]

The last clause would prove to be vitally important because it legally bound all mines to the $2 per ton payment, whether or not the owners had previously signed a contract with the Sutro Tunnel Company. So far Sutro had been aided by powerful cooperation and had met little or no opposition.[9]

As soon as the Tunnel Act passed, Sutro traveled from Washington, D.C., to New York to persuade the leading merchants, bankers, and financiers to invest in his project. Despite all that Sutro had done in gaining governmental and private support, skepticism remained. The magnitude and endurance of the Comstock Lode were unproven, Eastern investment in other Western mines had proven to be risky, the prospective profits of the tunnel were vague and uncertain, the cost was enormous, and the project was larger than anything of a similar nature.

Sutro had answers for all of the objections. He was especially expansive regarding the question of profits. Royalties for ore extraction at the current rate would amount to $3,000 per day. Hauling out waste rock would bring $1,000 per day. Transporting the 3,000 miners presently employed in the mines would add $1,500 per day. Sales of building lots in the town that would rise near the mouth of the tunnel (of course, the town would be named "Sutro") would add another $3 million. In total, Sutro projected annual revenue from the tunnel of between $2.3 and $6 million.[10]

During his discussions with potential New York investors, Sutro predicted a major population shift from Virginia City and Gold Hill to the new town of Sutro at the mouth of the tunnel. He said that Virginia City and Gold Hill would shrink with or without the tunnel, because with existing mining methods, involving pumping enormous amounts of water and hoisting ore and waste rock hundreds or thousands of feet to the surface, costs would soon exceed the value of bullion produced. The assessed value of property in Virginia City and Gold Hill was $6.8 million and included major investments in mills for refining the ore. Sutro said of these mills, "The only course left to them is to remove to the tunnel company land." He was essentially predicting that control of the mines and mills of the Comstock would shift to the tunnel company (that is, to Sutro himself). Sutro's statements raised the eyebrows of residents and mill-owners alike.[11]

It is a tribute to Sutro's enthusiasm and salesmanship that he obtained consideration for his scheme and a virtual pledge from several New York capitalists. But one objection remained. If this tunnel idea was so great, why was there no financial support from either Nevada or California investors? If he could get backing of a few hundred thousand dollars from western investors, eastern sources would add $3 million of funding. Sutro urged the New Yorkers to write a letter stating their concerns and pledging support if those concerns were resolved.

A letter from potential New York investors dated October 5, 1866, summarized the situation. After describing the lack of western investment as a "fatal objection," the letter said that if a portion of the required money, "say $400,000 or $500,000," were raised in the west and construction of the tunnel started, "we think you will find it comparatively an easy task to obtain the balance of the funds here." The letter continued:

> Let some of the leading men on your coast, who are known here for their commercial standing and their integrity, form a preliminary board of directors, and you may then, while the tunnel is daily progressing, return to New York, we think, with confidence of success, and we shall use our best effort to assist you in accomplishing your object.

The letter was signed by 40 individuals or companies who, in Sutro's judgment, represented $100 million in capital.[12]

With this assurance, Sutro returned to California. In January 1867, he convinced the Nevada Legislature to petition the U.S. Congress to grant material aid (money) to accelerate construction of the Sutro Tunnel, claiming that this work was of vital importance to the mining interests of the whole country and certain to increase the revenues of the nation.[13]

He then discussed the results of his New York negotiations with the mining companies interested in the success of the tunnel. He convinced them that dividends on tunnel stock would easily cover the $2 per ton fee they were obligated to pay. His arguments, whether valid or not, were so convincing that $600,000 (including $150,000 from the Savage Mining Company) was subscribed conditionally by the mining companies on the lode before the end of May 1867.[14] He also received an extension of one year's time, to August 1, 1868, to raise the capital needed to build the tunnel. That extension was signed by 11 mining companies, the product of whose mines in 1867 was 71 percent of the total yield of the lode for that year.[15]

Sutro believed that his struggles to obtain financing were nearly over, and that construction of the tunnel would start soon. He stated, "I had a fair prospect of raising $1 million in San Francisco, and the whole amount required, perhaps, in California."[16] What could go wrong?

Chapter 15

Rejection

In the end we will remember not the words of our enemy, but the silence of our friends.
—Martin Luther King, Jr.

The annual meeting of the Crown Point Mining Company would be tomorrow, June 7, 1867. Stockholders would ratify the $75,000 pledge the trustees had made to the Sutro Tunnel Company. In Sutro's words, this ratification would be another milestone "on the full road to success."

But that script was shredded during a secret meeting called by the Bank of California the night before. At that June 6 meeting, the decision was made not to ratify the pledge of $75,000 to the tunnel company. In addition, the president and superintendent of Crown Point were fired and replaced with bank loyalists. Annual meetings of other Comstock mines likewise failed to ratify previous pledges, and pledges that had been ratified were canceled unilaterally. The $600,000 previously pledged by the mines was just a memory.[1] What caused this dramatic overnight reversal?

Of course, the change from support to opposition was not an overnight occurrence. We can gain some insight by examining a series of comments by Alpheus Bull, president of the Savage Mining Company, whom Sutro characterized as "a mere tool of the Bank of California."[2] Both the timing and the content of Bull's comments are critical. For a timing reference, recall that by April 1866, Sutro had reached agreement with 23 of the mining companies, including Savage, to build a tunnel and to charge $2 per ton of ore to use the tunnel for drainage and ventilation. That agreement required Sutro to raise $3 million by August 1, 1867.

Bull's first comment, in his official report to stockholders dated **July 10, 1866**, just after the initial agreements with the mining companies were reached, read:

> The importance of affording drainage at a great depth, if it can possibly be obtained, cannot be too highly estimated. The Sutro Tunnel Company is the only party that proposes to undertake this important enterprise, and your trustees have entered into a contract with that company, for the purpose of effecting this great object. It is much to be desired that success may attend the effort, for it is, in my opinion, a work upon which depends the future value and profitable working of the mines of the Comstock lode. I recommend that this contract be ratified by the stockholders at their present meeting.[3]

Sutro received from the mining companies an extension of one year to raise the $3 million to build the tunnel, thus moving the deadline to August 1, 1868. The extension was explicitly agreed to by the Savage Mining Company in a document signed by Alpheus Bull in his capacity as president on **March 7, 1867**.

Bull next commented on the tunnel on **July 18, 1867**:

> On the 26th of April, 1867, the board of trustees entered into an agreement with the Sutro Tunnel Company to subscribe $150,000 towards the construction of the proposed drain tunnel, upon two conditions: first that the tunnel company were to procure *bona fide* subscriptions to the amount of $3,000,000; and second, that the agreement should be submitted to this annual meeting and ratified by the stockholders. The tunnel company have failed to fulfill the first condition.
>
> In addition to this, I consider there are grave reasons for doubting the policy of such an agreement on the part of this company. Suffice to say that I recommend the stockholders to refuse to give their approval to the agreement.[4]

Finally, in **April 1868**, Bull wrote in the official report of the Savage Mining Company:

> I am so strongly impressed with the importance of the early construction of this railway,[5] and the great benefits it would confer upon this company, that I earnestly recommend to the stockholders the repeal or amendment of the 4th article of the by-laws, so as to enable the incoming board of trustees, if in their judgment they deem it advisable, to increase the subsidy of this company to the railway enterprise by an additional sum of fifty thousand dollars.
>
> With this road constructed and in operation, and with a deep-drain tunnel which in a few years will be run, and with further saving in the reduction of ore, and also to increase the returns of the assay value of them from 65 percent, the present standard, to 80 or 85 percent, it is reasonable to believe, with all these advantages secured, we can transmit the danger of profits from silver mining at Virginia and Gold Hill to another generation.[6]

There are many dates and statements to consider, so let us attempt to make sense of them.

- By April 1866, 23 of the Comstock mining companies agreed to support a tunnel and to pay $2 per ton of ore once the tunnel was completed.
- On July 10, 1866, Bull strongly supported the Sutro Tunnel in his annual report to stockholders.
- On March 7, 1867, Bull signed an agreement to extend the deadline for Sutro to procure money for the tunnel until August 1, 1868.
- On April 26, 1867, Bull and his trustees agreed to provide $150,000 to support the tunnel construction.
- On June 6, 1867, the meeting called by the Bank of California decided not to support the previous pledge by the Crown Point Mining Company to provide $75,000 to the tunnel company.
- On July 18, 1867, Bull wrote that the tunnel company had not met its obligation to raise $3 million, although the deadline to raise that money was originally August 1, 1867, and had been delayed, with Bull's agreement, to August 1, 1868. Based on this alleged failure, Bull recommended against complying with his commitment of three months earlier to provide $150,000 to the tunnel company.
- In April 1868, Bull switched his support to a railroad project (which would become the Virginia and Truckee Railroad). He also envisioned a "deep-drain tunnel which in a few years will be run" similar to the Sutro Tunnel but obviously not built by the Sutro Tunnel Company.

The fingerprints of the Bank of California are all over this series of occurrences. Sometime between April 26 and June 6, 1867, Ralston and Sharon must have realized that allowing Sutro to build his tunnel would threaten their stranglehold on the Comstock and jeopardize their flow of cash. What triggered that realization?

Sutro believed that the Nevada Legislature's January 1867 petition to the U.S. Congress to provide money for the tunnel worried Ralston. If the tunnel construction were financially supported by the federal government, Sutro would not be dependent on the Bank of California and would be much harder to control.

Another concern for Ralston was the massive profit that Sutro projected from the operation of the tunnel, part of which derived from the $2 per ton fee on ore. With annual bullion production in the state of Nevada of $16.5 million, Sutro was projecting tunnel revenues of up to $6 million. Tunnel revenue would not flow to Ralston- or Sharon-controlled properties and would certainly reduce their cash flow.

A third issue concerning Ralston and even more so Sharon was Sutro's prediction that much of the population and investment in mills would leave Virginia City and Gold Hill in favor of the new town of Sutro. Remember that when the conservative directors of the Bank of California wanted to close the Virginia City bank branch, Sharon had bought the mills that had been foreclosed by the bank at the price the bank had paid and incorporated them into the Union Mine and Milling Company. So he certainly did not want the tunnel to open and thereby force the mills to relocate to the mouth of the tunnel at Sutro.

Whatever the reason, Ralston, Sharon, and the other investors who benefited from a close relationship with the Bank of California (whom Sutro dubbed the "Bank Ring") decided that Sutro's tunnel must not be built.

Adolph Sutro was devastated by the rejection of those he had counted as friends. Wherever he went in Virginia City, people avoided him. No one dared talk to him for fear someone would tattle to the Bank of California, and the Bank would withdraw credit from their business. He was Don Quixote with no Sancho Panza to support him.

But the tunnel was his obsession, and he would not concede defeat. He had persevered in the jungles of Panama, he had persevered in the snowstorm when returning from his first trip to the Comstock, and he would persevere now. In his words, "I was not going to give it up, because I had said I would carry it out, and I was more determined than ever not to give it up under any circumstances."[7]

When Sutro was a tobacco merchant in San Francisco in the 1850s, he bought from the wholesale firm of Weil and Company, and there he met Joseph Aron. Along with Sutro and August Helbing, Aron was a member of the Eureka Benevolent Society. He was capable and ambitious and had recently become a partner in the Weil firm. Sutro and Aron had discussed the tunnel project, and Aron was impressed with the need for the project and offered to help Sutro in any way he could. At the time of their discussion, Sutro did not need any help, but now he did. Sutro outlined the initial support of the Bank of California followed by its recent opposition. After many discussions, Aron finally agreed to invest $1,000 in tunnel company stock and gave Sutro $3,000 for a trip to Washington, where he planned to lobby for the tunnel.[8] He also committed to send Leah Sutro $200 a month to support her and the five children (soon to be six, with the birth of Clara in October 1867). Aron's support of Leah and the children continued for several years.[9]

Sutro realized that it was impossible to raise money in Nevada or California against the opposition of the Bank of California. So he decided in July 1867 to return to New York, where he had received a supportive audience just eight months earlier. But Ralston was ahead of him. Upon entering Leese and Waller's, the New York agent of the Bank of California, Sutro saw a large placard declaring that the stockholders of the Savage Mining Company had refused to ratify the commitment made by its trustees to subscribe $150,000 to the stock of the Sutro Tunnel Company, and that commitment was null and void. Sutro said of the placard, "I was astonished to find in a banking office in New York a placard like that. Everybody from the Pacific coast would come in and read it, and would think I had committed some crime."[10]

How could Sutro keep his pledge to continue against such strong and far-reaching opposition?

Chapter 16

Starting Over

The only real battle in life is between hanging on and letting go.
—Shannon L. Alder

With financing from both the West Coast and New York closed to him, Adolph Sutro decided to travel to Europe. He had two purposes for the trip: first to visit mines like the those on the Comstock Lode and consult with European mining experts about the feasibility and effectiveness of the Sutro Tunnel; and second, to negotiate financing for his tunnel.

Before leaving for Europe, Sutro obtained several letters of introduction. He already had a glowing one from William Ralston to the Oriental Bank of London, but of course, that letter was useless given Ralston's current opposition to the tunnel. But Sutro succeeded in obtaining a favorable letter from James W. Nye, senator from Nevada, who either did not know of the Bank of California's new position or chose to ignore it. Sutro visited his family in Baltimore and, probably through his brothers, gathered more letters of introduction.[1]

In Europe, Sutro visited Ireland, England, and ten countries on the continent. He met with many mining experts who virtually all endorsed the possibility of building the proposed Sutro tunnel, its positive impact on the mines of the Comstock Lode, and its profitability. The Report of the Commissioners,[2] discussed in Chapter 20, includes extensive testimony about Sutro's interactions with these European experts.

Regarding Sutro's second objective, negotiating for financial support, he was less successful. In 1867, the general sentiment in Europe was that war between France and Prussia was inevitable. Although actual hostilities did not begin until July 19, 1870, the unsettled atmosphere in 1867 made foreign investment untenable. Sutro later said, "...everybody in London told me that nothing could be done with American enterprises, either railroads or tunnels or anything else because war was bound to come."[3]

Adolph Sutro departed from Liverpool on December 1, 1867, aboard the ship *Russia*, and arrived in New York on December 12. Mark Twain, whom Sutro had met previously in Virginia City, greeted Sutro with his usual satirical style:

> Mr. A. Sutro of the great Sutro Tunnel scheme arrived yesterday from Europe on the *Russia*. He brought his tunnel back with him. He failed to sell it to the Europeans. They said it was a good tunnel, but that they would look around a little before purchasing; if they could not find a tunnel to suit them

nearer home, they would call again. Many capitalists were fascinated with the idea of owning a tunnel, but none wanted such a long tunnel or one that was so far away that they could not walk out afternoons and enjoy it.

Then Twain went on to say that Sutro had gone to Washington to try for federal funding, and he expressed his great admiration for Sutro's "industry and tenacity."[4]

Upon hearing that Sutro was in Washington, Ralston and Sharon sent telegrams to Nevada senators Stewart and Nye, and several others. Until the reversal by the Bank of California in mid–1867, Stewart had been the president of the Sutro Tunnel Company. And Senator Nye had written a letter of introduction for Sutro before his European trip just six months earlier. The telegrams read as follows:

Virginia, Nev., January 15, 1868

To Hon. Wm. Stewart and James W. Nye:

We are opposed to the Sutro Tunnel project and desire it defeated if possible.

    WM. SHARON
    CHARLES BONNER, Superintendent of Savage Company
    B.F. SHERWOOD, President Central Company
    JOHN B. WINTERS, President Yellow Jacket Company
    JOHN P. JONES, Superintendent Kentuck Company
    J.W. MACKAY, Superintendent Bullion Company
    THOS. G. TAYLOR, President Alpha, and Superintendent Crown Point and Best & Belcher Company
    F.A. TRITLE, President Belcher Company
    ISAAC L. REQUA, Superintendent Chollar-Potosi Company[5]

Despite the telegrams, Sutro had a series of productive meetings with the Committee on Mines and Mining of the U.S. House of Representatives. Sutro reported of those meetings,

... they often met twice a week, nearly every member present.

I went into all the details of mining; explained it all to them, and they became deeply interested in it, so much so, that they were anxious for me to come before them and talk about everything connected with mining, independently of this tunnel question. I became acquainted with nearly all the members of the House, and I found a great many friends. After this lengthy examination of the subject, they made an able report to the House, recommending a loan of $5,000,000, with a mortgage to the Government on all the property.[6]

Unfortunately for Sutro, before the full House could consider the loan recommendation of the committee, the House voted on February 24, 1868, to impeach President Andrew Johnson. The impeachment proceedings occupied the House for four months, and the loan recommendation for the Sutro Tunnel never reached the full House. Sutro returned home, disappointed but determined.

Sutro returned to Washington for the 1868-69 session of Congress in November. Ulysses S. Grant had just been elected president and the lame-duck Congress accomplished nothing. Sutro met President-elect Grant in February and was able to insert a brief and veiled reference to the Sutro Tunnel into Grant's inaugural address. But Grant was opposed to government spending on any such project until the country fully recovered from the trauma of the Civil War.

It seemed that Sutro could not win. Not only was the all-powerful Bank of California against him, but the looming Franco-Prussian War, the impeachment hearings against President Andrew Johnson, and the difficult recovery after the Civil War all stacked the odds against him.

The Yellow Jacket Disaster

On April 7, 1869, a tragedy occurred that would alter the course of Sutro's search for financing. Lord,[7] in his seminal book on the Comstock, devotes eight pages to the Yellow Jacket fire. A condensation of his account follows.

A warning cry of fire was heard in the Crown Point Mine. The fire originated in the 800-foot level of the adjacent Yellow Jacket Mine. The cause of the fire was never verified, but it is generally believed that a lighted candle was left near the timbers and the dry wood caught fire. Once the timbers burned enough to weaken them, the unsupported rock fell with a crash, choking up the gallery and expelling a blast of foul air and smoke through connecting drifts into the shafts of the Crown Point, Kentuck, and Yellow Jacket mines. Because shifts were changing, fewer men than usual were at work in the mines, and this saved many lives. John Murphy, station-man at the 800-foot level of the Yellow Jacket shaft, heard a sound like a gust of wind roaring through the drift and saw the 15 candles in the station extinguished at once. The foul blast stifled him, and he crouched on the floor, wrapping his rubber coat around his face. In a moment he lost consciousness, but he could remember when rescued that he heard a pitiful cry come up the shaft from a lower level: "Murphy, send me a cage; I am suffocating to death!"

Two miners at work in the 800-foot level of the Kentuck Mine, which also adjoined the Yellow Jacket, heard a similar gale roaring through the drift and were instantly overwhelmed by its fierce blast of smoke and gas. One struggled through the stifling atmosphere to the Crown Point shaft and survived; the other fell dying in the drift beyond hope of rescue.

It was in the Crown Point Mine, however, that this gust was most deadly. Forty-five men had just been lowered into the mine, getting off the cage at different levels. The cage was again descending with its load of men when it plunged into a rising current of foul air at the 700-foot level; still, it went down steadily to the 800-foot level, where men were found crying for help in the dark, amid the stifling smoke. The terrified sufferers rushed toward the cage as the last hope, and they crowded in and upon it. All could not be saved, and those who saw the cage rise toward the surface from the station knew that they had been left behind to die. As soon as the rescued miners could leave the cage at the surface, it was lowered again to the 800-foot station, and after a moment's pause the signal was given to hoist, and the cage was once more pulled up at full speed. As it surfaced, observers witnessed a ghastly and pitiful sight. Two brothers from Yorkshire, England, worked in the Crown Point Mine. George Bickle stood on the cage insensible, leaning over his dead brother, Richard. Richard Bickle had sunk down upon the bottom of the cage as it was drawn up, and his head and arm were torn almost completely from his body by the side timbers of the shaft. Gentle hands parted the dead and dying brothers. George Bickle was laid on a rude couch in the hoisting-works by the side of other sufferers, who, like him, were past all help of medicine. They gasped faintly for some hours, and then their troubled breathing ceased forever.

Dense volumes of black smoke began to rise in the Kentuck, Crown Point, and Yellow Jacket mineshafts, steam whistles sounded an alarm, and fire engines from Gold Hill and Virginia City drove to the burning mines. With the firemen also came a great company of men, women, and children, who crowded about the smoky works, pressing in at every opportunity, and trying to peer into the blackness of the pits where fathers, sons, and husbands were imprisoned.

Miners and superintendents, especially John Percival Jones,[8] made all possible efforts to rescue the doomed men. As soon as the smoke cleared away somewhat from the Yellow Jacket shaft, small parties of miners and firemen went down repeatedly into the burning pit, but at first without success. At 10 o'clock, however, two dead bodies were taken out of the Kentuck shaft, and about noon four more were found and brought to the surface from the Yellow Jacket.

No one could live for a moment in the reeking chimney of the Crown Point shaft, but in the faint hope that some in the depths of the mine might still be alive, a cage was sent down to the 1,000-foot level with a lighted lantern and a note to survivors. The note read, "We are fast subduing the fire. It is death to attempt to come up from where you are. We shall get you out soon. The gas in the shaft is terrible and produces sure and speedy death. Write a word to us and send it up on the cage, and let us know where you are." When the cage reached the 1,000-foot level, there was a pause for a few

Grief and despair during the Yellow Jacket Fire. Lithograph from Dan DeQuille's *The Big Bonanza*, published in 1876.

moments while all waited breathlessly for an answering signal. When the cage was drawn up to the surface, the lantern had gone out, and there was no reply to the message.

The roll of the three mines was then called. Of the men in the Crown Point Mine, 23 were missing; in the Yellow Jacket one; and in the Kentuck four. Six bodies had been recovered; thus 34 miners were likely dead. About midnight it was decided to attempt to descend through the Yellow Jacket Mine into the lower levels of the Crown Point. Three Gold Hill firemen and one from Virginia City reached the 1,000-foot level of the Crown Point Mine alive, groping their way with dimly burning lanterns through the darkness and choking atmosphere of the drifts. They saw dead men on the floor of the level where they had fallen, turning everywhere for one last breath of fresh air. Their faces were flushed and swollen, but the features of well-known friends were still recognizable. Farther on, however, in the well at the bottom of the shaft, mangled bodies were found. The bodies were tied securely to planks and hoisted, one after another, to the surface. All night long the crowd of relatives and friends had stood about the hoisting-works. As the bodies were at last carried out, pitiful cries of women were heard, "My God! Who is it this time?"

The bodies of the dead men were borne to their graves by the largest and most solemn funeral procession that had ever been seen on the eastern slope of the Sierra Nevada. Guards from Virginia City and Gold Hill, with reversed arms, and bands playing requiem marches, paid the last honors to the dead, and the long line of bearers was followed by the Miners' Unions and the Canadian Society, after whom moved the sorrowful relatives and friends.

Meanwhile, the miners and firemen were battling valiantly with the unsubdued fire in the mines. As they made their way farther and farther into the burning drifts, the danger grew more deadly. As fast as the firemen extinguished the flames, the miners cleared away the charred wood and fallen rock and set new timbers in place. Streams of water were sprayed to cool the heated rock of the walls. Hot water stood ankle-deep on the floor of the levels, and its rising steam mingled with the smoke of the burning wood. Another cave-in could occur at any time, which would block the men in a stifling prison or expel a blast of foul air that would smother them. In placing hosepipes on the levels of the Kentuck Mine, miners repeatedly fell on the floor of the drifts and were carried fainting to the surface.

Fresh air was pumped into the drifts by blowers through long-jointed pipes, but when air entered the drifts, the smoldering wood was likely to reignite. No one wanted to suggest the fatal measure of closing the shafts and filling the mines with steam while even the faintest hope remained of rescuing the imprisoned miners. Sealing of the mines was done, however, at noon on April 9, and for 72 hours steam was forced from the boilers of the hoisting-works into the mines. At noon on April 12, a stream of water was directed down the Crown Point shaft to purify the air as much as possible; and after several attempts to descend in the cage, small parties of miners explored several levels and brought up the bodies of three more victims. The final tally was 45 miners dead.

On April 17, the Yellow Jacket mineshaft was reopened, and efforts were made to ascertain and repair damages. During the days immediately following, all passages connecting with the Crown Point and Kentuck mines were closed by bulkheads, so that, although the air continued bad in several levels for more than a month, work could be resumed with a portion of the former force. On April 28, ore was hoisted from the upper levels of the Kentuck Mine, but on May 3, it was necessary to close both the Kentuck and Crown Point shafts, as the fire appeared to be gaining. Even six months later, men working in the upper levels of the mines would occasionally drive their picks into a recess where cinders were still smoldering. Once several miners were asphyxiated by a sudden influx of gas while extracting ore, but they were taken out of the mine by fellow workmen on other levels, and all recovered in a few hours.

The damage caused by the great fire was never fully repaired; some of the closed galleries were never reopened. The bodies of several miners remain to this day where the fallen roofs of the galleries entombed the men.

Safety First

All the residents of the Comstock mourned the victims of the Yellow Jacket disaster. Underground fire is the constant fear of all miners, and that such a devastating one had occurred forced Adolph Sutro to reexamine the functions of his tunnel. If the tunnel had been in place, the lives of many miners might have been saved. By climbing down shafts, away from the rising gas and flames, they could have avoided suffocating smoke and heat. Sutro decided to appeal directly to the miners, to show them how the tunnel would provide them with an escape route in the event of a mine fire.

At Sutro's request, the miner's unions of Virginia City and Gold Hill called a joint meeting for August 25, 1869. Through talking with the miners, he found that their primary concern had shifted from better working conditions (due to improved ventilation and elimination of the standing water) to an escape route from any future fires. So, at the joint meeting, he emphasized the safety aspects of the proposed tunnel. He encouraged the miners to support the tunnel financially, and they responded by pledging $50,000 by a unanimous vote.

This pledge was a major turning point for Sutro's campaign. On September 1, he opened a stock subscription office at 76 C Street in Virginia City. To encourage public participation, he published the text of the miner's resolution and also a long appeal for stock subscriptions daily in the *Territorial Enterprise* for the next two months.

Sutro's momentum peaked at the next event, a public meeting at Piper's Opera House in Virginia City on September 20, 1869. The Opera House was the prime performance venue and hosted every important performer who visited Virginia City. It was the perfect place for Sutro to rally support for his tunnel.

Sutro had presented this material

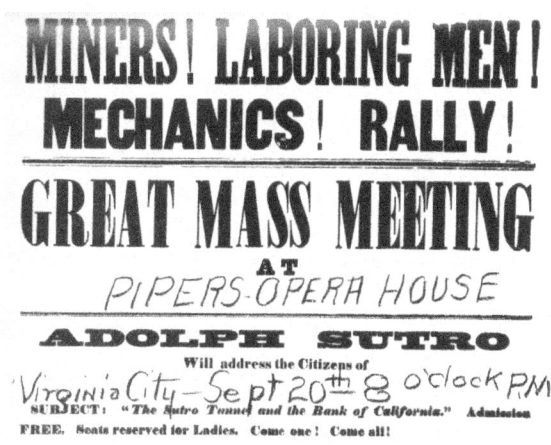

Piper's Opera House poster from 1869.

before: to financiers in San Francisco, New York, and London; to government officials in Carson City and Washington; and to mine owners and mine superintendents in Virginia City and Gold Hill. But now he would present it to the people who would most directly benefit from his tunnel, the miners and other citizens of the Comstock. Sutro spoke of the stranglehold the Bank of California, the Bank Ring, had on life in Virginia City, and of his battles with the Ring—how they had at first supported him and then turned against him. He spoke honestly and from the heart, and told of his humiliation:

> Fellow citizens: Have you ever been in a position where your friends shunned you? If you have you know how mortifying it is on meeting an old acquaintance to have him pass by pretending not to see you, instead of shaking you by the hand and welcoming you. Have you noticed them cross over on the other side of the street when they saw you at a distance? Have you seen their nervous hurry, trying to get off when you happen to engage them in conversation? You may possibly have made similar experiences if you were ever broke and your good friends were afraid you might ask them for a loan.[9]

Sutro turned his pain into an advantage, eliciting both sympathy and empathy.

Sutro then told of his efforts to acquire financing by appealing to capitalists in San Francisco, New York, and Europe, and to the federal government in Washington. He told of the mismanagement that resulted in expenses eating up most of the $16 million per year in precious metals extracted from the mines, and how the tunnel would reduce expenses and increase yield.

Sutro finished his speech by encouraging the audience to buy stock in the tunnel. He concluded:

> Miners and laboring men, what is the price of your health, your liberty, your independence? Are they not worth more than all the filthy lucre you could possess? Who is there among you so avaricious as to refuse to give and donate outright a few paltry dollars per month to a cause ... which will ensure to you liberal wages ... a cause which will make you the power of this land, make powerless your oppressors, and break up your arch enemy, the California Bank?
>
> Let a noble rivalry spring up among you who shall come in first; drop all prejudice; let all trifling objections fall to the ground; let one excel the other in magnanimity; let all make one joint, grand, unanimous effort and victory will be ours.[10]

Sutro's speech was a sensation. An editorial in the *Territorial Enterprise* the next day summarized his main points, and the full speech was reprinted two days later. Sutro was encouraged to have the miners behind him as evidenced by their monetary commitment, and the enthusiastic acceptance of his speech restored his self-confidence. Only the Bank Ring begrudged his success, and they had a way to sabotage any profits that might result from Sutro's tunnel.

Chapter 17

Workin' on the Railroad

Railroad iron is a magician's rod, in its power to evoke the sleeping energies of land and water.
—Ralph Waldo Emerson

Because of their incessant demand for water, the mills that extracted bullion from the ore of the Comstock mines had moved from Virginia City to the Carson River Valley. While that location solved the water problem, it meant that ore must be transported from the mouths of the mines to the mills 13 miles away and 1,575 feet below. Endless lines of mule teams hauled often overloaded wagons carrying tons of ore down steep grades. On the return trips, the wagons brought loads of timbers to construct Philip Deidesheimer's square-set boxes used to stabilize the mines. Such trips were difficult enough when the weather cooperated, but snow and ice in winter made the trails impassable and shut down operations.

Visionaries, starting with Adolph Sutro in 1860, had for years proposed a railroad line to streamline transportation on the Comstock. From the first Nevada Territorial Legislature in 1861 to the first State Legislature in 1865, three different franchises for various railroad schemes were authorized. But the cost and engineering challenges of such a line prevented any actual construction.

Adolph Sutro recognized the transportation problems, and he identified hauling ore from the mines to new mills to be built near the mouth of the tunnel (at the rate of 25¢ per mile per ton) as a source of profit for the tunnel. As with the mule wagons, return trips of train cars in the Sutro Tunnel would carry timbers for mine support, adding another revenue stream.

Ralston and Sharon could not allow Sutro to establish a monopoly on transportation via his tunnel; they wanted the money from hauling ore and timber for themselves. So, in December 1868, Sharon met with Isaac E. James, the official surveyor of the Comstock. Their conversation is recorded in Lord's treatise, *Comstock Mining and Miners*.[1] Sharon asked, without any preface, "Can you run a (rail)road from Virginia City to the Carson River?' 'Yes!' answered the surveyor with equal brevity. 'Do it, then, at once!' said Mr. Sharon; and the surveyor began work immediately to carry out the direction without further instructions." Lord claims that this brief interchange, although sounding like a movie script, is accurate.

James knew the region and worked quickly and efficiently. His judgments were rapid and accurate, but the task was formidable. Most railroads involve tunnels and bridges, but the terrain of the Comstock is extreme. Lord says, "The turns and twists and convolutions of this railroad are indescribable; it winds along like the trail of a serpent on a rock. The maximum grade is 116 feet to the mile (2.2% grade), and the total curvature in the distance traversed is 17 × 360°; or, in other words, the aggregate curves of the railroad would make 17 full coils of the track in the space of 13½ miles."[2]

Incredibly, the survey was completed within 30 days, and even before it was finished, grading of the route began. During that 30 days, Sharon was busy. He acquired the rights from the previous franchises, obtained financial pledges from wealthy friends, secured a charter from the Nevada Legislature for his new Virginia and Truckee Railroad, and convinced Ormsby and Storey Counties to issue bonds for the new railroad totaling $500,000. Soon afterward, Lyon County issued bonds for $75,000 in support of the railroad, and Sharon used his influence to convince the mining companies to loan and contribute a total of $700,000 to the effort. In less than two months, Sharon had raised over $1.2 million for his railroad, much of that amount with no conditions or guarantees. Sutro was undoubtedly envious.

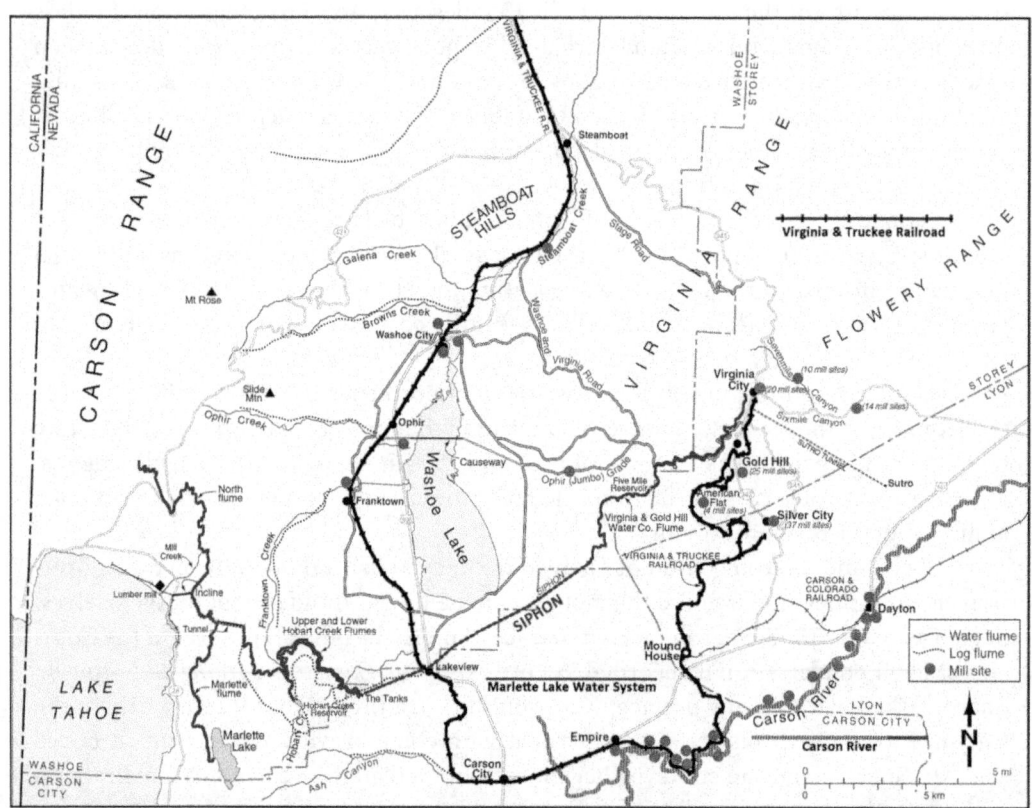

Map showing the Virginia & Truckee Railroad, Marlette Lake water system, and mills along the Carson River (courtesy Nevada Bureau of Mines and Geology; modified from Purkey and Garside, 1995, pp. 54–55).

17. Workin' on the Railroad

Train of the Virginia & Truckee Railroad on trestle at the Crown Point Mine (courtesy St. Mary in the Mountains Museum, Virginia City, Nevada).

The initial route of the railroad extended from Virginia City to the Carson River and then to Carson City, a total distance of 21 miles. The map on page 100[3,4] shows the tortuous path of the Virginia and Truckee Railroad.

Groundbreaking took place on February 18, 1869, just two months after Sharon had asked Isaac James whether such a railroad was possible. Within one month, 750 men were at work building the railroad. By June, this number had increased to 1,200, most of whom were Chinese. Thirty-eight work camps along the route housed the workers. The line included seven tunnels, each requiring two to five months of excavating; and an 85-foot-tall, 350-foot-long trestle over the Crown Point ravine.[5]

Sharon ordered iron rails from England in January, and they were shipped early in March. He even ordered extra rails in case any were lost to a shipwreck. Before the rails arrived, engines were ordered and built, and ties were cut and shaped.

On September 28, 1869, H.M. Yerrington, superintendent of the railroad, drove a silver spike (what else!) to secure the first rail laid at Carson City. By November all rails were laid, and on November 12, 1869, the first train arrived at Gold Hill to cheers from the crowd and the din of steam whistles at every mine along the way. Sharon stepped down from the engine and gave a mercifully brief speech recounting the difficulties of designing and building the railroad and emphasizing the expected benefits.

Six days later, on November 18, the railroad carried its first ore shipment. The Gold Hill *Daily News* reported,

> The first lot of ore from the Yellow Jacket mine and in fact from the Comstock ledge—yet shipped over the railroad was sent down yesterday to the Yellow Jacket mill on the Carson River. There were seven car loads of it, about eight and a half tons to the load, not far from 60 tons. This was from the 700 foot level of the old north mine, and dumped directly into the cars, the railroad passing within a few feet of the shaft. It is low grade ore, assaying $26 or $28 to the ton, and will yield under the stamps (after processing in the mill) not far from $17 per ton. It is ore which heretofore was considered too poor to work and was accordingly used to fill up drifts with. The railroad affords for the first time a chance to work this low grade ore profitably.[6]

The *Daily News* article touches some important points. First, transporting 60 tons of ore by mule-drawn wagons would have required at least three 10-mule teams and wagons with drivers. Second, the railroad provided "mine-to-mill" service for most of the mines. Third, because it was faster and cheaper, low-grade ore became profitable to haul and process, thus increasing profits for the mines.

The mule-drawn wagons almost immediately became obsolete, and soon 30 to 45 loaded trains ran daily from Virginia City to Carson City.[7]

Not everyone was pleased with the financing of the railroad. Dan DeQuille (pseudonym for William Wright), wrote about William Sharon and his Virginia and Truckee Railroad:

> Mr. Sharon is the father of the Virginia & Truckee Railroad, undoubtedly the crookedest railroad in the world, and a wonderful road in many other respects. In building this road, Mr. Sharon secured a subsidy of $500,000 from the people of Washoe in aid of the project, constructed as much of the road as the sum would build, then mortgaged the whole road for the amount of money required for its completion. In this way, he built the road without putting his hand in his own pocket for a cent, and he still owns half the road—worth $2,500,000 and brings him in, as Mr. Adolph Sutro says, $12,000 per day.[8]

DeQuille expressed the popular sentiment, and the double entendre "crookedest railroad in the world" became widely popular. But Lord provides a more balanced accounting. He says, "the personal outlay of Mr. Sharon and his associates was very large. The cost of the road was $1,750,000 ... without reckoning the necessary equipment of rolling stock, machine shops, etc., and when," (in 1871–72), "it was extended to Reno, a station on the line of the Central Pacific Railroad, this original outlay was more than doubled."[9]

Regardless of how it was financed, the Virginia and Truckee Railroad was another great engineering accomplishment on the Comstock, built in record time, and it forever ended Adolph Sutro's dream of transporting ore and timber through his proposed tunnel to mills that would now never be built at the mouth of the tunnel, at least not in Sutro's lifetime.

Chapter 18

Mines, Mills and Money

Mining is like a search-and-destroy mission.
—Stewart Udall

Geology and Mines

The Comstock Lode, named for hard-luck miner Henry Comstock who prospected there, is in the Virginia Mountains (earlier called the Washoe Mountains) of west-central Nevada. Volcanic activity created the Comstock and deposited massive amounts of gold- and silver-bearing ore in the hills east of Mount Davidson, at 7,864 feet the highest mountain in the area. Virginia City, the focus of the gold and silver deposits, is 0.7 miles east of Mount Davidson and 1,700 feet lower.

Unlike most silver deposits, which occur in long, thin veins, the ore deposits of the Comstock are large, shapeless masses often hundreds of feet thick, randomly distributed throughout the Lode,[1] some near the surface, some as far down as 2,550 feet. Extensive and redundant exploration by numerous mining companies, costing many millions of dollars, was required to locate the deposits.

R.W. Raymond, U.S. Commissioner on Mines and Mining, in his 1868 report to Congress, commented on the inefficient organization of the mines relative to the configuration of the Lode:

> One great cause of trouble is the fact that mining has not on the whole been profitable to individual adventurers; and of this fact the Comstock Lode has furnished a striking example. Nearly $100,000,000 have been extracted from that lode within the past eight years, yet the aggregate cost to the owners has been almost as much. The reason is simple. Unnecessary labor has been employed, and vast sums of money have been wasted in extravagant speculations and litigations, and the root of the whole evil lies in the system of scattered, jealous, individual activity, which has destroyed, by dividing, the resources of the most magnificent ore deposit in the world. Thirty-five or forty companies, each owning from 1,000 to 1,400 feet along the vein, and each (almost without exception) working its own ground independently; 40 superintendents, 40 presidents, 40 secretaries, 40 boards of directors, all to be supplied with salaries, or, worse yet, with perquisites, or, worst of all, with opportunities to speculate; an army of lawyers and witnesses, peripatetic experts, competing assayers, thousands of miners uniting to keep up the rate of wages—these explain the heavy expense of Comstock mining. Aside from this immense drain of money, amounting to 20 percent of the whole production, the labor actually performed has been, for want of united action, often useless. There have been tunnels enough run by different companies into the Comstock Lode to make, if put together, the whole length of the

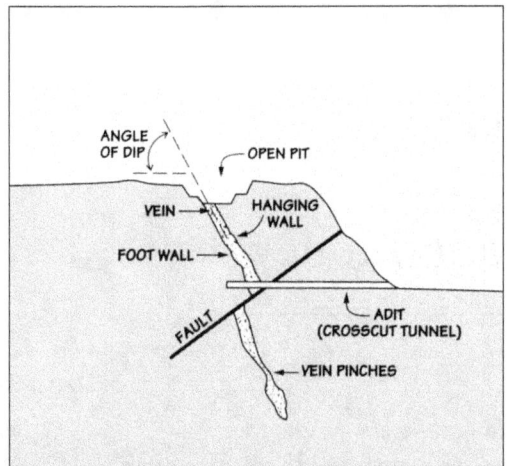 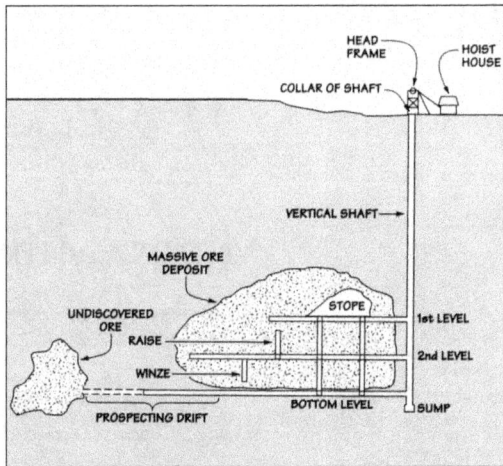

Mining techniques used on the Comstock. *Left:* **Open pit surface mining diagram.** *Right:* **Deep-shaft mining diagram (both diagrams courtesy Nevada Bureau of Mines and Geology, modified from Purkey and Garside, 1995, 58).**[2]

Sutro tunnel. Hardly one of them is good for anything today. The Bullion company, which has the deepest shaft on the lode, never had any ore but has spent more than a million of dollars in prospecting, while some neighboring mines, like the little Kentuck, have been in bonanza for long periods. Now, this division of a vein, which gives the rich chimney to one owner and the barren intervals to another, is not conducive to economy. The result has proved to be that both owners waste money. All the explorations in the barren mines of the Comstock could have been executed with the money flung away by the mines that have had for a time rich ore.[3]

As Commissioner Raymond stated, just a few of the mines were profitable. To understand profitability, we must consider the nature of mining shares. Such shares were assessable; that is, the trustees of the mining company could require stockholders to contribute money to support the purchase of new equipment, digging an exploratory drift, litigation expenses, or for any reasonable business expense that could not be financed from operating profits. If the stockholders refused to cover the assessment, their shares would be auctioned to the highest bidder. Conversely, in times of bonanza, when the mine was producing high-quality ore, dividends might be paid to the lucky stockholders.

The power to levy assessments along with inside information on the present quality of ore being mined encouraged the trustees of the mining companies to manipulate the price of their stock. If miners encountered high-quality ore, the trustees might keep that information secret while levying a large assessment. With no knowledge of future prospects, stockholders would likely refuse to pay the assessment and thus forfeit their shares. The trustees or their friends would then snap up the shares at a low price before news of the high-quality ore became public. Such stock-price manipulation was a common practice on the Comstock.

Of 103 mining companies analyzed by Eliot Lord,[4] just six had dividends greater than their assessments. Only 14 of the companies paid any dividends at all, and 102 levied assessments on their stockholders. The six mining companies that showed a profit were Belcher, California, Consolidated Virginia, Crown Point, Gould & Curry, and Kentuck.

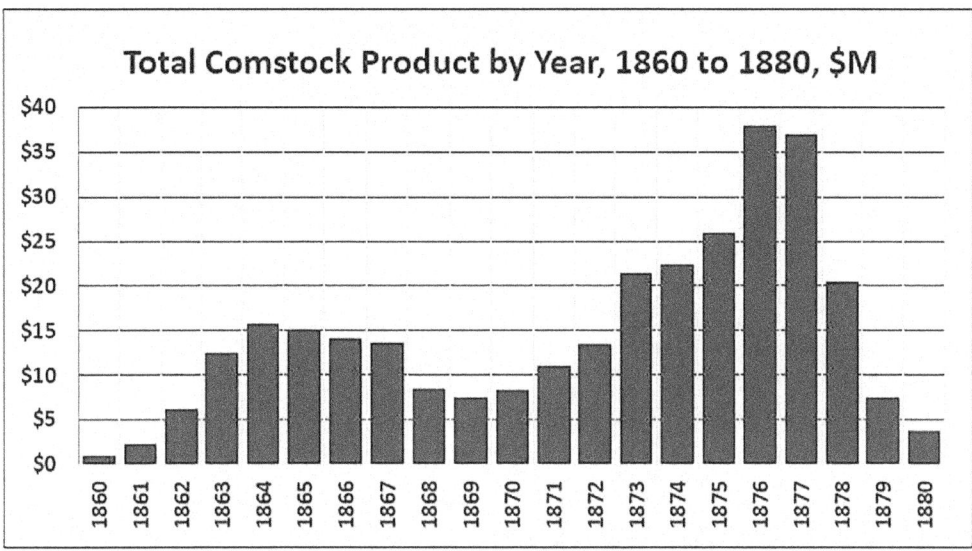

Mines did not produce high-quality ore continuously. Some had just one good year. Others, such as Crown Point, produced millable ore for over 13 years. Looking at the value of bullion produced by year (combined gold and silver) reveals the financial health of the Comstock as a whole. Of this amount, 45 percent was from gold and 55 percent from silver.[5]

Role of Mills

Mills on the Comstock took the tons of ore from the mines and processed it to extract the precious metals, generally using the Washoe Pan Process, as described in Chapter 7.

Initially, mills were located near the mine mouths to minimize transporting heavy ore. But mills need water to operate, and lack of water near the mines became a limiting factor. The tradeoff between proximity to the mines and lack of water forced construction of new mills along the Carson River.

The map below[6] shows the locations of over 130 mills that were built on the Comstock. Note the concentration of mills along the Carson River. The Virginia and Truckee Railroad, built by William Sharon, transported ore from the mines to the mills there.

Another change occurred in the ownership of the mills. In the early days of the Comstock, when Adolph Sutro built his Sutro Metallurgical Works, mills to obtain bullion from raw ore were independent operations, separate from the mining companies. But mining company investors soon realized that they could make more money through vertical integration; that is, by building and controlling their own mills.

Ownership of mills was far different than ownership of mines. William Ralston and William Sharon, with just six associates, owned most of the mills on the Comstock. Their Union Mill and Mining Company was formed in June 1867, and consolidated ownership of mills foreclosed on by the Bank of California. Dozens or even hundreds of stockholders owned each of the mines, but Sharon and his friends usually held a controlling

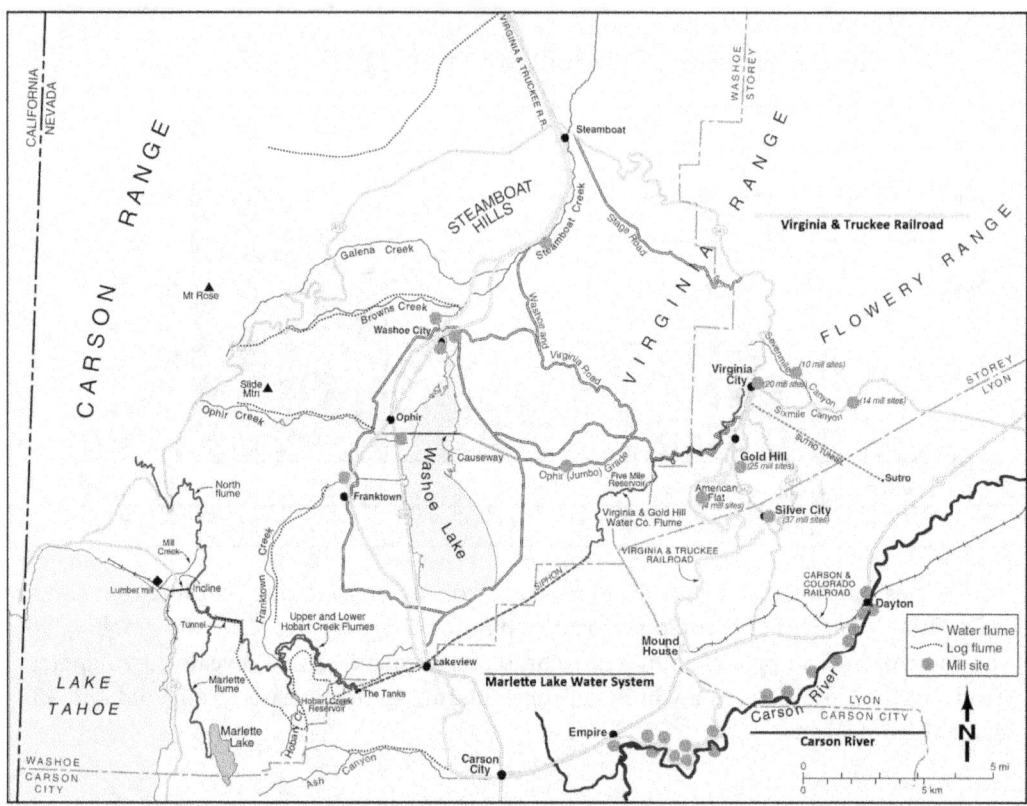

Map showing mills on the Comstock, indicated as dots (courtesy Nevada Bureau of Mines and Geology (modified from Purkey and Garside, 1995, 54–55).

interest. Ore quality was all-important to the profitability of the mines. But the mills were paid based on how many tons of material were processed, regardless of the ore quality. This basic difference in the importance of ore quality, combined with the different ownership of mills and mines, led to deceitful practices.

For example, at the Yellow Jacket Mine, the trustees (controlled by Sharon) ordered that all ore be processed at Sharon-owned Union Mill and Mining Company mills, while the Morgan Mill, owned by the mine itself, sat idle. Then Sharon ordered the mine superintendent to add waste rock to the material sent to the mills. That meant that the mills, running 24 hours per day, processed more ore and made more money. The mines had to pay for processing all the material, but the waste rock degraded the yield of bullion per ton. During one two-week period, the cost of processing by the mills exceeded the value of bullion recovered by $58,000. The Yellow Jacket stockholders had to pay the loss through an assessment. Of course, Sharon and his associates, being mine stockholders themselves, also had to pay that assessment. But because they shared the assessment with all the mine owners, their cost was far less than they gained from the mill profits.[7]

The Comstock was not about mining silver and gold; it was about making money.

Chapter 19

Start Digging!

We know that suffering produces perseverance; perseverance, character; and character, hope.

—Romans 5:3b–4 (NIV)

Now that he had $50,000 from the miner's unions, Sutro was anxious to start the actual work of digging the tunnel. In September 1869, he hired Hermann Schussler to survey the area and establish the tunnel route. Schussler, born in 1842 in Rastede, Germany, studied civil engineering in Zurich from 1862 to 1864. During that time, he also worked at the Lucerne Vulcan Iron Works in Germany, where he learned to fabricate iron pipe. This experience would serve him well on the various water projects he would later design in the United States. Schussler emigrated to California in 1864, where he worked for the Spring Valley Water Company of San Francisco. With the population of the city burgeoning, the need for more water led to the purchase of land west of the San Andreas Valley, and Schussler assisted in building dams there as part of the Crystal Springs Reservoir and San Andreas Lake. Both projects survived the massive 1906 San Francisco earthquake.[1,2]

On September 27, 1869, Schussler started to survey the route of the tunnel from the base of the Flowery Range near the Carson River to a point under Virginia City where it would meet the main shaft of the Savage Mine. This date marked the first official work on the Sutro Tunnel. Just one day later, H.M. Yerrington drove the silver spike to install the first rail of the Virginia City & Truckee Railroad.

Hermann Schussler (1842–1919), engineer for Spring Valley Water Company, 1864–1908: "If you seek his monument, look about you."

How do you dig a tunnel so that it hits a mineshaft target four miles away and 1,800 feet underground? That was the problem that Schussler had to solve. He started by establishing a straight line on the surface from the tunnel portal to the top of the Savage mineshaft in Virginia City. The mountainous terrain made that task quite difficult.

> The first rail of the Truckee and the Virginia City Railroad was laid to day.
> The work on Sutro Tunnel was commenced yesterday.

News items from the *New York Herald*, September 29, 1869, 7.

Theodolite from 1851.

He used a surveying instrument called a theodolite along with triangulation to find locations for alignment posts along the straight line. A theodolite is capable of precisely measuring horizontal and vertical angles and dates to 1720.[3]

Schussler then marked the line with cast-iron posts with winged tops. Each post had a clear line-of-sight to its neighboring posts, and marked what was referred to as "The Line."[4] The Line was intended to be precisely above the route that the tunnel would take from its entrance to the Savage Mine under Virginia City.

Once the posts were set, he placed the theodolite on each one, in turn, to make sure they were on a straight line.

Schussler's next step was to place a theodolite on a pedestal directly in front of the tunnel mouth and on the straight line already established to the Savage shaft. That theodolite appears on top of a pedestal on the left side of the photo on the next page. Note also the slanted line on the hill above the theodolite. That line is a pole to mark the location of the closest alignment marker.

The next photo shows the structure of the theodolite sitting atop the pedestal at the mouth of the tunnel.

As the tunnel progressed, alignment posts like those used to establish The Line could be installed in the tunnel. One other requirement for the tunnel was that it have a slope of at least 1 inch per 100 feet. The theodolite assured the slope by measuring the vertical angle of the tunnel.

While Schussler was surveying the line of the tunnel, his workers strung telegraph lines to provide communica-

Schussler's survey alignment marker (courtesy the Historical Society of Dayton Valley, image from Don and Elaine Bergstrom).

Theodolite at the mouth of the Sutro Tunnel (courtesy Society of California Pioneers).

tion between Virginia City and the tunnel portal, with extra stations at each of the four shafts along the tunnel route. Sutro bought the very latest equipment for the telegraph, a new terminal that eliminated the requirement that the operator know Morse code. With these terminals (shown next page) at each station, an operator would type normal alphabetical letters and the terminal automatically generated a corresponding code. At the other end, the code was automatically converted back to letters.

With the survey showing where to dig and the telegraph facilitating communication, Sutro was ready to dig his tunnel.

The official groundbreaking for the Sutro Tunnel was set for October 19, 1869. Sutro used newspaper ads to invite the entire populations of Nevada and California, some

Detail of theodolite at the mouth of the Sutro Tunnel (courtesy Society of California Pioneers).

200,000 people, to celebrate the occasion. Tunnel superintendent John D. Bethel organized a massive barbecue, including an oven to roast eight pigs and a pit five feet wide by 14 feet long to roast beef. The day dawned, not bright and sunny, but dismal and rainy. A rainstorm pelted Sutro and his party as they descended from Virginia City to the site of the ceremony at Dayton, Nevada. Fortunately for Sutro and the cooks, the rain and previous commitments prevented 199,800 of those invited from attending. At 1:00 p.m., the brass band hired for the occasion started playing, and the 200 guests mounted horses or boarded carriages for the three-mile trip through Dayton and north to the site of the tunnel opening.

Upon arrival, the flag was raised, and the band played "The Star-Spangled Banner." Then Sutro gave one of the shortest speeches of his life and swung the ceremonial pick to make it official. Following Sutro, Dan DeQuille of the *Territorial Enterprise* was invited to excavate a bit more, because any publicity his newspaper provided would benefit Sutro and the tunnel.

The crowd cheered, guns fired, and a dynamite blast accented the festivities. Even the sun appeared briefly, causing a rainbow to form within 200

Top: **Automatic telegraph terminal (courtesy the Historical Society of Dayton Valley, image from Don and Elaine Bergstrom).** *Left:* **Famous (and fake) photo of Sutro digging the tunnel. This photo was taken thousands of miles from the Comstock, in Europe, when Sutro was seeking finances for the tunnel. Note the shiny, black shoes, not typical of a hardworking miner (courtesy Western States Jewish History Association Archives).**

19. Start Digging!

Location of Sutro Tunnel, looking from town of Sutro toward Mount Davidson. Adolph Sutro named the local mountain peaks for three of his daughters (photo by author).

yards of the tunnel mouth. The tunnel was started, and Sutro vowed to keep work going until it was completed.

In 1866, Sutro and the mining companies had agreed on basic dimensions for the tunnel, seven feet high and eight feet wide, with a grade of not less than 1 inch per 100 feet. Now that actual work had started, more specific details were added. The tunnel would be at least nine feet wide at the bottom. Two sets of railroad tracks along with a covered conduit to carry drainage water would be placed on the floor.[5]

As money was scarce, Sutro reduced Bethel's crew to nine men. They worked three men per shift, three shifts a day, seven days a week. Using only hand tools, they excavated 52 feet and installed track in the first 10 days. If they maintained that rate of progress, it would take 10.5 years of 365 days/year of work to complete the tunnel. Ironically, that is close to how long it actually took.

With an eye toward impressing potential investors, Sutro wrote to Bethel saying,

> Try to push the drift ahead all you can, it is of the highest importance to make a big showing in the beginning. It will help me wonderfully to raise money. People will wonder what fast progress we make and figure out in how short a time the tunnel might be finished.[6]

Under Bethel's leadership, the crew built an office for himself and a boarding house for the men. By November 26, the tunnel reached 254 feet into the mountain. Three days later, Sutro filed a certificate of incorporation for the new Sutro Tunnel Company, a California corporation. Joseph Aron, Sutro's old friend and benefactor, was named to the Board of Trustees. The company issued 1.2 million shares of stock with a par value of $10 per share.

Contrary to the common practice with mine shares, the Tunnel Company shares were non-assessable, which made them more attractive to both small and large investors. The 1.2 million shares were allocated as follows:

- 400,000 shares to the company treasury;
- 296,084 shares to those who had provided money to the predecessor Nevada Sutro Tunnel Company; and
- 503,916 shares to Adolph Sutro in exchange for his Nevada company shares.

Sutro had the title of general superintendent but drew no salary.

Money continued to be the biggest problem, and Sutro continued to look to the U.S. Congress to solve that problem. In early 1870, Sutro headed for Washington. For the first time, he was able to travel by rail, as the Transcontinental Railroad had inaugurated service on May 10, 1869. As he traveled in comfort, he must have remembered his trip from New York to San Francisco in 1850. Sutro's original journey had taken 41 days including six tortuous, steamy days traveling across Panama. On the new railroad, the trip from San Francisco to New York averaged seven days.

Little did Sutro know how much that pleasant train ride would cost him. The construction of the Transcontinental Railroad resulted in the Crédit Mobilier Scandal, which would directly impact funding for his tunnel.

When Sutro reached Washington, he had to fight the Bank Ring's attempt to pass a bill that would eliminate the critical royalty clause in the Sutro Tunnel Act. With that clause gone, the mining companies would no longer be obligated to pay $2 per ton of ore mined, and the Sutro Tunnel would be dead. Fortunately, Sutro's friends in the capital detected the threat. Sutro called on the friends he had made in the House of Representatives and convinced them to vote against the bill. Sutro's forces prevailed, 124 to 42. That victory was tempered by the unwillingness of the House to provide any money for the tunnel, and Congress adjourned without considering a loan or grant to Sutro.

Adolph stayed in the east for four more months, continuing his quest for supporters and money. The possibility of French investment caused him to schedule a voyage there on July 20, 1870. But on July 16, just four days before Sutro's departure, France declared war on the German Kingdom of Prussia and the long-anticipated Franco-Prussian War started, dashing any hopes for French money. The odds against Sutro were increasing.

By September, Sutro had returned to San Francisco. Money was so scarce that he had told Bethel to scale back to just one shift at the tunnel.

Sutro went back to Washington in December and tried a new approach. He requested Congress to send a special commission to Nevada to determine the worth of his tunnel. Somewhat to his surprise, both houses agreed. On April 4, 1871, President Grant signed the bill creating the Sutro Tunnel Commission, which was to consist of three engineers reporting to the chief of engineers in the War Department.

One month later, Sutro was in New York to greet George T. Coulter, a possible investor who was important for several reasons. Coulter was the second cousin of Robert and Hugh McCalmont of the banking house McCalmont Brothers and Company in London. Also, Coulter, with McCalmont backing, had brought the stock of the Sierra Buttes Gold Mining Company of California to the London market. The Sierra Buttes mine was financially successful and paid its investors 20 percent per year. As a result, Coulter had an excellent reputation in London financial circles. Sutro met Coulter and his friend, Lewis Richard Price, who had been named the chairman of the board of directors of the Sierra Buttes Company. Price had come to the states to visit the Sierra Buttes mine. While Sutro, Coulter, and Price traveled west on the train, Sutro had a captive audience and flooded Price with information about the Sutro Tunnel. Suddenly Sutro had two groups of people interested in his tunnel.[7]

The Sutro Tunnel Commission arrived in Virginia City in late June 1871 and stayed until late August. The Commission members were H.G. Wright and John G. Foster, both lieutenant colonels of engineers and brevet major generals of the U.S. Army; and Dr. Wesley Newland, a civil and mining engineer from Cornell University. They were to examine the condition of the Comstock Lode, both as to past production and likely future outlook; and the tunnel as to its importance, feasibility, cost, construction time, and geological and practical value as an exploring work, and its impact on national interests. The commissioners prepared a list of 17 detailed questions regarding the mines and mining practices, which they submitted to the mine superintendents.[8] Of course, those superintendents were under the thumb of the Bank of California, so the answers they provided were undoubtedly weighted against any possible need for or benefits of a tunnel. As an extreme example, Isaac Requa, superintendent of the Chollar Potosi Mine, said "that if the Sutro Tunnel were then in existence and all of its many proposed services were absolutely free to the mining companies, it would still be of absolutely no use to them."[9]

The commissioners went into the mines and visited the site of the tunnel. But their mine visits were carefully controlled by the superintendents. Pumps ran day and night to remove as much water as possible. Areas with water were boarded up or "out of order." No hot areas were on the itinerary. Miners were warned that they faced termination if they disclosed any water or heat problems or commented favorably about the tunnel. And the commissioners were served excellent champagne each morning as they arrived for their inspections.

On July 6, as the commissioners were getting started with their explorations, George Coulter and Richard Price arrived in Virginia City. After arriving in San Francisco, they had spent several weeks in California. They were now returning east and were anxious to see the famous Comstock Lode and Sutro's tunnel. Sutro immediately became their host and took them to see the tunnel and the ore body being worked at the Crown Point Mine. Price spoke with Professor Newland, one of the commissioners, and reported that he was "wonderfully impressed" with the tunnel's advantages.[10]

Sutro's choice of the Crown Point was no accident. The ore body there was at the 1,100-foot level, and the temperature at that depth was quite high. After just ten minutes the visitors were sweating profusely, "as though in a vapour bath." Price wrote, "And in this atmosphere the poor miners have to work!!! They die in great numbers from miner's consumption, but all this will be changed & ventilation be perfect if the Sutro Tunnel be carried out."[11]

Both Coulter and Price were impressed by what Sutro showed them, and Coulter agreed to buy some tunnel company stock with his own money. In addition, he signed an agreement with Sutro that gave him one share of tunnel stock for every four shares that he sold.

In early August, Coulter cabled Sutro with encouraging news. The McCalmont brothers might be interested in investing. Although he did not invite Sutro to come to

England, Sutro read between the lines and left Nevada for London on August 15, 1871. He was not going to allow a possible investment to slip away.

In London, Sutro met with Robert McCalmont and found him to be a sincere believer in the tunnel project. He was willing to invest $650,000 of his own or bank funds in Sutro Tunnel Company stock. Sutro must have broken his Prussian reserve with at least a big smile, and Coulter had just been handed $162,500 in stock for himself. Whether Coulter had disclosed his deal with Sutro to his cousins was never positively established.

Now work on the tunnel could begin in earnest. By December Sutro had purchased drilling machinery, and 300 to 400 men were digging away to create the tunnel.

On November 30, 1871, the Sutro Tunnel Commission submitted their report on the Comstock Lode and the feasibility and effectiveness of the proposed tunnel. After passing through several levels of authority, it reached the Committee on Mines and Mining on January 9, 1872. The report contained both good and bad news for Sutro and his tunnel. The major conclusions regarding various aspects of the tunnel are summarized here.[12]

Ventilation

The commissioners stated the following. "It is, therefore, the opinion of the commission that, while the proposed tunnel would increase and improve the ventilation of the mines and possibly dispense with the use of some part of the means for artificial ventilation now employed, it is not a necessity for ventilation. Even with all the aid that the tunnel can be expected to afford, it is the opinion of the commission that mechanical ventilation blowers, operated by steam or other power, would still be needed at the headings and in the stopes where the air from the tunnel would not penetrate."

Economy of Working through the Tunnel

(Carrying ore and waste rock through the tunnel; transporting miners to and from the mines through the tunnel)

The commissioners provided two cost estimates for working through the tunnel, the first assuming 25¢ per ton per mile for ore and waste rock and 50¢ round trip per miner, and the second assuming 10¢ per ton per mile for ore and waste rock and 20¢ round trip per miner.

Based on answers given to the commissioner's list of 17 questions by the mine superintendents, the cost of hoisting ore, transporting it to the mills, pumping water, and transporting miners to and from their work stations, with no tunnel, totaled $1.035 million per year for the entire Comstock.

Under the 25¢/50¢ assumptions and including the $2 per ton of ore royalty to be paid to the tunnel company, the corresponding cost for these operations by working through the tunnel would be $1.772 million per year. The commissioners concluded, "This is not a favorable showing for the economy of working through the tunnel."

Under the 10¢/20¢ assumptions, and again including the $2 per ton of ore royalty, the corresponding cost of working through the tunnel dropped to $1.17 million. Again, the commissioners concluded, "Even with this reduction in tariff, the balance would be against working through the tunnel." "(T)he opinion of the commissioners would necessarily be against the tunnel in the point of economy of operating the mines."

Feasibility of the Tunnel

On the issue of feasibility, the commissioners had no doubts. They stated, "Of the practicability of the project there is no doubt." "So many tunnels have been run in this, as well as in other countries, through material much more difficult, that no reasonable grounds exist for questioning the feasibility of the one we are considering." "We, therefore, dismiss this portion of the investigation with the expression of the opinion of the commission in favor of the entire feasibility of the tunnel project, so far as its construction is concerned."

Cost of the Tunnel

"In making the estimate of cost, the commission has been governed mainly by costs of shafts and drifts in the mines on the Comstock, and by the actual expenditures as reported by the tunnel company in running its preliminary tunnel or drift, which, as has been stated, has already penetrated over 2,500 feet under the mountains lying between its mouth and the lode."

On that basis, the commissioners provided the following estimates for the total costs of constructing both the main tunnel and the branch tunnels needed to connect to all the mines:

"For the main tunnel and four (air) shafts	$2,707,595.15
For the branch tunnel and two (air) shafts	$1,710,734.35
Total in gold	$4,418,329.50"

Time Required for Construction of the Tunnel

Based on working from four air shafts and using manual labor only, the commission estimated that the main tunnel would require 3.25 years to complete. By also starting work on the branch tunnel from its two air shafts, the branch and main tunnels could both be completed in 3.4 years. Use of machinery to augment manual labor would reduce the total time for both tunnels to 2.3 years.

Value of the Bullion Extracted from the Mines on the Comstock Lode

For the period 1859–1871, the commissioners estimated that total bullion production from the Comstock Lode was $125 million.

Present and Probable Future Production

"The present annual production may, it is believed, be taken with sufficient accuracy at $15,000,000.

As regards the probable future yield, no claim can be made to anything like accuracy, excepting the few instances in which ore-bodies are now developed. The commission has already stated its belief in the lode being what is known as a true fissure vein, or as continuing downward indefinitely in the crust of the earth; but whether the vein will continue to be ore-bearing cannot be predicted with any degree of certainty. It is a matter of opinion, to be based, however, upon probabilities and the actual results experienced in deep mining in other parts of the world. These, in the judgment of the commission, favor the finding of ore down to the lowest depths that can be reached; and that this opinion is shared by most of the mining authorities seems to be shown by their continued downward search."

On the "Geological and Practical Value" of the Sutro Tunnel "As an Exploring Work"

This section of the report is quite lengthy, but the following quotations provide a fair summary of the important points.

"We know that for a distance of five miles, with a varying width of from 50 to 500 feet, and to an unexplored depth, the Comstock lode is found one of the richest, most productive and extensive in the records of mining.

It is, however, of very great importance to determine whether the Comstock be a true fissure-vein, as declared by most intelligent geologists or be but a gash-vein, with its material filled in from adjacent rocks. The permanency of the mining interests of Nevada depends upon which of these views prove correct. In the first contingency we may claim that no true fissure vein has ever been worked out, and from analogy we may draw the conclusion, with a good degree of certainty, that the Comstock cannot be exhausted by the labor of man. If but a gash-vein, the conditions are so changed that exhaustion must at no distant day be the result."

"The value of the proposed Sutro Tunnel simply as an exploring work is so evident as to be scarcely called in question. Cutting, as it does, at right angles two or more lodes before reaching the Comstock, that, in Europe, would be deemed valuable; the determination of their wealth or poverty would prevent further ruinous outlays in prospecting. There is no certainty that rich bonanzas will be met within the progress of the work, but that an abundance of moderately rich ores will be found is quite probable."

"As an exploring work, we think the Sutro Tunnel may claim to determine with sufficient certainty the ore-bearing character of the Great Flowery and Monte Christo lodes, and settle definitely the question whether the Comstock lode at great depths continues in richness; or, as is believed by some, becomes worthless as deep levels are opened."

"We cannot but think, therefore, that, as an exploring work for deep mining, the Sutro Tunnel may justly claim favorable consideration."

Eliot Lord, in summarizing the report of the commissioners said, "This commission reported favorable on the geological and practical value of the tunnel as an exploring work to determine the ore-bearing character of the Comstock and other ledges lying to the east, at great depths; but its utility as a drainway and as affording ventilation to the mines was judged to be small in comparison with its cost." "(T)the commission did not consider that the extension of the tunnel would prove an economical method of operating the Comstock Mines." "(T)the report of the commission was practically a serious blow to Mr. Sutro's hopes of aid from the National Government in his project."[13]

Would this largely negative report of the Sutro Tunnel Commission, prepared by three acknowledged mining experts, doom the Sutro Tunnel?

Chapter 20

Mr. Sutro Goes to Washington

The most terrifying words in the English language are: I'm from the government and I'm here to help.
—Ronald Reagan

For most people, an unfavorable report by a panel of experts chartered by a committee of the U.S. House of Representatives would end their endeavor. Not so for Adolph Sutro. Because he knew mine superintendents beholden to the Bank of California had unduly influenced the experts, Sutro resolved to fight the conclusions of the report. To do so, he requested a hearing before the Committee on Mines and Mining, where he proposed to question the experts who had prepared the report. The Committee granted his request, and the hearings began on Monday, February 12, 1872. The hearings extended over 22 days and concluded on Friday, March 29, 1872. Nine different witnesses were called, including all three of the commissioners (General John G. Foster, Professor Wesley Newcomb, and General H.G. Wright). The hearings were to be conducted by the rules of the Committee, not courtroom rules. Attorneys could represent each party, but Sutro decided to confront the commissioners himself, as no one knew more about the Comstock than he did. Thomas Sunderland represented the Bank of California, but acknowledging that would be to admit one of Sutro's key arguments, that the Bank controlled the Comstock. So, Sunderland did not mention the Bank of California but claimed to represent the whole Comstock. The following discussion of the hearings is drawn from REPORT OF THE COMMISSIONERS AND EVIDENCE TAKEN BY THE COMMITTEE ON MINES AND MINING.[1]

General J.G. Foster was the first witness called, and Sutro immediately set the stage for some devastating questions on the cost of hoisting materials from the mines. At issue was the commissioner's conclusion that "Working through the Tunnel" (carrying ore and waste rock through the tunnel; transporting miners to and from the mines through the tunnel) would not be economical compared to the current practice of hoisting everything to the top of the mines by steam power.

Sutro quoted from the Commissioner's Report:

Under the present system of operating the mines, the ore and the refuse rock are raised to the surface, through the shafts, by steam power; the ore being transported to the mills by wagons, or by the railroad before alluded to, and the refuse rock deposited at the dumps contiguous to the shafts. The items of expense, as given by the superintendents, vary somewhat, as might have been expected, in view of the different circumstances in each. The average of certain of the more important of them may, however, be stated with sufficient accuracy, as follows: Cost per ton hoisting from depths varying from 1,200 to 1,750 feet, being the average reported for seven of the principal mines the lode, 51.17 cents. Cost of pumping for the year ending June 30, 1871, as arrived at by the commission, by taking the cost of the mines as far as reported, and estimating for the rest $124,674.

After setting up the General, **Sutro continued,** "Now, I want to ask you, General Foster, how you arrived at these figures: whether you simply took the statements of the superintendents of the companies, or whether you had an opportunity of examining the books of the companies as to the correctness of those statements?"

General Foster replied, in part, "We did not seek access to the books.... My answer to your question, therefore, is that we based our estimates upon the statements they made in reply to our inquiries—upon their official statements.

Sutro: "Have you made any comparison between the statements which were made by the superintendents and the statements furnished by their annual reports? Have you been able to make a comparison, or has it been possible for you to make one, as far as the accuracy of these statements is concerned?"

Foster: "Well, we made certain comparisons; but with us it was not a question of invalidating their reports. We did not make comparisons with a view to test the complete accuracy of what they wrote us. As the basis of estimates, we had no reason to question the veracity of their statements, and we took their statements."

The critical point that Sutro made with Foster's testimony is that the commissioners accepted the mine superintendents' answers to the 17 questions posed by the commissioners, and did nothing to verify or reconcile those answers to the official annual reports filed by every mine.

Sutro then analyzed the cost of hoisting materials based on the official annual reports and concluded that the actual cost was 2.36 times what the commissioners reported. The questioning and testimony were detailed and complex, but at no time did General Foster dispute Sutro's conclusions.

Other people entered the hearing room, so the following discussion summarized the discussion up to this point:

Mr. Banks (Committee Member): "Two or three gentlemen have just come in since the discussion began. I do not understand what particular proposition is intended."

Mr. Waldron (Committee Chairman): "Mr. Sutro is attacking the report made by Captain Day, superintendent of the Ophir silver mine, which report is attached to the report of the commissioners, and introducing figures and statistics to show that the report of Captain Day is incorrect, so far as the cost of making shafts and drifts in the mines are concerned."

Mr. Banks: "Is it above the cost, or below the cost?"

Mr. Waldron: "Below the cost."

Mr. Sutro: "What I am trying to show is this: In the report of the commissioners, on page 9, it is stated, in a comparison between the cost of mining as it is done now, and the cost of mining through the tunnel, that under the present mode of mining it costs 51.17 cents per ton to hoist. I am trying to show that it costs in some mines more than $10 per ton to hoist. General Foster has stated that this estimate of 51.17 cents is arrived at by taking the statements of the various mine superintendents and averaging them. That is it, is it not, General?"

Mr. Foster: "Yes, sir."

Mr. Sutro: "The commissioners had no access to the books over there, and the only figures they could make were by taking the statements of these people and averaging them and basing their report on the data furnished. I want to show that these people have not told the whole truth, have not told the whole thing, as I have already shown in the case of the Ophir company. In this mine, where the expenditures amounted to from six to eight hundred thousand dollars during the time they had been constructing this shaft, according to the statement of the superintendent, it only cost $178,000. Consequently, there is a discrepancy of from four to six hundred thousand dollars."

Mr. Banks: "It is an under-estimate to that amount."

Mr. Sutro: "It is an underestimate absolutely, and it makes an unfavorable showing as regards the comparative working of the tunnel. It is my endeavor to show that these people here who have made these figures have not told the whole truth; they have withheld certain facts which are highly important to know; and they can only be brought out by having these gentlemen state, of their own knowledge, what they know of the accuracy of these figures, and what we can arrive at by examining the official reports which are made from year to year to Congress by the Commissioner on the mineral resources of the country."

At that point, James Negley, committee member from Pennsylvania, raised a relevant issue.

Mr. Negley: "Mr. Chairman, right here I would like to ask one question of General Foster."

Mr. Waldron: "Certainly."

Mr. Negley: "During your investigations there, Mr. Foster, did you discover any feeling of antagonism among the owners of these properties to the projected tunnel?"

Mr. Foster: "Yes, sir; decidedly."

Mr. Negley: "That feeling was general?"

Mr. Foster: "Not to obstruct their giving information of all kinds." "They gave information freely, verbally and in writing; but there was a decided feeling of antagonism, as shown by their published reports. In their conversations, they said about the same things you find in their reports, made here and in the appendix. Some of them were quite violently opposed; others less so. Some, whose names appear here, appeared to be rather lukewarm in their opposition. Still, as a general thing, with one or two exceptions, they were opposed to the tunnel. The feeling was against it."

Mr. Negley: (Regarding the feelings of the miners about the tunnel) "My inquiry arose from the fact that miners in our coal mines are almost invariably opposed to any innovation or new custom in the old established rules of mining?"

Mr. Foster: "Now that you have mentioned that, I will say the miners, as far as I could get information from prominent men, seemed to be in favor of the tunnel. I believe the Miners' Union is in favor of the tunnel."

Mr. Sutro: "General, do you know who are opposed to the tunnel, or at least who are charged with being opposed to it over there by these people you speak of? Who is at the bottom of it?"

Mr. Foster: "If you want a straightforward answer, I would say that the property-owners in Virginia City, those that have money invested in the mills around there, the Bank of California, through its agent, and the railroad company."

Q.: "May I ask you who the owners of the railroad are, as far as you know: whether it is owned by the Bank of California or its men?"
A.: "I don't know who the owners are."
Q.: "Who has control of it?"
A.: "Mr. Sharon seemed to control it."
Q.: "The agent of the Bank of California?"
A.: "Yes, sir."
Q.: "Who owns the majority of the mills over there?"
A.: "On the Carson river?"
Q.: "Yes, sir; and the other mills—the majority of the mills."
A.: "A very large number of the mills is owned by the Union Mill and Mining Company."
Q.: "Do you know whether the Bank of California has anything to do with that?"
A.: "Mr. Sharon has a large amount of stock in that, I believe, but I am not positive."
Q.: "Is he the agent of the Bank of California?"
Mr. Foster: "I heard so."
Mr. Sutro: "Well, then, the opposition to it is by the Bank of California, by the railroad, and by the mills—which means the Bank of California."

By the above testimony, which occupied the daytime portion of the first day of the hearings, Sutro established the following facts for the Committee:

- The commissioners trusted and relied on the answers to their 17 questions as provided by the mine superintendents. No significant cross-checking of official annual reports of the mines was done to verify the answers given by the mine superintendents. These facts alone cast doubt on, if not destroyed the credibility of the report of the commissioners in the eyes of the Committee.
- The costs for hoisting materials as reported by the commissioners greatly underestimated the actual costs (by a factor of 2.36). Therefore, the report's comparison of costs of the current mode of operation (by hoisting) to working through the tunnel were invalid and highly misleading.
- The mine superintendents "have not told the whole truth; they have withheld certain facts which are highly important to know."
- Among the mine officials and residents of the Comstock, there was general animosity and opposition to the tunnel. However, the miners were generally in favor of the tunnel.
- The Bank of California and its agents controlled the mines, mills, and railroads in the Comstock.

The results of this first hearing were essentially repeated with each of the three commissioners. Realizing that he was losing the battle, Sunderland, the representative for the Bank of California, called two mine superintendents as witnesses in an attempt to bolster his case. Isaac Requa, superintendent of the Chollar-Potosi Mine, and General C.C. Batterman, superintendent of two other mines, traveled to Washington to testify.

Requa testified about the cost and desirability of moving existing mills from the Carson River to the area near the mouth of the Sutro Tunnel; the possibility and utility of building a dam on the Carson River to provide water power for potential mills at the tunnel mouth; the amount of stock he owned in the mine that he managed; and other miscellaneous topics.

Batterman also testified about a possible dam on the Carson River; the impact of the tunnel on the Virginia & Truckee Railroad; and the potential benefits of the tunnel (none, in his opinion).

The next witness was Professor R.W. Raymond, U.S. Commissioner of Mines and Mining. After establishing the impressive credentials of Professor Raymond, Sutro asked questions about the use of tunnels at the bottom of mines in Europe, and how the European experience applied to the Comstock Lode:

Mr. Sutro: "I wanted to ask you, Professor Raymond, whether you do not consider that they (European mining engineers) look upon tunnels as of very high importance, and if we find they have constructed a tunnel 14 miles in length, which is but 300 feet below the tunnel which had been previously constructed to the same mines?"

Professor Raymond: "I know they look upon tunnels as of very high importance. It does not need any argument to prove that. I know it."

Q.: "And that they arrive at the conclusion that these tunnels contribute very much to the development of their mines?"

A.: "Yes, sir. Wherever tunnels are feasible, I think they run them, in connection with the development of the mines."

Q.: "Would you consider that the tunnel to the Comstock lode, which in a distance of 4 miles, cuts the mines to the depth of 2,000 feet, would be a desirable point to be attained?"

A.: "Yes, sir; I have always thought so."

Mr. Sutro: "Do you think that such a tunnel, as a general mining proposition, would contribute largely to the profitable working of those mines?"

Professor Raymond: "Why, yes, I think that such a tunnel would be a very important assistance in the proper working of the Comstock lode."

Sutro then asked Professor Raymond if he knew, personally or by reputation, 15 specific European mining experts. Raymond knew most of the men, at least by reputation. Sutro had previously obtained support for his tunnel from all of these men and detailed that support to the Committee in his questions to Professor Raymond.

Based on the favorable opinion of one unbiased expert, Professor Raymond, Sutro completely overcame the negative testimony of two clearly biased mine superintendents, Requa and Batterman.

The next witness, Mr. C.A. Luckhardt, provided fascinating testimony regarding the financial interest of the Bank of California in the Comstock mines. Sutro established that Luckhardt studied mining engineering and chemistry, and that he had held various positions at the Justis Mining Company, the Ophir Mine, and the North American Mine before being employed by the Bank of California. The most important portions of Luckhardt's testimony follow:

Mr. Sutro: "How long have you been employed by the Bank of California?"

Mr. Luckhardt: "Nearly five years."

Q.: "What were the special duties that were assigned to you?"

A.: "To examine the mines that they wished to have examined, and report the appearance and probable product of those mines."

Q.: "You were employed, then, as a general agent, or as an expert to report on all the mines?"

A.: "Yes, sir; on all the mines to which they sent me; on all those mines they wished to have examined."

Q.: "What was the object of the Bank of California in employing you as mining engineer?"

A.: "Well, I suppose it was to receive truthful information as regards the state of the mines."

Q.: "The Bank of California is supposed to be a banking institution, is it not?"

A.: "Well, I suppose so."

Q.: "And they employed you to render a report of the condition of the mines?"

A.: "Yes, sir. They employed me through their agent, Mr. Sharon, to examine such mining property as they wished to have examined."

Q.: "How often did you report to the Bank of California?"

A.: "Every day."

Q.: "Did you make a written report every day?"

A.: "Well, for the first two years I made a written report, as soon as I could get the opportunity to complete such. Sometimes it took me three days to make one report, but afterwards I sometimes made a report every two days, when there was nothing new to report upon."

Q.: "What was the special object they had in view, in employing you to give them specific information about the mines or condition of the mines, etc.?"

A.: "I have my opinion about it. I do not know what their object was, but from the conversation and the injunctions put upon me, I inferred that they wished to know the exact truth of the state of the ores, etc."

Q.: "Was it for the purpose of stock operations?"

A.: "Well, I could not say that—what it was for."

Q.: "What interest could the Bank of California have in sending you to a mine in which they had no interest in getting information?"

A.: "Probably the interest they had in sending me there was to see what the state of the mine was, so that they might—these parties interested—buy into the mine, by stock, or obtain ores from the mine. The injunction was put upon me, when I was employed, to keep all that I saw there for their especial benefit and no one else's."

Q.: "In other words, you were to keep secret all you found out about the mines, and report to them?"

A.: "That was the purport of it, I suppose."

Q.: "How did you gain admission to those mines?"

A.: "By an order to the superintendent or foreman from the agent of the Bank of California."

Q.: "Please state who he was."

A.: "Mr. Sharon."

Q.: "Did that order from Mr. Sharon gain you admittance to all the mines?"

A.: "It always gained me admittance where he gave me an order."

Q.: "Did other people have a chance to go into those mines any time they pleased?"

A.: "Not as a general thing."

Q.: "Don't you account for it (that mine superintendents were almost never trained mining engineers) by the fact that they want men who are connected with them in a manner, so as to manage affairs to suit them?"

A.: "I think that mining has been carried on in Virginia City, not alone for the purpose of developing mines and making them remunerative institutions, but also for the purpose of stock speculations."

Q.: "In making a report upon a mine, would you go to work and visit every portion of that mine, try to get into every drift, take out samples of ore, assay them in that manner, and examine the mine from the lower level to the uppermost?"

A.: "Yes, sir."

Mr. Sutro: "Then the reports you made to the Bank of California at that time must possess great value?"

Mr. Luckhardt: "As far as throwing light upon the conditions of those mines, they may be worth something as records; but whether they were of great value, that, of course, those people have to judge of who read them, and not I, who made them."

As an expert witness myself, I cringe at the number of opinions, speculation, and hearsay contained in the testimony of General Foster and especially that of Mr. Luckhardt. Such testimony would never be allowed in a courtroom, but this was a House of Representatives Committee hearing, and they made their own rules. Mr. Sunderland, the attorney representing the Bank of California, was powerless to object.

Based on Mr. Luckhardt's testimony, it was clear that the Bank of California, at Sharon's and probably Ralston's direction, was gathering information that they used to determine when to buy and when to sell stock in the Comstock mines. Such "Insider Trading" is illegal under current laws, but it was not uncommon in the 1860s and '70s. The most famous cases concerned railroads, specifically Jay Gould's manipulation of Erie Railroad stock,[2] and the Crédit Mobilier scandal involving the Union Pacific Railroad.[3]

The full record of testimony before the Committee on Mines and Mining consumed 810 pages, and the discussion and closing arguments took another 141 pages. Adolph Sutro's closing argument alone took three hours to deliver. In it, he began with the history of the tunnel, from when it was the germ of an idea during his first trip to Washoe to the present, when construction was underway. He refuted the biased testimony of mining superintendents Requa and Batterman by emphasizing the testimony of mining experts Raymond and Luckhardt. He made clear the control over the Comstock exercised by the Bank of California and its reasons for opposing the tunnel. Near the end of his closing argument, Sutro took the unusual step of praising his friend and supporter, Joseph Aron. He said, "I want to pay tribute right here to a noble-hearted, far-seeing, generous, and true man, who has stood by me in the darkest hours of my trials, who has counseled and assisted me at all times, who has appreciated the magnitude and importance of the work to which I have devoted myself. That man's name is Joseph Aron, a resident of San Francisco."[4]

Finally, as with any good sales pitch, Sutro asked for the order, in this case, a $3 million government loan to advance his tunnel project.

It took three weeks for the Committee on Mines and Mining to review the testimony and develop a final report. The result, released on June 3, 1872, was far different from the report of the three commissioners. The report listed 60 points in support of the tunnel, and then stated, as point 61:

> 61. We would, in conclusion, indorse the language used in the closing paragraph of a report to Congress, made by a former committee, recommending a loan of five millions of dollars, in the following words:
> That, taking into consideration the magnitude of the undertaking, the great yield of bullion which will be directly secured thereby, the great influence by its successful completion upon all our mining interests, the stimulus it will give to mining generally, the positive proof it will furnish of our immense mineral wealth, and considering the importance of attaining these results in view of our large national debt, ordinary wisdom and foresight should command that the aid asked for the construction of this important work, or a much larger sum if it were necessary, should be granted, even were no security whatever offered for its repayment.

The Committee also prepared a companion bill, H.R. 2966, calling for a loan of $2 million to the Sutro Tunnel Company, and urged its passage.

But the Crédit Mobilier scandal intervened. Because four senators, the speaker of the House, the vice president, and the secretary of the treasury were caught up in the scandal,[5] Congress conducted virtually no regular business, and the full House of Representatives never even considered H.R. 2966, the bill for Sutro's loan.

CHAPTER 21

That Sounds French

As so often happens with Washington scandals, it isn't the original scandal that gets people in the most trouble—it's the attempted coverup.
—Tom Petri, U.S. House of Representatives, 1979–2015

Adolph Sutro had enjoyed his comfortable journey across the United States on the Transcontinental Railroad, but he certainly did not enjoy losing the opportunity for government funding of his tunnel because of the Crédit Mobilier of America scandal. But the railroad and the scandal were inseparable.

The idea for a transcontinental railroad originated in 1845 when New York entrepreneur Asa Whitney proposed a route from Lake Michigan to the mouth of the Columbia River in present-day Washington state.[1] In 1853, the U.S. Congress commissioned Jefferson Davis, then secretary of war in the Pierce administration, to survey three potential routes, northern, central, and southern.

Onto the scene came Theodore Judah, who had recently completed the Sacramento Valley Railroad between Sacramento and Folsom, which Adolph Sutro rode on his journey to Washoe in 1860. Judah, like Sutro, was a visionary. His vision, which he discussed endlessly with everyone he encountered, was to build a railroad to connect the west to existing railroads near Omaha, thus forming a transcontinental railroad. Judah pushed his idea so hard that he was often called "Crazy Judah." In pursuit of his dream, Judah had studied the terrain of the Sierra Nevada to find a gap or other natural feature that would allow construction of a railroad.

When Judah heard of the possibility of government support for a transcontinental railroad, he headed for Washington, D.C., to make his voice heard. By now, William Aspin-

Theodore Judah (1826–1863).

wall of the Pacific Mail Steamship Company had completed a railroad across Panama, so Judah and his wife, Anna, took that faster route east. Upon arrival in the unfinished and muddy town of Washington, Judah found a tense atmosphere between Northern and Southern interests regarding the issue of slavery.

To promulgate his ideas, Judah prepared a pamphlet called *Practical Plan for Building the Pacific Railroad*. Just as Sutro had done with his tunnel proposal, Judah lobbied Congress. He proposed a detailed survey of what he thought would be the best route for the railroad. But no one could focus on a railroad when their attention was on the possible secession of some or all of the southern states.

Judah and his wife returned to California, where they convinced the state legislature to call a railroad convention. Judah believed that the federal government would be forced to act if the state of California and other western states actively supported a railroad. A convention in September–October 1859 and a subsequent one in February 1860 solidified western support for the railroad and identified details of funding, but still, Washington was frozen in inactivity.[2]

Abraham Lincoln was elected president in November 1860, and South Carolina became the first state to secede from the Union in December. War was on the horizon, and the Battle of Fort Sumter in Charleston Harbor, South Carolina, on April 12, 1861, marked the official start.

Theodore Judah realized that the federal government would support the railroad only if California investors started building it. So through intense effort, he found four Sacramento merchants who each initially invested $1,500: Collis Huntington, a hardware merchant; Leland Stanford, a grocer; Mark Hopkins, Huntington's business partner; and Charles Crocker, a dry-goods merchant.[3,4] They filed incorporation papers for the Central Pacific Railroad on June 28, 1861, just 18 days after Leland Stanford was nominated for governor of California.

On October 9, 1861, the board of directors of the Central Pacific Railroad sent Theodore Judah back to Washington yet again, with the following resolution:

> Resolved that Mr. T.D. Judah, the Chief Engineer of this Company, proceed to Washington on the steamer of the 11th October inst. as the accredited agent of the Central Pacific Railroad of California for the purpose of procuring appropriations of land and U.S. Bonds from the government to aid in the construction of the road.

Judah arrived in Washington in November to find the city an armed camp. Congress was paralyzed because half of its seats were empty, either because Confederates had occupied them or because Union members had gone to battle. Even though he was not an elected member of Congress, Theodore Judah took advantage of the power vacuum and got himself appointed secretary of the Senate Committee on Pacific Railroads and clerk of the House Main Committee on Railroads. From these powerful positions, Judah was practically able to write bills in his own words and in his own way. He sent for Collis Huntington, who was a master of one-on-one lobbying, and Huntington called on each legislator personally. On June 20, 1862, the Senate passed the Pacific Railroad Act, 35 to 5. The House passed the final bill four days later, and President Abraham Lincoln signed the Act on July 1, 1862.[5,6]

In 1864, the government granted two charters, along with financing, to build a railroad from Council Bluffs, near Omaha, Nebraska, to Sacramento, California. This new railroad would link to the existing eastern rail network at Council Bluffs, and was comprised of the following segments (although the mileages and meeting point at Promontory Summit were not specified)[7]:

- Union Pacific Railroad—1,087 miles from Council Bluffs to Promontory Summit, Utah Territory;
- Central Pacific Railroad Company of California (CPRR)—690 miles from Promontory Summit to Sacramento.

To say that the financing plan for the railroad was complex would be a gross understatement. The Pacific Railroad Act and subsequent legislation authorized the federal government to issue 30-year bonds at 6 percent interest. The railroad companies also issued company-backed bonds and stock. Once a 20-mile section of track was laid on level grade, the government would pay the railroad company $16,000 per mile. For track on the plateau between the Rocky Mountains and Sierra Nevadas, the amount increased to $32,000 per mile. For track in mountainous areas, the amount increased again to $48,000 per mile. As a further incentive, federal and state governments granted land to the railroads: 400-foot-wide right-of-way corridors and also 10 sections (640 acres each) per mile on both sides of the track.[8] The total area of land grants to the Union Pacific and Central Pacific was larger than the state of Texas; over 200,000 square miles from the federal government and over 76,000 square miles from state governments.[9]

The Union Pacific had trouble selling its stock. One of the few investors was Mormon leader Brigham Young, who also supplied workers for building the Utah portion of the railroad. The primary investor was Dr. Thomas Durant, a former ophthalmologist, who ended up owning or controlling about half of the railroad stock.[10]

Dr. Thomas C. Durant (1820–1885).

The financial reward system invited fraud, and government oversight was insufficient to monitor the railroad companies. The Union Pacific under Thomas Durant built track on land that Durant owned, and also built excess miles of track in the form of unneeded oxbows. After two and a half years of construction, it had progressed just 40 miles from its starting point.[11]

Both railroad companies knew that ongoing operations after the railroad was completed would not be profitable for years, if ever, so they decided to make as much money as possible during the construction phase. The Union Pacific and the Central Pacific each established what appeared to be independent companies to do the actual construction. But these companies were controlled by the same management team as their parent railroads. This self-dealing allowed the construc-

Clockwise from top left: **Collis Huntington, Leland Stanford, Mark Hopkins, and Charles Crocker.**

tion companies to charge exorbitant profits and the railroads to add "management fees" on top of the construction company invoices.

The Central Pacific chose a prosaic name for their puppet company, the "Contract and Finance Company."

The Union Pacific was far more creative, calling their construction firm "Crédit Mobilier of America."[12] The name was chosen to establish separation from the Union Pacific, and also to gain credibility. A French bank, Crédit Mobilier, was one of the most important financial institutions in the world in the mid–19th century and financed numerous railroad and other infrastructure projects.[13] But except for the similar name, the French bank was unrelated to the U.S. company.

By charging excessive amounts for construction, Crédit Mobilier of America and the Union Pacific billed and were paid by the federal government over $94 million for construction that had actually cost less than $51 million. But this overbilling was just part of the fraud.

In 1867, Crédit Mobilier replaced Thomas Durant as its head with U.S. Congressman Oakes Ames. Ames offered to members of Congress shares of stock in Crédit Mobilier at its discounted par value rather than the market value, which was much higher. Because of its excessive billing, the management of the Union Pacific would soon need to request additional funding from Congress. By providing key members of Congress stock in Crédit Mobilier of America, their self-interest would prevent them from disclosing any wrongdoing and assure their support for additional construction funds. The bribes went undetected until 1872.

During the presidential election campaign of 1872, the *New York Sun* newspaper was opposing the reelection of President Ulysses S. Grant. Because of a disagreement with Congressman Oakes Ames, a business associate leaked incriminating letters to the *Sun*. The newspaper reported that Crédit Mobilier of America had been paid $72 million for building a railroad worth just $53 million. A subsequent Department of Justice investigation revealed that 30 politicians from both parties had been provided discounted shares of Crédit Mobilier of America. Among those accused were Representative James A. Garfield (later elected president) and incumbent vice president Schuyler Colfax. The Crédit Mobilier scandal became one of the best-known examples of graft in American history.[14,15,16]

Congressman Oakes Ames (1804–1873).

Theodore Judah did not live to see the scandal or the realization of his dream with the driving of the golden spike at Promontory Point, Utah, on May 10, 1869. He died of yellow fever in New York City on November 2, 1863. Judah contracted the disease while crossing Panama, a trip that his railroad would make obsolete.[17]

Because of the construction of the Transcontinental Railroad, Adolph Sutro was able to ride in comfort across the country in 1872. But the resulting Crédit Mobilier of America scandal paralyzed the House of Representatives and prevented it from passing H.R. 2966, which would have granted Sutro a loan of $2 million for his tunnel.

CHAPTER 22

Sutro Builds Sutro

The undiscovered places that are interesting to me are these places that contain bits of our disappearing history, like a ghost town.
—Ransom Riggs

When the U.S. Congress passed the Tunnel Act in 1866, it granted to Adolph Sutro the right to buy up to two sections (1,280 acres) of land near the mouth of the tunnel for $1.25 per acre. Adolph envisioned a shift in population from the established towns of Virginia City and Gold Hill to the new town of Sutro, and he put his vision into writing in a pamphlet published on September 1, 1866. The assessed value of property in the two towns was $6.8 million (excluding mining property), but Sutro saw their demise as inevitable because of pure economics. Transporting miners to their work site via the tunnel, as well as carrying timber, ore, and waste rock through the tunnel, would be far cheaper than using a steam-powered hoist to move men and materials. Furthermore, with mills at the mouth of the tunnel in Sutro, the cost of moving ore from the mine mouth to the mills would be minimized. While all that Sutro proposed might be true, the people who lived in Virginia City and Gold Hill, and the Bank of California, were understandably and violently opposed to Sutro's vision for their towns, and therefore to the tunnel project.[1]

Until late 1872, the prospects for a tunnel were dubious, and Sutro lacked money to do much of anything. But then, with money from the miners' unions and English banker Robert McCalmont, and the positive recommendation from the Committee on Mines and Mining (Sutro hoped that the bill authorizing a government loan would eventually pass), it was time to begin buying land and planning the town of Sutro.

Adolph hired Ross E. Browne to survey and plan the town, centered on the tunnel. The drawing[2] on the next page shows Browne's plan, drawn in 1873.

Tunnel Avenue extended from the mouth of the tunnel and was 200 feet wide. Streets perpendicular to Tunnel Avenue bore female names in alphabetical order, from Adele through Zeline, and were 100 feet wide, except for Florence, which was 150 feet. Streets parallel to Tunnel Avenue were designated as 1st through 50th Street (Tunnel Avenue replaced 27th Street) and were 80 feet wide. Each town lot measured 25 by 60 feet.

Sutro must have remembered the words of his botany teacher when the two went

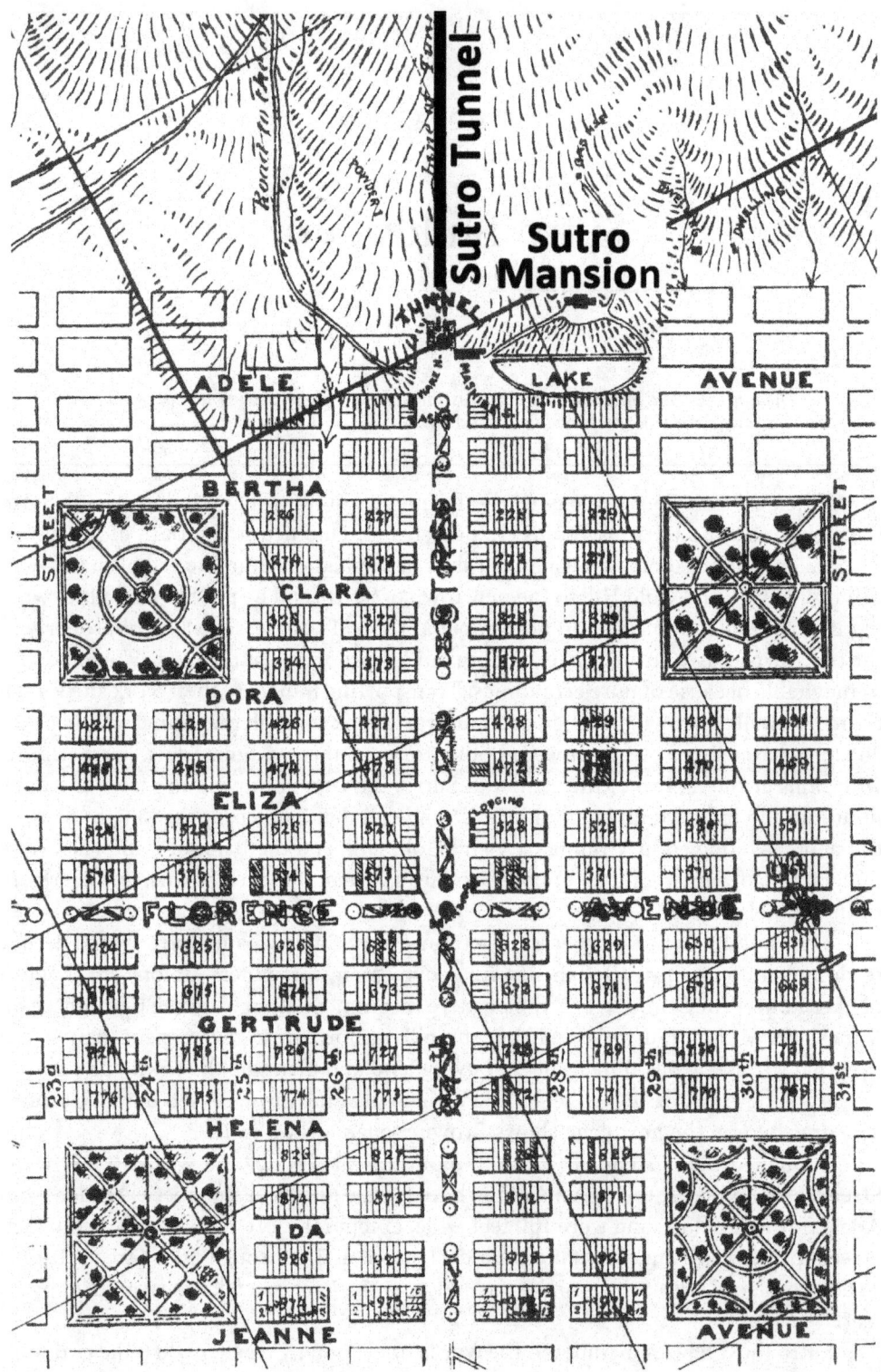

Enlarged view of the town of Sutro, as planned by Ross E. Browne, 1873.

for walks in the forests near Aachen when Adolph was a youngster. His teacher said, "My son, live ever near to nature's heart, for to depart from nature is to depart from happiness. Choose companions among such as love trees and little children. The man who loves these can never commit a crime."[3]

Sutro bought and planted trees along Florence and Tunnel Avenues, and he required anyone who purchased a lot to plant and care for a tree in front of his house. Six large squares (four shown on the opposite figure), 680 feet on each side, were reserved for parks, which Sutro planned to plant with trees and flowers. He established a tree nursery across the Carson River and ordered every variety of tree suitable for the soil and climate of the region.

The Tunnel Company received its first income by selling two lots for $500 each on September 9, 1872, one for a livery stable and one for a butcher shop.

Now that the town of Sutro existed, at least on paper, it was time for Adolph to build a house for himself and his family. He chose an elevated site northeast of the tunnel mouth, near Adele Avenue and 28th Avenue, and asked an architect to design a large, gracious home devoid of frills but well-lighted (with candles at first, then with gas lights), heated, and with lots of plumbing. It was to cost between $15,000 and $20,000 and be large enough for him, Mrs. Sutro, and their six children.[4]

Patrick Neylan, curator of the Historical Society of Dayton Valley Museum, recently measured the foundation of the house at 40 feet square, so the three-story building

Sutro Mansion in Sutro, Nevada. Note the pond in front (courtesy Laura Tennant Collection).

Sutro Mansion. Note the guy rods to anchor the building against strong winds.

contained about 4,800 square feet. As usual, Adolph spent more than he had planned. The mansion, owned by the Sutro Tunnel Company, cost $40,000.

The mansion looked out over a large pond, 1,000 feet long by 200 feet wide and 14 feet deep. The pond was filled with water draining from the tunnel and became home for ducks, frogs, turtles, salmon, and trout. These animals in turn often filled the dinner plates of the Sutro family.[5]

A 2007 article by a man who lived in the mansion in the 1940s describes the building[6]:

> There were three floors to the building. I remember there was a marble fireplace in every room except the bathrooms and kitchen. There was two huge chimneys so there must have been quite a network of pipes to connect all the fireplaces. On top there was a penthouse where we kids used to play and of course you could see up and down the valley for miles. I remember the downstairs rooms had 12 foot ceilings. As you entered the big hallway the stairs were straight ahead. To the left was a large parlor with the most beautiful Victorian furniture as was the furniture throughout the house. A library was to the right that had an untold number of books. Past the pantry a door opened into a huge dining room. It had all the accommodations (hutches, serving tables, etc.). I remember the dining table could be extended to accommodate at least 24 people.
>
> Outside was a small lawn on the left as you walked up to the big porch (ran the full length of the main house). There were guy rods from the ground up to the third story to keep the wind from blowing the thing away.[7] These were located on the left and back side. They were made in sections and about an inch in thickness.

Sutro and his family moved into the mansion around November 1872, but Adolph did not stay long. He left in December for Washington, still hoping to obtain government funding for his tunnel.

Fire truck that served Sutro from 1879 to 1894. Photo by author at the Historical Society of Dayton Valley.

When Adolph left, 18 men were working directly on the tunnel; 140 more on the four airshafts along the tunnel route; 21 in the machine shop; and 17 others in various positions. Many of these workers built homes in the town of Sutro, and the population peaked at about 800 people. But Sutro never became the population center that Adolph envisioned. As the silver and gold ore in the Comstock ran out, the population of the town of Sutro declined. In 1880 there were 435 residents, by 1890 just a few buildings survived, and by 1900 the town had been virtually abandoned.

Chapter 23

Water, Water

Water, water everywhere, nor any drop to drink.
—Samuel Taylor Coleridge

Instead of a sea of undrinkable saltwater faced by the sailors in Coleridge's classic *Rime of the Ancient Mariner*, Virginia City residents confronted a barren landscape covering buried deposits of porous rocks laden with solutions of sodium sulfate and calcium sulfate.[1] Average annual precipitation in Virginia City is just eight inches, so cisterns were not practical.[2] Early settlers relied on either the barely potable underground water or small local springs. As the population grew, residents cut tunnels into mountains west of town to tap larger springs, but still the water was scarce and tasted bitter. When Adolph Sutro visited Virginia City in 1860, he found the water to be cloudy and foul-tasting. That description was valid until late 1873.

German engineer and surveyor Hermann Schussler had surveyed the Sutro Tunnel in 1869 and served as the first chief engineer on that project. From that work, Schussler was familiar with the geography of the Comstock area. In 1871, hearing that Virginia City was desperate for better drinking water, Schussler wrote to the Virginia and Gold Hill Water Company. The company had recently been purchased from William Sharon by John Mackay and James Fair. In his letter, Schussler presented a plan to obtain water from the Sierra Nevada Mountains and pipe it to the Comstock.

Upon receiving Schussler's proposal for a solution to their water problems, and knowing of his previous successful work around San Francisco, the directors of the Virginia and Gold Hill Water Company hired him as their chief engineer.

The closest usable source of water was more than 20 miles west of Virginia City, from spring- and snow-fed lakes in the Carson Range east of Lake Tahoe. The distance was not the biggest problem; the elevation change was. The Washoe Valley, between the source of the water and Virginia City, was at an elevation of 5,143 feet, and holding tanks that would have to be constructed above Virginia City would be at 6,525 feet. The water would somehow have to be raised almost 1,400 feet.

Schussler recognized the enormity of the task but had the knowledge and experience to tackle it. When completed, the water system would have over 15 miles of wooden flumes and seven miles of iron pipes. The pipes would form a U-shape and act as an inverted siphon. Water pressure in the pipe at the bottom of the Washoe Valley would be over 800 pounds per square inch (psi), which would be sufficient to push it up to Virginia City. But no water system in the world had ever been constructed with such massive pressure.

Drawing on his earlier experience at the Lucerne Vulcan Iron Works, Schussler developed a plan to bend wrought-iron plates into a cylindrical shape and rivet them together to form sturdy pipes. Each one-foot diameter, 26-foot-long section of pipe was custom-designed, with wall thicknesses tailored to the specific pressure load and topology of that location. Three-feet-by-ten-feet sheets of iron in ten different thicknesses were shipped from Scotland to San Francisco, where they were cut and rolled into cylinders at the Risdon Iron and Locomotive Works. Before shipping, each length of pipe was coated inside and out with a mixture of asphalt and coal tar to prevent rusting.

Pipe fabrication started in March 1873, and by August 2, 1873, water was flowing to Virginia City. The 21-mile system delivered 2.2 million gallons of water to thirsty Virginia City residents every 24 hours.

A *Mining and Scientific Press* article about Schussler's Nevada pipeline stated, "After three months of use, the pipe has proved wonderfully successful. It is worthy of remark, as showing the kind of pipe turned out by the San Francisco contractor Risdon Works, that there was absolutely no leakage in the pipe joints...."[3]

A Virginia City newspaper reported:

> The pouring into this city and Gold Hill of a large stream of water from the Eastern Summit of the Sierra Nevada Mountains at 6:45 last evening, marked an epoch in the history of the Comstock, and was the signal for a general jollification and rejoicing of 12 or 13 thousand people. Bonfires and rockets girdled old Mt. Davidson for hours and cannons continued to roar until a late hour in the night. A stream of about 1,717 gallons per minute poured through the flume at Bullion Ravine, between this city and Gold Hill.[4]

In June 1875, the Virginia City *Territorial Enterprise* noted:

> One of the boasts of the Comstock is that in this land of barrenness—of shifting sands and burning alkali, we have the purest and best mountain water and plenty of it. Nor is the boast lightly made. There is no place in the world where so many natural difficulties have been overcome and so many triumphs achieved as in bringing the pure, fresh and soft water of the Sierra to our communities.[5]

A second parallel system was built in 1875 to handle the needs of an increasing population, this one drawing water from Marlette Lake, whose level had been increased by raising the dam. The two systems together cost $3.5 million. A third pressure pipe was added in 1887, increasing the capacity of the system to 10 million gallons per day.[6] The system, started in 1871, continues to be the sole source of fresh water for the Comstock region.

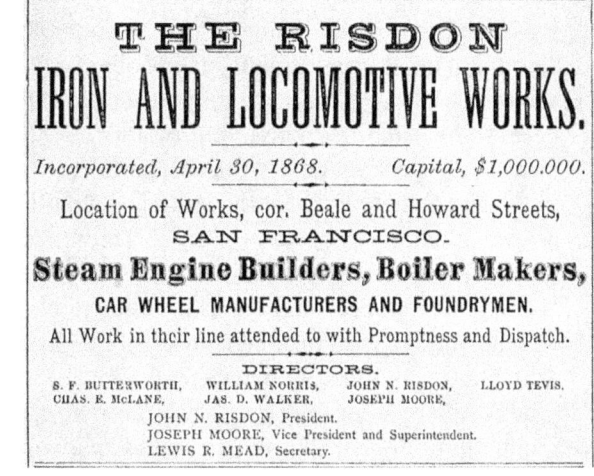

Risdon Iron and Locomotive Works advertisement.

Chapter 24

The King Is Dead; Long Live the Kings

Fortune does not change men, it unmasks them.
—Suzanne Curchod Necker

On July 4, 1864, William Ralston formed the Bank of California and immediately started investing in the mines and mills of the Comstock Lode. In November 1864, Ralston appointed William Sharon as manager of the Virginia City branch of the Bank of California. By practices (such as stock manipulation, insider trading, and restraint of trade) that today would be illegal, Ralston, Sharon, and their friends and investors gained almost total control of the Comstock, from mines to mills to transportation to lumbering to water. What their Bank Ring did not own outright, they controlled through friendships and proxies. This growing and ultimately almost total control of the Comstock enriched the Bank, Ralston, Sharon, and a handful of others. Understandably the Bank Ring was loath to surrender that control and money to any outsider, especially Adolph Sutro. But starting in early 1869, a group of outsiders challenged the control of the Bank Ring.

One of the most valuable Comstock properties that was not controlled by the Bank Ring was the Hale & Norcross Mine. George Low owned the H & N, which was actively producing ore. A producing mine not controlled by the Bank Ring was anathema to Sharon, so he resolved to gain control. He started buying shares so that he could achieve a majority and thus elect the mine trustees at the next annual meeting in March 1868. Because he often had inside information, other investors watched every transaction made by Sharon. So, despite his attempts at secrecy, Sharon's plan was discovered, and those who owned shares of the H & N held out for higher prices. Share prices rose from below $300 in early January to $2,925 a month later. With Low and Sharon both bidding for the few shares that would swing the election, the price rose to $4,100 on February 11 and $7,100 on February 15. As the annual meeting approached, bids reached $10,000 a share. Sharon, with the deep pockets of the Bank of California behind him, eventually won, but it was an expensive victory. The H & N "pinched out" and therefore stopped producing ore soon afterward, and the shares dropped to $41.50 in September. With production stopped, Sharon eliminated dividend payments and levied a series of assessments. Not wishing to pay the assessments himself, Sharon sold most of his shares at a great loss. He knew that he would receive advance notification from his handpicked trustees and mine superintendent if a new body of ore was discovered, and he could then repurchase the shares.

But in 1869, two new players entered the game. John Mackay was the largest owner of a small but profitable mine in Gold Hill, the Kentuck. James Graham Fair was superintendent of the Ophir Mine; he had recently been assistant superintendent of the Hale and Norcross and was quite familiar with the mine. Mackay and Fair thought that the prospects for the H & N were far better than the stock price indicated, and agreed to attempt to gain control of the mine from Sharon. To carry out their plan, Mackay and Fair realized they would need a presence on the floor of the San Francisco Mining Exchange.

Mackay and Fair had previously met and worked with two fellow Irishmen during the fight between Sharon and Low for control of the H & N. James G. Flood and William S. O'Brien owned the Auction Lunch Saloon at 509 Washington Street in San Francisco. Based on bar talk, they had achieved considerable success trading in Comstock stocks. In 1868, Flood and O'Brien sold the Auction Lunch and moved around the corner to upstairs offices on Montgomery Street to become Flood and O'Brien, Stockbrokers.

The four Irishmen met in San Francisco and agreed to buy enough H & N shares to give them control. Mackay would hold a three-eighths share; Flood and O'Brien together another three-eighths; and Fair the remaining two-eighths. Only Mackay had sufficient funds to finance his portion of the purchases. The other three had to borrow money, or, in Fair's case, sign promissory notes to his partners secured by future earnings.

Flood quietly began to purchase H & N shares, and the Hale & Norcross Mine was again in play. Despite being alert for signs of abnormal trading, the other San Francisco brokers remained unaware of any unusual activity in H & N shares.

Finally, on February 27, 1869, the *Gold Hill News* printed the following paragraph: "As J.G. Fair and J.W. Mackay, of Virginia City, own over four hundred shares of Hale & Norcross stock, they will be likely to control the election of officers in March."

Owners of all but 100 shares of the H & N had been identified. Those 100 shares would determine the outcome of the election, so both sides desperately sought to find the owner. On March 9, the night before the meeting, Sharon discovered the owner of the 100 shares was a San Francisco widow who was unaware of the importance and value of the shares. He immediately sent a coded telegram with the widow's address to Ralston and told him to get the stock at any cost. But the Virginia City telegraph operator was an ally of John Mackay, and he hated William Sharon. The operator had studied other coded dispatches sent by Sharon and had developed a way to decipher Sharon's code. He translated Sharon's message to Ralston and gave the result to Mackay. Thirty minutes after Sharon sent his coded message to Ralston, Mackay sent a similar message to Flood. Ralston did not appreciate the urgency of reaching the widow, and when he called on her in the morning, he was devastated to find that Flood had already paid her $8,000 a share for her holdings.[1]

It was the first major defeat that Sharon had experienced in his five years as King of the Comstock, and he and Ralston vowed to seek vengeance on the four rank amateurs who had outwitted them.

At the Hale & Norcross annual meeting, Flood was elected president of the H & N, succeeding Sharon; O'Brien and Mackay were elected trustees. The new board dismissed the former superintendent and replaced him with Fair. An $80,000 assessment that had been levied by Sharon was canceled and money already paid was returned. The next events were even more frustrating for Sharon and the Bank Ring. Almost immediately, promising new ore bodies were discovered and quickly put the mine on a paying basis. For the rest of 1869, the H & N paid dividends of almost $200,000. With the discovery of another rich vein, dividends rose to $500,000 in 1870. As the ore deposit was depleted, dividends dropped to $80,000 in 1872, and assessments resumed in 1873.[2]

The four Irishmen, soon dubbed the Bonanza Kings, had proven that the Bank Ring was not invincible. Now they struck at the cash cow of the Bank of California, the Union Mill and Mining Company. The Bonanza Kings were certainly not going to allow the Bank Ring to profit by processing their H & N ore. So, they started buying mills not controlled by the Bank Ring and processed their ore at those mills. Ralston and Sharon quickly recognized this new threat to their dominance.

What was the next move for the Bonanza Kings? They needed an encore to their Hale & Norcross triumph. The region between two profitable mines, the Ophir and the Gould & Curry, looked promising. Five different mining companies claimed the 1,310 feet between these mines, but despite intensive exploration, virtually no worthwhile ore had been discovered. Another ownership group had previously gained control of all but 100 feet of the region and merged the mines into a property called the Consolidated Virginia Mine. Again, exploration by the new group to the 500-foot level (dotted line 1 in the figure to the left) yielded no workable ore, and the experts concluded that the area was barren.

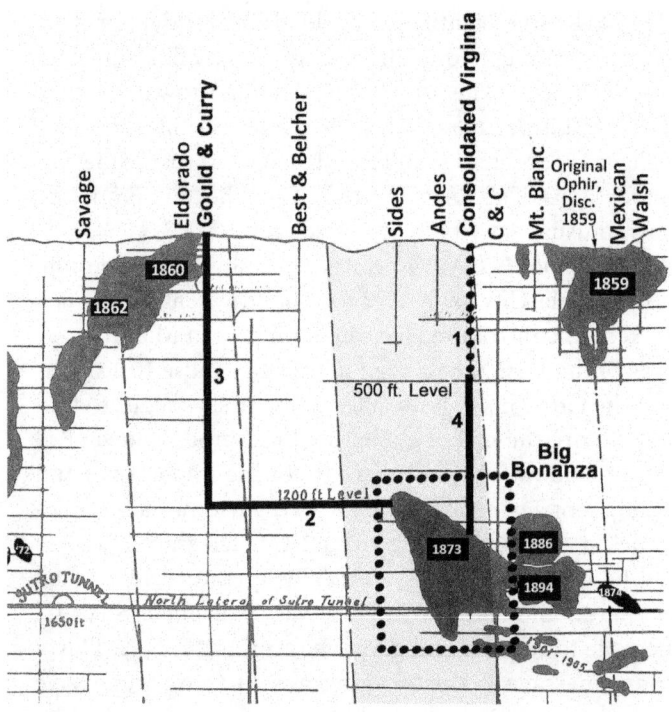

Comstock cross-section at consolidated Virginia mine, adapted from Lord, Comstock Mining and Miners; (1) initial consolidated Virginia shaft to 500 feet; (2) drift at 1,200 feet from Gould & Curry Shaft (3); (4) extension of consolidated shaft from 500 feet to Big Bonanza. Consolidated Virginia region in light gray.

If those experts had available to them a map such as the one to the left, they would have seen that the region was indeed barren to about 1,100 feet. But starting below that level was the greatest bonanza ever found on the Comstock.

Foresight is always infe-

The Bonanza Kings: John William Mackay (1831–1902); James Graham Fair (1831–1894); James Clair Flood (1826–1889); and William Shoney O'Brien (1825–1878).

rior to hindsight, so shares of Consolidated Virginia fell to one dollar in 1870. Mackay and Fair had either superior foresight or incredibly good luck. They decided to gain control of the Consolidated Virginia and adjacent California Mines. In February 1872, with an investment of $100,000, they achieved their goal.

Fair and Mackay then made a fateful and inspired decision. Rather than working down from the 500-foot level of the deserted Consolidated Virginia shaft (dotted vertical line 1 on the map), they decided to dig a drift (solid horizontal line 2) north from the bottom of the Gould & Curry shaft (solid vertical line 3), which then extended to 1,200 feet. Cutting a drift is generally easier than digging a shaft; because in a drift, waste rock can be accumulated and removed more effectively. Although Sharon controlled the Gould & Curry, he encouraged Fair and Mackay, thinking that they would be wasting their money exploring in a barren region.

It was not easy. After starting in May 1872, by September the drift was 1,000 feet long and within Consolidated Virginia territory. The solid rock they encountered gave no hint of silver-bearing ore, and had to be carried back to the mineshaft and then hoisted 1,200 feet to the top of the mine before being carried to the dump. With no direct access to the surface, the air was both foul and hot, and working shifts had to be cut to 15 minutes with 30-minute cooling-off breaks.

In mid–September, Fair spied a thin sliver of ore at the face of the drift. Three weeks later the sliver was seven feet wide, and in one more week 12 feet wide. The ore assayed at $60 per ton, 50 percent higher than the average for the Comstock and well into the profitable range. With a proven strike, the abandoned Consolidated Virginia shaft was reopened and extended down to the ore body (solid vertical line 4 on the map), thus negating the need to use the drift from the Gould & Curry shaft.

In late October, after the partners, including Flood and O'Brien, had accumulated more than three-fourths of the Consolidated Virginia shares at just $50 per share, they announced the discovery.

Reporters, starting with Dan DeQuille of the Virginia City *Territorial Enterprise*, visited the mine and wrote glowing reports of the riches found there. They competed for superlatives, and indeed this Big Bonanza, as it was called, was the richest strike in the 14-year history of the Comstock.[3] Eliot Lord, in his 1883 *Comstock Mining and Miners*, said,

The lid, so to speak, of that wonderful ore-casket, termed commonly the Big Bonanza, had been lifted off. Of its magnitude and richness all were then ignorant. No discovery which matches it has been made on this earth from the day when the first miner struck a ledge with his rude pick until the present. The plain facts are as marvelous as a Persian tale, for the young Aladdin did not see in the glittering case of the genii such fabulous riches as were lying in that dark womb of rock. The miner's pick and drill are more potent than the magician's wand. Under their resistless touch the bars of the treasure-house were broken through and its hoard revealed to the dazzled eyes of the invaders. The wonder grew as its depths were searched out foot by foot. The bonanza was cut at a point 1,167 feet below the surface, and as the shaft went down it was pierced again at the 1,200-foot level; still the same body of ore was found, but wider and longer than above. One hundred feet deeper, and the prying pick and drill told the same story; yet another hundred feet, and the mass appeared to be still swelling. When, finally, the 1,500-foot level was reached and ore richer than any before met with was disclosed, the fancy of the coolest brains ran wild. How far this great bonanza would extend none could predict, but its expansion seemed to keep pace with the most sanguine imaginings.[4]

The Big Bonanza was dreadful news to the Bank Ring. The largest ore strike on the Comstock and the processing of that rich ore would yield hundreds of millions of dollars to the Bonanza Kings, not to the Bank Ring.

Trouble at the Bank of California

In San Francisco, Ralston was worried. The financial status of the Bank of California was precarious. Capitalization of the Bank was supposed to be $5 million. But of that amount, $3.5 million had been loaned to George P. Kimball & Co. (carriage builders), the New Montgomery Street Real Estate Company, and the Pacific Woolen Mills Company. All three of these companies were owned by William Sharon & Co., which was in turn owned in equal shares by William Sharon and William Ralston. Now, after years of paying interest on their loans, money was tight, and the three companies had stopped paying interest. On February 19, 1873, Ralston laid out the facts to the Bank's Board of Trustees. They were not pleased and ultimately demanded that Ralston take personal responsibility for the loans. J.D. Fry, a bank trustee and Ralston's father-in-law, was one of the signers of an agreement to that effect that was ratified by the full Board.[5]

Now there were newspaper reports of the Big Bonanza at the Consolidated Virginia mine, controlled not by the Bank Ring but by four Irishmen! Reputable experts, including the director of the U.S. Mint and Philip Deidesheimer of square-set timbering fame, placed the value of the Big Bonanza at from $275 million to $1.5 billion. Ralston could not believe his eyes. All the while that Sharon had assured him that the Irishmen were squandering their money exploring barren ground, they had been finding the biggest ore body on the Comstock. Just when he needed support from the mines and mills to shore up the finances of the Bank, that support had slipped through his fingers.

Outwardly Ralston retained his legendary composure. He continued his daily early-morning visits to the site of his latest extravaganza, the Palace Hotel, which occupied the entire city block bounded by Market, New Montgomery, Jessie, and Annie Streets. The Palace, initially estimated at $1.75 million, would end up costing over $6 million. With 755 guest rooms, the Palace was the largest hotel in the western United States.[6] Andrew Carnegie said of the Palace,

> A palace truly! Where shall we find its equal? Windsor Hotel, good-bye! you must yield the palm to your great Western rival, as far as structure goes, though in all other respects you may keep the foremost place. There is no other hotel building in the world equal to this. The court of the Grand at Paris is poor compared to that of the Palace. Its general effect at night, when brilliantly lighted, is superb; its furniture, rooms and appointments are all fine, but then it tells you all over it was built to "whip all creation," and the millions of its lucky owner enabled him to triumph.[7]

The Palace survived the April 18, 1906, earthquake, but it was consumed by the fire that followed.[8]

After visiting his Palace Hotel, Ralston lunched at the Union Club. If he was not entertaining in the city or at his opulent Belmont Estate, he swam in the evenings off North Beach in San Francisco Bay. No one could see Ralston's inner turmoil caused by Bank of California problems.[9]

Still, Ralston looked to the Comstock for salvation. The mine just north of the Consolidated Virginia was the Ophir, site of the first silver strike on the Comstock in 1859. Ralston believed that the Big Bonanza was likely to extend to the Ophir, so he decided to gain control and harvest the reward. He started buying shares in December 1874 at a cash price between $75 and $80 per share. Later in the month, those same shares rose to about $175. In January 1875, Ophir peaked at $350 per share. Those who sold out at that price made fortunes. Ralston was not one of them. But he had succeeded in gaining control of the Ophir Mine. Unfortunately, the Big Bonanza did not extend into Ophir territory, and despite Ralston's attempts to support the stock price, it fell to $50 per share in February 1875. Ralston and his Bank had lost over $3 million on his gamble.[10]

Ralston had one last card to play, this one far from the Comstock. He sought to control the Spring Valley Water Company, which supplied water to San Francisco and the surrounding area. To obtain funds to buy Spring Valley stock, he started selling his own assets, including his 16,000-acre estate in Kern County, California. That property went for the bargain-basement price of $90,000. Ralston's interest in his beloved Palace Hotel went to Sharon. A friend, Michael Reese, loaned Ralston over $3 million at 6 percent interest. All of this money went to buy Spring Valley shares. Eventually, Ralston acquired 49,608 of the 80,000 shares of Spring Valley. He expected to sell the water company to the city for $15.5 million, but the sale depended on electing a city Board of Supervisors favorable to the purchase. That election would take place on September 1, 1875, and Ralston campaigned for candidates who supported his cause.

When the proposed selling price for the water company was announced, two San Francisco papers launched a campaign to discredit Ralston and prevent the sale. The *Call* and the *Bulletin* ran daily editorials accusing him of profiting at the city's expense. Typical was the following rant:

> Ralston's Ring is entrenched behind bank-counters and installed in comfortable chairs. His ring is powerful by reason of wealth. It is above the law. The influences which it yields are not of the barroom, ward-gathering or sailors' boarding-houses. Its methods resemble Washington rather than New York. Its head is depraved. It hatches the worst designs against its own body. Its dangers smack of the villa, bank and palace rather than the back-alley and slum. For all that, its bite is more vicious than that of New York's Tweed Ring.

The *Bulletin* claimed that the city could have purchased the Spring Valley Water Company for $6 million in 1874. Now that Ralston had gained control, the price was to be $15.5 million; a profit for Ralston and his ring of $9.5 million.[11]

But it was not to be. At 1 p.m. on August 26, 1875, after a morning of frantic trading on the San Francisco Stock Exchange had relentlessly driven down Comstock share prices, Ralston noticed the run. Depositors in successive waves approached the bank counter demanding withdrawals. Checks for $100,000 were common. By 2 p.m., Ralston, always unflappable, was worried. The lobby was packed, with no room for more customers. From his window, Ralston could see that California Street was full of waves of people, all trying to approach the bank steps. By 2:30, the run had intensified to a

The Bank of California suspends operation, August 26, 1875. From *Harper's Weekly*.

near-riot. Bank clerks were almost pouring gold coins through their teller windows. At 2:35, a white-faced clerk entered Ralston's office and confided that the vault held just $40,000. Normal closing time was 3 p.m., but money was almost gone. Ralston strode to paying-teller Nicholson's window and said, "Close the door," pointing to the open teller's window. Despite the crowd's protests, the bank closed.

After a brief meeting of the bank trustees, Ralston talked to reporters. One asked, "Shall you resume business tomorrow at the usual hour?" Ralston replied, "No, we shall not resume business." "How soon do you propose to resume?" Ralston concluded, "We do not expect to resume at all."[12]

The next morning, August 27, 1875, Ralston dressed with his usual care and met with the contractor at the nearly completed Palace Hotel to offer some suggestions. Then he rushed to the bank, where he was met with crowds as dense as the previous day. Inside the bank, Ralston resumed his duties, reassuring frightened employees and encouraging them to meet the crisis with equanimity. His first action was to surrender all of his remaining property to the benefit of his creditors by executing a deed of trust conveying everything to William Sharon. Sharon assured Ralston that he would stand by him until his last dollar was spent.

About noon, Ralston convened a meeting of the Board of Trustees and proposed that he be allowed to remain in charge of the bank until the crisis passed. The Board refused his request and asked him to leave the room while they deliberated.

As soon as Ralston departed, Sharon rose and made a motion that Ralston be requested to resign from the Bank of California. After a second, the motion passed unanimously. D.O. Mills, the first president of the bank, was tasked with telling Ralston. At about 2 p.m., Mills entered Ralston's office and told him the decision. Ralston's face turned red, and perspiration covered his forehead. He quickly wrote the following message:

San Francisco, Aug. 27, 1875.

To the Board of Trustees of the Bank of California:

You will please accept my resignation as president of the bank and also as a member of the board of trustees to take effect immediately.

Most respectfully yours,
W.C. Ralston

After recovering for several minutes, Ralston rose and strode toward the Sansome Street entrance and out onto the street. On this hot August day with the load of the bank off his shoulders, Ralston wanted nothing more than to swim in the familiar, cool waters of San Francisco Bay. He headed toward North Beach and arrived at the water about 3:30 p.m. At the Neptune Beach House, he rented two coarse towels and changed into his bathing suit. As was his normal practice, he swam through the waves and out into the bay. Suddenly he threw up one arm and then the other. Then his body lay motionless, facedown in the swirling water. At 49 years old, the King of the Bank of California was dead. It was never determined whether the primary cause of his death was a stroke or drowning.[13]

Chapter 25

A Hole in the Ground to Pour Money Into

It's hard to beat a person who never gives up.
—George Herman "Babe" Ruth, Jr.

The Comstock mines needed a tunnel. Sutro needed money to build it. Those basic facts had not changed in the eight years since the state of Nevada had granted Sutro a franchise to build a tunnel in early 1865. Even the challenge to the power of the Bank Ring by the Bonanza Kings changed little for Sutro. Both groups were opposed to paying $2 per ton of ore, and so the fight against his tunnel proceeded unabated.

By February 1873, the $700,000 provided by the Miners' Unions and Robert McCalmont was running out. Expenses for salaries and wages totaled over $1,000 per day, and Sutro had invested in expensive equipment such as pumps and mechanical drills. Sutro also purchased two steam locomotives designed for 36-inch track and costing a total of $10,400.

If they were to be used in the tunnel, these locomotives had two insurmountable problems: the use of steam engines in a long tunnel was dangerous to life, and the track in the tunnel was 21 inches wide. The locomotives were never used. Work on the tunnel would cease in May if more money was not forthcoming.

Sutro ordered severe cutbacks. He curtailed orders for new pumps and boilers. He closed the Virginia City office of the Tunnel Company. He stopped work on air shaft number one even though it was just four feet from reaching the tunnel level. He stopped work on shaft numbers two and four.

The vertical shafts were crucial to the construction of the tunnel, both for ventilation and to allow workers to dig the tunnel in both directions from the point where the shaft reached the level of the tunnel. With the four planned shafts, it would be possible to have nine crews working simultaneously. But "the best-laid plans of mice and men oft go awry."[1] Only two of the shafts were completed.

In Washington, the Crédit Mobilier scandal interrupted all other business, and Sutro began to despair about ever obtaining a U.S. government loan. Europe was the only hope. The London bankers, Robert and Hugh McCalmont, disagreed on the prospects for the Sutro Tunnel, so their McCalmont Bank would not buy more tunnel

25. A Hole in the Ground to Pour Money Into

Hoist House at top of shaft #1 (courtesy the Historical Society of Dayton Valley.

company stock. But Robert McCalmont, his faith in Sutro unimpeded, invested significant personal funds to support work on the tunnel.

In late 1873, Sutro and the McCalmont Brothers Bank, along with the London banking house run by Isaac Seligman, developed a rather complicated new approach. The tunnel company would offer first mortgage bonds to the public at a discount below face value. The bonds went on sale on January 6, 1874, and subscriptions on the first day totaled $750,000. But the banking houses squabbled over terms of the offering, and it was withdrawn. The failed offering was yet another setback for Sutro.[2]

Fortunately, Robert McCalmont's personal investment was sufficient to keep the tunnel moving forward. But ominous news came in the form of a letter from Nevada Congressman C.W. Kendall, for whom Sutro had campaigned in the 1872 election. Kendall said that there was as yet no movement to check the rights of the tunnel company, but told Sutro, who was still in London, "You ought to be here (in Washington), however, as soon as possible."[3]

On January 12, 1874, the Board of Trustees of the Ophir Gold and Silver Mining

Miners' boardinghouse at top of shaft #2 (courtesy the Historical Society of Dayton Valley.

Company met and approved a plan to assess the various mining and milling companies on the Comstock. The purpose of the assessment was to finance "such legal proceedings as may be necessary to secure a final judgment denying the validity" of the claim of the Sutro Tunnel Company to a royalty of two dollars a ton on ore raised from the mines. Joseph Aron, Sutro's friend and benefactor, was a stockholder in the Ophir Mine and discovered the plan to support legislation to eliminate the ore royalty. Aron sent a copy of the plan to Washington, and someone (probably Congressman Kendall) forwarded it to Sutro in London.[4] Sutro takes up the story in his own words:

> On the 1st day of February, 1874, I addressed letters to all Senators and members of Congress,[5] informing them of the fact of the existence of this corruption fund, and asked them to be on the lookout for underhanded legislation which I expected would be attempted at that session of Congress. I considered afterward that it would be safer for me to be there myself, and accordingly appeared in Washington on the 22nd of February. I examined all the bills which had been introduced, and found one which had been introduced by my old enemy, Sargent,[6] who had been elected to the United States Senate. This bill was called Senate Bill 16, and was evidently intended to allow those mining companies on the Comstock Lode that had not taken out their patents, as yet, to escape doing so, by making all proceedings for patents had by them null and void. By the Sutro Tunnel Act of 1866, each mining company on the Comstock lode was compelled to take its patent, subject to the provisions of that Act, which had to be distinctly set forth in each patent.[7]

Requiring each mine to take out a patent was crucial to the Sutro Tunnel Company because the terms of the patent bound the patentee to observe the provisions of the Sutro Tunnel Act, including the $2 per ton of ore royalty. Sutro had his friends in Congress introduce amendments to gut Senate Bill 16:

> An amendment was offered thereto by the Hon. William Holman, of Indiana, to the effect that nothing in the bill should affect our rights.
>
> The Hon. James S. Negley, of Pennsylvania, offered another amendment requiring parties on the Comstock lode who had not yet taken out their patents to do so within six months, in default of which they would forfeit their rights.
>
> Senate Bill No. 16, with both the amendments of Holman and Negley, went over to the Senate, where it was referred to the Committee on Mines and Mining.
>
> (The Bank Ring) "managed, by some means unexplained, to get Senator Chandler, of Michigan, to resign (from the Committee on Mines and Mining), while Senator Jones, of Nevada, a large owner in the Crown Point mine, was placed in his stead on that committee. When the day was set for the argument of the case, I went before it, together with the Hon. Jeremiah Black, of Pennsylvania, who had been retained as our counsel, and I asked permission to put a few questions to some of the members of that committee. My request having been granted, I showed clearly that Senator Jones owned large interests antagonistical to us, and that he was the bitter enemy of the Sutro Tunnel. Turning next to Senator Sargent, I asked him whether he was opposed to our work. He said that he considered our undertaking a great iniquity."[8]

Having established a conflict of interest by Senator Jones and clear bias by Senator Sargent, Sutro requested that Senate Bill 16 be referred to another committee, whose members were not predisposed to a decision. His request was granted, and Senate Bill 16 died in the Senate Judiciary Committee. Sutro's active presence in Washington saved the Sutro Tunnel Company from another attack by the Bank Ring.

Tunnel Digging Continues

While the power shift from the Bank Ring to the Bonanza Kings had little impact on the tunnel, the discovery of the Big Bonanza in 1872–73 was transformative. First, it became imperative for Sutro to complete his tunnel quickly so that he could collect the $2 per ton of ore royalty on the ore from the Big Bonanza. Second, the riches flowing from the Big Bonanza encouraged investment in all parts of the Comstock, including Sutro's tunnel.

In 1873, using hand-powered drills, the tunnel advanced almost 2,000 feet. Based on this rate of progress and accounting for all factors, the tunnel would not be completed before 1885. Something had to change.

Burleigh drills, powered by compressed air, were tried in the Hoosac Tunnel in Massachusetts, but they broke down every five days.

Burleigh drill in the Best & Belcher Tunnel (photo by author).

But it was essential to improve the rate of rock removal, so the first Burleigh drill entered service in the Sutro Tunnel on April 25, 1874. By mid–August, four such machines were in constant use. In September 1874, the tunnel advanced 310 feet, well over twice the distance cut in March 1874 (130 feet), the last month when only hand drills were used.[9]

Robert McCalmont and the Seligman Bank were providing loans of $25,000 per month to cover expenses for the tunneling operation, but that commitment would drop to $15,000 on December 1, 1874.

Early on December 30, 1874, disaster struck. Two tunnel workers, John Delaney, the shift foreman, and Samuel Richards, chief blaster on the shift, were killed in an explosion. Four others were injured. Some loose dynamite powder had collected near the blasting battery, and when the intended blast at the tunnel face was triggered, the powder near the battery also exploded.

Compared to similar projects, the death rate on the Sutro Tunnel was quite low. In all, 12 people died while working on the tunnel. On the five-mile Hoosac railway tunnel in Massachusetts, 185 workers died. But any loss of life was devastating, and Sutro, who was again in London seeking funds, wondered if the benefits of his unwanted tunnel justified the horrible working conditions and loss of life.[10]

Not surprisingly, workers digging the tunnel encountered many of the same problems as the Comstock miners. Sutro described those problems in an 1879 article published in *The Engineering and Mining Journal*.[11]

Inside the Sutro Tunnel during excavation. The pilot tunnel on the right was cut quickly, leaving enlargement and support timbers for a follow-up crew (courtesy the Historical Society of Dayton Valley).

OBSTACLES TO PROGRESS

In carrying on a work of this kind, we meet all sorts of difficulties. Now and then, we would get indications of water. The men would put in a blast, and the water would pour out in a perfect torrent, and the men would have, at times, to quit temporarily to escape it, and wait until the water had subsided sufficiently, so that they could go to drilling again. Every now and then, we would come to a clay, that would swell and cave, so as to reduce our progress of 150 feet (and afterward with improved machinery of 300 feet) per month to less than fifty feet per month. Sometimes we could not keep the roof up. As soon as we would get started a little way in our work of excavation, the rock would yield, and hundreds of feet would come pressing down on the timbers with such force that it was almost impossible to resist it. The worst ground that we came to was the swelling ground. This is sometimes clay, and some times it is rock. The moment you dig into it, it swells out; and no matter what size of timbers you use, it will snap them off as if they were but matches. Nothing will resist it. You must let it swell.

Mule pulling workers in a mine car (courtesy Special Collections Department, University of Nevada–Reno).

In one place, the swelling was so great that the track swelled up a foot or two seven different times, and each time we had to cut it down. The timbers used are a post and a cap. The pressure on this cap would be so great that the post would be pressed through the cap in twenty-four hours—just as though the cap were a piece of cheese.

The greatest obstacle encountered by us was the heat and the poor air. Our last opening to the surface was at shaft No. 2, about 9000 feet from the tunnel entrance. From there, we had to go to the Comstock lode, a distance of 11,000 feet, without any natural air connection. After we got in to a distance of 17,000 feet from the mouth of the tunnel, the heat became so intense and the air so bad that it was almost impossible to keep the air sufficiently cool and pure to sustain life. There was not oxygen enough in the air to make our candles burn. Although we blew in air by means of blowers and air-compressors, still at times there was not sufficient air to enable the men to work.

In addition to describing the problems encountered in digging the tunnel, Sutro added interesting comments about the animals used to haul supplies to the workers and debris from the tunnel.

A CHAPTER ON MULES

We have been using mules for years, and have found out that they are tolerably good animals; but there is a prejudice against mules, though they are very intelligent. I think that I could write a chapter on their traits, as I have had a very extensive experience with them. It has been said that they have a strong propensity for kicking, but I have never seen them kick when in the tunnel. They become very tame under ground; in fact, they become the miners' pets. The men become quite attached to them; and as the shift-mules pass along by the men at lunch, they will often receive from one a piece of pie and from another a cup of coffee, etc. When a signal is given to fire a blast, the mules understand the signal, and will try to get out of the way of it just as the men do.

Of course, under ground it is very dark, and the mules become so accustomed to the darkness that even when they go out into the sunlight they can not see very well, and when they go back from the sunlight into the mine, they can not see at all. So we are in the habit of covering one eye with a piece of cloth whenever they go out, and keep the covering over the eye until they go into the tunnel again; we then remove the cloth, so they have one good eye to see with. We had to adopt this plan for preserving their sight, because the mule is so stubborn that he will not pull unless he can see his way ahead. We have found out another thing about mules. We tried horses at first, but we found that whenever any thing touched the ears of a horse, he would throw up his head and break his skull against the overhanging rock; but if you touch a mule's ears, he drops his head. For that reason, we could not use horses; we employed mules, and they have answered very well.

Trouble in Virginia City

William Ralston had died in San Francisco on August 27, 1875. Two months later, on October 26, 1875, Virginia City, the town that had been the source of his wealth, burned to the ground. An overturned oil lamp in one of the many boardinghouses ignited the wooden building, and the flames, driven by the ever-present wind, spread to adjacent buildings. With no rain for several weeks, the wooden buildings that comprised most of the town needed only a spark to set them ablaze. Even the few brick buildings could not withstand the heat and wind and collapsed in piles of rubble. Despite the valiant efforts of firemen and citizens, the main business district was a total loss. Miners attempted to create a firebreak by dynamiting dwellings and other buildings near the mines, but the flames leaped over the break. The great hoisting houses at the mouth of the mines burned, exposing massive piles of cordwood meant to fuel steam boilers, along with timbers for supporting underground drifts. All this wood caught fire, sending flames, smoke, and sparks upward. At the Consolidated Virginia, more than 1,000,000 feet of lumber burned to ashes. At the Ophir Mine, 1,000 cords of wood and 400,000 feet of timber burned. The last great treasure, the mineshafts themselves, were in danger. Only a concerted effort by miners and firemen and a continuous stream of water down the shaft for 36 hours stopped the flames at 400 feet below the surface of the Ophir Mine. Two thousand buildings were destroyed; property damage totaled $10 million; and hundreds of people were made homeless and destitute.[12]

Rebuilding started the next day and continued the next and far into the night. A tornado blew down much of the newly created buildings during the week after the fire, but the wrecks were cleared as soon as the storm passed and building resumed. Sixty days after the fire, the principal streets of the business district were lined with new buildings.

Recovery at the mines, mainly the Ophir and the Consolidated Virginia, was equally impressive. At the Ophir, timber and machinery were ordered, new engine foundations built, and the burnt shaft restored. By December 15, 1875, the Ophir was back in business. Workers at the Consolidated Virginia rebuilt the hoisting works and ore house and were raising 600 tons of ore daily by the same date.[13]

Tunnel Excavation Continues

The massive fire had little impact on tunnel construction 1,800 feet below the streets of Virginia City. In reality, the fire was a plus for the tunnel, because no ore, at $2 per ton royalty, was hoisted during the break in mine production.

During 1875 and 1876, through extensive use of the Burleigh drills, the tunnel advanced 7,398 feet.[14] In late 1876, the McCalmonts agreed to a $1 million loan using the tunnel as collateral. This loan was provided to the Sutro Tunnel Company at the rate of $24,000 per month.[15] But again, an explosion seriously injured one of the most optimistic of the tunnel employees. Henry L. Foreman, an engineer in his late twenties, wrote Sutro daily reports on the status of the tunnel. Those reports stopped on December 3, because dynamite blasting fuses, called exploders, that Foreman was storing exploded. Foreman was blinded and paralyzed. After a month of treatment in a San Francisco hospital, doctors were hopeful that he would have sight in his right eye and some use of one arm. Sutro was a paternalistic employer and continued to pay an allowance to Foreman through good years and bad.[16]

Sutro was greatly disturbed by the unintended explosions of exploders, so he undertook some experiments to determine the cause. He placed several exploders in a strong wooden box, enclosed that box in another, and connected long wires through the boxes to the exploders. Sutro then shuffled his slippered feet through a thick carpet to generate static electricity.[17] When he extended his finger toward the wires, the exploders exploded. Sutro repeated the experiment with various brands of exploders. Some brands were more susceptible to exploding from the static electricity; some less so.[18] To eliminate the problem, Sutro ordered that steel plates be fabricated and installed on the floors of all areas where exploders and dynamite were processed and stored. The plates were connected by wires to the streams of water flowing from the tunnel, effectively grounding them and preventing the buildup of static charge. Once the steel plates were installed, there were no more exploder accidents at the Sutro Tunnel.[19]

Because injuries were inevitable, Sutro established a hospital in the town of Sutro. To support it, he docked each worker's pay three dollars a month. But the miners' union complained that his workers were no longer receiving the required wage of four dollars a day, so Sutro was forced to pay for the hospital himself.

When Sutro was in town, he often took his turn at the face of the tunnel. In air so hot and foul-smelling that workers had to stop for relief after just 20 minutes, Sutro suffered beside his men, demonstrating endurance that they could emulate.[20]

Eliot Lord's overwrought description from his 1883 book captures the scene at the tunnel:

> Sutro's untiring zeal kindled a like spirit in his co-workers. Changing shifts urged the drills onward without ceasing; skilled timberers followed up the attack on the breast and covered the heads of the assailants like shield-bearers. The hot rocks blown from the face of the heading hardly ceased rattling on the floor of the tunnel before they were thrown and shoveled into iron tram-cars and borne away by mule-trains. Lanterns bound to the shoulders of the mules threw straggling rays of light on the dark pathway; the dripping walls and roof reflected the beams through a myriad of water-prisms, and streaks of mottled gray, green, and black rocks shone out at intervals with vivid distinctness, as if illuminated by lightning flashes. A foreground and background of utter blackness inclosed the moving cylinder of changing lights and shadows, a fitting frame-work to the weird picture.
>
> The dump at the mouth of the tunnel grew rapidly to the proportions of an artificial plateau raised above the surrounding valley slope; yet the speed of the electric currents which exploded the blasts scarcely kept pace with the impatient anxiety of the tunnel-owners to reach the lode when the extent of the great Consolidated Virginia bonanza was reported; for every ton raised from the lode before the tunnel cut it was a loss to them of $2, as they thought. Urged on by zeal, pride, and natural covetousness, the miners cut their way indomitably toward their goal, though at every step gained the work grew more painful and dangerous.

From the 1st day of May, 1878, it was necessary to change the working force four times a day instead of three, as previously, and the men could only work during a small portion of the nominal hours of labor. Even the tough, wiry mules of the car-train could hardly be driven up to the end of the tunnel, and sought for fresh air not less ardently than the men. Curses, blows, and kicks could scarcely force them away from the blower-tube openings, and more than once a rationally-obstinate mule thrust his head into the end of the canvas air-pipe.[21]

By July 1, 1878, the men in the Savage mine could hear the explosions in the tunnel below. On July 8, just a few feet of rock separated the Savage Mine from the Sutro Tunnel. Sutro sent a telegram to Superintendent Gillette of the Savage Mine:

To M.G. Gillette: Should your men succeed in knocking a drill hole through, let them stop and not enlarge it until I am fully notified. There should be ample time for your men and ours to retire, for I am afraid a column, several thousand feet in length, of hot, foul air, suddenly set in motion, might prove fatal to the men.

Adolph Sutro[22]

A few hours later, Sutro telegraphed again:

The men report a drill hole knocked through near the north side. Put in your blast, and let your men retire to the incline. Will be at the header at 11 o'clock.

Adolph Sutro[23]

Rosa, Kate, Charles, and Edgar Sutro with their father at Sutro Tunnel-Savage Drift Junction, July 8, 1878. The other people at the sides and kneeling in front are unidentified, but Savage Mine Superintendent Milton Gillette is probably on the left (courtesy Historical Society of Dayton Valley).

The Savage miners inserted eight powder cartridges into as many holes, and all retreated to safety. A blast joined the Savage drift to the horizontal tunnel; Sutro's dream and the Bank Ring's nightmare were simultaneously fulfilled. Dust, smoke, and fetid air rushed upward, blinding and suffocating the Savage crew and extinguishing all the lanterns. At that time, Sutro turned around and was amazed to see four of his children, Rosa, Kate, Charles, and Edgar, standing behind him. They had come to help their father celebrate his victory.[24]

Savage Mine Superintendent M.G. Gillette ordered a ladder lowered to the floor of the tunnel, and a jubilant, dust-covered, and half-naked Adolph Sutro climbed up. A sudden gust of wind pushed him through the opening and dropped him against the opposite wall. Bruised, bleeding, and overcome with excitement, Sutro shook every hand within reach, then hurried to

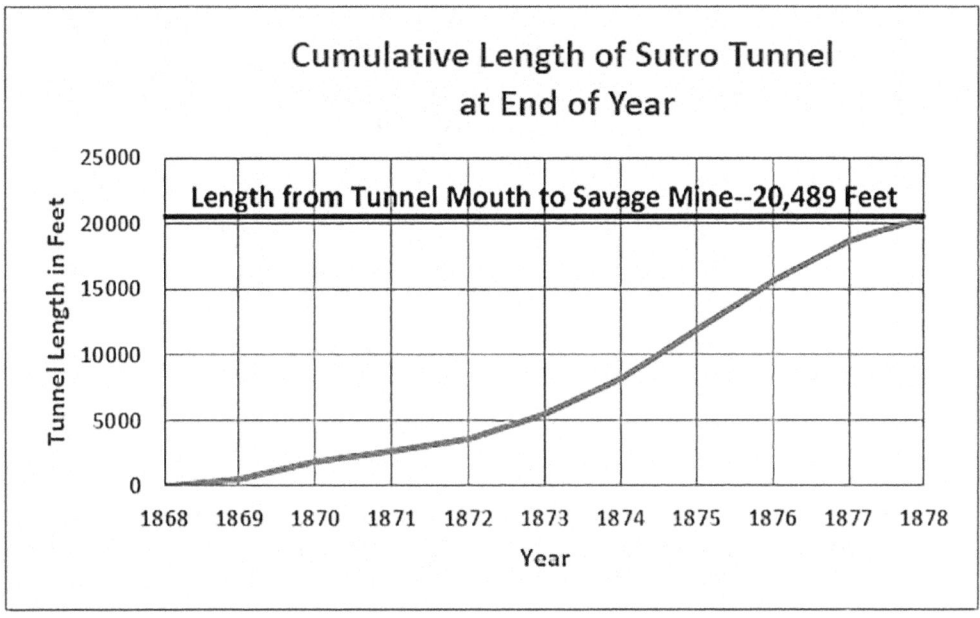

Cumulative length of the Sutro Tunnel by year.

the Savage rest station for some well-earned cool water and air. Then Adolph and his children returned by way of the tunnel to the town of Sutro, where speeches and toasts celebrated the great event.[25]

Overview of Tunnel Progress

The graph above shows the cumulative length of the Sutro Tunnel by year from the first shovel of earth on October 19, 1869, until connecting the main tunnel to the Savage Mine on July 8, 1878, eight years, eight months, and 19 days later.[26]

CHAPTER 26

The Devil Is in the Details

Beware the person who won't be bothered with details.
—William Feather

The tunnel had reached the mines, but would the mining companies honor their commitments? The April 1866 agreement required the mining companies to pay Sutro $2 per ton of ore extracted once the tunnel reached their respective regions. The Sutro Tunnel Act passed by the U.S. Congress three months later confirmed that agreement. But now the abstract clause was becoming real money.

As gravity acts without prejudice, any mining company connected to the tunnel could have dumped their water into the tunnel and worried about payment later. But Sutro had anticipated such an action and had included a watertight bulkhead in the tunnel to block any unauthorized drainage. In May 1878, Sutro's workers were completing the bulkhead comprised of a masonry frame 52 inches thick and sugar-pine doors 30 inches thick and capable of withstanding a column of water 5,000 feet high.[1] Isaac Requa, the superintendent of the Chollar-Potosi Mine who had testified against the tunnel in the 1872 Washington, D.C., hearing before the Committee on Mines and Mining, visited the tunnel and observed the bulkhead. He "was rather astonished" at how substantial it was. Sutro commented, "As to closing it, that is a question to be left open, and I do not propose to vitiate any of our legal rights until I am driven to it."[2]

For once, God seemed to be on Sutro's side. In February 1879, a pump-rod broke at the Hale & Norcross Mine, causing the water to rise and overflow into the combination shaft of the Hale & Norcross, Savage and Chollar-Potosi Mines. To protect the underground workings, mine superintendents pumped the excess water, at 130 degrees, into the Sutro Tunnel without notifying workers there. The tunnel workers and mules had to flee for their lives in the face of the oncoming flood of hot water. Then the Julia Mine struck an underground reservoir and flooded. The Belcher Mine also flooded. Even the Bonanza Kings with their Consolidated Virginia and California Mines sought relief from rising water.[3] It was time to reach a compromise.

Sutro told of the negotiations and resulting agreement in an 1879 talk:

> We commenced, last spring, to negotiate the terms of a new agreement. They were pretty stiff-necked about it, and so were we. We thought, as they had held back so long, and as they had to have the aid of our tunnel finally, that we were entitled to make fair and equitable terms. And thus it took

about three months to negotiate an arrangement. At last we came to an understanding, which is looked upon as being a fair arrangement for all parties concerned.

Under the original agreement, we had contracted not only to run a tunnel to the Comstock lode, a distance of four miles, but we were also to construct a (lateral) tunnel along the Comstock lode for three or four miles more. A part of the settlement is, that we agreed to reduce our royalty, on all ores yielding under forty dollars per ton, from two dollars to one dollar per ton, while all ores yielding above forty dollars still pay two dollars. They, on their part, agree to pay for these lateral tunnels in the form of a loan; but it is really no loan at all, for we pay no interest upon it, and it is not repayable except by deducting half the royalties that we earn.

We are now engaged in constructing these lateral branches, and the mining companies pay us from $20,000 to $40,000 on the fifth day of every month, which fully pays for the work. We have, also, already commenced earning some royalty, though not a great deal, as yet. We probably receive from $7000 to $8000 per month from that source; and as soon as the lateral tunnels are extended past each mine, it commences to pay, and our royalty, therefore, will increase gradually.[4]

Under the revised agreement, the mining companies who had so bitterly opposed the Sutro Tunnel were now providing money for extending it to their mines. Adolph Sutro must have felt justified and victorious.

Over 1,300 workers began modifications to the main tunnel and cutting of the lateral tunnels. In the main tunnel, they cut and boxed with three-inch-thick Sierra Nevada pine a drainage channel five feet wide and three and a half feet deep to handle the water. At 6:00 a.m. on June 30, 1879, several mines, including the Savage and Hale & Norcross, began to drain water into the drainage channel. Eighty minutes later, the water, at a temperature of 101 degrees, arrived at the mouth of the tunnel. As intended, the wooden drainage boxes were water- and steam-tight. The water level in one of the flooded mines dropped by 100 feet in just eight hours. "As an engineering work the success surpasses all expectations."[5] In 1880, 3.5 million gallons of water per month drained from the mines through the tunnel; a total of 1.3 billion gallons of water drained in that year.[6]

Work on the lateral tunnels progressed quickly because of the use of Burleigh drills driven by compressed air. The total length of the North Lateral was 4,403 feet, and it was completed in just over one year. The longer South Lateral, at 8,424 feet, took just over two years.

With the main and lateral tunnels completed, it was clear that the mining experts, including Baron Ferdinand Richthofen, were wrong about the Comstock Lode. Although many shafts, laterals, and drifts were cut below the level of the Sutro Tunnel, very little ore was found there. The ore bodies, rather than extending downward to a large but indefinite depth, were virtually all located above the level of the tunnel.

All the workers added to dig the drainage channel and laterals made 1879 a boom time for the town of Sutro. Building lots sold, stores and rooming houses opened, and five saloons did a brisk business. Two thousand Lombardy Poplars were planted in the North Square, and cottonwoods adorned the South Square.

On April 27, 1879, two of the Bonanza Kings, John Mackey and James Fair, who were formerly Sutro's antagonists, visited the town of Sutro. The newspaper article describing their visit commented,

> The town of Sutro is building up, and presents a scene of much activity. The place is thronged with people, town lots are in demand, and buildings are going up in every direction. It is generally believed that several mills will be in operation at this point on the low grade ores of the Comstock by next fall, and that eventually this will be the largest town in the state.

Mackey and Fair returned to Virginia City by way of the Sutro Tunnel and the Savage mineshaft.[7]

But with the completion first of the drainage channel and later the laterals, work became scarce, and the town of Sutro started to decline. Although Adolph Sutro estimated that monthly royalties from the mining companies to the Sutro Tunnel Company would reach $100,000,[8] he realized that the heady days of Comstock mining were over and that his tunnel had arrived too late.

Sutro Tunnel Entrance, circa 1890.

Sutro began selling his shares of Sutro Tunnel Company stock. Some of the sales were handled by Adolph's youngest sibling, Theodore Sutro, who was a former president of the Sutro Tunnel Company. Theodore sold 900 shares at $4.375, less a commission of $0.125.[9]

Edward Adams, a partner in the New York banking firm of Winslow, Lanier and Company, handled the bulk of the stock sales with great discretion. Adams sold 50,000 shares in January 1880 at an average price of $3.69 a share. By March 27, a total of 200,000 shares had been sold at an average price of $3.19. In all, Sutro cleared between $709,000 and $769,000 from his Sutro Tunnel Company stock.[10] Adolph Sutro resigned as superintendent of the Sutro Tunnel Company effective March 1, 1880.[11]

The Sutro Tunnel remained in use for drainage for over 50 years, but it was never a financial success. The stock that had been purchased by the McCalmont Brothers Bank and many smaller investors soon became worthless.

The Sutro Tunnel Company went into bankruptcy in 1887, but some of the former stockholders reorganized it under the leadership of Theodore Sutro, who was a Harvard- and Columbia-educated New York attorney. Theodore had faith in the tunnel and urged the stockholders to voluntarily contribute 50¢ per share to buy out the McCalmont Brothers Bank. The McCalmonts, realizing that they could do no better, accepted $800,000 for notes and interest totaling almost $1.6 million.[12] Theodore awarded himself a controversial fee of $100,000 and became president of the new Comstock Tunnel Company.

In his 1887 report to stockholders, Theodore provided estimates of the total cost of the tunnel. He wrote that the direct cost of the tunnel without laterals was $3.5 million. The laterals added another $1.5 million, for a total of $5 million. These amounts are without interest. When interest is added, the total cost comes to about $10 million.[13] Based on 1875 dollars, $10 million then would correspond to about $229 million in 2018 dollars.

But financial concerns no longer bothered Adolph Sutro. At the age of fifty, he would again follow the advice attributed to Horace Greeley, and "go west."

Chapter 27

A Family Man?

A man who doesn't spend time with his family can never be a real man.
—Vito Corleone in *The Godfather*

No one would ever call Adolph Sutro "a family man." He was married more to his Sutro Tunnel than he was to his wife, Leah. Adolph Sutro and Leah Harris wed in 1855, but even the exact date of that important detail of his family life is unclear. Leah was of English ancestry, and a far more conservative Jew than Adolph. She had simple tastes focused on home, husband, children, and synagogue, and was certainly not adventuresome.[1]

The couple had their first child, Emma Laura, on December 15, 1855.[2] Emma would always be Adolph's favorite.

Their next child, Rosa Victoria, was born July 1, 1858; but Adolph was away in Victoria, British Columbia, attempting to establish a store there to serve prospectors at the Fraser River gold strike. When Adolph returned from Canada, poorer but wiser, the Sutros rented two houses, and Leah operated them as lodging houses to earn enough money to sustain the family.[3]

The couple's first son, Gussie Emanuel Sutro, was born in 1859 but survived only until December 25, 1864. Although they were Jewish and so did not celebrate Christmas, the joy of the Christmas season around them would have been a stark contrast to their grief over the loss of their son.

A third daughter, Kate Sutro, was born in 1862; and a second son, Charles Walter Sutro, on June 24, 1864. The Sutros celebrated two more births, Edgar Ernest Sutro on March 4, 1866, and Clara Angela Sutro in October 1867. Adolph Sutro II was stillborn in 1870.

From his first trip to Virginia City and the Washoe area in early 1860, Adolph Sutro was away far more often than he was home with his family in San Francisco. He constantly traveled to Virginia City, Washington, New York, and Europe. Leah was on her own to raise the children, and only Emma remained close to her father.

In late 1872, the Sutro Mansion in Sutro, Nevada, was ready to welcome Adolph, Leah, and two youngest children, Clara, age five, and Edgar, age six. The other children were away at school: Emma, age 16, in New York, possibly at Vassar; Rosa, age 14, in

159

Children of Adolph and Leah (Harris) Sutro			
Name	Birth Date and Location	Marriage Date, Location, and Spouse	Death Date and Location
Emma Laura[4]	December 15, 1855; San Francisco	March 27, 1883; London, England; George W. Merritt	October 17, 1938; San Francisco
Rosa Victoria[5]	July 1, 1858; San Francisco	Pio Alberto Morbio	October 5, 1942; San Francisco
Gustavus Emanuel[6]	August 1859; San Francisco		December 25, 1864; Dayton, Nevada
Kate[7]	January 19, 1862; San Francisco	Moritz Nussbaum	January 10, 1913; Bonn, Germany
Charles Walter[8]	June 24, 1864; San Francisco	Lillian Edith Eckhoff	April 26, 1936; San Francisco
Edgar Ernest[9]	March 4, 1866; San Francisco	Marion McLarty	March 13, 1922; San Francisco
Clara Angela[10]	October 1867; San Francisco	December 25, 1898; Chicago; William J. English	January 24, 1924; France
Adolph II[11]	1870; San Francisco		1870; San Francisco

Baltimore; Kate, age 10, in Oakland, California; and Charles, age eight, in San Francisco. Adolph stayed at the Mansion for under two months, then left for Washington in December. Leah and her young children remained behind to entertain any celebrities who came to examine the tunnel.

Sutro hired Frank Mercer to publish a newspaper in the town of Sutro starting in 1876. In 1918, Mercer recalled the happy times at the Mansion with Sutro.

> Home life was much to Mr. Sutro. He certainly dearly loved his children, and without an exception that I can recall, they loved him. Frequently he would invite a town friend or one or two of the young men about the works to spend an evening at his home. That usually meant a full attendance of his family. He was an excellent entertainer. There was seldom a lack of sociability, conversation and pleasure. On one occasion, I recall, he requested during the evening that each one present read a selection, recite a piece, sing a song, or tell a story. When it came to my turn I was somewhat embarrassed, but read a selection from Shakespeare's "Julius Caesar." Each did his or her part.[12]

In the spring and summer of 1877, Adolph and Leah returned to San Francisco together and stayed at the luxurious Baldwin Hotel for 10 days. Emma was immersed in her medical education,[13] but the other five children stayed with their parents for between four and eight days.[14] This time together was probably the longest that the Sutros had ever enjoyed.

In mid–1879, with mine water flowing through the Sutro Tunnel, the hard work of raising money and digging the tunnel was mostly behind Adolph Sutro. He was able to relax, as much as he would allow himself, with his family in the Sutro Mansion in the town of Sutro. As their school vacations permitted, the children came to visit, and

27. A Family Man?

General U.S. Grant (fifth from left) and company at the Bonanza Mine in Nevada, October 28, 1879. From *Harper's Weekly*.

what others would see as normal family life prevailed. But two events would disrupt that peaceful time.

We will discuss the second event first because it is less controversial. Former President Ulysses S. Grant was completing a two-year world tour and wanted to visit the Comstock Lode. Grant and his group started with a tour of the Consolidated Virginia mine on Tuesday, October 28, 1879. The engraving above, originally published in the November 29, 1879, issue of *Harper's Weekly*, shows the party emerging from the mine and captures some of the important people of the Comstock.

From left to right are:

- John Mackay, one of the Bonanza Kings;
- Mrs. M.G. Gillette, whose husband was superintendent of the Savage Mine when it connected to the Sutro Tunnel;
- U.S. Grant, Jr., son of the former president and his wife;
- Mrs. U.S. Grant;
- General U.S. Grant;
- S. Yanada, the guide for the tour;
- Mrs. James Fair;
- J.H. Kinkead, third governor of Nevada;
- James G. Fair, another of the Bonanza Kings.

The next day, Grant and his party left Virginia City to tour the other towns of the Comstock: Gold Hill, Silver City, and Dayton, ending at the Sutro Mansion, where Leah Sutro greeted them. Mr. Alexander Summerfield, a store owner in Sutro,[15] welcomed the general and his party on behalf of the citizens of Sutro. He said, in part,

> I echo the sentiment of every child, woman and man in the town of Sutro, for, General, we love you. In a short time, you will behold one of the great enterprises of the world, constructed by these brave, hard-working men.[16]

The general's speech in response was characteristically brief: "I thank you."[17] After a hearty breakfast, the Grant party, joined by about 200 townspeople, boarded seven rail cars for a tour of the Sutro Tunnel. The raucous group enlivened the ride by singing "The Star-Spangled Banner" and "John Brown's Body."[18]

The second event occurred about four months earlier and explained why Adolph Sutro did not meet with General U.S. Grant during his visit. Leah Sutro had heard rumors about her husband, but she tried to ignore them.[19] The rumors involved a new resident of Virginia City, Mrs. George Allen, who dressed all in black but not in mourning. To accent her unusual apparel, Mrs. Allen added feather boas, willow plumes, and diamonds. She was promptly nicknamed "The $90,000 Diamond Widow." Sutro, at the peak of his success and popularity, soon met Mrs. Allen. The pair seemed to hit it off and often dined together on champagne and pheasant at the best restaurant in Virginia City, the International Hotel.

After such a dinner on July 3, 1879, hotel guests were startled by women's screams. The *San Francisco Chronicle*, published on July 9, picks up the story:

> A general rush was made in the direction of the cries, which led to the room of Mrs. Allen, where Mrs. Sutro was beating her over the head with a champagne bottle and making outcries, calling her all sorts of names. Mrs. Sutro declared that she had caught her husband with Mrs. Allen. Mrs. Sutro was removed to her room and commenced making things lively for Mr. Sutro, accusing him of infidelity and holding questionable relations with the woman. It is stated that E.B. Stonehill has been retained as attorney for Mrs. Sutro in a suit for divorce which will be begun immediately.[20]

After hearing rumors that their meetings in Nevada were far from the first time they had met, Leah Sutro had hired Major Stonehill to gather evidence about possible indiscretions in Washington. Adolph admitted that he had dinner with Mrs. Allen and that he had been in her room several times but denied any impropriety. Mrs. Allen said that her real name was Miss Hattie Trundle and that she was just out of finishing school, implying that she had been heavily chaperoned and could not possibly have been asso-

Mrs. George Allen, aka Hattie Trundle, a.k.a. "The $90,000 Widow."

ciating with any man in Washington. For his part, Adolph maintained to his death that Hattie had been falsely accused. In his will, he tried to compensate for the injury done to her reputation by bequeathing her $50,000.[21] He never saw Hattie again, but his marriage to Leah, already shaky, was ruined.

Leah Sutro filed for divorce, but two years later, on October 6, 1881, her suit was dismissed.[22] The reason for the dismissal became clear many years later. The Sutros had agreed to a settlement with no divorce. Under the terms of the agreement,

- Leah was to go to Europe and stay for three years;
- She would receive $2,000 for travel expenses, and $10,000 more if she remained for three years;
- Her debts, totaling $22,000, were to be paid;
- She would receive, until her death, $500 per month;
- The six children would receive between $100 and $200 per month, based on their respective ages until they reached age 30.[23,24]

Leah did go to Europe, but not until April 1889. She returned in mid–1890 because she was ill.[25]

On Wednesday, October 29, 1879, immediately after General Grant's visit to the Sutro Mansion, Leah Sutro took her belongings and left Nevada for San Francisco. There Adolph had bought for her a spacious home with extensive gardens at Hayes and Fillmore Streets,[26] and they lived separately until Leah's death on December 8, 1893, at the age of 60.

Chapter 28

Return to San Francisco

Those who know how to win are far more numerous than those who know how to make proper use of their victories.
—Polybius (200–118 BC)

Adolph Sutro had won his battle with the Bank Ring and had kept his promise to drain the Comstock mines with his four-mile tunnel, but it was a Pyrrhic victory. He had lost his wife, Leah; his friend Joseph Aron was accusing him of mismanagement or worse; and his long-time supporter in London, Robert McCalmont, was understandably upset at losing millions of dollars. The tunnel had taken so long to complete that its economic value was minimal. But Sutro emerged from the experience with over $700,000 and the knowledge that he could achieve what others deemed impossible. It was time for Don Quixote to find another windmill.

Having seen so little of the United States, Sutro did not know where he wanted to live. But Leah would be in San Francisco, and he knew something of that city, so he chose to return there. The city was experiencing one of its periodic downtimes. The Bank of California reopened on October 7, 1875, but William Ralston, the bank founder and sugar daddy of San Francisco, had drowned earlier that year. The almost unlimited wealth pouring in from the Comstock was ending. Investments that should have been building industry and infrastructure in the city had gone instead to chase riches from silver and gold in Nevada. Everyone seemed to be dispirited and depressed. For someone with money and ambition, it was a wonderful time to be in San Francisco.

In early 1880, Adolph moved into the Baldwin Hotel on Market and Powell Streets, where he and his family had enjoyed happier times just three years earlier. He decided to invest in real estate at a time when no one else was doing so. As a result, he was able to obtain valuable property at bargain prices and to purchase land viewed as sand dunes for next to nothing. His first purchase consisted of two adjacent three-story buildings on Battery Street, near the center of town. Income from these buildings was for the support of Leah Sutro and the children. Sutro made other high-quality investments on Market Street and California Street, as well as another property on Battery. But these purchases in and near the central business district were dwarfed in area by Sutro's investments in what were called the "Outside Lands." Sutro is quoted as saying, "I took my money and invested in real estate ... when everyone was scared and thought the city was going to the dogs. I bought every acre I could lay my hands on until I had 2,200 acres in this city."[1]

The map of San Francisco on the next page is from a 1902 Market Street Railway Company map with areas of particular interest to Adolph Sutro overlaid.[2,3] Sutro purchased several large tracts in the Outside Lands, including the 46-acre Byfield Tract for $46,294 and the massive, 1,350-acre Rancho San Miguel Tract for $240,000. In 1880, Sutro acquired 40 separate parcels of real estate.[4]

Before he finished buying property, Sutro owned one-twelfth of the land in San Francisco, over 2,200 acres. He also bought land outside of San Francisco, in San Mateo, Alameda, Napa, and Lake counties.[5] Later, when economic conditions improved, Sutro sold hundreds of building lots in the Outside Lands to finance his massive expenditures for world travel and new construction projects.

On March 2, 1881, Sutro and his daughter Emma explored the Outside Lands during a fateful carriage ride. Such excursions had become popular with San Franciscans since the development of Golden Gate Park starting in the early 1870s. In addition to providing a much-needed recreational area, Golden Gate Park also encouraged the extension of residential areas to the undeveloped Outside Lands. When Adolph and Emma reached the Pacific Ocean, near a place later appropriately called Lands End, they were overwhelmed by the sight. Standing on a promontory, they saw below them a restaurant called the Cliff House; Seal Rocks with a resident population of sea lions; the Pacific Ocean; and to the north, the Marin Headlands and Mount Tamalpais.

Sutro was entranced. When he turned around, he saw a small frame four-room cottage possessing that breathtaking view. He knocked on the front door, and the owner, Samuel Tetlow, invited Adolph and Emma inside. Tetlow was the owner of the Bella Union Music Hall, located in the notorious and dangerous Barbary Coast section of San Francisco. His cottage at Lands End, bought from Charles Butler in 1860, was physically and emotionally as far from his business as possible.

Tetlow had recently shot and killed his business partner but had been acquitted

Seal Rocks and the Cliff House from Lands End, ca. 1868.

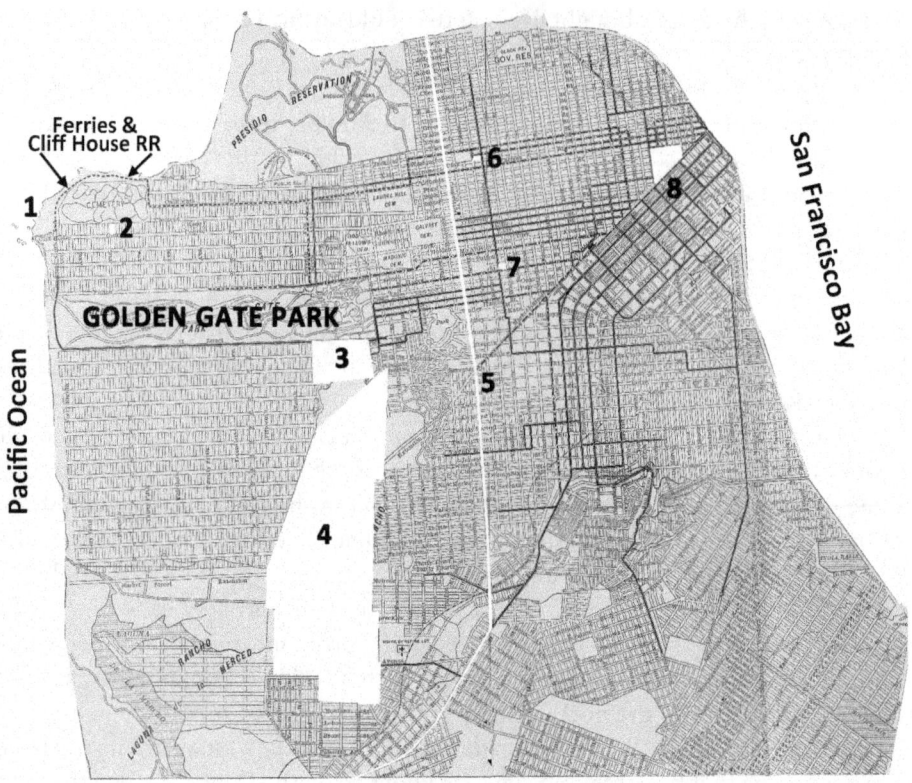

San Francisco Market Street Railway map from 1902, Courtesy University of Texas Libraries
1—Seal Rocks, Sutro Heights, Cliff House, and Sutro Baths
2—Block of property Sutro deeded to Clara Kluge in 1895
3—Byfield Tract
4—Rancho San Miguel Tract
5—Region to the left (west) of Divisadero Street was called the "Outside Lands."
6—Location of home Sutro built for Clara Kluge, at Clay and Steiner Streets
7—Location of home Sutro built for his wife, Leah Sutro, at Hayes and Fillmore Streets
8—Central Business District in 1880. Most of the rest of the city was sparsely developed.

based on a plea of self-defense just three months before the Sutros' visit. He was anxious to sell his property and move on, and Sutro was anxious to buy. After a brief negotiation, he gave Tetlow $1,000 as a deposit to buy the property for $15,000.[6] Although it was far smaller than the Sutro Mansion in Nevada, Adolph Sutro now had a permanent home in San Francisco.

In the ensuing years, Sutro purchased one parcel of land with 22 acres, and another extending 1.5 miles north and east along the Pacific Ocean and containing 80 acres. The Cliff House, directly west and below Sutro's property, had been a favorite of wealthy San Franciscans in the 1860s and '70s but lost its allure in the late '70s. It gained favor again as a house of gambling and prostitution, but that did not suit the new neighbor, Adolph Sutro, so he bought the Cliff House and surrounding property in 1883.

Of course, Sutro was not ready to retire. From this base at the extreme west end of San Francisco, he would undertake more unbelievable projects.

Chapter 29

Sutro Heights

God Almighty first planted a garden. And indeed, it is the purest of human pleasures.
—Francis Bacon

With over two thousand of acres of land around San Francisco and beyond, an oceanfront cottage situated on 100 acres, and his own money to work with, Adolph Sutro was no longer constrained by the limitations imposed by others. Unlike other rich men such as William Ralston, James Fair, and Mark Hopkins, Sutro did not build a many-gabled, turreted mansion. Rather than tearing down the modest four-room cottage he had bought from Samuel Tetlow, he added rooms, glassed in the porch, and installed statues by the front door. Instead of spending millions on an enormous new house, he invested in the grounds around the existing house.

Adolph predictably named his estate Sutro Heights. He was always good at spending money, and he spared little in designing and implementing Sutro Heights. He created "The Old Grove," comprised of cypress, pine, and eucalyptus trees planted 10 to 15 feet apart around the cottage.[1] Once mature, the trees were pruned to provide an overhead canopy that shaded the lawn below. Eight axial walkways radiated from a central point, providing a focal point for the landscaping.

The grounds included a rich mix of flower beds, gardens, forests, wide walks, hedge mazes, and Parterre gardens. Open areas within the forest featured specific ornamental plants, a piece of sculpture, or a scenic view. One dominant garden feature was a 130-foot-long hedge of American arborvitae that

Sutro in front of one of the Parterre Gardens (courtesy National Park Service).

Above: **Adolph Sutro residence at Sutro Heights, ca. 1886. Image from Cliff House Project (courtesy Dennis O'Rorke).** *Below:* **Statues, urns, and a cannon on the parapet, looking south.**

eventually reached 40 feet in height. Norfolk Island pines planted near the arborvitae added contrasting textures to the hedge. Flowering shrubs included hydrangeas, roses, and rhododendrons. Annual and perennial flowers such as geraniums, salvias, chrysanthemums, and violas added varying colors.

Sutro utilized a spring located near the Pacific Ocean to provide water for the plants. He designed a system in which windmills pumped water into a 50,000-gallon tank on the property, and also to a 15,000-gallon tank on top of a tower attached to the house. Gravity then fed water from those tanks to the plants below.

The tower itself, built of sandstone, sat at the highest point of Sutro Heights and provided spectacular views of the coastline to the north, west, and south. Below the tower was the parapet, comprised of a curved sandstone wall extending in a semicircle for 280 feet. At the ends of that wall were matching 100-foot walls, thus creating a "D"

Cottage and tower above parapet and Dolce far Niente Balcony (courtesy Golden Gate National Recreation Area).

shape. Crushed native sandstone covered the parapet floor. The top edge of the curved wall included 30 stone crenellations, each topped with either a statue or a planting urn.

Another prominent feature at Sutro Heights was the *Dolce far Niente* (pleasantly doing nothing) Balcony, a 250-foot-long wooden terrace cantilevered over the cliff face and overlooking the beach and ocean below.

Prominent gates marked the primary and smaller private entrances to Sutro Heights. The main gate, pictured on the next page, was a wooden structure over 25 feet high, with a central carriage entrance flanked by two pedestrian entries. Carved lions, a common theme at Sutro Heights, guarded the gates. The lions were created by Willem Geefs, a prominent Belgian sculptor.

In addition to the lions, most of the statuary at Sutro Heights resulted from a stop Sutro made in Belgium during his 1883 tour of Europe. There he commissioned the casting of over 200 pieces of sculpture. Upon completion in 1884, they were shipped from Antwerp, around Cape Horn, to San Francisco.

While far less costly than originals, Sutro intended the sculptures to show visitors examples of European gardens and culture. He had the sculptures, along with planting urns, chairs, and tables, placed at prominent positions around the grounds of Sutro Heights.

Maintenance of all these lawns, gardens, statuary, and paths required a full-time staff of 17 people: 10 gardeners, a tree man, a coachman, driver, gatekeeper, machinist and helper, and a road maker.

Adolph opened Sutro Heights to the public in 1885. Visitors from downtown San Francisco paid 20 cents for a round trip to the Heights, and their enthusiastic descriptions

Main entry gates to Sutro Heights. Image from Cliff House Project (courtesy Dennis O'Rorke).

made it clear that such a trip was worth the cost. A reporter from the Salt Lake City *Daily Tribune* wrote the following appraisal:

> There are two very massive gateways with lodges, the first being guarded by two huge sphinxes, and through which is a narrow drive leading to the private gardens a quarter of a mile up the Cliff House Road, and nearer town in the main entrance, even larger than the lower or private one. This is guarded by two enormous lions couchant, copies of Sir Edwin Landseer's lions at the base of the Nelson Column, Trafalgar Square, London. The main drive is very wide, perfectly level, and forms a junction with the lower drive in the center of the grounds, and extends round the bluff rock overhanging the sea, and from which you look down on the seals. Above you to the right, the bluff still rises about twenty feet, and on the extreme summit is built a massive stone wall, castellated in true Norman style, that resembles a piece of the terrace at Windsor Castle, or the battlements of Northallerton, and much admired, especially by those who have seen it from the ocean. The gardens are laid out beautifully, in the center of which is a very large conservatory, and to which, in addition is being made, and at every turn, or junction of roads, or foot paths, is placed some piece of statuary, rustic chairs, tables, and in fact everything that luxury or comfort can demand. There are several hundred chairs and not less than one hundred pieces of fine statuary.[2]

Visitors to Sutro Heights ranged from 220 six-year-olds who picnicked on the grounds to 23rd U.S. President Benjamin Harrison.

Sutro played host to the president of the University of California, 60 female kindergarten teachers, William Jennings Bryan, Andrew Carnegie, Oscar Wilde, and a production of *As You Like It* with an audience of 5,000.

Poet E.J. Jackson was so inspired by the place that he wrote a 13-page poem titled "Sutro Heights." The last stanza reads:

29. Sutro Heights

President Benjamin Harrison (sixth from left) and party, April 27, 1891.

> Lord of the manor, he who thus confers
> A public boon, which gratitude bestirs
> In all who visit and enjoy delights,
> Such as are only found on Sutro Heights.[3]

The map below provides an overview of the Sutro Heights area.

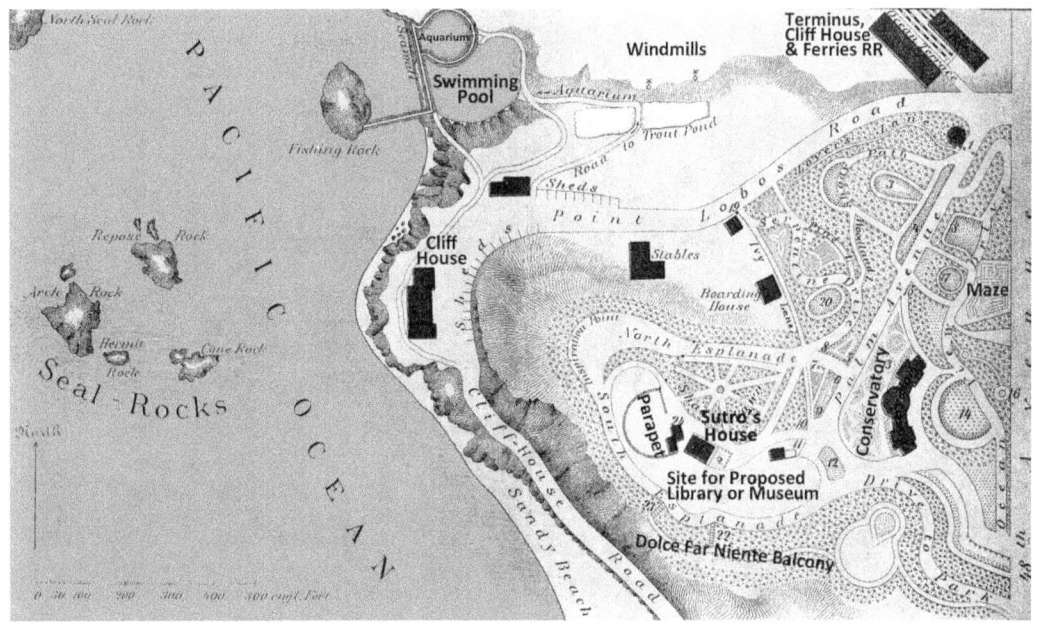

Map of Sutro Heights and surrounding area.

Despite his wealth, Sutro was sensitive to the plight of the working man. At a time when a clerk earned about 12 dollars a week, Sutro felt that even the 20-cent round-trip fare to Sutro Heights was too high. So, he and his cousin Gustav supported the development of a new steam rail line from downtown San Francisco to Sutro Heights. This new line would charge just 10 cents for a round trip and would also provide scenic views of the rugged shoreline at the entrance to San Francisco Bay, the Marin Headlands, Fort Point, and the Golden Gate. A newspaper article said, "This new line will be along the edge of the cliffs above the Pacific, at a height of 170 feet from the ocean, and when completed will afford one of the grandest views and most charming excursions to be found on the continent."[4] When the new line, called the Cliff House and Ferries Railroad, opened on March 1, 1886, it was immediately popular. Two special locomotives pulled filled-to-capacity open-air coaches on Sundays, while four lighter engines handled weekday traffic.

The Sutros sold their franchise for the new line to the Powell Street Railroad Company in 1887, but the deed of sale required that the new owner retain the 10-cent roundtrip fare from downtown to Sutro Heights.

Now that cheap transportation to Lands End was available, Sutro could capitalize on his Cliff House Restaurant and other property bordering the Pacific Ocean.

Sutro, the Conservationist

From his boyhood in Prussia, Sutro had enjoyed being outside and enjoying natural surroundings. Now that he could sit on the parapet or the Dolce far Niente Balcony at Sutro Heights and look out to sea, his eyes were drawn to Seal Rocks and the resident sea lion population.

Cliff House and Ferries steam train at Golden Gate Park Terminal, circa 1895.

Sea lions at Seal Rocks. The largest sea lion was named Ben Butler, and after his death on July 6, 1895, his preserved carcass adorned the entrance to Sutro Baths. Image from Cliff House Project (courtesy Gary Stark).

He campaigned for a law to afford them protection from predators of all kinds, including humans with rifles. On February 23, 1887, the U.S. Congress granted Seal Rocks to the city and county of San Francisco, which placed the rocks and sea lions under the care and custody of the Board of Park Commissioners. Thus, Sutro was instrumental in passing the first environmental protection law.[5]

Sutro did not limit his beautification efforts to Sutro Heights. He established a tree nursery adjacent to the Laguna Honda Reservoir west of the Twin Peaks and south of Golden Gate Park. There he experimented to determine which trees would flourish in the moist air and stabilize the sandy soil.[6] Sutro's nursery provided hundreds of thousands of seedlings for planting on his properties and elsewhere in San Francisco. Sutro was celebrated as the father of tree planting in California on the state's first Arbor Day on November 26, 1886.[7] At that ceremony, Sutro said,

> It is my pleasure to plant trees and watch their progress. They are the children of my old age, that will live long after I am laid to rest. Whoever places a seed in the earth is king over unreckoned forces. In my visionary moments I can see spreading branches and hear the rustling of leaves around which future generations will live, and strive, and achieve their successes; for this is, indeed, a country of glorious possibilities. If only we do our part, these rivers and lakes, the beautiful bay of San Francisco, the solitary cliffs, and the pallid snow peaks, shall one and all become classic ground. It is man's labor, and the heroic deeds of men, which put new and more divine seal to nature's fairest scenes. I have crossed the Atlantic twenty times, and lived in every European capital. I have traveled in every country endeared to worshippers of art, literature, science and religion ... and yet I return to Sutro Heights satisfied to live out my allotted time, here beneath these matchless skies, and repose, at last on the sands that have favored my efforts at fertilization. These green-robed hills and beds of blooming flowers you see, were not so many years ago, quite bare and barren of vegetation.... There are thousands of acres yet to be cultivated.... I would encourage both by precept and example, a taste for horticultural

pursuits, as may be inferred by the gift of trees to school children, to be planted by them upon approaching Arbor Day.... It is the refinement which comes from a love of nature, the simplicity fostered in rural homes, that restless Americans need. Tired people will, I trust, learn to ramble every year in ravine and forest, and find renewed health in the presence of the wonderful mountains....

Among the millions of trees already planted, 400,000 of which have been placed south of Golden Gate Park, those that grew most prolifically in sandy soil were chosen from the cypress, the eucalyptus, and Mariana, a species of the pine originally found near the Black Sea. The special virtue of the eucalyptus consists in its rapid growth and its shelter to the trees which surround it. Betwixt the ocean and the Industrial School, occupying a space of a mile and half each side of the road, the same species can be selected.

In this work of planting trees, which extends from an altitude of 920 feet.... I have naught else but the interest of humanity at heart ... when an unemployed situation arose in the city, I employed a gang of men out of work to dig holes, to plant, and to water the trees.... The work of setting out the young trees ... gave employment to from forty to sixty men.[8]

Sutro's efforts to beautify the barren dunes of the Outside Lands continued from 1882 to 1896.[9] Trees supplied by Sutro still cover some of the iconic mountain peaks within the city, including Mount Davidson and Mount Sutro; and even today grace residential developments such as St. Francis Woods, Forest Hill, Westwood Park, Westwood Highlands, and Sherwood Forest.

Mount Davidson Cross surrounded by Sutro's Trees, memorial to the 1.5 million victims of the Armenian Genocide of 1915. Image from mountdavidsoncross.org (courtesy Ara Harmandarian).

Triumph of Light

In addition to the 200-plus statues at Sutro Heights, Adolph commissioned a large work by Belgian sculptor Antoine Wiertz. Called the *Triumph of Light*, it depicted Lady Liberty conquering despotism, and Sutro donated the statue to the City of San Francisco.

The 12-foot-high statue was installed on the top of a hill named Mount Olympus at what was then the geographic center of San Francisco. On Thanksgiving Day, 1887, the San Francisco Board of Supervisors, a band, the entire student body from the Sanchez Street School, and dozens of other onlookers came to witness the dedication of the statue.[10] Sutro made an uncharacteristically brief dedication speech, saying, "May the light shine from the torch of the Goddess of Liberty to inspire our citizens to good and noble deeds for the benefit of mankind."[11]

After Sutro's death in 1898, both he and the *Triumph of Light* faded from memory, and the statue deteriorated. By 1947, vandals had broken off the torch and otherwise defaced the statue.

Sometime in the 1950s, the statue was removed, leaving only the base, which remains today. Instead of the *Triumph of Light*, the site on top of Mount Olympus became the Triumph of Entropy.

Top: Triumph of Light **by Antoine Wiertz (courtesy San Francisco History Center, San Francisco Public Library).** *Above:* **1947 photo of the** *Triumph of Light* **(courtesy San Francisco History Center, San Francisco Public Library).**

Chapter 30

Clara and Leah

Men will bear many things from a kept mistress, which they would not bear from a wife.
—Samuel Richardson

Sewing was not one of Adolph Sutro's talents. But to make his cottage at Sutro Heights livable and attractive, he wanted to add curtains, draperies, and other decorations. The place needed a woman's touch, and that woman was Clara Kluge. No references describe how Sutro found Clara, but she was probably recommended by a friend or appeared in a newspaper advertisement. But in 1885, Clara started working as a seamstress at the Sutro Heights home of Adolph Sutro.[1]

Clara Louisa Kluge was born February 12, 1863, in Leipzig, Saxony, Germany.[2] Leipzig is about 280 miles east of Aachen, the birthplace of Adolph Sutro.

With a shared German heritage, Sutro found Clara attractive, and they struck up a friendship. By 1890, the 60-year-old Sutro and the 27-year-old Clara had become lovers, and on August 9, 1891, Clara gave birth to a son whom she named Adolph Newton Kluge.[3] Just over one year later, on November 5, 1892, the couple had a daughter named Adolphine Charlotte Kluge.[4]

Sutro had been supporting his wife, Leah, and their children since their separation in 1879. In April 1893, news came that Leah's death was imminent. Adolph and four of their children, Emma, Charles, Edgar, and Clara, came to be with Leah. She had suffered from the complications of diabetes for two years and became more seriously ill in February.[5] The immediate crisis passed, but Leah died on December 9, 1893. At her death, Adolph said, "But for her I should have lost heart altogether. My wife never repined, never reproached me for the poverty with which we struggled, and she never wavered in her devotion."[6] Her obituary stated, "The life of this good woman was devoted to her family and to charitable deeds. In early womanhood before riches came, when assistance to other could be rendered only through self-deprivation, Mrs. Sutro was more than generous to the poor. Later in life, with ample means, her generosity was proverbial."[7]

Rabbi Jacob Voorsanger conducted Leah's service at her home at Hayes and Fillmore Streets. He mentioned "the numerous unostentatious charities which had characterized the daily life of Mrs. Sutro. Even her family had never known what a large number of poor and destitute pensioners she had supported. It was her delight to do good in secret, not to let her good deeds be known."[8]

Leah left a handwritten will dated March 29, 1893, in which she left specific items of jewelry, furniture, glassware, and silverware to each of her daughters (Emma, Rosa, Kate, and Clara). To her sons (Charles and Edgar), she bequeathed items of furniture including a billiard table. The balance of her personal property was to be sold at auction with the proceeds divided among her children. Leah named her daughter, Emma, and her son-in-law, Albert Morbio (husband of Rosa) as executors.[9]

Leah is buried at Home of Peace Cemetery and Emanu-El Mausoleum, Colma, California,[10] along with stillborn son, Adolph Sutro II,[11] and his brother, Gustavus Emanuel Sutro.[12]

Memorial to Leah Sutro and stillborn son, Adolph Sutro II, Plot E, Section 5, Lot 1 (courtesy Bryan Winter).

Candi McMahan describes the background of the Sutro family burial vault in a note on the FindaGrave page of Gustavus Emanuel Sutro:

> Adolph Sutro paid $82.50 to have Gustavus Emanuel disinterred from the Jewish Cemetery in Virginia City and transported, on October 20, 1894, properly boxed and with accompanying papers, to San Francisco, arriving on October 22, 1894, to be re-interred at the Home Of Peace family vault in Colma, upon the one-year anniversary of the passing of his mother, Leah. Adolph Sutro paid $918 on December 5, 1894, to Home Of Peace, for the cost of the family vault and monument, which can accommodate 12–even though only 3 are there: Leah, Gustavus Emanuel, and Leah and Adolph's stillborn infant, Adolph, II.[13]

Clara Kluge claimed that she and Adolph married in late December 1893, immediately after Leah's death. However, she was never able to provide any documentation confirming that marriage.

Two revealing real estate transactions were reported in 1895 issues of the *San Francisco Call*. The first of these, on April 26, conveyed "outside land block 219, bounded by Thirty-eighth and Thirty-ninth avenues, Point Lobos avenue and Clement street" from Adolph Sutro to Elliott J. Moore.[14] Moore was Sutro's long-time attorney, and such property transfers were commonplace. But the second transaction was far more interesting. The exact same property was conveyed from Elliott J. Moore to Clara Kluge less than one month later, on May 16, 1895.[15] The location of the property was just seven-tenths of a mile from Adolph's home at Sutro Heights.

On September 2, 1895, Clara purchased a lot on the northeast corner of Clay and Steiner Streets in San Francisco from Charles L. Beal for a reported amount of $10.[16]

Current view of Clara Kluge home at 2302 Steiner Street (courtesy Jacquie Proctor).

Even now, many real estate transactions list an amount of $10, possibly for privacy or tax reasons. The actual amount paid by Clara (or Adolph) was later reported to be $5,500.[17]

In October 1896, Clara filed a building permit to start work on the house. Sutro oversaw and paid for construction, which included inlaid mahogany floors and carved mantles. When it was completed, Adolph provided money to furnish the 17-room home.

Sutro's frequent visits to the home and young family there attracted a great deal of attention, especially because he was the mayor of San Francisco until January 1897. Sutro's visits ended when his health declined in early 1898.[18]

Clara exchanged the Steiner Street house for property on Grattan Street in June 1898, when Sutro was on his deathbed.[19] She claimed that she could no longer pay the mortgage on the house. Adolph Sutro's death in August 1898 exacerbated Clara's problems, but she, like Adolph, persevered and was ultimately victorious in gaining a share of Sutro's estate, as detailed in Chapter 37.

Chapter 31

The Cliff House—Before Sutro

The coldest day I ever spent was a summer's day in San Francisco.
—Mark Twain

When Adolph Sutro and his daughter Emma first surveyed the view from Lands End in 1881, the Cliff House they saw was not the first restaurant built near that spectacular location. In 1858, Samuel Brannan, the ex–Mormon official who had proclaimed, "Gold! Gold! Gold on the American River!" built the Seal Rock House just south of where the Sutros saw the Cliff House. Brannan had purchased the cargo of a lumber ship that foundered on the rocky shore and hauled the lumber up the cliff to construct his hotel and restaurant. Because it was so far from civilization with no roads to ease travel, Brannan's Seal Rock House never prospered.

But other visionaries saw the potential of the seaside location. Soon after Brannan opened his place, Charles Butler purchased the promontory where the Cliff House would be located along with 160 surrounding acres. Butler originally planned to hold the land until the next investor came along, but soon decided to build a hotel and restaurant of his own. He opened the first structure called the Cliff House on October 15, 1863. Like Brannan's building, the first Cliff House was a wooden structure, and a local critic described it as looking "...something like a barracks."[1] Butler's Cliff House offered food, drinks, rooms, and spectacular ocean views.

Because there were still no roads, patrons had to brave a treacherous six-mile horse ride to reach the first Cliff House. But Butler had recognized this problem, and in 1862 formed the Point Lobos Road Company with Senator John P. Buckley. To gain Buckley's support for the granting of a franchise for the road, he was awarded a partnership in Butler's Cliff House. By 1865, the new road was open with a round-trip toll of one dollar. The main road was paved with macadam that was "as smooth as a dollar."[2] A two-mile high-speed clay track for trotter horses alongside the main road attracted the city's horse owners. Friendly races were commonplace, to the delight of the travelers on the main road. Wealthy families such as the Crockers, the Hearsts, and the Stanfords, flocked to the Cliff House, where they relaxed on the veranda sipping drinks and watching sea lions cavort on Seal Rock just offshore.

To keep his upper-class clientele satisfied, Butler leased the Cliff House to Captain Junius Foster, an experienced hotel operator who had also been purser on a Panama-to-San Francisco steamship. A guest at the time recalled, "meals were on 'the American plan,' and not at all bad. Long tables were each adorned with a center line of pies, the line broken by an occasional jelly cake in a high glass dish with glass cover."[3] The Cliff House was so popular that a sunny day might see 1,200 teams of horses tied up at the hitching posts and more teams tethered farther down the coast.

On June 25, 1864, less than one month after he left Virginia City, Mark Twain reported on his visit to the Cliff House:

> If one tire of the drudgeries and scenes of the city, and would breathe the fresh air of the sea, let him take the cars and omnibuses, or, better still, a buggy and pleasant steed, and, ere the sea breeze sets in, glide out to the Cliff House. We tried it a day or two since. Out along the rail road track, by the pleasant homes of our citizens, where architecture begins to put off its swaddling clothes, and assume form and style, grace and beauty, by the neat gardens with their green shrubbery and laughing flowers, out where were once sand hills and sand-valleys, now streets and homesteads.... Then away you go over paved, or planked, or Macadamized roads, out to the cities of the dead, pass between Lone Mountain and Calvary, and make a straight due west course for the ocean. Along the way are many things to please and entertain, especially if an intelligent chaperon accompany you. Your eye will travel over in every direction the vast territory which Swain, Weaver & Co. desire to fence in, the little homesteads by the way, Dr. Rowell's arena castle, and Zeke Wilson's Bleak House in the sand. Splendid road, ocean air that swells the lungs and strengthens the limbs. Then there's the Cliff House, perched on the very brink of the ocean, like a castle by the Rhine, with countless sea-lions rolling their unwieldy bulks on the rocks within rifle-shot, or plunging into and sculling about in the foaming waters. Steamers and sailing craft are passing, wild fowl scream, and sea-lions growl and bark, the waves roll into breakers, foam and spray, for five miles along the beach, beautiful and grand, and one feels as if at sea with no rolling motion nor sea-sickness, and the appetite is whetted by the drive and the breeze, the ocean's presence wins you into a happy frame, and you can eat one of the best dinners with the hungry relish of an ostrich. Go to the Cliff House. Go ere the winds get too fresh, and if you like, you may come back by Mountain Lake and the Presidio, overlook the Fort, and bow to the Stars and Stripes as you pass.[4]

But just a week later, Twain was not so enchanted by the same journey. The quotation opening this chapter probably resulted from this second trip.

> The wind was cold and benumbing, and blew with such force that we could hardly make headway against it. It came straight from the ocean, and I think there are icebergs out there somewhere. True, there was not much dust, because the gale blew it all to Oregon in two minutes; and by good fortune, it blew no gravestones, to speak of—only one of any consequence, I believe—a three-cornered one—it struck me in the eye. I have it there yet.... From the moment we left the stable, almost, the fog was so thick that we could scarcely see fifty yards behind or before, or overhead; and for a while, as we approached the Cliff House, we could not see the horse at all, and were obliged to steer by his ears, which stood up dimly out of the dense white mist that enveloped him. But for those friendly beacons, we must have been cast away and lost.... We could scarcely see the sportive seals out on the rocks, writhing and squirming like exaggerated maggots, and there was nothing soothing in their discordant barking, to a spirit so depressed as mine was.[5]

Despite Twain's ambivalence, patronage at the Cliff House increased, aided by daring attempts to cross by tightrope to Seal Rock. On September 27, 1865, circus performer James Cooke navigated from the Cliff House to Seal Rock, a distance of 400 feet, on a thin steel wire suspended 90 feet above the water.

The following report appeared in the Marysville (CA) *Daily Appeal*.[6]

> A crowd of 5,000 watched in tense silence as Cooke stepped on the rope at 12:15 p.m. He progressed across the void without problems until he was about 100 feet from the rock. Then an improperly attached guy wire came loose, and a strong breeze, common at this exposed location, caused the wire

James Cooke walking a tightrope from the Cliff House to Seal Rock (author's collection).

to sway violently from side to side. Cooke slipped and fell across the wire, losing his balancing pole in the process. Those watching, who had been holding their collective breath, gasped as he fell. Undaunted, Cooke knelt on the wire and used his hands to pull himself the remaining distance to the rock. A boatman who had retrieved the balancing pole handed it to Cooke while he gathered his strength and resolve. After five minutes, Cooke mounted the wire again and walked steadily towards the shore. Near the middle of his journey, the rope again swayed, but he continued on undeterred. When Cooke stepped off the wire onto land, the crowd, which covered the balcony and roof of the Cliff House as well as the beach below, cheered wildly and gave him a tremendous ovation.

In June and July 1866, eighteen-year-old Rosa Celeste matched Cooke's feat on three separate occasions, and the Cliff House capitalized by selling balcony seats for one dollar each. Finally, Millie Lavelle crossed to Seal Rock by gripping a bit, connected to a trolley, between her teeth. Millie coasted under the wire to Seal Rock and back.[7]

The Cliff House needed more room. The smooth road, excellent food, and daring feats brought more patrons than the small building could handle, so in 1868 extensions were added on each end, effectively tripling the size of the structure. The new south wing contained "a ladies' parlor and accessories," while the north wing included, "a barroom, reading-room, restaurant, card room, and other conveniences for gentleman's use."[8]

But times were changing. San Francisco, finally recognizing its dearth of parks, initiated work on Golden Gate Park in 1870. This massive park, 20 percent larger than New York City's Central Park, made the citizens more aware of what were called the Outside Lands west of the city. The first public road through the park opened in 1877, making the Point Lobos Toll Road obsolete. The most important change, however, was the end of the wealth pouring into San Francisco from the Comstock Lode. As the ore in Nevada became depleted, rich San Franciscans started to reduce their spending. No

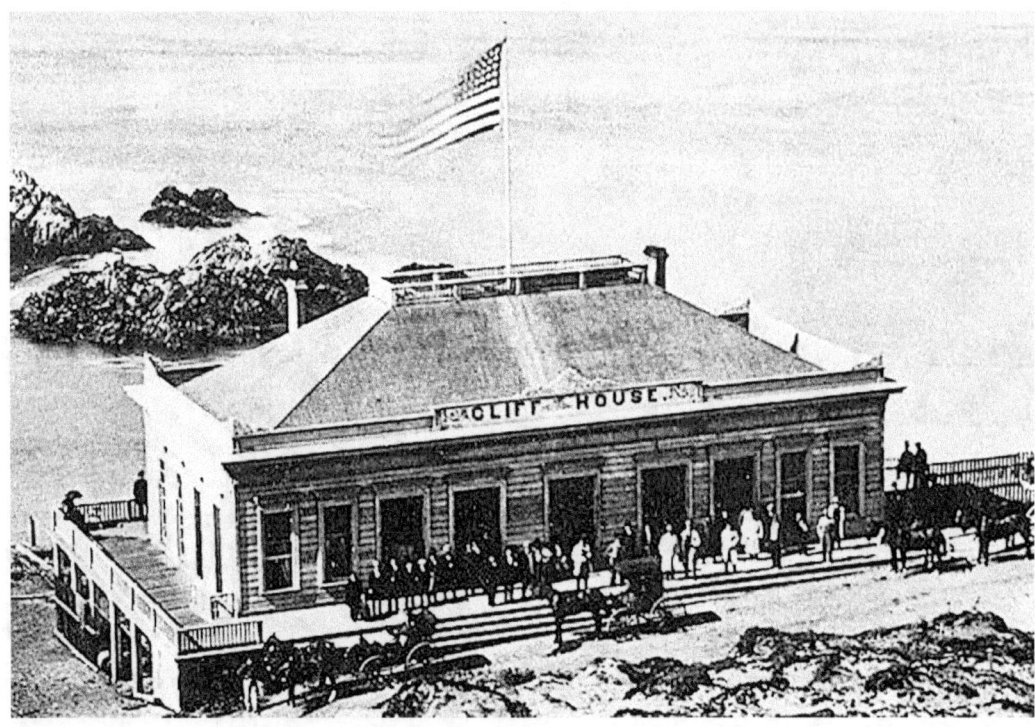

Top: **Original Cliff House.** *Above:* **Cliff House with additions on each end. Image from Cliff House Project (courtesy Dennis O'Rorke).**

longer could they afford days spent in leisure watching sea lions from the balcony of the Cliff House.

The Cliff House clientele changed from the wealthy to the average, and the new crowd wanted gambling, later hours, and rowdier entertainment. Cliff House manager Junius Foster reluctantly adapted to their demands. But it was a slippery slope. The Cliff House soon descended to a gambling and dance hall, with private rooms for those who wanted to do more than dance. Parties were loud and long but bothered no one except maybe Samuel Tetlow in his nearby cottage. Tetlow's Bella Union Music Hall in the Barbary Coast section of San Francisco catered to the same boisterous crowd, so he could hardly complain.

But in 1881, Adolph Sutro bought Tetlow's cottage and then the land surrounding the Cliff House. Sutro was not pleased with the tawdry reputation of the Cliff House, or with its late-night noise and traffic. He solved the problem by buying the Cliff House from Charles Butler in late 1881, reportedly for $169,000.[9] The new era of the Cliff House had begun.

Chapter 32

The Cliff House—With Sutro

*But all who came through the Golden Gate,
And those who traveled the continent o'er,
The thing to do first was to do the Cliff,
See the lions and hear them roar.*
—Jen Kirk

When Adolph Sutro bought the Cliff House in 1881, he retained Junius Foster, who had managed the restaurant for more than 20 years. But looking for a change in direction, Sutro dismissed Foster effective January 1, 1884.

For seven months, Sutro tried to run the Cliff House himself. He attempted to increase patronage by adding other attractions. In early March 1884, he had a wire suspension bridge constructed between the shore north of the Cliff House and nearby Flag Rock, about 160 feet away. Guests who ventured from dry land to the massive rock found themselves surrounded by the ocean. The trip across the bridge was thrilling, as it swayed from side to side in the strong ocean breezes.

Unfortunately, the bridge tended to tip if too many people stood or walked on one side or the other, and this is what happened on March 16. An elderly man attempted to cross, but halfway over he became terrified and stopped, forcing the rest of the adventurers to pass him on the left. With so many people on one side, the bridge tipped, dumping most of them onto the sandy beach or into the shallow surf. No one was hurt seriously.

Guy-wires and other reinforcements were added to stabilize the bridge, but just a few weeks later, on April 7, 1884, disaster struck. With about 30 people on the bridge, some reckless boys periodically pushed the bridge back and forth so that the amplitude of the oscillations increased. Eventually, the bridge overturned, throwing everyone to the sand, the rocks, or the water. Many were injured, with bruises and broken bones. At least three lawsuits were reported in the *Daily Alta California* newspaper, with claims for damage ranging from $299 to $15,000.

After the bridge disaster, Sutro leased the Cliff House to Stroufe & McCrum, a local liquor wholesaler. That arrangement did not work out either. Finally, in 1885, James M. Wilkins took over and remained as the Cliff House proprietor for the next 22 years.

32. The Cliff House—With Sutro

Cliff House Suspension Bridge. Image from Cliff House Project (courtesy Gary Stark).

Wilkins recalled how he got the job in a 1918 article in the San Francisco *Chronicle*:

> ... I went to a mutual friend, William Lewis, who knew me very well and also had been a friend of Sutro in Virginia City, Nev., and asked him to introduce me.
> Lewis said to me, "I will speak to Sutro in Hebrew and tell him I know you very well and that you are all right."
> During the interview that followed it was agreed that I should take over the Cliff House, at a rental of $760 a month, and that I could retain it at that figure as long as Sutro remained alive. The only condition imposed was that the establishment should always be maintained as a respectable resort, that there should not be bolts on any of the doors and there should be no beds in the house.
> I said: "All right. Your terms please me. I will take the place tomorrow."
> Then Sutro said, "I wish to speak to Mr. Wilkins privately." He then took me aside and looked me squarely in the eyes with a penetrating gaze.
> "Why did you bring Mr. Lewis with you?" he asked.
> "Mr. Sutro," I replied, "Mr. Stroufe told me that if I could get a prominent Hebrew to introduce me to you it would help me in my bargaining with you."
> "It has not done you a bit of good," said he. "But I see you have told me the truth, and that will help you very much. I knew why you brought Mr. Lewis with you."
> At the end of the article, Wilkins said, "I found Adolph Sutro a good man. He was my friend and neighbor, and I think I knew him better than anyone else did. When he died I lost a good friend."[1]

Under Wilkins's management, the Cliff House regained its luster and "again drew crowds of local people with its renewed focus on families, good food, and entertainment."[2]

Ship's Graveyard

Many ships ran aground on the rocky shore west of the Cliff House. A whaler, the *Atlantic*, hit the rocks and disintegrated there on December 17, 1886. At least 30 sailors lost their lives, and 12 survived.

Another stranded ship resulted in major damage to the Cliff House and other Sutro-owned buildings in the area. On January 12, 1887, the 142-ton schooner *Parallel* under Captain Miller left the port of San Francisco loaded with hay, coal, kerosene oil, pig iron, lumber, a salmon boat, a large case of detonating caps, and 42 tons of dynamite. Light winds impeded progress, and three days later she had barely cleared the headlands of San Francisco Bay. When the winds died completely, the vessel started drifting toward Seal Rocks, and the captain, fearing an explosion when the ship hit the rocks, decided to abandon ship. He and his crew of seven escaped in a lifeboat and rowed 2.6 miles across the Golden Gate to Point Bonita Lighthouse in Marin County,[3] but did not launch flares or otherwise announce their distress.

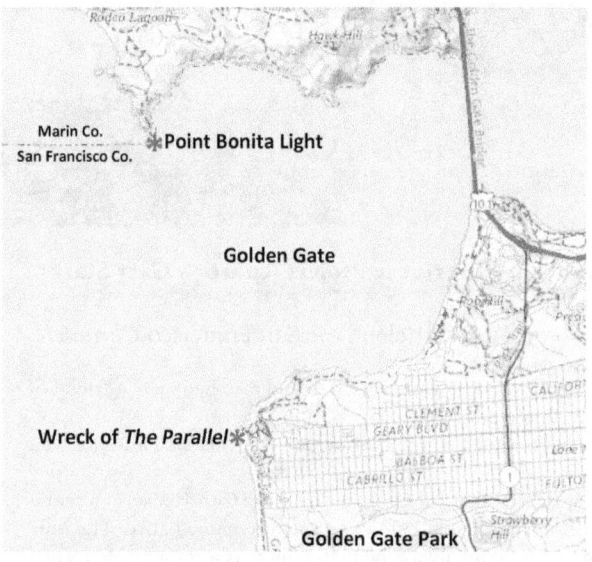

Map showing the *Parallel* and Point Bonita Lighthouse.

On Saturday, January 15 at 9:30 p.m., the schooner hit the rocks just north of the Cliff House at the cove where Adolph Sutro was building an aquarium. Sutro, James Wilkins, and several of the gardeners arrived at the Cliff House and lowered ropes to the beached ship for the crew to climb to safety. When no one appeared, they realized that the captain and crew had abandoned ship. A lifesaving crew arrived, but with no one to save, the captain placed two men, Henry Smith and John Wilson, on watch on the cliff above the ship. With the excitement over, everyone but Smith and Wilson departed to get some sleep.

At 12:34 a.m., that sleep ceased, as the gunpowder on the ship, possibly ignited by oil lamps that the crew had left burning, exploded. The blast was compared to an earthquake in power. It was felt as far away as Sacramento, Vacaville, and San Jose. Smith and Wilson, the two sentries, were thrown about 200 feet by the blast and both suffered broken bones and head injuries. Amazingly, there were no fatalities from the blast. But the damage to buildings was enormous. The entire north end of the Cliff House was blown off; both balconies collapsed; all windows in the Cliff House, the Seal Rock House, Sutro's cottage and conservatory, and every other building within a mile were shattered. Every room of the Cliff House was filled with rubble, and in the bar room, shattered glasses and whiskey bottles littered the floor.[4]

SCHOONER PARALLEL "BLOWN TO ATOMS" 1887

THE TWO-MASTED, 148-TON PARALLEL LEFT SAN FRANCISCO FOR ASTORIA, OREGON, WITH A MIXED CARGO & 42 TONS OF BLACK POWDER & DYNAMITE. CAPT. W.C. MILLER, FOUGHT AGAINST DIFFICULT WINDS FOR TWO DAYS & FINALLY GAVE UP. THE ABANDON-SHIP ORDER PUT THE 7-MAN CREW INTO A LIFEBOAT BEFORE THE SHIP WENT ON THE ROCKS OFF PT. LOBOS & THE CLIFF HOUSE. THE CREW ROWED TO SAUSALITO BUT TOLD NO ONE OF THE DANGEROUS CARGO. MILLER LATER WAS CRITICISED FOR HIS ACTIONS.

A CREW FROM THE LIFE-SAVING STATION AT GOLDEN GATE PARK WENT TO THE WRECK. THEY FOUND NO CREW ON BOARD BUT DID SAVE A FORGOTTEN DOG. ABOUT 1:30 A.M. 16 JANUARY 1887 THE SHIP EXPLODED. BADLY DAMAGED WERE THE: CLIFF HOUSE & COTTAGE; ADOLPH SUTRO'S RESIDENCE ON THE HEIGHTS; & OTHER STRUCTURES. THE BLAST INJURED 3 OF THE LIFE-SAVERS, BLEW DEBRIS FOR A MILE & WAS FELT 15 MILES AWAY AT SEA. FORTUNATELY, NO LIVES WERE LOST. 40,000 CURIOUS SPECTATORS CAME TO SEE THE WRECKAGE.

THIS PLAQUE IS DEDICATED TO THE COURAGEOUS MEN OF THE U.S. COAST GUARD (FORMERLY LIFE-SAVING SERVICE).

DEDICATED 26 MARCH 5999 (1994) BY THE A&HO E CLAMPSUS VITUS

CAPITULUS REDIVIVUS   YERBA BUENA NO.1

CREDO QUIA ABSURDUM

Plaque commemorating the explosion of the *Parallel*, dedicated March 26, 1994, below the Cliff House (photo by author).

On Sunday, sightseers skipped church to view the devastation. One estimate said that they numbered 80,000, and public transportation was overstretched to carry them. Other than shattered windows and the wreckage of the Cliff House, there was little to see. A pile of rubble was all that was left of the *Parallel*. People collected scraps of charred wood or twisted metal as souvenirs. Ever-enterprising James Wilkins cleared the debris from the bar of the Cliff House and hand-lettered in charcoal a "HOUSE OPEN FOR BUSINESS" sign for the door. The bar reported record sales of liquid refreshments on that Sunday after the explosion.

Repair work started that same Sunday, and Wilkins had the Cliff House ready to reopen within a month. Business and various wire-walking, swimming, and parachuting stunts continued as usual for the next several years, until the nationwide Panic of 1893 struck. At the beginning of the downturn, Sutro purchased 1,000 meal and bed tickets from the Salvation Army to distribute to the newly unemployed. Later, as the Depression deepened, even he was forced to borrow money to keep his various enterprises afloat. On February 9, he borrowed $120,000 at 6½ percent annual interest from the Hibernia Savings and Loan Society of San Francisco. But Sutro was far from destitute. He felt secure enough to continue buying land in Napa County for a hideaway away from the city.[5]

A final disaster hit the Cliff House on Christmas Day, 1894. A fire that had started about 8 p.m. in a chimney in the building quickly spread. For a while the nearby Sutro Baths were threatened, but the wind blew the fire away from that structure. The combination of a 30-year-old wooden building and a strong breeze from the northeast doomed the structure. Within two hours, flames consumed the walls and attacked the wooden supports and beams. James Wilkins, who leased the building from Adolph Sutro, provided details of the fire in the San Francisco *Morning Call* of Wednesday, December 26, 1894:

> Everything seemed as usual about the Cliff House this afternoon. The day was chilly and we had fires burning in the grates. I had made up the cash and gone up to Sutro Heights, where I have made my home.
>
> The bell rang the annunciator shortly after half-past 7 o'clock. Smoke was discovered in a little room off the bar and I was hastily summoned. I went to the parlor and found the fire just beginning to break through where the flue passed above the ceiling. Smoke was coming out of the crevices in many places. We were helpless from the start to fight the flames. I grabbed one of the fire extinguishers and attempted to subdue the fire in the parlor. Then I went to the shell room and used one of the extinguishers there. None of us realized at the outset that the fire was to prove so serious. It was supposed that the timbers about the flue had merely begun to char. In the shell room the fire had begun to break through the ceiling when I reached the room. The first extinguisher had no effect. I tried another. It proved useless.
>
> We went to the hall next which had begun to smoke. We rushed over and unrolled the hose which leads from Sutro Heights and has a water pressure of 150 pounds to the inch. This hose connects with the reservoir on the hill. It was too late. Five minutes after I reached the Cliff House, having been summoned from Sutro Heights, the fire was breaking through the roof. This gives an idea of the rapidity with which the flames worked. With all the splendid apparatus with which the Sutro Heights is equipped to fight fire we were helpless to put out the flames.
>
> When we saw that we couldn't save the building, we turned our attention to such articles as might be hastily removed. Many of the pictures were saved. We secured the mirrors and the silverware, and we saved quite a portion of the stock of wines and liquors.
>
> Mr. Sutro owned the building. He estimated its value at $10,000. It cost much more than that to construct the Cliff House, and I think that he underestimates its value as it stood before the fire. The building was uninsured.[6]

A poem by Mr. Jen Kirk captured the love and loss felt by the people of San Francisco for their Cliff House:

THE OLD CLIFF HOUSE
By Jen Kirk, January 13, 1895

Dear old house, thou hast fallen low,
A heap of dust and gray ashes light.
Desolation has trailed her mantles o'er
Thy lofty perch and sunny height.

Thou art today but a smoldering pile,
On thy cliff by the side of the sea—
A tangled mass of pipes and bands,
Red bricks a few, and a heap of debris.

For hours the fires had smoldered unseen,
But a breath of air sent then all aglow,
Far out to sea went tongues of flame,
Defying the surging waters below.

The seals on their rocky home took flight
As smoke and cinders around them came
And quickly into the ocean plunged
To watch from below the sheets of flame.

The flag of our country no longer waves
Over thy gay and festive halls;
No more shall we hear the trampling feet
Of the crowds that gather within thy walls.

No smoothly chiseled brownstone front,
No granite gray or massive walls;
No mansard roof, with tiles of slate,
No cold, forbidding marble halls;

No stately pillars, or portals grand,
No frescoed ceilings, or tapestried walls;
Yet kings and queens have deigned to stand
In thy plain and unpretentious halls!

Thou wert our quaint, old-fashioned house,
Built with timbers so strong and light—
With old-time window-shutters green,
And rustic boards, all painted white.

But all who came through the Golden Gate,
And those who traveled the continent o'er,
The thing to do first was to do the Cliff,
See the lions and hear them roar.

Far out below spreads the beautiful beach,
Where the breakers curl o'er the hard gray sand,

>Leaving ribbons of foam as they backward roil;
>Ever held in check by our Father's hand.
>
>Towering above hangs Sutro Heights,
>And at thy feet old ocean breaks.
>While just outside runs the sea's highway
>For ships that pass through the Golden Gate.
>
>Thy fame, old house, has journeyed far
>Over continents broad and wide;
>Also in every isle of the sea
>Thy traveled patrons now abide.
>
>On thy sunny crag by the sea
>A palatial pile will bear thy name,
>But to us who loved the dear old house
>It will never be quite the same.[7]

The poet was correct; a "palatial pile" would be planned and built by Adolph Sutro, and it would be called, of course, the Cliff House. Despite shipwrecks and fires, Sutro would persevere.

Chapter 33

Gingerbread Palace

The one who falls and gets up is stronger than the one who never tried. Do not fear failure, but rather fear not trying.
—Roy T. Bennett

When interviewed the day after the Cliff House burned to the ground on Christmas Day, 1894, a reporter asked Adolph Sutro if he would rebuild. He replied, "Will I rebuild the Cliff House? No, not the Cliff House as it was, but one of the greatest hotels in the land. I think I will build upon the site of the old house, but not immediately."[1] Sutro didn't wait long. In early 1895 he commissioned Emil Lemme, a university-trained architect and structural engineer, and his partner, Charles Colley, who worked as a carpenter and millwright before his architectural work, to design the new Cliff House. On April 13, 1895, Sutro let the contract for construction to Campbell & Pettus, with a completion schedule of four months and a price of $42,000.[2]

Thousands of San Franciscans watched progress from Sutro Heights and the beach below. The new structure was built to withstand the earthquakes common to the region as well as strong hurricanes. Eight steel rods, each 1½ inch in diameter and anchored 20 to 40 feet in the rock, extended all the way up to the roof joists. The foundation rested on 12-inch-by-12-inch beams double-coated with tar and cemented into solid rock.[3]

The new Cliff House would be spectacular, nothing like the one it replaced. There would be four main floors each 91 feet by 140 feet, a 27-foot square tower, and a basement, all accessible from a fast elevator. Starting at the top, here is the arrangement of the floors:

7. An observatory on top of the tower, with a camera obscura to provide 360-degree images of the surrounding region

6. Meeting rooms in the tower

5. Photograph gallery, receptions rooms, and parlors

4. Two large parlors, one for ladies only, about twenty private lunch rooms, a large art gallery for displaying treasures that Mr. Sutro collected from around the world, and an open veranda

3. The main floor, at street level, with a large dining room, parlor, ten small dining rooms, barroom, kitchen and pantry, and a glassed-in veranda

2. "Popular-Price Floor," where food and drink prices were to be comparable with those in the city; with a kitchen, barroom, one large and four small public dining rooms, parlor, butcher shop, employee dining room, lavatories, and glassed-in veranda
1. (Basement) Boiler room, a dynamo for emergency power, laundry, workshops, and 10 sleeping rooms for employees

All verandas were to be 20 feet deep on the ocean side and 16 feet deep on the north and south sides.[4,5]

The photos below show the new Cliff House in various stages of construction.

Opposite, top: Second Cliff House, early construction 1895. Note diagonal supports from cliff at far left. *Opposite, bottom:* Second Cliff House, later construction, 1895. *Current page, top:* Victorian Cliff House from above Sutro Heights parapet with ship in background, 1895. Image from Cliff House Project (courtesy Gary Stark). *Above:* Victorian Cliff House from the beach (author's collection).

The second Cliff House had two opening nights, the first during a full moon on January 4, 1896, featuring a masquerade ball. After window repairs necessitated by a fierce storm on Friday, January 17, the formal opening occurred on Saturday, February 1. It was a momentous day, as two other major developments reached completion. The Sutro Baths were dedicated, and the Sutro Electric Railway opened the same day. Sutro, who was now mayor of San Francisco, used the occasion to rail against big corporations. His specific target was the Southern Pacific Railroad, and in particular its president, C.P. Huntington. Sutro said, in part, "Monstrous corporations are the bane of the people. Railroads are grinding the substance out of our farmers and our workingmen." Other speakers supported the attack and praised Sutro for his accomplishments and for fighting big business throughout his career.[6] With three of his major projects completed at once, February 1, 1896, was quite likely the proudest day and the high point of Adolph Sutro's life.

Ironically, given Sutro's attack on the railroads, among the first visitors to the new Cliff House were Cornelius Vanderbilt, who made his immense fortune in railroads, and Chauncey Depew, his attorney and the president of the New York Central Railroad. The *San Francisco Chronicle* of April 6, 1896, said, "Both Mr. Vanderbilt and Mr. Depew declared that in all their travels around the world they had never seen anything to compare with the (Sutro) baths, and were profuse in their expressions of praise."[7]

Later visitors included three of the Bonanza Kings, James Flood, James Fair, and John Mackay. Also, U.S. presidents Ulysses S. Grant, Rutherford B. Hayes, William McKinley, Theodore Roosevelt, and William Howard Taft, as well as celebrities Sarah Bernhardt, Mark Twain, and Bret Harte all visited the second Cliff House.[8]

Adolph Sutro did not live to see the great San Francisco earthquake. As we will discuss in Chapter 37, he died on August 8, 1898.

Top: **Cornelius Vanderbilt, ca. 1860.** *Above:* **Chauncey Depew, ca. 1908.**

CLIFF HOUSE WAS SAVED AFTER ALL

SAN FRANCISCO, April 22. — A thorough inspection made by a representative of the Associated Press, who made the trip in an automobile, shows that comparatively little damage was done in the vicinity of the Cliff House. The Cliff House itself not only stands, but the damage sustained from the earthquake shock to this historic building will not exceed, according to the statement of Manager Wilkins, $500. In fact, the escape of the Cliff House is one of the curious features of the disaster which has befallen San Francisco. The famous Sutro Baths, located near the Cliff House, with its hundreds of thousands of square feet of glass roofing, also was practically unharmed. Only a few of the windows in the Sutro Baths and in the Cliff House were broken and the lofty chimney of the pumping plant of the former establishment was cracked only slightly.

Manager Wilkins of the Cliff House notified the General Relief Committee that he would turn over his establishment, as well as the immense stables of his resort, which are unharmed, to the housing of the homeless. The only difficulty about the acceptance of this tender would be the difficulty of transporting supplies that distance. The water supply of the Cliff House and buildings in that vicinity has been cut off, but it is expected that an independent supply will be arranged for some time to-day.

The entire district lying west of Golden Gate Park and along the beach from Golden Gate southward suffered less from the earthquake than probably any other section of the San Francisco peninsula.

Despite rumors to the contrary, the second Cliff House survived the cataclysmic April 18, 1906, earthquake and fire with less than $500 in damage.

But it was to be a short reprieve. On September 7, 1907, while the Cliff House was closed for renovations, James Wilkins, the former proprietor, and watchman Owen Mulvaney discovered smoke rising from an opening in the floor of the south porch. Within minutes the wooden structure was engulfed in flames. Wilkins was overcome by smoke and had to be carried out of the building by firemen. Despite immediate response by the nearby fire company, the building, after a spectacular 11-year life, was a total loss.[9] Disaster had struck the Cliff House yet again.

Left: Article from *Sacramento Union*, April 23, 1906. *Above:* Victorian Cliff House burning on September 7, 1907. Images from Cliff House Project (courtesy Gary Stark).

Chapter 34

Glass Houses

The cure for anything is salt water: sweat, tears or the sea.
—Isak Dinesen

When he was planning and building the Sutro Tunnel in Nevada, Adolph Sutro faced many challenges, both natural and man-made. In addition to digging through four miles of rock and soil to hit a target buried 1,800 feet below ground, he had to raise $3.5 million despite the relentless opposition of the Bank Ring.

Now that he had his own money, both from the sale of his Sutro Tunnel stock and from profitable real estate transactions in San Francisco, the financial problems no longer existed. But his projects at Lands End, especially Sutro Baths, posed significant engineering problems that no one had previously encountered. By the time the Sutro Baths were completed, Sutro had conceived and executed a plumbing system that would fill the Baths with 1.8 million gallons of heated ocean water in as little as one hour. He also had to address more mundane issues; an on-site laundry could wash and dry 20,000 rental bathing suits and 40,000 towels daily.

More than any of Sutro's other projects, the Sutro Baths evolved. That's not to say that Sutro did not have plans, but he kept changing them.

His first plan was for a simple but ingenious self-maintaining saltwater aquarium. In mid–1884, Sutro decided to combine natural features of the coastline with his intimate knowledge of tunnel construction. When exploring the westernmost point of his Lands End property, he discovered a natural catch basin that filled with water when particularly strong waves crashed onto the rocks. Just south of this point was a cove with a large natural depression. Sutro reasoned that if he could transport water from the catch basin to the depression, he would have an aquarium that would be filled with sea creatures.

Sutro had spent his life moving water from one place to another, first with a pipeline to supply water to the new woolen mill at Memel, East Prussia, and then with the Sutro Tunnel to drain water from the Comstock mines, so the aquarium project was second nature to him.

The aquarium complex was completed around 1890, but no photos from that time clearly show its operation. The following current photos illustrate how it worked:

At high tide, waves carried water and sea creatures over a natural rock wall and into the catch basin at the center.

Sutro dug the eight-foot-high, 153-foot-long tunnel on the right side of this photo to carry the water and sea creatures from the catch basin. The opening to the left carried excess water from the aquarium back to the Pacific Ocean.

The water and ocean life were deposited in the aquarium so Sutro and his guests could observe them. The 14-foot-high seawall shown above, separating the aquarium from the ocean, required three tries before it was stable. The first two walls, including $70,000 of concrete, sank into the sand. The third attempt, built on top of the previous two, was successful and survives today.

The aquarium, which captured water and small creatures, soon bored Sutro. He had a bigger and better plan. He decided to convert the aquarium to a settling pond for an adjacent saltwater swimming pool.

Sutro's idea was for a single large pool filled with unheated seawater. Then he realized that 55-degree water would not be conducive to swimming, so he decided to heat the water.

In this version, the aquarium area clarified the seawater by allowing silt to drop to the bottom of the pond. A powerhouse would heat and filter the water and a large pool would provide ample area for swimming.

But what temperature should the water be? Sutro had an answer for that too—he would create multiple pools at different temperatures. John Martini, a former National Park Service Ranger, a guide at the Lands End area, wrote the definitive book on the Sutro Baths.[1] The following description is derived from his book.

The Settling Pond (previously the Aquarium) at the north end held 500,000 gallons of seawater.[2]

There were seven pools or tanks, six saltwater and one freshwater:

- Tank 1, the largest, was L-shaped, 275 feet long and 150 feet wide on the south end, with water between 78 and 82 degrees, containing 1,310,000 gallons. A deeper diving tank was later added on the north end of Tank 1.

- Tanks 2 through 5 were each 28 feet by 75 feet, with progressively warmer water, containing 65,000 gallons each. Tank 2 was usually covered to provide a stage and exercise area for swimmers.

- Tank 6 was 50 feet by 75 feet, with water as warm as 90 degrees, containing 115,000 gallons. Tank 6 was designated for women and children, but this limitation was generally ignored.

- The freshwater plunge tank was set at 62 degrees.

This plan was far more ambitious than just a single swimming area and required a 286-foot-long concrete wall six feet thick and nine feet high on the west side to protect the tanks from the sea. Construction of the wall and other features was underway by November 1890.

One problem remained. With no covering, the heated water would rapidly cool. And remember the quote attributed to Mark Twain, "The coldest day I ever spent was a summer's day in San Francisco." Who would want to swim outdoors on the cool, breezy Pacific Coast?

Of course, Adolph Sutro had an answer: He would enclose the entire swimming area in a massive wood, steel, and glass structure. On August 5, 1891, Sutro advertised for the design of the Sutro Baths:

> To Architects. The undersigned invites Architects to furnish designs for structures at his proposed bathing establishment, consisting of arrangements of bathhouses and offices: also for glass to cover

Baths construction in progress, 1891.

baths. Premium for best approved design, $500, designs to be submitted on or before August 31, 1891. For particulars inquire F.T. Newberry at his office, Room 30, Montgomery Block.

Adolph Sutro[3]

Allowing less than one month for such a monumental design task seems unreasonable, but Sutro was always impatient. He awarded the architectural contract on November 11, 1891, to the San Francisco firm of Emil Lemme and C.J. Colley.

In an interview with a *San Francisco Chronicle* reporter, Sutro said, "At first I will run the place myself, but when its success is assured and everything is in perfect working order I will probably lease the whole place."[4] Sutro was driven by the challenge. He did not shirk difficult tasks; he sought them. But when he had met the challenge, he moved to the next one.

Sutro Baths was an enormous project. It took the architects nearly a year to find a supplier and write a contract for the steel-framed glass roof, which included over 100,000 square feet of glass.

With an area of just under three acres, Sutro Baths were the largest enclosed swimming facility in the world.[5]

An August 27, 1893, article in the *San Francisco Morning Call* was headlined, "THE SUTRO BATHS ARE RAPIDLY NEARING COMPLETION."[6] The article speaks with wonder about the transformation of the area:

> Once there was a huge depression on the north side of the road that runs to Sutro Heights, and in the depression or gully was a sea of sand, and rock, and seaweed and spray, and the gulls went there to roost. "That will always remain a wild and barren place," people said.
> When it is completed San Francisco will have an institution of which she may be justly proud. There is no bathing establishment in this country as large, as complete, as convenient or as luxuriously appointed.

The writer was overoptimistic about the completion date for Sutro Baths. He wrote, "If the work be rushed it can be finished in a little over a month's time." It took another eight months, until April 1894, to complete construction and interior finishing. But on May 1, 1894, Adolph Sutro announced that the opening of the Baths would be delayed indefinitely.

The problem was not with the facility. The largest indoor swimming facility in the world did open in May 1894 for tours, concerts, professional swimming competitions, and trick diving, but not for public swimming.

The problem was the hated Southern Pacific Railroad. The SPRR bought the Cliff House and Ferries Railroad from the Powell Street Railroad Company in 1893. Under Powell Street RR management, roundtrip fares were kept at the 10¢ level specified in the purchase agreement when they bought the line from Gustav and Adolph Sutro in 1887. But when the SPRR bought the line, they eliminated the use of transfers, effectively doubling the roundtrip cost to 20¢. That amount, which Adolph Sutro thought far too expensive for the working man, was the very reason he had built the Cliff House and Ferries RR in the first place. Never one to dodge a fight with the SPRR, which he called "The Octopus" for the way it controlled everything, Sutro not only delayed the opening of the Sutro Baths but he also erected fences around Sutro Heights and the Cliff House. Anyone seen arriving on the SPRR trains was charged 25¢ to pass through the fences. Patronage on the SPRR trains soon dropped by 75 percent.[7]

Doubling down on his opposition to the SPRR, Sutro obtained a franchise for a new electric street railroad running mainly along Clement Street north of Geary Boulevard. Work on the new line started on October 26, 1894. Also, as the Populist Party candidate for San Francisco mayor, Sutro campaigned against "The Octopus," further emphasizing the greed of the Southern Pacific. Finally, in November 1894, just five days

Sutro Street railway, depot, and baths. Image from Cliff House Project (courtesy Dennis O'Rorke).

before Sutro won the election for mayor, the SPRR relented and reinstated the use of transfers. But it was too late. Sutro continued work on his street railway, and it opened to great acclaim on February 1, 1896.

The *San Francisco Call* gushed, "The opening of the new road was an epoch in the history of San Francisco. It punctuated the time when the domination of the Market-street Railway Company (controlled by Huntington's SPRR) ceased and the rights of the people began." "The new road is well equipped. It is an electric line and excellent time is made. There was a great contrast yesterday, exemplifying the feeling of the people between the crowded cars of this road and the empty vehicles of the octopus."[8] Later the same week, the *Call* reported, "The Sutro electric railroad..." "carried last Sunday 20,000 passengers, or 10,000 each way." "Yesterday afternoon the cars were running on a 7½ minute schedules and were fairly well crowded with passengers."[9]

With the 10¢ roundtrip fare issue decided, it was time to open the Sutro Baths officially. After a dedication on February 1, 1896, the same day the Sutro Street Railway and the new Victorian Cliff House opened, Sutro Baths opened to the public on March 14. At last, the public could swim in comfort in heated saltwater pools. Visitors paid 10¢ to enter the building, and for that price could see exhibits that Sutro had gathered from his world travels. A swimsuit (suits issued by Sutro Baths were mandatory until the mid–1930s), towel, and private changing room cost an additional 15¢.

What would a visitor to Sutro Baths see? It was a wonderland. Just past the ticket booth was a massive stuffed sea lion, nicknamed Ben Butler, who had been king of Seal Rocks west of the Cliff House until his death on July 6, 1895. Beyond Ben were glass cases holding Egyptian mummies and sarcophagi; stuffed polar bears, pythons, and birds; seashells and geology specimens; and twin staircases down to the Promenade Level.

The Promenade ran along the south and east sides of the building and overlooked the pools 50 feet below. Descending from the Promenade, the Grand Staircase took visitors down to the Bathers' Promenade at pool level. Bleachers along the Grand Staircase allowed spectators to observe the swimmers below.

Marilyn Blaisdell, long-time proprietress of the Cliff House gift shop and collector of San Francisco memorabilia, and her son Robert published an iconic book of Sutro Baths photos. In the introduction to that book, Robert includes a description of the entertainment and activities at the Baths. He lists these and other performers:

Woolen swimsuits were standard for women and men. Image from Cliff House Project (courtesy Gary Stark).

- Professor Karl, "the marvelous Anthropic Amphibian who eats, drinks, smokes, writes, and sleeps underwater";
- "Charmian, Queen of the air, the greatest girl aerialist in the world," whose "leaps and dives into a net from the trapeze have never been accomplished by a woman";
- Professor M.H. Gay and his wonderful dog, Jack, "...the highest diving dog act in the world"; and
- Zeda, "the boneless boy wonder."

Activities included:

- A "Monster May Day Festival with ... a beautiful queen, triple May poles, 1,000 children in grand march and the butterfly ballet." This annual event often drew 9,000 spectators.
- A Grand International Tug of War;
- Underwater walking race with each racer carrying a 50-pound dumbbell in each hand;
- Diving for gold (coins); and
- A 50-yard doughnut race, where each contestant had to eat six doughnuts before starting.[10]

One of four ceramic muses that greeted visitors to Sutro Baths, presently in the Cliff House (photo by author).

May Day at the Sutro Baths, 1897.

Sutro Baths broadsides (courtesy Sutro Library, California State Library).

Dr. Ron Rohrer, a professional colleague and friend of mine, recalled his time at Sutro Baths when he was a youngster: "I remember once whacking my head going down the slide and getting a bloody nose. I also remember getting right back on the slide once the bleeding abated. We didn't even bother with the Cliff House; Playland at the Beach and Sutro Baths were the destinations."

There are hundreds if not thousands of photos of Sutro Baths on the internet. I have chosen a few to illustrate the size and appearance of the building.

Sutro examining Sutro Baths during construction, ca. early 1890s.

Thousands of people at the Baths, May 1, 1896. Image from Cliff House Project (courtesy Dennis O'Rorke).

According to a 1900 article in the *San Francisco Examiner*, the Sutro Baths averaged 500 bathers on weekdays and 8,000 on Sundays and holidays.[11] Assuming the 8,000 figure applied to Saturdays as well as Sundays, at 25¢ per swimmer, the weekly gross would have been $4,625. By 1910, after Adolph Sutro had died and his daughter Emma Sutro Merritt was administering his estate, an appraisal placed the value of Sutro Baths at $242,500.[12] Profits then were just $12,000 per year.[13] Sutro himself once claimed that the building had cost him "over a half a million dollars."[14] As unique and amazing as Sutro Baths were, they had been a poor investment.

Opposite, top: Cliff House, Sutro Baths, and SS *Ohioan* shipwreck from above, 1936.
Opposite, bottom: Sutro Baths and Victorian Cliff House (both from GGNRA Collection).

Chapter 35

The Philobiblist

To build up a library is to create a life. It's never just a random collection of books.
—Carlos María Domínguez

From his childhood, Adolph Sutro had loved books. When he was just seven and living in Aachen, Prussia, he often overspent his allowance at local book sales. Much later, during his many trips overseas to seek financing and support for his Sutro Tunnel, he visited bookshops and made small purchases.

Acquisitions

In 1882 Sutro started buying in earnest. While work was progressing on the conversion of Sutro Heights from sand dunes to landscaped gardens, Sutro traveled to Europe, the Near East, the Far East, and South Asia. In addition to commissioning copies of classical statues for Sutro Heights, he bought books. Robert E. Cowan, a veteran San Francisco bookdealer, described some of Sutro's book-buying tactics in a 1917 article:

> He had a queer way of buying which was particularly successful in Italy. He'd go into a book shop and see ten or fifteen thousand volumes, mostly in pigskin or parchment. He'd ask how much was wanted per volume for the whole collection. Perhaps the dealer would say, "four lire." He'd offer two lire, and get the whole stock. And usually, it would be a bargain. Or he'd go to the old monasteries and ask the monks to sell their old treasures. They'd refuse, whereupon he'd draw from his pockets handfuls of American gold, and the impoverished monks would yield. These methods of buying account for the enormous heterogeneous mass of books in the Sutro collection. He didn't live long enough to round the collection out.[1]

But Sutro was not a collector of random titles; he had a clear focus for his library. He said,

> The wealth of man can be enjoyed only a short portion of the immeasurable span of time, ... and I resolved to devote some portion of this wealth for the benefit of the people among whom I have so long labored. I first resolved to collect a library, a library for reference, not a library of various book curiosities, but a library which shall compare with any in the world.[2]

Sutro's perseverance and compulsion, repeatedly demonstrated during the tunnel project, carried over to his book buying. If a publication met his criteria of having undisputed historical or literary value and of documenting the development and growth of Western civilization from antiquity to modern times and the spread of that civilization, it qualified for his library. Sutro did not limit his acquisitions to English; French, German, Italian, Spanish, and Latin were equally acceptable. Likewise, books were not the only format. Pamphlets, prints, periodicals, manuscripts, and broadsides were fair game. Because he had been to London so often seeking tunnel money, he felt at home and would go sightseeing there. But he could not pass an antiquarian bookstore without stopping, and it was not unusual for him to pile so many books in his taxi that he had no room to sit down. He became known as the "California Book Man."[3]

Private book collections of deceased owners were another favorite source of publications for Sutro. The Sunderland Library, originally founded by Charles Spencer, third Earl of Sunderland in the 1690s, was described as "the finest in Europe" in 1703.[4] It featured material from the period of the English civil wars and also political and social works from the 18th and 19th centuries. Sutro bought about 30,000 items from this library.[5]

In Belgium, Sutro bought several thousand volumes originally from the Buxheim Library. Started by the Carthusian Monastery in Buxheim, Bavaria, in 1402, the library was confiscated by Prussia under the June 20, 1875, law and placed in the hands of trustees.[6] When that trustee needed money in 1883, Sutro met his need and obtained manuscripts, incunabula,[7] and 16th- and 17th-century books with woodcut illustrations.

In Augsburg, Germany, Sutro bid at the auction of the library of Baron Wolfgang Heribert von Dalberg. He prevailed on 8,000 volumes, largely in the natural sciences and medicine, including transactions and journals of several learned societies.

Sutro's travels in Europe gave him the opportunity to attend daughter Emma's marriage to George Merritt. The wedding took place in London on March 27, 1883. By then both George and Emma were medical doctors.

The downside of being in Europe was that Adolph missed the gala celebration of his mother's 80th birthday. Adolph's brother Theodore had arranged the party for Rosa, which took place in New York City on March 14, 1883. Thirty-six of Rosa's fifty-one living descendants attended, but none of Adolph' family were among them.[8] Less than six months later, on August 1, 1883, Rosa died.[9]

After the break for Emma's wedding, Adolph continued traveling and buying books. In 1883, the Kingdom of Bavaria needed money, and Sutro obtained permission to review the holdings of the Royal State Library in Munich and purchase duplicate imprints. Anxious to continue his travels, Sutro engaged Carl Friedrich Mayer, a Munich book dealer whom Sutro had dealt with many times, to examine the library contents. While Sutro traveled on to the Near East, Mayer diligently scanned the holdings and ended up purchasing 13,000 volumes for Sutro. When packaged for shipment, these books filled 86 cases, of which 33 held precious and unique incunabula.

Upon seeing the quality of Mayer's work, Sutro realized that he could not accomplish his objectives for his library by himself. He had business and projects in California that demanded his attention. Mayer was in the book trade and had the required specialized knowledge, contacts, and language skills. Sutro made him an offer, and Mayer agreed to move to London, where he would become Sutro's purchasing agent and also manage the storage, cataloging, packing, and shipping of the books. He started this full-time position in May 1884 and received £20 per month.[10] Sutro expected all of his senior employees to be in frequent contact with him, and Mayer wrote weekly and later biweekly letters detailing all aspects of his work. Sutro continued to stress that he wanted to establish a reference library, one that would have practical value. He decided to focus on science and technology, with a secondary emphasis on political and cultural history, and Mayer followed Sutro's instructions faithfully. He sometimes bought directly from bookshops, but mainly at book auctions.

Most auctions sold books by the lot, usually 25 books tied together without separate descriptions. Thus, it was difficult to ascertain the content or even the subject matter of the individual books. But Mayer solved this problem by studying the preauction catalogs and examining the lots in advance to determine which ones were of interest, especially those containing books in the natural and physical sciences, medicine, and engineering. For example, in January 1885, Mayer was able to obtain a complete set of 76 volumes of the *Journal and Proceedings of the Royal Geographical Society of London*.[11] Occasionally, the sale catalogs were published early enough for Sutro to examine them himself and select the offerings he was most interested in, but it was mostly up to Mayer to make the selections.

Sutro allocated about £300 per month for book purchases, and resisted Mayer's encouragement to buy rare items, sticking instead to his plan for a reference library with practical value.[12] As purchases increased, Sutro found it necessary to appoint a business manager to oversee the London operation. Robert Warner filled that position and managed all financial transactions, including paying Mayer and his assistant, E. Hofstätder. Sutro's book-buying hobby had become a book-buying business.

Near the end of 1886, Sutro apparently decided that he no longer needed an overseas agent and started to close the London operation. By late spring 1887, Sutro was back to buying books himself, and he purchased on a wide variety of subjects. He bought a collection of theater-related works, early plays, manuscripts, and dramatic works from San Francisco actor Walter Leman; 18th- and 19th-century British newspapers and journals from dealers in England and Scotland; and a high-quality collection on the natural sciences from another San Francisco collector, Robert Woodward.

In 1889, Sutro traveled to Mexico and Cuba, and this trip led to a significant expansion of the growing Sutro collection. The distinguished Librería Abadiano bookstore was going out of business, and Sutro bought the entire inventory, consisting of "tens of thousands" of items representing "the most important and complete collection of 19th-century Mexican political, religious and related imprints and ephemera to be found anywhere in the world."[13] There were titles published in Mexico in the 16th century from the earliest printing presses in America. Other holdings included religious tracts and other church documents, and early reports of the Spanish conquest and colonization. The most important portion of the holdings was a collection of 35,000 pamphlets, broadsides, and flyers documenting the Mexican War of Independence and the subsequent political conflicts.[14] This single purchase greatly expanded the size of Sutro's library and placed it among the most important repositories of Mexican heritage documents.

What to Do with All These Books?

Purchasing books and other printed materials was only the beginning. More important but far less exciting were the problems of fumigating, repairing, sewing, binding, storing, and cataloging these publications, which now numbered well over 100,000. With no library building yet in existence, Sutro sent the books first to a warehouse on Battery Street and then, when that facility was filled, to offices on Montgomery Street. While he studied European theories on library design and organization, Sutro hired George Moss as his chief librarian and Fredric Perkins as his assistant to do the less glamorous work. They worked at the Montgomery Street location along with a bookbinder, a book sewer, and several clerks. Expenses for salaries, furniture, shelving, bookcases, office supplies, janitorial service, and a night watchman were a constant financial drain, but Sutro was not concerned. In 1887, he authorized the construction of a room dedicated to fumigation, and in 1892 a separate room for bookbinding.

The burgeoning library was a curiosity to the general population, and they created a carnival-like atmosphere when hundreds of cases of books arrived at the San Francisco wharves. But students and faculty from Stanford and the University of California at Berkeley showed a more serious interest when they started using the Montgomery Street facility as a research resource. Eventually, scholars across the country learned of the Sutro Library, even though there was no formal building of that name. Cornell University cofounder and president Andrew Dickson White wrote of the library after his 1892 visit and in a later letter to Sutro:

> With considerable acquaintance among the libraries of the United States, I should rank this one already among the first four in value, and it is rapidly increasing." "All to whom I have spoken ... joined me in my wonder at the foresight and depth of thought which has prompted you not to create a popular public library, which any one can do, but one of the great libraries of the World for scholars....[15]

By then (1892), the Sutro Library comprised over 250,000 volumes and was one of the largest private libraries in the United States.[16] Included in the collection were 3,000 volumes of incunabula, estimated to be one-seventh of all such books in existence.[17]

A Permanent Location

In his plan for Sutro Heights (see Chapter 29), Adolph designated a prominent location for a "Library or Museum." In 1886, President Edward S. Holden of the University of California and other dignitaries toured the proposed site, and Holden expressed his strong support. But various "experts" had reservations. They advised Sutro that the fog and sea air at that location would damage the books.

Of course, Sutro had other property in San Francisco. A few years later, he decided on a 26-acre site near the geographic center of San Francisco, then called Mount Parnassus (now called Mount Sutro). An article in the June 15, 1893, *San Francisco Morning Call* announced the plans for the library:

> His plans, which will probably be changed but little, if at all, provide for a building 200 feet long by 100 feet in width, running from north to south, with a large circular space in each end for reading-

rooms and for files of periodicals. Over the center of the building will be a dome, which would be on the line of First Avenue if it were continued in a southerly direction. The interior of the building will be open up to the glass roof with rows of stacks for books twenty feet deep and seven feet in height. There will be ten stories of these. As the height of each story of stacks will lie only seven feet, all the books may be reached without the use of ladders. Elevators will be put in for convenience in going from one story to another. In the basement, which will be entirely above ground, there will be numerous study rooms, a bindery and storerooms. The height of the shelving will be seventy feet, and the capacity of the shelves not less than 500,000 volumes. The cost of the building will be about $300,000 on the plans proposed. The library will not be a circulating but a reference library, and entirely free to the public.

In speaking of his library yesterday, Mr. Sutro said: "When the plan was conceived of putting up a library building for the use of the public, I first thought of building it on Sutro Heights, for I thought that the town would soon build out there and the library will last for centuries. However, there was some objection to going out to the edge of the peninsula, and in looking around for another suitable site, I found that I owned one near the park, just south of the present music stand. It is between those two hills and is a beautiful site, well adapted for a library, and entirely secure against fire. I consider that security against fire is the most important of all considerations in locating a library that is to last for centuries and is being built for the future. History shows us that libraries have been partly or entirely consumed by general conflagrations from the time of the loss of the great library in Alexandria down to the present day. In this locality, with the large grounds surrounding and the high hills on either side, there will be as much security as can be obtained in any part of the city.

Some people suggest that this is very far out, but the place chosen is very near the geographical center of the city of San Francisco, and the city is pretty well built up from the east, and before many years buildings will stretch out westwardly toward the ocean."[18]

Adolph Sutro was elected mayor of San Francisco in 1894. But his beloved books still occupied his thoughts, and in September 1895 he presented a formal proposal to the regents of the University of California regarding the Mount Parnassus site for a library building. He summarized the advantages of that location, which was to include the "Affiliated Colleges" so that students and staff would have easy access to research materials. Those Affiliated Colleges included the Toland Medical School, from which his daughter Emma had graduated. Then he provided quotations from leading scholars confirming the superiority of the Sutro collection. Sutro ended his presentation by noting the close association of respected centers of learning with their libraries: Oxford with its Bodleian Library; Cambridge; Rome and the Vatican Library; Harvard; Yale; Princeton; and Cornell. He concluded, "San Francisco and California may well feel proud to have at the command of their students such a library, which will redound more to the credit of the State than anything that has up to this time been accomplished in that direction."[19]

Finally, the regents accepted Sutro's offer of land, and it was conveyed to them on October 10, 1895.[20]

Sutro's fitting motto, captured on his library bookplate, was ***Labor Omnia Vincit—Labor Conquers All***.[21]

By the time his term as mayor was over in January 1897, Sutro's health was compromised, and he was unable to continue with his many ambitious plans. The proposed library building near Mount Parnassus (now Mount Sutro) was never started. Sutro's impressive collection did not find a permanent home until August 1, 2012. As we shall see in the Epilogue, the journey to that home was long and tortuous.

CHAPTER 36

His Honor, the Mayor

If you got good elective officials in your day, it was a happy accident, better than you deserved.
—Robert A. Heinlein

According to that source of all information, Wikipedia, Adolph Sutro "was a German-American engineer, politician and philanthropist who served as the 24th mayor of San Francisco from 1895 until 1897."[1] Of those few people who have heard of Adolph Sutro, most know him as a former mayor of San Francisco. Ironically, being mayor was, without doubt, the least successful of his many ventures. In a recap of Sutro's life, a columnist for the *San Francisco Call* wrote,

> The mistake of Mr. Sutro's life was permitting himself to be elected Mayor of the city. He was not equipped with the peculiar gifts which fit a man for municipal administration, nor was his temper calm and serene enough to endure the wearing friction of office. For nearly twenty years he had been successful in everything he tried; he was intolerant of opposition and irascible when he was thwarted. The good-humored ridicule which he drew on himself by his assaults on the octopus diverted public attention from his noble qualities and blinded people to his lofty merits. It exposed him to being called a demagogue by politicians of small caliber. It led people who were quite incapable of understanding him to sneer at his noble schemes of public benevolence.[2]

How did it happen that on Thursday, November 8, 1894, Sutro was victorious in the election for mayor of San Francisco?[3]

Sutro had long harbored political ambition and had run unsuccessfully against William Sharon, John P. Jones, and William Stewart for U.S. Senator from Nevada.[4] After returning to San Francisco, he became popular with the laboring class by constructing the Cliff House and Ferries Steam Train so that a trip to Sutro Heights would cost just five cents. He was a soft touch for those in need, always carrying $2.50 and $5 gold pieces for those he met in the streets.

In early 1893, the Salvation Army inaugurated its Lifeboat program to give either two meals or one meal and lodging for the cost of a ten-cent ticket. Sutro immediately supported the charity by buying and distributing 1,000 tickets that he purchased for $100. Word spread quickly and the initial distribution point, Sutro's office on the Montgomery Block in San Francisco, was overwhelmed. After the first week, Sutro moved the ticket distribution to the Salvation Army Depot at Kearny and Sacramento Streets, where 100 tickets per day were handed out courtesy of Adolph Sutro.[5]

The public loved Sutro for his fights against the avarice of Collis Huntington and his monopolistic Southern Pacific Railroad (SPRR).[6] The SPRR had gained a near-monopoly on San Francisco streetcar service and eliminated transfers and raised fares. Sutro had resisted by charging SPRR riders a fee to enter Sutro Heights and the Cliff House. Then, to provide competition to the SPRR, Sutro built the Sutro Street Railway and charged one-half the fare.

As we saw in the chapter on the building of the transcontinental railroad, Collis Huntington was one of "The Big Four" in the founding and financing of the Central Pacific Railroad. Huntington and Sutro provide an interesting study in similarities and contrasts. Both were large, strong men. In his twenties, Huntington weighed 200 pounds; in his twenties, Sutro weighed 225. Both men were drawn to California by the siren song of gold, but neither was a gold-seeker. Rather, both saw the ready market for merchandise provided by the thousands of prospectors in an area that had no supplies or stores. Both Huntington and Sutro were too impatient to take the overland or around-the-Cape routes to California; both elected the challenging shortcut across Panama. Both men found Panama to be a horrid experience, filled with rain, mud, disease, filth, and lack of basic necessities. But both made it to San Francisco. Huntington became a merchant in Sacramento, and Sutro became a merchant in Stockton, both in 1850.

Then their paths diverged. Huntington saw the potential of Theodore Judah's vision for the transcontinental railroad and became the leader in making that vision a reality, with massive U.S. Government support, in 1869. Sutro saw the potential of the Comstock Lode and visualized a tunnel to drain and ventilate it. He made that tunnel a reality, with no U.S. Government support, in 1878. Both made fortunes, Huntington's an order-of-magnitude larger than Sutro's.[7] Huntington was focused on making money; Sutro was focused on solving challenges. When their paths crossed in San Francisco, these two men, who had so much in common, became bitter enemies.

The consensus of the population of San Francisco was that Huntington was a cold, avaricious monopolist; and that Sutro, although rich, cared for the common man.

Sutro fought Huntington and the railroad monopoly on the so-called Funding Bill, which would have allowed the Central Pacific Railroad to pay off its multimillion-dollar debt to the U.S. government, due in 1894, in 99 years, at 0.5 percent interest. Sutro saw this delay as a cancellation of the original debt and argued that the railroad was exploiting the public through unfairly high rates. At a mass meeting of citizens in San Francisco on June 19, 1894, Sutro led the speakers in attacking Collis Huntington and his Central Pacific Railroad. Among the resolutions passed by acclamation at that meeting were the following:

> That we believe, and we are so advised by able lawyers that the Government may recover the largest part of the $76,000,000 owing by the Central Pacific Railroad Company, by proceeding legally against the principal stockholders, who are multi-millionaires, and make them disgorge the money belonging to the United States.
>
> That C.P. Huntington, now in Washington, is self-convicted by the Colton letters as a corruptionist and a briber of courts, Legislatures and Congresses.
>
> That the secretary of this meeting is hereby instructed to forward copies of these resolutions to the President of the United States, to the members of both houses of Congress, to the press, to the Governors of States, to the chairmen of the State Central committees of all parties in every State of the Union; and resolved, that if the Associated Press is not muzzled it will telegraph these resolutions broadcast over the land.[8]

Another of Sutro's contributions to the public good was his support for the kindergarten movement, first conceived in Germany by Friedrich Froebel. Sutro, along with Justice Solomon Heydenfeldt and insurance magnate Samuel Levy, established in San Francisco the first nonsectarian, tuition-free, privately financed kindergarten in the United States. The founders believed that early education would lessen the impact of slums on children, and they aimed the program primarily at urban immigrants. By 1895, the founders and their large group of contributors had established 40 kindergarten classes in the city, serving more than 3,500 young students.[9]

The Populist Party, which was a distinct minority, noticed Sutro and approached him about running for mayor on their ticket. At a Sutro Heights breakfast in July 1894, two members of the executive committee of the Populist Party joined several Sutro friends and associates to discuss the upcoming election. The Populist Party needed a candidate who could win the election, and Sutro was that man. They overlooked the responsibilities that Sutro had as well as his failing physical health. More importantly, they ignored his personality—Sutro was not a compromiser; he was a general who gave orders to be carried out. He rarely delegated responsibility or authority, and if he did, he micromanaged. He was not a politician. Regardless of his unsuitability, the Populist Party offered,[10] and Sutro accepted the position as candidate for mayor.[11]

His campaign emphasized his opposition to the Southern Pacific Railroad, and to big business in general. Sutro was a man of the people.

Every daily paper and recognized political organization in the city opposed Sutro's candidacy.[12] But he won the election with an absolute majority over five other candidates, taking 31,254 votes out of about 60,000 total.[13] He became the first Jewish mayor of a major American city.

On election night, once it was clear that he had won, Sutro said,

> I shall endeavor to be just and fair to all, but the moment the aggressive corporations overstep the bounds of law I shall firmly oppose them, and if corrupt means are used I shall in my official capacity, endeavor to unearth and bring both the bribers and the bribed to justice. I shall try to bring about an honest, business-like, and economical administration to the affairs of the city.[14]

In his inaugural address, Sutro proposed a large number of new programs, especially improved education, better streets, and city-owned gas, water, electric, and sewer systems. None of these programs would come to fruition. One statement Sutro made on inauguration day was prescient, "Our climate makes us particularly susceptible to a general fire."[15] That fire would come in 1906, after Sutro's death.

As mayor, Sutro sup-

Sutro campaign poster emphasized his opposition to the Octopus, a.k.a. Southern Pacific Railroad (courtesy Sutro Library, California State Library).

ported women's suffrage and continued to oppose Collis Huntington and his Southern Pacific Railroad. But the city charter gave the mayor little power, and Sutro had no allies on the more-powerful Board of Supervisors.

After just six weeks in office, Sutro expressed his frustration to a newspaper reporter. He was quoted as saying:

> I am sick and tired of this filthy business of politics. Everywhere I look it is money, money, money; men are plundering and looting the city in a small and in a large way; if I expose them I am abused by my opponents. But it is humiliating to me, at my time of life, to be thrown into conflict with such men, and I wish I were a thousand miles away from politicians. I don't know why the board (Board of Supervisors) acts as it does. The members seem to be opposed to me and appear to delight in showing their hostility.[16]

After his first year in office, most days would find him escaping to a sanctuary, either the home of Clara Kluge on Steiner Street or his 2,000-acre Arcadia Ranch near Calistoga in the Napa Valley.[17,18] By April 1896, Sutro was disgusted and physically exhausted, and asked for and received a two-month leave of absence. He retreated to his Arcadia Ranch to recuperate. By early July, with unsigned documents piling up on his desk and city government grinding to a halt, the *San Francisco Call* printed a story titled, "Who is Mayor of this Town?"[19]

Regarding his term as mayor, Sutro commented:

> What have I accomplished as Mayor? Very little. The Mayor is little more than a figurehead.... I have always been master of a situation; I have always had a number of men under my employ, and they did as I told them. I could not manage the politicians.[20]

On New Year's Day, 1897, Sutro happily entertained at Sutro Heights. In two days, he would no longer be mayor of San Francisco. He, the politicians, and the citizens were pleased with that prospect. No one asked him to run for reelection.

Sutro left office on January 3, 1897. On January 7, the U.S. House of Representatives began consideration of the Railroad Funding Bill. On January 9, toward the end of the acrimonious debate, California Congressman Samuel Hilborn took the floor to express his opposition to the funding bill. In a speech so full of details and numbers that all his fellow representatives must have fallen asleep, Hilborn concluded as follows:

> What are the admitted facts as they will go down in history?
> The United States advanced for the construction of these roads, in principal and interest which it has paid or will pay up to maturity, $178,884,249, and donated over 26,000,000 acres of land worth $65,073,836; in all, $243,935,595. These advances of money were not donations to the companies, or to the individuals controlling them, in consideration of the construction of the roads. On the other hand, the terms of the act require them to repay the Government every dollar of principal and interest.
> The difficulties were not so great as were anticipated, and the sum advanced by the Government was greatly in excess of the necessities for construction. These men could have dealt honestly with the Government and still have become millionaires; but they chose the opposite course. Nearly half of the great sum placed in their hands by a confiding Government for the performance of a trust was misappropriated and diverted to their own use by the parties charged with the trust, who are now fabulously rich, while the companies in whose names they acted are left at last stripped of all means to pay, while the individual directors are millionaires.
> In other words, the directors have the money and the companies owe the debts.
> Congress ought not to condone such monstrous frauds, such misuse of public funds. To do so, especially after publishing to the world the particulars and proofs, as we have done, will be to say to

all the world that the American Congress considers these transactions quite up to the American standard of morality in dealing with public trusts.[21]

On January 11, 1897, the House of Representatives voted 168 to 102 to defeat the Southern Pacific Funding Bill,[22,23] much to the delight of private citizen Adolph Sutro. The Southern Pacific loss was the high point of Sutro's previous two years.

Chapter 37

Decline, Demise, Disputes

If you want a happy ending, that depends, of course, on where you stop your story.
—Orson Welles

Within a year of leaving office as mayor of San Francisco in January 1897, Adolph Sutro, age 67, was suffering from diabetes and senile dementia. He returned to Sutro Heights to live out his days walking in his gardens, watching the Pacific Ocean with its fog banks, and hearing the sea lions bark and roar. Sutro had never been a man to make close friends. He said of himself, "I am not (of) a social disposition. I am very much alone.... I can spend more hours alone than any man you ever saw."[1] So he was content with his Sutro Heights estate, his Victorian Cliff House, Sutro Baths, and his library of books.

This sweet retirement did not last long. Adolph suffered apoplexy (now called a stroke) in September 1897 and was unconscious for several hours. He recovered, but had another occurrence in late November 1897 and was near death. Again he recovered, but his mental faculties were impaired.[2]

In early 1898, the Red Bluff, California, *Daily News* reported, "He is both mentally and physically incapable of attending to business," and "his relatives are talking of having a guardian appointed for him."[3] In just two weeks the talking became action. On Saturday, February 5, 1898, Superior Court Judge Edward A. Belcher declared Sutro mentally incompetent and appointed his favorite child, Dr. Emma Sutro Merritt, as his guardian.[4]

Two of Sutro's children, Charles and Clara, had moved to Sutro Heights to live with and care for their father.

Just three months later, on May 5, Emma Sutro Merritt arrived at Sutro Heights with a carriage and two attendants with the intention of moving her father to her home at Van Ness and Sutter Streets in downtown San Francisco. In a soap opera–worthy scene, despite the pleas of siblings Charles and Clara, the two attendants carried the oblivious Adolph Sutro to the carriage. Before they could load Sutro onto the carriage, Clara grabbed the whip from the seat and swung it over the horses, causing them to gallop across the landscaped yard of Sutro Heights. She had hoped to damage the carriage and thus delay the removal of her father until she could rally the rest of her siblings. A few overturned statues later, the horses returned to the driveway and Sutro was successfully loaded aboard and carted off to Emma Sutro Merritt's home. Emma claimed that she, as a doctor, would be better able to care for her father at her home. Other observers suspect that her motives were not so altruistic and that she wanted to prevent Sutro from signing any papers that would threaten her inheritance.[5]

Nothing that Emma Sutro Merritt or anyone else could do would deny the inevitable. Although he had a few lucid moments after arriving at Emma's home, he died there three months later, on Monday, August 8, 1898. In a rare show of unanimity, the children agreed that his funeral should be at Sutro Heights, and his body was moved there early on the morning of August 9. While the rest of the country celebrated the imminent conclusion of the Spanish-American War, the Sutro family mourned.

Adolph Sutro's funeral was private, with only about thirty family members and intimate friends attending.[6] Though Sutro was not religious, he maintained Jewish ties. At the funeral, the rabbi of San Francisco's Congregation Sherith Israel, Jacob Nieto, observed, "So long as one stone remains above the other in San Francisco.... Sutro will be remembered as the one man who fearlessly fought against overwhelming odds to protect the rights of the people."[7] Despite his earned wealth, Adolph Sutro was a man of and for the people. Sutro's body was taken to the crematory at Odd Fellows Cemetery. His ashes were moved several times, lost at least once, and in 1979 were allegedly discovered in an urn on Sutro Heights, overlooking his beloved Seal Rocks. James Delgado, then an historian with the Golden Gate National Recreational Area, was quoted as saying, "We are 98 percent sure that it is Sutro."[8] The urn was taken to a mortuary for evaluation but subsequently disappeared. Where's Adolph?

Many people believed that Adolph Sutro had written a will sometime around 1895. But the only will ever discovered was dated May 22, 1882, soon after Adolph and Leah had separated. The 18-page document was read to Sutro's children on August 11, 1898, and published in its entirety in the August 12 edition of the *San Francisco Call*.[9]

The most interesting contents of most wills are who was excluded, who received the smallest bequest, and who received the largest. Sutro's wife, Leah, who was alive when the will was written but who died on December 9, 1893, was not mentioned in the will. Likewise, Clara Kluge, whom Sutro did not meet until 1886, was not mentioned. Contrary to expectations that were based on Sutro's repeated verbal statements, neither Sutro Heights nor the Sutro Library collection was bequeathed to the city of San Francisco.

The smallest bequest went to Adolph's youngest sibling, Theodore Sutro. When Adolph was ending his association with the Sutro Tunnel Company, Theodore, a New York attorney, assisted in quietly selling Adolph's stock. Because Theodore was simultaneously promoting the fortunes of the tunnel company, he was afraid that Adolph's stock sales would depress the value of the shares. The two feuded bitterly, both about Adolph selling stock and about payment for the work Theodore did for his older brother. Adolph had the last word with his bequest of $1.00 to Theodore.

Hattie Trundle

Hattie Trundle, who notoriously rendezvoused with Sutro in Virginia City in 1879, received the largest bequest, as follows:

XVIII. Unto Miss Hattie Trundle of Washington D. C, heretofore known as Mrs. George Allen, the sum of fifty thousand dollars ($50,000) as a reparation, as far as it may be possible, for the injury done her by a scandalous charge, falsely and maliciously, at Virginia City State of Nevada, in the month of July 1879, then and there brought against her.

Finding Hattie Trundle, aka Mrs. George Allen, to give her the money turned out to be fruitless. She was reported to have returned to Washington, D.C., after the confrontation with Mrs. Leah Sutro in Virginia City in 1879. But according to an article in the August 19, 1898, *Topeka State Journal*,

> ... all the Trundles and George Allens in the city (Washington) have been visited. None of them knows anything of the woman named in the will. The Trundles in Washington all come from the Maryland family of that name. Even the older members have no recollection of the Virginia City story. The same is true of the Allens.[10]

One month later, the same newspaper reported,

> It has been learned that Mrs. Hattie Trundle, one of the beneficiaries under the terms of the late Adolph Sutro's will to the amount of $50,000, died near Washington, D.C. about two years ago. An effort is being made to trace her heirs.[11]

As would be expected when a large amount of money is at stake, the heirs eventually surfaced. They filed suit to claim the bequest, and their case made it to the California Supreme Court. The court held that the legacy lapsed with the death of the beneficiary. The only way it might have been arranged for the heirs would have been for Sutro to have named a substitute for Miss Trundle.[12,13] The $50,000 bequest went back into the Sutro estate, becoming a further reason for continued disputes.

Other Beneficiaries

Each of Sutro's six children was to receive $10,000 from the initial distribution of funds and then split the residual estate. The only exception was Emma, who was also to receive all of her father's books and papers. This seemingly simple bequest further inflamed ill will between Emma and her siblings and resulted in protracted discussions and litigation with the city of San Francisco over Adolph's library.

Sutro named at least 75 other beneficiaries. These included other relatives (his mother, siblings, cousins, nieces, and nephews), judges, members of the U.S. House of Representatives and other politicians who had helped Sutro by supporting his tunnel, and Vassar College. Bequests ranged from $1 (as discussed above, this went to his youngest brother, Theodore) to $30,000 (to each of his three sisters). Because the will had been written more than 16 years earlier, many of the beneficiaries predeceased Sutro,[14] so their bequests were added back to the estate.

Sutro's will described his real estate holdings (about 1,150 acres) in excruciating detail and established a complicated trust to manage those properties until after the death of his last child. At that time, the trustees were to sell the properties and devote the proceeds, "...for such charities, institutions of learning and science and for premiums to be set apart for distinguished scholarships and scientific discovery and inventions as shall be directed by my executors."[15] The will identified the trustees, as follows:

XXVI. The said board of trustees shall consist of the Governor of the State of California, the Chief Justice of the Supreme Court of the State of California, the Presiding Judge of the Superior Court of the city and county of San Francisco, the United States Circuit Judge for the District of California, the Mayor of the city of San Francisco, the president of the Chamber of Commerce of San Francisco, the president of the board of regents of the University of California and their successors in office and six other members to be chosen by the above-named officers, three from amongst the leading bankers of San Francisco and the other three from amongst my male descendants or those of my brothers bearing the name of Sutro.[16]

Who Will Get the Money?

The maneuvering and fighting over Adolph Sutro's wealth started even before he died. On March 10, 1898, Clara Kluge, who later claimed to be Sutro's wife, gave a lengthy interview to a newspaper reporter. Portions of the story follow:

> Mrs. Kluge lives with her two little children, a boy and a girl, in a handsome stone and frame residence at the northeast corner of Steiner and Clay Streets. In the two years that she has occupied the house, she has furnished considerable gossip for her neighbors. Always well-dressed, conducting an expensive household and distant toward strangers, she has attracted the attention of several people whose interest has been heightened by the frequent visits which she received from Adolph Sutro. The millionaire, until his last illness, was seen at the house in his carriage almost daily, staying there often for hours at a time.
>
> In the Kluge ménage are two interesting children—a girl of 5 named Adolphine and a boy of 8 called Adolph. The boy is a blonde, while the girl is dark, with snapping brown eyes and curling hair, and bears a very striking resemblance to the Sutro family. Her mother, who claims to be a Sutro, has none of the family traits, but in the child they are very apparent.
>
> The children were ingenuously frank and obviously truthful. They said that Mr. Sutro, their "Papa," was very sick and that he had not been to see them for some time. They remembered that when he was well they often went to the Heights with their mother, when they lunched with "Papa," and that he often came to see them, on which occasions he usually came in the morning and went the next morning.[17]

Even though she was not mentioned in Adolph Sutro's will, Clara Kluge was using the newspaper to help establish her claim to a portion of the Sutro estate.

- Adolph's son, Edgar, filed suit on September 6, 1898, alleging that Adolph died intestate[18] because he was not of sound mind when he signed the 1882 will.
- A majority of the heirs, led by Sutro's children (excluding Emma) filed suit on October 6, 1898, to nullify the Trust clause of the will as it related to Sutro's real estate holdings. On January 18, 1899, Superior Court Judge James M. Troutt ruled that the Trust clause was invalid, thus placing Sutro's real estate holdings into the residual estate to be distributed to the heirs. Probate Judge James V. Coffey affirmed Judge Troutt's ruling in an October 30, 1905 decision.[19] On October 28, 1909, the California Supreme Court issued a final ruling that the trust described in Sutro's will was invalid, thus releasing 1,200 acres of valuable real estate back into the Sutro estate.[20] In May 1910, professional appraiser A.S. Baldwin issued his valuation for the real estate holdings of the Sutro Estate. Baldwin placed the total value at that time at just under $4 million, and said that amount could be increased to over $4.6 million if the properties were "put in shape."[21]

- On October 25, 1898, Clara Kluge filed a petition to be appointed guardian of her two children, whom she named as Adolph Newton Sutro, age 7, and Adolphine Charlotte Sutro, age 6. Clara claimed that Sutro had built a home for her and the children at Steiner and Clay Streets in San Francisco, and was providing support for the family.[22] No one objected, and Clara's petition for guardianship was granted by Judge Troutt on November 15.[23]
- On January 18, 1899, Edgar Sutro's suit against the will was dismissed.
- On January 19, 1900, Sutro's children (excluding Emma Sutro Merritt and Charles Walter Sutro) filed suit against the will alleging that there was a will executed later than the one signed in 1882. The same day Clara Kluge filed a similar suit alleging that there was a will dated 1895. A search of the Sutro Heights house failed to locate any such document.[24] Clara Kluge claimed a widow's portion of the estate and said her children, Adolphine Charlotte and Adolph Newton, should receive one-fourth of decedent's entire estate. She also asked for a jury to try the issues of fact raised by any answer to the petition.
- Between mid–1902 and early 1906, Clara Kluge sold 16 properties and contracted for the construction of a two-story frame home with attic and basement.[25,26] When or how she obtained those properties is not known.

On August 5, 1908 (10 years after Adolph Sutro died), the Sutro heirs asked the court to partition the estate, excluding the assets covered by the Trust clause, and distribute the portions.

There were three sets of claimants to Sutro's estate:

1. Clara Kluge;
2. Emma Sutro Merritt and Charles Walter Sutro; and
3. Sutro's other four children and over 75 other beneficiaries.

After two years of posturing and legal actions by all groups, Group 2, Emma Sutro Merritt and Charles Walter Sutro, agreed to pay Clara Kluge and her children a total of $100,000 to settle her claims. This money was to come from Emma and Charles's share of the estate and thus did not impact the amount that those in Group 3 would eventually receive. On January 21, 1902, the *San Francisco Call* reported that Clara agreed to accept $80,000 and each child $10,000 to rescind her claim on the Sutro estate.[27]

First Division Monument in President's Park, Washington, D.C.

Loading the Ship by Adolphine Sutro Fullerton (courtesy Christine A. Miller Collection).

But it took another 10 years for formal agreements to be signed. In a "DEED" signed June 8, 1912, "CLARA KLUGE, Also sometimes called CLARA KLUGE SUTRO," agreed in tortured legalese to withdraw all claims against the Sutro estate in return for "A VALUABLE CONSIDERATION."[28] Clara's daughter, Adolphine Charlotte Sutro, executed a similar document.[29] It is likely that Clara's son, Adolph Newton Sutro, signed a similar document, although I have not discovered it.

In later years Clara and her children bought and sold real estate in San Francisco.[30]

Adolph Newton Sutro became chairman of the California Committee of First Division Monument Association and worked for the erection of the battle monument honoring the First Division for its heroic efforts against the Germans in World War I.[31] The efforts of the Association succeeded, and the resulting monument is shown on page 220.

Portrait of a Woman (Standing) by Adolphine Sutro Fullerton (courtesy Christine A. Miller Collection).

Adolphine Charlotte Sutro lived in San Francisco, where she married N.N. Fullerton. She studied at the San Francisco Institute of Art during 1910–13 and moved to Los Angeles in 1937. Adolphine became an accomplished watercolorist and an untrained but talented architect.[32]

Her paintings are still available at galleries and on eBay. Two examples, both from the Christine A. Miller Collection are shown on page 221.

Clara Kluge Sutro died at age 80 on December 31, 1943, in Hollywood, California.[33] Adolphine Charlotte Sutro Fullerton died in Los Angeles on January 2, 1974, at age 81.[34] Adolph Newton Sutro died in Los Angeles on March 8, 1981, at age 89. He is buried at Arlington National Cemetery.[35]

There are four axioms to be learned from what happened to Adolph Sutro's estate:

- If one generation makes money, the next generation will fight over it.
- Be absolutely clear about how your assets are to be distributed after your death.
- Avoid probate court.
- The surest way to avoid conflict is to spend it all before you die!

CHAPTER 38

Epilogue—Nevada

There is no real ending. It's just the place where you stop the story.
—Frank Herbert

When Adolph Sutro left Nevada in 1879, he had resigned from the Sutro Tunnel Company and sold all his stock. The Comstock was in decline, and the Sutro Tunnel was not earning enough to pay back its investors. The town of Sutro was temporarily prosperous, but with reduced ore production, it, too, would decline. Let us explore what happened to the Comstock, the Sutro Tunnel, and the town of Sutro in the intervening years up to the present.

The Comstock

From 1859 to 1896, the Comstock mines produced about 192 million ounces of silver and 8.3 million ounces of gold, with 80 percent of that production before 1880.[1]

Exploration and production on varying scales and in varying locations have been undertaken on the Comstock Lode in every decade since its discovery. Because of excessive water and the expense of pumping it up to the level of the Sutro Tunnel (about 1,640 feet below Virginia City), all mining from 1920 to the present has taken place above the level of the tunnel. Major activities on the Comstock since 1920 include:

- In 1920, United Comstock Silver Mines consolidated ownership of the entire Gold Hill section of the Comstock Lode. They constructed the 2,500-ton-per-day capacity American Flat cyanide mill, the largest in the world at the time. The economics of this project were tenuous, and with a drop in silver prices, it closed between 1924 and 1926.[2,3]

- In 1933, Arizona Comstock Company began underground mining through the Hale & Norcross tunnel, followed by a surface mine known as the Loring Cut. Arizona Comstock processed its ore at a 110-ton-per-day flotation mill, but it was not economically effective, and money was not available to build a more efficient cyanide plant. The Arizona Comstock operation shut down in 1938.[4]

- In 1935, after several years of exploration and development on the Crown Point claim in Gold Hill, the Sutro Tunnel Coalition built a 100-ton-per-day cyanide mill to process both underground and surface mined ore. The Crown Point Mill operated profitably, treating primarily ores from the Crown Point and Yellow Jacket claims until it was shut down by order of the War Production Board in 1942. During WW II, the government deemed gold mines "nonessential" for wartime purposes. The intention was to shift resources to copper mining.[5]
- Since 2010, Comstock Mining Inc. has been operating old underground mines and two open pit mines, Lucerne and Billy the Kid, southwest of Gold Hill.[6] They reported a net loss of $12.9 million for 2016.[7]

Perhaps nothing shows the transformation of the Comstock region so clearly as the following photos of the Chollar-Hale & Norcross-Savage Combination Mines. Beneath the headframe is the deepest shaft on the Comstock, at 3,250 feet. Over $28 million of gold and silver were extracted from these mines from 1866 to 1874.[8] The building and equipment are gone, and only the massive hoisting structure remains.

An objective observer would conclude that gold and silver mining on the Comstock is now a marginal business at best. However, the area in general and Virginia City in particular have become a tourist destination, drawing more than 2 million visitors a year.

Underground tours of the Best & Belcher and Chollar Mines are among the most popular attractions.

Chollar-Hale & Norcross-Savage Combination Shaft circa 1880 (courtesy Special Collections, University of Nevada, Reno Libraries).

Above: In 2018, the hoist mechanism is all that remained of the Chollar-Hale structure. *Below:* The Ponderosa Saloon occupies the site of the Virginia City branch of the Bank of California. William Sharon lived upstairs. The underground tour of the Best & Belcher Mine starts inside (both photos by author).

Virginia City is a National Historic Landmark District and contains numerous historic properties that are separately listed on the National Register of Historic Places.

The Historical Society of Dayton Valley Museum in Dayton, Nevada, has a fine collection of relics, documents, and photos related to Adolph Sutro's time in Nevada. Patrick Neylan is the curator and a Sutro expert.

Sutro Tunnel

After the Sutro Tunnel Company went into bankruptcy in 1887, several of the former stockholders, led by Adolph Sutro's youngest brother, Theodore, reorganized under the name, The Sutro Tunnel Company and The Sutro Tunnel. In his 1887 report to the stockholders, Theodore sought to assure them that the tunnel was undamaged and functional.

> Mr. John Landers, the newly-elected Vice-President of the Company, ... writes under date of May 21, 1887, after a visit of inspection to the Sutro Tunnel, as follows: "The examination of the tunnel and property belonging to the Company resulted in finding everything connected with this great work in fine condition. The tunnel proper, over twenty thousand feet in length and it's south and north lateral branches, nearly eleven thousand feet additional, were in perfect repair.
>
> "Mr. C.C. Thomas (the tunnel superintendent), ... told me, when I inspected the tunnel on April 8, 1887, that it was then in better condition than it had ever been—far better than when he took charge of it in 1880.
>
> "...I may add my own testimony, after a thorough inspection of the property, that every part of the six and one-third miles of tunnels is at present open and in working order. There is no obstruction anywhere for mule teams on the many miles of track-rails."[9]

In that same report, Theodore Sutro provided a summary of income and expenses for the Sutro Tunnel. Net income for the three years prior to July 1887 totaled about $350,000. He painted a glowing picture for the future of the Comstock mines and therefore the Sutro Tunnel.

In 1898, mines below the level of the Sutro Tunnel attempted to reopen by pumping water up to the tunnel level. The 24 mining companies still operating on the Comstock formed the Comstock Pumping Association to coordinate the pumping operation.[10] But the wooden boxes meant to carry the water through the Sutro Tunnel had rotted, allowing hot water and steam to escape into the tunnel. This humid atmosphere caused the timbers in the tunnel to deteriorate, thus threatening the collapse of the entire tunnel.

New York lawyer Franklin Leonard, Sr. had been on the Board of Directors of Theodore Sutro's tunnel company and was a frequent critic of salaries paid to its officers. He finally made an offer to the stockholders that he would serve as president of the company without salary until it was in a better financial position. Tired of the criticism and faced with massive repair costs for the damaged tunnel, Theodore Sutro sold his stock in the tunnel company to Leonard in 1898. Five generations of the Leonard family have managed and maintained the Sutro Tunnel and the town of Sutro since 1898.[11,12]

To manage the tunnel company, Franklin Leonard, Sr., his wife, Sarah Lee, and their children moved into the Sutro Mansion in 1899. It was a traumatic transition for the family who had lived in luxury in New York, but they adapted to the isolation and desert-

Large drainpipe in Sutro Tunnel, ca. 1910.

like climate. Leonard's title was superintendent of the new Sutro Tunnel Company, and his job was to keep the tunnel open not only for mine drainage and ventilation but also for transporting ore and people.[13,14]

Leonard had to find a way to repair the damage to the tunnel caused by the hot water and steam. Based on Sutro's agreement with the mining companies, the tunnel company's only source of revenue was based on ore mined. But the mining companies could mine no ore unless they could pump water from levels below the tunnel. This Catch-22 situation was resolved in April 1905, when Leonard signed a contract with the Comstock Pumping Association. The Association agreed, over the next five years and at its own expense, to make all required repairs to the tunnel including the installation of 1,500 sets of new timbers, thus retimbering nearly the entire tunnel. In addition, they would build a 30-inch diameter wooden-stave pipe within the tunnel to carry the hot water to the tunnel portal.[15] The Sutro Tunnel continued to drain water from the Comstock mines until it was closed in 1932.

After Franklin Leonard, Sr. died, his son, Franklin, Jr., took over the management of the Sutro Tunnel properties. Franklin, Jr. developed the Crown Point mine and cyanide mill in 1935, as discussed in the previous section.

Government action can directly affect precious metal prices, and therefore the viability of mining. As part of U.S. Government action to control inflation, on August 15, 1971, President Richard M. Nixon suspended the convertibility of U.S. dollars into gold, thus making the price of gold free-floating. Released from its artificially imposed price constraint, from 1971 to 1979 gold rose in price from $44.60 to $459.00 per ounce, over a factor of 10.[16] That increase made gold mining far more attractive. The Leonard family (by now Jim Schryver, a Leonard relative, had become president of the Sutro

Interior of Sutro Tunnel, 1984 (courtesy Tim Roth, Virginia City, Nevada).

Tunnel Company) hired Greg Hess of Virginia City to reopen the first 1,600 feet of the Sutro Tunnel.

By 1984, the outside of the tunnel was still dilapidated, but Hess and his crew had replaced the supporting timbers and made the initial portion of the tunnel passable.

Schryver leased rights to the tunnel to the Houston Oil and Minerals Company. But rotting timbers and frequent cave-ins made the tunnel repair effort too costly, so Houston Oil instead turned to open-pit mining. By 1999, the tunnel supports had collapsed.

The nonprofit Comstock Foundation for History and Culture encourages the preservation and promotion of historical and cultural resources within the Virginia City National Historic Landmark District. In 2016 and 2017, the Foundation offered tours of the Sutro Tunnel and surrounding area. While no tour was offered in 2018, they hope to resume similar tours in the future.

Town of Sutro

The original town of Sutro is not on the National Register of Historic Places; in fact, it is on few maps. Since its peak population of 800 in 1879, the population has declined to zero today.

Having a man named Sutro and a town named Sutro is confusing. To compound that confusion, there is now a subdivision about three miles northeast of Dayton, Nevada, that is called Sutro. This settlement includes a new Sutro Elementary School

Top: Old Sutro Elementary School (courtesy Laura Tennant Collection). *Above:* New Sutro Elementary School (photo by author).

and is adjacent to but not on the land originally deeded to Adolph Sutro. For clarity, I shall refer to this modern subdivision as New Sutro and Adolph's town as Old Sutro.

From 1900 to about 1925, a few people lived in Old Sutro and used the warm mine drainage for agriculture. The warm water extended the growing season. The agricultural activity ceased in 1925 when the farmers moved to Dayton, and the original Old Sutro Elementary School was dismantled for building materials.

A 1909 article from the *Goldfield News* described ore being shipped through the Sutro Tunnel to a mill operating at the mouth of the tunnel, just as Adolph Sutro had envisioned:

> The Savage Mining Company is now running the Comstock Tunnel Company's mill at the mouth of the tunnel to full capacity and ore is being shipped daily through the tunnel to the mill. A new track has been built practically throughout the tunnel and a large amount of transportation is being handled early and without delay. The drainage facilities of the tunnel are now perfect to take care of the large increase of water being sent through from the C & C shaft. The pumping is being steadily increased every day and more water is now being raised from the lower levels than at any time since pumping was resumed some years ago.[17]

The milling activity at the mouth of the tunnel continued until the 1930s, milling mostly "custom ore" (i.e., on a contract basis). The mill was destroyed by fire in 1967.[18]

In October 1940, Albert and Lyla West and their three children (daughters, Corlene

Mill near the mouth of Sutro Tunnel. Photograph by Gus Bundy (courtesy Special Collections, University of Nevada, Reno Libraries).

Mill and mansion near the mouth of the Sutro Tunnel, circa 1939 (courtesy Nevada Department of Transportation.

and Mary, and son, Francis) moved into the vacant Sutro Mansion in Old Sutro. Albert was working as a laborer (later promoted to foreman) for the Sutro Tunnel & Drainage Company, which was owned by the Leonard family.

Francis West, about seven years old at the time, later recalled the mansion and other buildings remaining in Old Sutro.[19] He remembered an assay shop for evaluating ore samples, and a long warehouse full of "odds and ends of material." The warehouse had "a loft where there were some boxes of old books about Sutro." Other buildings surviving at that time included the office, a steam plant to provide power, a garage, a small stamp mill for refining ore, a machine shop, a blacksmith shop, a bathhouse fed with pure spring water, and a large barn.

Francis described the only time he was permitted to enter the Sutro Tunnel:

> The one time I was allowed to go into the tunnel for any distance was the occasion of a cave-in located a couple of miles in. After supper one summer evening Dad noticed the water had almost stopped in the drainage ditch. He let me get on the electric car (used for inspections and tours) with him to go in for a look see. You can imagine the excitement of a young lad not knowing what was beyond the headlight beam of that electric car. I not only was able to see a partial cave-in (it didn't completely fill the tunnel) but I got to see some of the tunnel I had only heard about. I saw the massive doors that

were installed when the mine owners decided not to pay for drainage rights shortly after the tunnel was built. I guess when the tunnel was closed off and flooded their mines they were glad to pay (even higher rates I was told). I understand one of the reasons for the tunnel was the steam pumps of that period could only pump water so high. The mines were going so deep they were having trouble getting the water to the surface.[20]

One night in later 1941 a fire broke out and quickly consumed the tinder-dry mansion. Only some furniture was saved, and the West family had to live in the assay shop until they moved to Oregon in July 1945.

In 1965, Robin Larrson of Berkeley, California, leased land near the tunnel portal and, with Stony Tennant, converted the old tunnel company warehouse into a western-themed bar. The bar had no formal sign or name but predictably was called the Sutro Bar. Adolph would have been proud. Robin and Stony even added a hot tub fed by hot mine water for the bar patrons. The bar venture lasted about a year, until late 1966.[21]

The hippie movement of the '60s was in full bloom, and the Red Dog Saloon in Virginia City became a center of psychedelic experimentation and counter-culture music from new entertainers such as Janis Joplin and bands such as Big Brother and the Holding Company.

Some of that activity spilled over into the town of Old Sutro, resulting in the Sutro Bar losing its liquor license and going out of business. The hippies did not really care, as drugs were more important to them than alcohol. Some of them stayed in the aban-

A few of the mustangs living in Old Sutro (photo by author).

doned buildings of Old Sutro and eventually established a small artist colony there that lasted until about 2000.

A developer installed infrastructure for a subdivision in Old Sutro in 2006, but the economic crash of 2008 ended those plans.

Now Old Sutro is deserted again, except for a herd of about 80 wild horses, called mustangs.

The photo on bottom of page 232 shows the current residents of Old Sutro, with Mount Davidson in the background. Note the trees thriving around the pond in front of the former Sutro Mansion. As these horses are free-range, they often mingle with the residents and graze on flowers and shrubbery in the yards of adjacent New Sutro.

Sutro's name and fame live on in the Comstock, but there are almost no physical reminders of his time there.

Chapter 39

Epilogue—San Francisco

Build your life on your dreams; because dreams never have bad endings.
—M.F. Moonzajer

Sutro Heights

After Adolph Sutro's death, his eldest child and executrix, Emma Sutro Merritt, moved to Sutro Heights with her husband, George, and lived there until her death on October 17, 1938.

In 1920, Emma transferred ownership of Sutro Heights to the city of San Francisco with the proviso that it be "forever held and maintained as a free public resort or park under the name of Sutro Heights."

Between 1920 and 1933, the Merritts continued to allow visitors access to Sutro Heights, which by this time was starting to show its age and lack of maintenance. In 1933, at Emma's request, the city of San Francisco agreed to take over maintenance of Sutro Heights. However, little work was done by the city.

In 1937, the city submitted a proposal to the Works Progress Administration for the rehabilitation of the grounds at Sutro Heights. Some repairs were undertaken, and staircases were constructed at both ends of the wall to provide access to the parapet terrace. When Emma died in 1938, the city directed the WPA to demolish the aged home that had fallen into severe disrepair.

In 1976, San Francisco transferred ownership of Sutro Heights to the National Park Service, to be managed as

Dr. Emma Sutro Merritt was California's first female physician.

Emma Sutro Merritt.

39. Epilogue—San Francisco

part of the Golden Gate National Recreation Area.[1]

Visiting Sutro Heights is a study of what is no longer there as very little remains.

To the left of the entrance road stands a replica of the statue of Diana. A conservatory that once graced the garden at the end of the entrance road has been reduced to a single basin. The Parapet, sans statues, continues to provide spectacular views of the Cliff House and the Pacific Ocean.

Sutro Baths

The Sutro Baths were a source of aggravation for the Sutro Estate executrix, Emma Sutro Merritt, as well as a drain on resources. She repeatedly tried to sell the Baths. In 1912, a referendum permitting the city of San Francisco to buy the Baths for $687,000 failed at the polls.

Statue of *Diana* (note that the animal on the base has been vandalized) (photo by author).

The conservatory and statuary are all gone now—only a single basin remains (courtesy National Park Service).

Sutro Baths auction poster (courtesy Harold B. Lee Library, Brigham Young University).

A probate sale was attempted in 1913 (see poster above[2]) but failed. In 1919, Emma reduced the price to $410,000, but still there were no buyers.

Only minimal changes were made to the Baths until 1934. Then the Sutro estate, under the direction of Adolph's grandson Adolph G. Sutro[3] made significant changes, including:

Tropic Beach interior (*top*) and exterior (*above*) 1934 (author's collection).

- Reconfiguring the main pool (Tank 1) by walling off the north end to form a 28-foot-wide, 60-foot-long, and 15-foot-deep diving tank with four diving boards and two diving platforms;
- Walling off and draining the south dogleg of the main pool, and partially filling it with sand to form a picnic area called "Tropic Beach";
- Covering two of the small pools to form volleyball courts; and
- Hiring noted architect Harold G. Stoner to modernize the entrance with a bright, tropical design.

By 1937, it was clear that the Tropic Beach was not popular, so it was converted to an ice rink. Having an ice rink adjacent to heated swimming pools brought many more challenges, some of which were addressed successfully.

In 1952, the Sutro Estate gave up. They decided to close Sutro Baths on September 1st. At the last minute, George Whitney, owner of nearby Playland at the Beach and the Cliff House offered $250,000 for the Baths, and the Estate gratefully accepted. Whitney immediately cleaned house, disposing of many of Adolph Sutro's exhibits, which had deteriorated badly over the years. As was Sutro, Whitney was an inveterate collector, so he had no trouble filling the exhibit spaces in the Baths with his own "stuff." Part of the housecleaning involved the pools themselves. The concrete walls had deteriorated, the locker rooms were moldy, and people went to newer facilities for swimming. So, on January 1, 1954, Whitney closed the pools forever. He consolidated activities into the southern half of the building and closed off the northern half with a plywood wall.

Main swimming pool converted to ice rink, 1937 (author's collection).

Sky tram from Point Lobos to the Cliff House. Image from Cliff House Project (courtesy Frank Mitchell).

On January 25, 1954, Whitney announced an effort to attract thrill-seekers by installing an 850-foot-long aerial tram from the observation deck at the Cliff House to a new overlook constructed on Point Lobos. The tram would carry an operator and 20 passengers on cables suspended above the surf. The round trip would take about 12 minutes.

Making good on his word, Whitney opened the sky tram on May 2, 1955.

But the ride took just four minutes, not the 12 that Whitney had promised. And it was one-way; the tram riders had to walk back. Most importantly, the Sky Tram designers did not contemplate the problems inherent in suspending a steel tram with steel wheels on steel cables above saltwater spray. Predictably, everything rusted and sometimes the tram stopped midway through the ride. The novelty of the tram soon wore off, and it was never profitable. It closed in May 1966.

George Whitney died in 1958 at age 67. His family continued to operate his holdings, including Sutro's (no longer Sutro Baths, as the pools had closed in 1954), until 1964. Realizing that maintaining the massive glass, steel, and wood building was impossible, the Whitneys sold part of the Baths and the Cliff House to a Berkeley real estate developer, Robert Frasier. After an awkward period of joint ownership, Frasier bought the remaining portion of the Baths and promptly announced plans for high-rise luxury condominiums on the site. After removing the collections that George Whitney had installed, along with the remainder of Sutro's displays, demolition of the 72-year-old

Top: Sutro Baths burning, June 26, 1966. Image from Golden Gate National Recreation Area Archives. *Above:* Sutro Baths site in September 2018 (photo by author).

Sutro Baths building commenced on June 12, 1966. Two weeks later, on June 26, a fire broke out in the partially demolished structure. In a few hours, the five-alarm fire accomplished what it would have taken wrecking crews weeks of expensive work to do. Arson was suspected; the watchman, who had a past conviction for arson, was questioned, but lack of evidence prevented prosecution.

Robert Frasier never started his condos and sold the property to Mr. Zev Ben-Simon. Public sentiment had turned against any construction at the site. In 1972, Congress formed the Golden Gate National Recreation Area (GGNRA) as a unit of the National Park Service. The GGNRA included the site of Sutro Baths but did not own it. In May 1980, after much negotiation, the National Park Service finally purchased the site of Sutro Baths and the adjoining hillsides for $5.5 million.

The site is open to the public, although many portions are hazardous. The cove has returned to the appearance it had in the early 1890s when Sutro had constructed the aquarium and rock wall in front of the swimming area.[4]

Sutro Railroads[5]

Adolph Sutro built two different railroads in San Francisco; both were started to provide 5¢ one-way service from the downtown area to Lands End.

Cliff House and Ferries Railroad

- The "Cliff House and Ferries RR" started in 1888 as a steam train that ran on the edge of Point Lobos. Its western terminal was at 48th and Point Lobos, across from the entrance to Sutro Heights.
- Before completion, Sutro sold it to the Powell Street Railroad.
- In 1893, the Powell Street Railroad was sold to the Southern Pacific Railroad.
- In 1905, the Cliff House and Ferries steam train was converted to an electric streetcar line.
- Severe landslides in February 1925 destroyed large portions of the streetcar tracks, and service around Lands End ceased. The streetcars continued to run, but were rerouted along city streets instead of the unusable cliff route.

Sutro Electric Railroad

- On October 26, 1893, construction began on the "Sutro Railroad," an electric streetcar line south of the Cliff House and Ferries line and north of Golden Gate Park.
- On February 1, 1896, the Sutro Electric Railroad opened. Its western terminal, near the entrance to Sutro Baths, was a wooden structure called Sutro Depot.
- On October 17, 1899, the Sutro Electric Railroad was purchased by R. F. Morrow of the Sutter-street road for $215,000.[6]
- On February 13, 1949, the Sutro Depot burned,[7] and MUNI stopped all streetcar service to Sutro Baths and the Cliff House.

Ownership of these railroads changed over the years.

- In 1902, a new city-wide company, United Railroads, bought both the Cliff House and Ferries Railroad and the Sutro Electric Railroad.
- In 1921, the Market Street Railway bought United Railroads.
- In 1944, the San Francisco Municipal Railway (MUNI) bought out the Market Street Railway.

Sutro Library

As noted previously, Clause XXIII of Adolph Sutro's will stated: "Unto my daughter, Emma L. Sutro, all the books, papers, scrapbooks, manuscripts and pictures contained in my library; also all private papers, letters, accounts and account books, and all other written papers, whether contained in my desk, safes or safe deposit vault or elsewhere."[8] While the language of the clause appears clear and unambivalent, the meaning is inconsistent with statements made by Sutro in the years after the will was written. He repeatedly stated his intention to leave the contents of his library to the city of San Francisco.[9] As a result, lawyers fought over the clause for 13 years with disastrous results for Sutro's book collection.

When Sutro died in 1898, Emma attempted to keep the work on the library continuing, at least on a reduced scale. But most of her five siblings had no interest and wanted to sell the library. After a few years, even the low level of activity ceased. Librarian George Moss, who was essential to progress, had also died in 1898. His assistant, Fredric Perkins, left to return to the East. Thus, no one with knowledge of the operation was left. A custodian, Ella Weaver, was hired to watch over the collection, but she did little or nothing to advance the work of expanding or cataloging the collection.

At 5:12 a.m. on April 18, 1906, disaster struck. The San Francisco earthquake, with a rupture zone of 296 miles and a magnitude now estimated at 7.9, devastated the city and other cities as far away as San Jose and Santa Rosa. Fires fed by ruptured gas lines soon started and caused even more destruction. Within three days, fires destroyed about 28,000 buildings on 470 city blocks.[10] One of the buildings destroyed by the fire was the Battery Street warehouse, which contained about one half of the Sutro collection, including more than 90 percent of the precious incunabula. The other half of the holdings, housed in the Montgomery Street offices, survived. Among the items destroyed in the fire were several rare Bibles, including a German Bible printed by Eggesteyn about 1466; the Plantin of Antwerp Polyglot of 1569, which was printed in Hebrew, Chaldean, Greek, and Latin; and the Puritan favorite, the Geneva Bible, published in 1615.[11] Ironically, in describing the Mount Sutro location for the proposed library building, Sutro had emphasized the danger of fire to libraries and the advantage of the Mount Sutro location regarding fire danger.

In 1913, Emma Sutro Merritt's position as heir to the library contents was finally validated. But the question of where the library should reside remained. The University of California continued to express their interest, the State Library in Sacramento did the same, and some of Sutro's friends reminded everyone of Sutro's oft-stated desire to give the library to the city of San Francisco. Emma and the other heirs opted for none of these, instead giving the library to the California State Library. Minimal conditions accompanied the gift:

- The collection must be called the Sutro Library;
- The books must bear the Sutro bookplate;
- Rare volumes must not circulate;
- The library must remain in San Francisco;
- Books must be made available to the public by January 1, 1917.[12]

The California State Library accepted the gift and the conditions and in September 1913 moved the contents of the Montgomery Street offices to temporary quarters in Stanford University's Lane Medical Library on Sacramento Street in San Francisco. That move was the beginning, not of a favorable resolution to the fate of the Sutro Library, but to 46 years of political disputes and neglect. Bills to provide state funding for a permanent home were repeatedly defeated. Even the paltry sum of $4,000 to pay two librarians came under fire.

In August 1923, the trustees of the San Francisco Public Library offered space in the main library. At best that was a stop-gap solution.

The shameful neglect of the Sutro Library finally neared an end in late 1958, when the University of San Francisco offered 14,000 square feet on the ground floor of its new library to house the Sutro collection. The term of the offer was 20 years at a nominal cost of one dollar per year. Of course, someone objected. Because USF was a Jesuit institution, some claimed that placing a public library in a religious institution violated church-state separation. Finally, California Governor Edmund (Pat) Brown appointed a committee to study the issue. The committee unanimously recommended that the USF offer should be accepted. Then two of Sutro's daughters threatened to sue to repossess the library if it moved to USF. Their lawsuit never materialized, and in 1960 the Sutro Library moved to its new quarters inside the Gleeson Library at USF.[13]

By 1980, the Gleeson Library at USF was out of room and wanted to evict the Sutro Library. Fortuitously, buildings that had housed the California legislature during the renovation of the State Capitol were no longer needed for that purpose. Gary Strong, then state librarian of California, along with Paul Romberg, president of the San Francisco State University, lobbied to acquire those two buildings to house the Sutro collection and to move them the to the SFSU campus. Deconstruction, moving 36 truckloads of building materials, and reconstructing at 480 Winston Drive overlooking the Pacific Ocean, preceded the dedication of the new Sutro Library location in 1982.[14]

The Winston Drive location was comprised of two old buildings cobbled together, but the HVAC system was insufficient to maintain the temperature control and humidity required for a library, and mold was a problem. In addition, more space was needed, and the roof had to be replaced. It was clear that a permanent site for Sutro's collection was essential.

The main SFSU library, the J. Paul Leonard Library, was severely damaged during the October 17, 1989, Loma Prieta earthquake. Staffs of the two libraries suggested that

Above: J. Paul Leonard Library Housing the Sutro Library, at San Francisco State University. *Below:* Bust of Adolph Sutro, Sutro Library, San Francisco State University (both photos by author).

space for the Sutro Library be included in the reconstruction of the Leonard Library. Administrators accepted the suggestion for combining the two libraries, but costs escalated. Finally, after changing to a design-build firm and reallocating space, the new J. Paul Leonard/Sutro Library was completed in July 2012. Once again, the massive Sutro collection had to be moved, but this time to a permanent location.[15]

The final chapter of the saga of the Sutro Library was written on August 1, 2012, when the collection opened in its new home on the fifth and sixth floors of the J. Paul Leonard Library at San Francisco State University. It is a fitting home for the Sutro Library, complete with pictures and a bust of Sutro himself and other Sutro memorabilia. And to the northeast is a clear view of Mount Sutro.

The Cliff House

Adolph Sutro and his spectacular second Cliff House were both gone. His estate had been tied up because of bitter disagreements among his children, with favored daughter, Emma, on one side and siblings Kate, Rose, Clara, and Edgar on the other. Emma was the executrix of the estate but had to obtain court permission to make any significant decisions. Judge James V. Coffey, judge of the Superior Court for the City and County of San Francisco, had jurisdiction over Sutro's estate. On March 9, 1908, Emma obtained the go-ahead from Judge Coffey to use the $97,000 proceeds from insurance on the second Cliff House to build a replacement.[16] A later article, on September 27, 1908, revised the available insurance money to $40,000, but reported that the Sutro heirs had agreed to take $10,000 from the estate to pay for the third Cliff House.[17] In October, another article said that the new structure would have two floors below the level of the entrance road, both constructed of fireproof concrete, and the main floor above, of frame construction.[18]

The design of the third Cliff House, by the respected architectural and engineering firm of Reid & Reid,[19] was far simpler than its Victorian predecessor. One critic called the rectangular, neoclassical building a "giant gray shoebox," but others appreciated its simple, clean lines.

The first dinner and celebration at the third Cliff House was held on June 29, 1909, and was a private affair for city officials, public commissioners, hotel men, and press representatives. The public packed the place two nights later on July 1 and celebrated the reopening of a new building at a familiar and beloved location. The *San Francisco Call* reported:

> The new Cliff House, under the management of John Tait, was thrown open to the public on Thursday night. The restoration of this attractive feature of the city's life has been awaited with keen expectancy by the community. Like the Campanile in Venice, the Cliff House forms a famous and distinct physical feature of San Francisco.

Third Cliff House, ca. 1912. Image from Cliff House Project (courtesy Dennis O'Rorke).

> Under its new management, the Cliff House is destined to surpass its two predecessors as a place to be sought out by epicures. The facilities far exceed those of the former structures, and provision has been made by which the scenery may be observed to best advantage.
>
> A beautiful promenade has been constructed on the face of the rock, forming a concrete terrace above the breakers, where a brass band will play every afternoon from 3 to 6. On the floors above are located the banquet halls, private dining rooms and a ballroom.[20]

In the years after its opening in 1909, the fortunes of the third Cliff House ebbed and flowed. In 1918, as part of the war effort, President Woodrow Wilson ordered that all drinking establishments within a half mile of a military establishment must close. Without alcohol sales, the Cliff House could not survive, so it closed on July 1, 1918, exactly nine years after it first opened. It reopened as a fine restaurant featuring entertainment on December 8, 1920, but Prohibition was the law of the land. Again with no alcohol sales, the establishment was not viable, so it was forced to close in October 1925.

Charles Sutro, the owner of the Cliff House and the last surviving son of Adolph Sutro, died on April 26, 1936, at age 71. The Cliff House was sold by sealed bid to Whitney Brothers, operators of Playland at the Beach, a nearby amusement park. The winning bid for $200,000 was approved by the court on December 15, 1937. After investing $100,000 more to refurnish and redecorate the building, on August 5, 1938, the Whitneys reopened the Cliff House after 13 years of darkness.

George Whitney died in 1958, and his heirs operated the Cliff House until October 1964, when Robert Frasier, a Berkeley real estate developer, purchased a 50 percent interest in the Cliff House and Sutro Baths.

The Cliff House was acquired by the National Park Service in 1977 for $3.79 million and became part of the Golden Gate National Recreation Area. The GGNRA is an over-50-miles-long region centered around San Francisco and extending from the northwest to the southeast along the California coast.[21]

The October 17, 1989, Loma Prieta earthquake occurred just before Game 3 of the Oakland Athletics–San Francisco Giants World Series, causing major damage and 63 deaths in the Bay area. The only impact of the quake on the region around the Cliff House was to cause the sea lion population to desert Seal Rocks. Many of these sea lions moved to Pier 39 in San Francisco, but in 2009, a large colony of sea lions returned to Seal Rocks.

In 2004, the long-time Cliff House restaurant operators, Dan and Mary Hountalas, and the National Park Service extensively renovated the third Cliff House, restoring its original neoclassical architecture. They also added a new, modernist wing with exposed beams reminiscent of the Sutro Baths.

Adolph Sutro was never reluctant to place his name on everything he built, from the Sutro Metallurgical Works to the Sutro Baths. He would certainly approve of the names chosen for the new Sutro Wing and for the most elegant of the Cliff House dining rooms. The dining room has two-story floor-to-ceiling windows overlooking Seal Rocks and the Pacific Ocean and is called **Sutro's**.[22]

Adolph Sutro lived an immensely productive life. But his Sutro Tunnel was completed too late and has now collapsed. Sutro Heights, which he built from bare sand dunes, is virtually gone. His Sutro Baths burned to the ground, and now only foundation

Sutro's dining room at the Third Cliff House (photo by author).

walls testify to its existence. His beloved books took 114 years to find their permanent home. His Victorian Cliff House also burned to the ground and was replaced by a "giant gray shoebox."

We could be discouraged that the tunnel and buildings constructed by Adolph Sutro are almost completely gone. But because of his investments and foresight, the city of San Francisco is blessed with incredible scenic views at Lands End; unspoiled, forested land in the middle of a densely packed city on Mount Davidson and Mount Sutro; the upscale St. Francis Wood and Forest Hill Residence Parks built on land originally purchased by Sutro; and the University of California–San Francisco School of Medicine at Parnassus Heights, built on 13 acres of land donated by Sutro.

We must be inspired by Sutro's perseverance in doing amazing things in the face of overwhelming opposition. As Marie Curie said, "Life is not easy for any of us. But what of that? We must have perseverance and above all confidence in ourselves. We must believe that we are gifted for something and that this thing must be attained." Adolph Sutro would have agreed.

Chapter Notes

Foreword (Fracchia)

1. "Board of Directors—San Francisco Historical Society." n.d. *sfhistory.* https://sfhistory.org/board-of-directors/#CF.

Preface

1. R.E. Stewart, Jr., and M.F. Stewart. *Adolph Sutro—A Biography.* Berkeley, CA: Howell-North, 1962.

Introduction

1. Joellyn, Zollman. "Jewish Immigration to America: Three Waves." n.d. *My Jewish Learning.* https://www.myjewishlearning.com/article/jewish-immigration-to-america-three-waves/.
2. Howard, Sachar. "German Jewish Immigrants." n.d. *My Jewish Learning.* https://www.myjewishlearning.com/article/german-jewish-immigrants/.

Chapter 1

1. "Sutro's Will Is Read to His Children." *San Francisco Call* 12 August 1898. https://cdnc.ucr.edu/cgi-bin/cdnc?a=d&d=SFC18980812.2.72.

Chapter 2

1. "Charlemagne." 19 September 2018. *History.* Ed. History.com Editors. https://www.history.com/topics/middle-ages/charlemagne.
2. "Charlemagne and Aachen." n.d. *Victoria and Albert Museum.* http://www.vam.ac.uk/content/articles/c/charlemagne-and-aachen/.
3. R.E. Stewart, Jr., and M.F. Stewart. *Adolph Sutro—A Biography.* Howell-North, Berkeley, CA. 1962.
4. Betty Magovern. *Sutro—A Family Tree.* San Francisco, CA. 1992.
5. *Emanuel Sali Sutro.* n.d. https://www.findagrave.com/memorial/146723622/emanuel-sali-sutro.
6. *Juliana Sutro Jordan.* n.d. https://www.findagrave.com/memorial/25644103/juliana-jordan.
7. *Adolph Sutro.* n.d. https://www.findagrave.com/memorial/6639928/adolph-sutro.
8. *Emil Sutro.* n.d. https://www.findagrave.com/memorial/58043145/emil-sutro.
9. *Otto Sutro.* n.d. https://www.findagrave.com/memorial/178508916/otto-sutro.
10. *Hugo Aron Sutro.* n.d. https://www.findagrave.com/memorial/140641977/hugo-aron-sutro.
11. *Laura Sutro Drost.* n.d. https://www.findagrave.com/memorial/178542254/laura-drost.
12. *Ludwig Sutro.* n.d. https://www.findagrave.com/memorial/12604421/ludwig-sutro.
13. *Elise Sutro Schucking.* n.d. https://www.findagrave.com/memorial/98914311/elise-schucking.
14. *Emma Bertha Sutro.* n.d. https://www.findagrave.com/memorial/141124131/emma-bertha-winterberg.
15. *Theodore Sutro.* n.d. https://www.findagrave.com/memorial/126500043/theodore-sutro.
16. James Chastain. "March Revolution." 20 October 2004. *Ohio.edu.* https://www.ohio.edu/chastain/ip/marrev.htm.
17. *San Francisco—Its Builders Past and Present.* Chicago: S. J. Clarke Publishing Co., 1913. http://www.ebooksread.com/authors-eng/sj-clarke-publishing-company/san-francisco—its-builders-past-and-present—pictorial-and-biographical-vol-fna/1-san-francisco—its-builders-past-and-present—pictorial-and-biographical-vol-fna.shtml.
18. Stewart. Op cit.
19. Adolph Sutro. "Letter to his mother." Memel, Fall 1849.
20. *Loc. cit.*
21. $467 in 1850 would correspond to about $15,000 in 2018.
22. Adolph Sutro. "Letter to his mother." Memel, 6 December 1849.

23. Adolph Sutro. "Letter to his mother." Memel, 5 February 1850.
24. "Sutro." 1919. *American biography: a new cyclopedia, Volume 5*. Ed. William Richard Cutter. The American Historical Society. http://www.delabrede.com/Windmuller/Sutro.html.
25. Julie A. S. Edwards. *Immigrant Ships Transcribers Guild—Ship Peter Hattrick*. 31 January 2000. https://immigrantships.net/v3/1800v3/peterhattrick18500930.html#Sutro.

Chapter 3

1. "John Augustus Sutter." 2001. *New Perspectives on the West*. PBS. http://www.pbs.org/weta/thewest/people/s_z/sutter.htm.
2. Kathy Weiser. "John A. Sutter—Boom & Bust in California." May 2017. *Legends of America*. https://www.legendsofamerica.com/ca-johnsutter/.
3. *Life of John Augustus Sutter 1803–1880*. n.d. http://score.rims.k12.ca.us/activity/suttersfort/pages/sutter.html.
4. C.F. McGlashan. "History of the Donner Party." 1922. *Books-About-California*. A. Carlisle & Co. http://www.books-about-california.com/Pages/History_of_Donner_Party/Donner_Party_chapter_21.html.
5. *Donner Party*. n.d. https://en.wikipedia.org/wiki/Donner_Party#Rescue.
6. Theodore Hittell. "The Gold Discovery." 1897. *The Virtual Museum of the City of San Francisco*. http://www.sfmuseum.net/hist6/impact.html.
7. "Maps, Museums, Monuments and Markers." n.d. *Mormon Battalion Association*. http://www.mormonbattalion.com/Museums_Monuments_Maps_and_Trails.
8. *Mormon Battalion*. n.d. https://en.wikipedia.org/wiki/Mormon_Battalion.
Route map by Briancole at English Wikipedia, CC BY 3.0, commons.wikimedia.org/w/index.php?curid=34908983.
9. Brandon J. Metcalf. "Four Things to Know about the Journey of the Mormon Battalion." 24 January 2018. *Church History*. https://history.lds.org/article/historic-sites/journey-of-the-mormon-battalion?lang=eng.
10. James S. Brown. "California Gold: An Authentic History of the First Find With the Names of Those Interested in the Discovery." 24 January 1894. *The Virtual Museum of the City of San Francisco*. http://www.sfmuseum.net/hist6/grush.html.
11. Hittell, *op. cit.*
12. Henry W. Bigler. Coloma, 24 January 1848. Inscription on monument at site of Sutter's Mill.
13. John Sutter. "Capt. Sutter's account of the first discovery of the Gold." 1854. *The Virtual Museum of the City of San Francisco*. Britton & Rey. http://www.sfmuseum.net/hist2/gold2.html.
14. *Ibid*.
15. General John A. Sutter. "The Discovery of Gold in California." November 1857. *Virtual Museum of the City of San Francisco*. Hutchings' California Magazine. http://www.sfmuseum.net/hist2/gold.html.
16. McGlashan, *op. cit.*
17. *Sutter Hock Farm*. n.d. en.wikipedia.org/wiki/Sutter_Hock_Farm.
18. *Life of John Augustus Sutter 1803–1880*, *op. cit.*
19. Weiser, *op. cit.*

Chapter 4

1. Tom Gray. "The Treaty of Guadalupe Hidalgo." n.d. *National Archives Educator Resources*. https://www.archives.gov/education/lessons/guadalupe-hidalgo.
2. Justin Kuepper. "3 Of The Most Lucrative Land Deals In History." 23 August 2017. *Investopedia*. https://www.investopedia.com/financial-edge/1012/3-of-the-most-lucrative-land-deals-in-history.aspx.
3. From https://www.officialdata.org/, $500 million in 1850 would correspond to about $16 billion in 2018.
4. Staff, History.com. "The Gold Rush of 1849." 2010. History.com. http://www.history.com/topics/gold-rush-of-1849.
5. Wallace Ohrt. "Defiant Peacemaker: Nicholas Trist in the Mexican War." Texas A & M University Press. College Station, Texas. 1997.
6. Scott Bomboy. "The man who delivered California to the U.S., and was fired for it." 10 March 2017. *National Constitution Center*. https://constitutioncenter.org/blog/the-man-who-delivered-california-to-the-u-s-and-was-fired-for-it.
7. "San Francisco Gold Rush Chronology—1846–1849." n.d. *The Virtual Museum of the City of San Francisco*. http://www.sfmuseum.net/hist/chron1.html#TOP.
8. Will Bagley. *Scoundrel's Tale: The Samuel Brannan Papers*. Utah State University Press, 1999.
9. Eugene E. Campbell. "The Apostasy of Samuel Brannan." *Utah Historical Quaterly* 1959.
10. Reva Scott. *Samuel Brannan and The Golden Fleece: A Biography*. Kessinger Publishing, LLC, 2010.
11. Bob Young. *Empire builder: Sam Brannan*. J. Messner, 1967.
12. Joan Hamblin. "Voyage of the 'Brooklyn.'" July 1997. *The Church of Jesus Christ of Latter Day Saints*. https://www.lds.org/ensign/1997/07/voyage-of-the-brooklyn?lang=eng.
13. "Ship Passengers—Sea Captains." n.d. *The Maritime Heritage Project*. https://www.maritimeheritage.org/passengers/br073146.htm.
14. Paul Bailey. *Sam Brannan and the California Mormons*. Los Angeles: Westernlore Press, 1943.
15. *1st millionaire dies broke*. n.d. http://www.calgoldrush.com/profiles/pro_brannan.html.
16. "San Francisco Gold Rush Chronology—1846–1849," *op. cit.*

17. "The excitement and enthusiasm of Gold Washing still continues—increases." *California Star.* Saturday, June 10, 1848.
18. Richard Barnes Mason. "Official Report on the Gold Mines." 17 August 1848. *The Virtual Museum of the City of San Francisco.* http://www.sfmuseum.net/hist6/masonrpt.html.
19. James K. Polk. "Fourth Annual Message." n.d. *The American Presidency Project.* Ed. Gerhard Peters and John T. Woolley. http://www.presidency.ucsb.edu/ws/index.php?pid=29489.
20. Ralph J. Benko. "President Polk: '...as would scarcely command belief....'" 12 May 2012. *The Gold Standard Now.* http://www.thegoldstandardnow.org/key-blogs-6/1223-the-california-gold-rush-begins.
21. Dean Albertson. "The Discovery of Gold in California as Viewed by New York and London." Winter 1949. *The Virtual Museum of the City of San Francisco.* The Pacific Spectator. http://www.sfmuseum.net/hist5/albertson.html.

Chapter 5

1. *Rising Tide.* n.d. Smithsonian Institution. https://postalmuseum.si.edu/makingway/p3.html.
2. *The Tide Turns.* n.d. Smithsonian Institution. https://postalmuseum.si.edu/makingway/p4.html.
3. *Steamships on the Panama Route—Both Atlantic and Pacific.* n.d. http://www.theshipslist.com/ships/descriptions/panamafleet.shtml.
4. *Ad for Steamship to Panama and on to California (1850).* 8 October 1850. https://ghostsofbaltimore.org/2013/09/24/ad-steamship-panama-california-1850/.
5. Jack Leibman. *Adolph Sutro Travels to California (Part 1).* n.d. SF City Guides. http://www.sfcityguides.org/public_guidelines.html?article=247&submitted=TRUE&srch_text=sutro&submitted2=TRUE&topic=.
6. Leibman, *ibid.*
7. Jack Leibman. *Adolph Sutro in Panama (Part 2).* n.d. SF City Guides. http://www.sfcityguides.org/public_guidelines.html?article=320&submitted=TRUE&srch_text=sutro&submitted2=TRUE&topic=.
8. Jack Leibman. *Adolph Sutro Slogs Through Panama (Part 3).* n.d. SF City Guides. http://www.sfcityguides.org/public_guidelines.html?article=351&submitted=TRUE&srch_text=sutro&submitted2=TRUE&topic=.
9. n.d. http://www.in2013dollars.com/1850-dollars-in-2018?amount=1.
10. "Passenger Lists: San Francisco 1800s." n.d. *The Maritime Heritage Project—San Francisco 1846–1899.* http://www.maritimeheritage.org/passengers/SS-California-21November1850.html.
11. *Rising Tide, op. cit.*
12. Jack Leibman. *Adolph Sutro Arrives in SF (Part 4).* n.d. http://www.sfcityguides.org/public_guidelines.html?article=378&submitted=TRUE&srch_text=sutro&submitted2=TRUE&topic=.

Chapter 6

1. "August Helbing (1824–1896)." n.d. *American Jerusalem.* http://www.americanjerusalem.com/characters/august-helbing-1824-ae-1896/22.
2. "Eureka Benevolent Society (San Francisco, Calif.) records, 1850–1977." n.d. *The Magnes Collection of Jewish Art and Life.* University of California, Berkeley. https://magnes.berkeley.edu/collections/archives/western-jewish-americana/eureka-benevolent-society-san-francisco-calif-records.
3. Adolph Sutro. "Letter to his brother, Sali." 1 December 1850.
4. R.E. Stewart, Jr., and M.F. Stewart. *Adolph Sutro—A Biography.* Berkeley, CA: Howell-North, 1962.
5. "Bernard Frankenheimer." n.d. *Find A Grave.* https://www.findagrave.com/memorial/144032434/bernhard-frankenheimer.
6. Arnold Roth. "Stockton's Jewish Community and Temple Israel." n.d. *Temple Israel Stockton.* http://www.templeisraelstockton.com/about-us/our-history?tmpl=component&type=raw.
7. Stewart, *op. cit.*
8. Julieta Duek. "Committee of Vigilance of San Francisco." 2013. *FoundSF.* http://www.foundsf.org/index.php?title=Committee_of_Vigilance_of_San_Francisco.
9. Reva Holdaway Stanley et al. "A Mormon Mission to California in 1851: From the Diary of Parley Parker Pratt." *California Historical Society Quarterly,* vol. 14, no. 1, 1935, 59–73. JSTOR, JSTOR, www.jstor.org/stable/25160556.
10. Meredith May. "Sydney Ducks and vigilante justice in SF, 1851." 9 December 2012. *SFGate.* https://www.sfgate.com/entertainment/article/Sydney-Ducks-and-vigilante-justice-in-SF-1851-4097306.php.
11. *1851: Samuel Whittaker and Robert McKenzie lynched in San Francisco.* n.d. http://www.executedtoday.com/2015/08/24/1851-samuel-whittaker-and-robert-mckenzie-lynched-in-san-francisco/.
12. Adolph Sutro. "Letter to his family." Stockton, 29 August 1851.
13. Stewart, *op. cit.*
14. Stewart, *op. cit.*
15. There are no reliable resources describing how Adolph and Leah met (possibly through the Eureka Benevolent Society) or specifying their marriage date. Likewise, the birth date of their first child, Emma, is somewhat in doubt. Many authors claim Emma was born December 15, 1856. However, her Funeral Record shows her birth date, which must have been provided by a family member or someone else who knew her well, as December 15, 1855. Thanks to Dale Sheldon, a distant relative of Adolph Sutro, for providing a copy of

her Funeral Record. Based on this less-than-conclusive evidence, I believe that Adolph and Leah were married in 1855.
16. *Dr Emma Sutro Merritt*. n.d. https://www.findagrave.com/memorial/76268972/emma-merritt.
17. "Fraser River Gold Rush." n.d. *Canadian Encyclopedia*. https://www.thecanadianencyclopedia.ca/en/article/fraser-river-gold-rush/.
18. Daniel P. Marshall. "Fraser River Gold Rush." 30 May 2014. *The Canadian Encyclopedia*. https://www.thecanadianencyclopedia.ca/en/article/fraser-river-gold-rush.
19. Stewart, *op. cit.*
20. Otis E. Young, Jr. *Western Mining: An Informal Account of Precious-Metals Prospecting*. Norman: University of Oklahoma Press, 1970. https://books.google.com/books?id=EQedpB0bxVAC&printsec=frontcover&source=gbs_atb#v=onepage&q&f=false.
21. Dennis Drabelle. *Mile-High Fever*. New York: St. Martin's Press, 2009.
22. *Comstock Lode—Creating Nevada History*. n.d. https://www.legendsofamerica.com/nv-comstocklode/.
23. Young, *op. cit.*
24. *Comstock Mining District*. n.d. http://www.onlinenevada.org/articles/comstock-mining-district.
25. Stewart, *op. cit.*

Chapter 7

1. The same trip, from San Francisco to Virginia City, would take about four and a half hours by car today.
2. "California Steam Navigation Company." 15 January 2019. *Wikipedia*. https://en.wikipedia.org/wiki/California_Steam_Navigation_Company.
3. "Theodore Dehone Judah." n.d. *Who Made America?* http://www.pbs.org/wgbh/theymadeamerica/whomade/judah_hi.html.
4. Helen Hinckley. *Rails from the West ... A Biography of Theodore D. Judah*. San Marino: Golden West Books, 1969.
5. Adolph Sutro. "A Trip to Washoe." *Daily Alta California* 11 April 1860. https://cdnc.ucr.edu/cgi-bin/cdnc?a=d&d=DAC18600411.2.13&e=-------en--20--1--txt-txIN--------1.
6. Adolph Sutro. "A Trip to Washoe." 13 April 1860. *Daily Alta California*. https://cdnc.ucr.edu/cgi-bin/cdnc?a=d&d=DAC18600413.2.18&e=-------en--20--1--txt-txIN--------1.
7. Adolph Sutro. "A Trip to Washoe." *Daily Alta California* 14 April 1860. https://cdnc.ucr.edu/cgi-bin/cdnc?a=d&d=DAC18600414&e=-------en--20--1--txt-txIN--------1.
8. *Ibid.*
9. *Pony Express debuts*. n.d. https://www.history.com/this-day-in-history/pony-express-debuts.
10. Adolph Sutro. "A Trip to Washoe." *Daily Alta California* 14 April 1860, *op. cit.*
11. *Ibid.*
12. R.E. Stewart, Jr., and M.F. Stewart. *Adolph Sutro—A Biography*. Berkeley, CA: Howell-North, 1962.
13. An amalgam is an alloy of mercury with another metal that is solid or liquid at room temperature according to the proportion of mercury present.
14. Ronald James. "Milling Technology in the Nineteenth Century." 15 July 2011. *Online Nevada Encyclopedia*. http://www.onlinenevada.org/articles/milling-technology-nineteenth-century.
15. "Science of the Comstock—Chemistry." n.d. *Nevada Bureau of Mines and Geology*. http://www.nbmg.unr.edu/scienceeducation/ScienceOfTheComstock/Chemistry-Ore.html.
16. "The Sutro Tunnel." *Engineering and Mining Journal* November 1878: 380–384. https://books.google.com/books?id=FpggAQAAMAAJ&pg=PA386-IA8&lpg=PA384&focus=viewport&dq=adolph+sutro+antwerp+to+new+york&output=text.
17. Stewart, *op. cit.*
18. Dennis Drabelle. *Mile-High Fever*. New York: St. Martin's Press, 2009.
19. "Almarin B. Paul." *History of the New California, Its Resources and People*. Ed. Leigh H. Irvine. Vol. 2. The Lewis Publishing Company, 1905. https://oac.cdlib.org/findaid/ark:/13030/c8q244pv/entire_text/.
20. Donald Hardesty. *Mining Technology in the Nineteenth Century*. 10 December 2010. http://www.onlinenevada.org/articles/mining-technology-nineteenth-century.
21. "Science of the Comstock—Chemistry," *op. cit.*
22. James, *op. cit.*
23. David M. Lyons; John J. Wayne; Paul J. Warwick; Gary A. Lechler; W. Berry Gill. "Mercury contamination in the Carson River, Nevada: A preliminary study of the impact of mining wastes." December 1996. *Springer Link*. https://link.springer.com/article/10.1007/BF00283569.
24. *The Comstock Lode and the Mining Frontier*. 2016. http://www.digitalhistory.uh.edu/disp_textbook_print.cfm?smtid=2&psid=3149.
25. Andrew Bain. *Carson River Mercury Site—Dayton, NV*. n.d. https://cumulis.epa.gov/supercpad/SiteProfiles/index.cfm?fuseaction=second.Clean up&id=0903020#bkground.

Chapter 8

1. *William Wright, aka Dan DeQuille*. n.d. http://www.onlinenevada.org/articles/william-wright-aka-dan-de-quille.
2. Mark Twain. "Mark Twain's Letters, Volume 4: 1870–1871." 1995. books.google.com. Ed. Michael B. Frank Victor Fischer. University of California

Press. https://books.google.com/books?id=wDiDCnOP6lIC&pg=PA447&lpg=PA447&dq=Twain+and+Sutro&source=bl&ots=m4qVx5UDaT&sig=CRGwVJKz7jDbquF4Kq7_sOqxTmk&hl=en&sa=X&ved=0ahUKEwj30eLvuMzbAhVyp1kKHQnGBF4Q6AEIYzAI#v=onepage&q=Sutro&f=false.

3. Mark Twain. *Roughing It*. Hartford: American Publishing Company, 1872. https://www.gutenberg.org/files/3177/3177-h/3177-h.htm.

Chapter 9

1. *Dangers Below (Comstock Silver Mines)*. Ed. Robert R. Van Ryzin. n.d. http://numismaster.com/ta/inside_numis.jsp?page=dangers-comstock-silver-mines.
2. *Ibid.*
3. An open space underground where ore is to be extracted is known as a *stope*. "Stoped" describes the process of supporting such a chamber.
4. Dan DeQuille. "Philip Deidesheimer." *Territorial Enterprise (draft of article)*. Sutro Library, Box 14, Folder 444, Undated.
5. "Philip Deidesheimer: Jewish Mine Support Engineer of the Comstock Lode, Virginia City, Nevada." 5 September 2014. *Jewish Museum of the American West*. http://www.jmaw.org/deidesheimer-jewish-nevada/.
6. *Bonanza*. n.d. https://www.amazon.com/gp/video/detail/B0172XX15I?ref_=atv_dp_season_select.
7. John A. Church. "Heat of the Comstock Mines." *American Institute of Mining Engineers* (1878). https://ia800209.us.archive.org/20/items/heatofcomstockmi00churrich/heatofcomstockmi00churrich.pdf.
8. Drifts are horizontal tunnels used for exploration, ventilation, to connect vertical shafts, or a combination of these.
9. Augustus Locke. "The Abnormal Temperatures on the Comstock Lode." *Economic Geology* 1912: 583–587.
10. "law of parsimony." n.d. Dictionary.com. https://www.dictionary.com/browse/law-of-parsimony.
11. "Digging Deeper into the Comstock." 10 October 2009. *Guide for the Earth Science Week Field Trip*. Nevada Bureau of Mines and Geology. http://dwgateway.library.unr.edu/keck/mining/dox/e48.pdf.
12. Greg B. Arehart, Mark Coolbaugh, Simon Poulson. "Geothermal Resources Council Transactions." 12 October 2003. *Evidence for a Magmatic Source of Heat for the Steamboat Springs Geothermal System Using Trace Elements and Gas Geochemistry*. Great Basin Center for Geothermal Energy, University of Nevada. http://www.atlasgeoinc.com/wp-content/uploads/Arehart_etal_GRC_2003_Magmatic_Steamboat.pdf.
13. Van Ryzin, *op. cit.*
14. *Ibid.*
15. Eliot Lord. Comstock Mining and Miners. Vol. IV. Washington: United States Geological Survey, 1883. https://play.google.com/books/reader?id=jQA0AQAAMAAJ&printsec=frontcover&output=reader&hl=en&pg=GBS.PR3.
16. An adit is a horizontal cut with only one opening to the surface.
17. George D. Lyman. *Ralston's Ring*. New York: Charles Scribner's Sons, 1937.
18. Lord, *op. cit.*
19. Van Ryzin, *op. cit.*
20. Lord, *op. cit.*

Chapter 10

1. Dennis Drabelle. *Mile-High Fever*. New York: St. Martin's Press, 2009.
2. Eliot Lord. *Comstock Mining and Miners*. Vol. IV. Washington: United States Geological Survey, 1883. https://play.google.com/books/reader?id=jQA0AQAAMAAJ&printsec=frontcover&output=reader&hl=en&pg=GBS.PR3.
3. Drabelle, *op. cit.*
4. Michael J. Makley. *The Infamous King of the Comstock—William Sharon and the Gilded Age in the West*. Ed. Michael Green. Reno: University of Nevada Press, 2006.
5. George D. Lyman. *Ralston's Ring*. New York: Charles Scribner's Sons, 1937.

Chapter 11

1. George D. Lyman. *Ralston's Ring*. New York: Charles Scribner's Sons, 1937.
2. "Panama Railroad." n.d. M Kalano. http://www.dickholt.net/images/605_originalline.jpg.
3. *History of the Panama Railroad*. n.d. http://www.panamarailroad.org/history1.html.
4. *William Walker and the Transit Company in Nicaragua*. n.d. https://nicatips.com/news/william-walker-transit-company-nicaragua/.
5. *Cornelius Vanderbilt*. n.d. https://legacy.voteview.com/vanderb2.htm.
6. *SS Yankee Blade*. n.d. Maritime Heritage.org. http://www.maritimeheritage.org/captains/SS-Yankee-Blade-30September1854.html.
7. *Photographs of W.C. Ralston and His Mansion in Belmont, Calif., 1872–1874*. n.d. http://www.oac.cdlib.org/findaid/ark:/13030/tf3t1nb6b1/entire_text/.
8. John Harrison Morrison. *History of American Steam Navigation*. New York: W.F. Sametz & Co., Inc., 1903.
9. Gold had been discovered as early as 1849 near Dayton, Nevada, but attracted little attention until the Grosh brothers found significant gold and silver deposits in 1857.
10. Lyman, *ibid.*

Chapter 12

1. Makeley, *op. cit.*

2. Lyman, *op. cit.*
3. George D. Lyman. *Ralston's Ring.* New York: Charles Scribner's Sons, 1937.
4. Michael J. Makley. *The Infamous King of the Comstock—William Sharon and the Gilded Age in the West.* Ed. Michael Green. Reno: University of Nevada Press, 2006.
5. *Ibid.*
6. "Death of Sharon." *San Francisco Chronicle* 14 September 1885: 2.
7. Makley, *op. cit.*
8. *Ibid.*
9. Lyman, *op. cit.*
10. Sharon's concept predated Henry Ford's vertical integration of the automobile industry by some 40 years.
11. Makley, *op. cit.*
12. Interestingly, Nevada is one of 14 states that currently have no usury laws. "Nevada has no limit on the rate of interest to which parties may agree so long as the agreement reflects an arms-length transaction. Further, Nevada allows compound interest on loans." (Usury Laws in Nevada, http://nevadalaw.info/usury-laws-in-nevada/.)
13. *Ibid.*

Chapter 13

1. Adolph Sutro. *Closing Argument of Adolph Sutro on the Bill Before Congress to Aid the Sutro Tunnel.* Washington: House of Representatives, 1872. file:///D:/Word/Book%20Publication/Adolph%20Sutro/09%20Mr%20Sutro%20Goes%20to%20Washoe--1859-1860/Closing_Argument_on%20the%20Sutor%20Tunnel.pdf.
2. Not to be confused with Manfred von Richthofen, the Red Baron of WWI fame.
3. Adolph Sutro. *The Advantages and Necessity of a Deep Drain Tunnel for the Great Comstock Ledge.* San Francisco, 1865. https://ia800306.us.archive.org/30/items/advantagesnecess00sutrrich/advantagesnecess00sutrrich.pdf.
4. *Ibid.*
5. *Ibid.*

Chapter 14

1. "The Sutro Tunnel and Its Projector." *The Engineering and Mining Journal* 30 November 1878: 384. https://play.google.com/books/reader?id=8OQ-AQAAMAAJ&printsec=frontcover&output=reader&hl=en&pg=GBS.RA15-PA384.
2. Adolph Sutro. *The Advantages and Necessity of a Deep Drain Tunnel for the Great Comstock Ledge.* San Francisco, 1865. https://ia800306.us.archive.org/30/items/advantagesnecess00sutrrich/advantagesnecess00sutrrich.pdf.
3. Eliot Lord. *Comstock Mining and Miners.* Vol. IV. Washington: United States Geological Survey, 1883. https://play.google.com/books/reader?id=jQA0AQAAMAAJ&printsec=frontcover&output=reader&hl=en&pg=GBS.PR3. 417.
4. *Ibid.*
5. George D. Lyman. *Ralston's Ring.* New York: Charles Scribner's Sons, 1937.
6. Adolph Sutro. *Closing Argument of Adolph Sutro on the Bill Before Congress to Aid the Sutro Tunnel.* Washington: House of Representatives, 1872. file:///D:/Word/Book%20Publication/Adolph%20Sutro/09%20Mr%20Sutro%20Goes%20to%20Washoe--1859-1860/Closing_Argument_on%20the%20Sutor%20Tunnel.pdf.
7. R.E. Stewart, Jr., and M.F. Stewart. *Adolph Sutro—A Biography.* Berkeley, CA: Howell-North, 1962.
8. "THIRTY-NINTH CONGRESS." 25 July 1866. *Statutes-At-Large.* Congress of the United States. https://www.loc.gov/law/help/statutes-at-large/39th-congress/session-1/c39s1ch244.pdf.
9. Lord, *op. cit.*
10. Stewart, *op. cit.*, 54–55.
11. *Ibid.*, 55.
12. *Ibid.*, 56.
13. Adolph Sutro. "The Bank of California Against the Sutro Tunnel." May 1874. *Google Play.* https://play.google.com/books/reader?id=BeSreOw4McwC&printsec=frontcover&output=reader&hl=en&pg=GBS.PA33-34.
14. Lord, *op. cit.*, 236.
15. Adolph Sutro. "The Bank of California Against the Sutro Tunnel," *op. cit.*, 20.
16. Stewart, *op. cit.*, 58.

Chapter 15

1. R.E. Stewart, Jr., and M.F. Stewart. *Adolph Sutro—A Biography.* Berkeley, CA: Howell-North, 1962. 59–60.
2. Adolph Sutro. *Closing Argument of Adolph Sutro on the Bill Before Congress to Aid the Sutro Tunnel.* Washington: House of Representatives, 1872. file:///D:/Word/Book%20Publication/Adolph%20Sutro/09%20Mr%20Sutro%20Goes%20to%20Washoe–1859–1860/Closing_Argument_on%20the%20Sutor%20Tunnel.pdf.
3. *Ibid.*, 13–14.
4. *Ibid.*, 14–15.
5. The railway that Bull was referring to was later named the Virginia and Truckee Railroad.
6. *Ibid.*, 15–16.
7. *Ibid.*, 20–21.
8. Mark Abbott Stern. *Beyond the Tunnel: The Second Life of Adolph Sutro.* Self-published, 2018.
9. Stewart, *op. cit.*, 63.
10. Sutro, *op. cit.*, 21.

Chapter 16

1. R.E. Stewart, Jr., and M.F. Stewart. *Adolph Sutro—A Biography.* Berkeley, CA: Howell-North, 1962. 64.

2. U.S. Sutro Tunnel Commission. *Report of the Commissioners and Evidence Taken at the Committee on Mines and Mining of the House of Representatives of the United States, in Regard to the Sutro Tunnel, Together with the Arguments.* Washington, 1872. https://books.googleusercontent.com/books/content?req=AKW5QaeJPn3wa63cIMYOH8JRPIgm8_y1wEGdYi3CVvPXTXb6yT2LideNlpIr39RRPPU68Cj_7OsDmkjc5tEX5vTOtuqkSKzvfFz0ADzNCt48IPki-PugVPYUhgyyMkvQWDRdLEcBACu-rXmAxg7OOc5umQdsWh271wkZ1N4vQcBK8XT_JrAbs9qimdfSRK2F-0skLcqss.

3. Adolph Sutro. *Closing Argument of Adolph Sutro on the Bill Before Congress to Aid the Sutro Tunnel.* Washington: House of Representatives, 1872. file:///D:/Word/Book%20Publication/Adolph%20Sutro/09%20Mr%20Sutro%20Goes%20to%20Washoe--1859-1860/Closing_Argument_on%20the%20Sutor%20Tunnel.pdf.

4. Stewart, *op. cit.,* 66.

5. Adolph Sutro. "Lecture on Mines and Mining." *The Daily Independent—Supplement* 31 October 1874.

6. Adolph Sutro. *Closing Argument, op. cit.*

7. Eliot Lord. *Comstock Mining and Miners.* Vol. IV. Washington: United States Geological Survey, 1883. https://play.google.com/books/reader?id=jQA0AQAAMAAJ&printsec=frontcover&output=reader&hl=en&pg=GBS.PR3.

8. Jones went on to become a U.S. Senator from Nevada from 1873 to 1903. He cofounded the city of Santa Monica, California, in 1875. Jones died in 1912.

9. Stewart, *op. cit.*, 78.

10. Stewart, *op. cit.*, 79.

Chapter 17

1. Eliot Lord. *Comstock Mining and Miners.* Vol. IV. Washington: United States Geological Survey, 1883. https://play.google.com/books/reader?id=jQA0AQAAMAAJ&printsec=frontcover&output=reader&hl=en&pg=GBS.PR3. 251.

2. *Ibid.*

3. Map adapted from Tingley, Joseph V. *Geologic and Natural History Tours in the Reno Area.* Sparks: Bear Printing, 2005. https://books.google.com/books?id=ekf0wBY8LyUC&pg=PA73#v=onepage&q&f=false.

4. B.Garside, W. Purkey, and L.J. *Geologic and Natural History Tours in the Reno Area.* Vol. Special Publication 19. Reno: Nevada Bureau of Mines and Geology, 1995.

5. "Along the Road." n.d. *Virginia and Truckee.* http://www.virginiaandtruckee.com/.

6. *Ibid.*

7. Lord, *op. cit.,* 255–256.

8. Dan DeQuille. *History of the Big Bonanza.* Las Vegas: Nevada Publications, 1887 (Reprint).

9. Lord, *op. cit.*, 254.

Chapter 18

1. Eliot Lord. *Comstock Mining and Miners.* Vol. IV. Washington: United States Geological Survey, 1883. https://play.google.com/books/reader?id=jQA0AQAAMAAJ&printsec=frontcover&output=reader&hl=en&pg=GBS.PR3. Facing page 79.

2. B.W. Purkey, and L.J. Garside. *Geologic and Natural History Tours in the Reno Area.* Vol. SP19. Reno: Nevada Bureau of Mines and Geology, 1995. 58.

3. R.W. Raymond. *Report to Congress.* Washington, D.C., 1868. 51. Quoted in U.S. Sutro Tunnel Commission. *Report of the Commissioners and Evidence Taken at the Committee on Mines and Mining of the House of Representatives of the United States, in Regard to the Sutro Tunnel, Together with the Arguments.* Washington, 1872. 212.

4. Lord. Op cit. 421.

5. Lord. Op cit. 418.

6. C. Craig, C. et al. "Science of the Comstock—Environment—Influence of Mining." 1999. *Nevada Bureau of Mines and Geology.* http://www.nbmg.unr.edu/_images/ScienceEducation/ScienceOfTheComstock/NBMG_SP19_Map_Mills_Flumes_RR.png.

7. Michael J. Makley. *The Infamous King of the Comstock: William Sharon and the Gilded Age in the West.* Ed. Michael Green. 1. Reno: University of Nevada Press, 2006. 34.

Chapter 19

1. *Hermann Schussler: A water-systems engineer and architect of Bay Area dams.* 8 June 2009. *San Mateo Daily Journal.* http://www.watereducation.org/aquafornia-news/hermann-schussler-water-systems-engineer-and-architect-bay-area-dams.

2. Victor Elmo Perry. "Pass Bearer Through Lines." 18 April 1956. *Virtual Museum of the City of San Francisco.* http://www.sfmuseum.org/hist3/perry.html.

3. John Wilfrid Wright, and John Lyman. "Surveying." n.d. *Encyclopædia Britannica.* https://www.britannica.com/technology/surveying.

4. Hugh A. Shamberger. *The Story of the Water Supply for the Comstock.* 1972. U.S. Government Printing Office. https://pubs.usgs.gov/pp/0779/report.pdf.

5. Richard Lyle Gardner. *The Comstock: Economic History of Mining Bonanza.* 2009. http://www.comstockhistory.com/media//DIR_9001/mss1.pdf.

6. Adolph Sutro. "Letter to Mr. D. Bethel." San Francisco, 12 November 1869.

7. R.E. Stewart, Jr., and M.F. Stewart. *Adolph Sutro—A Biography.* Berkeley, CA: Howell-North, 1962.

8. U.S. Sutro Tunnel Commission. *Report of the Commissioners and Evidence Taken at the Committee on Mines and Mining of the House of Rep-

resentatives of the United States, in Regard to the Sutro Tunnel, Together with the Arguments. Washington, 1872. https://books.googleusercontent.com/books/content?req=AKW5QaeJPn3wa63cIMYOH8JRPIgm8_y1wEGdYi3CVvPXTXb6yT2LideNlpIr39RRPPU68Cj_7OsDmkjc5tEX5vTOtuqkSKzvfFz0ADzNCt48IPki-PugVPYUhgyyMkvQWDRdLEcBACu-rXmAxg7OOc5umQdsWh271wkZ1N4vQcBK8XT_JrAbs9qimdfSRK2F-0skLcqss.

9. Stewart, *op. cit.*, 94.
10. Stewart, *op. cit.*, 95.
11. W. Jackson, Turrentine. "Lewis Richard Price, British Mining Entrepreneur and Traveler in California." *Pacific Historical Review* November 1960: 331–348. http://phr.ucpress.edu/content/29/4/331.
12. U.S. Sutro Tunnel Commission. Op cit. 13–32.
13. Eliot Lord. *Comstock Mining and Miners.* Vol. IV. Washington: United States Geological Survey, 1883. https://play.google.com/books/reader?id=jQA0AQAAMAAJ&printsec=frontcover&output=reader&hl=en&pg=GBS.PR3.

Chapter 20

1. U.S. Sutro Tunnel Commission. *Report of the Commissioners and Evidence Taken at the Committee on Mines and Mining of the House of Representatives of the United States, in Regard to the Sutro Tunnel, Together with the Arguments.* Washington, 1872. https://books.googleusercontent.com/books/content?req=AKW5QaeJPn3wa63cIMYOH8JRPIgm8_y1wEGdYi3CVvPXTXb6yT2LideNlpIr39RRPPU68Cj_7OsDmkjc5tEX5vTOtuqkSKzvfFz0ADzNCt48IPki-PugVPYUhgyyMkvQWDRdLEcBACu-rXmAxg7OOc5umQdsWh271wkZ1N4vQcBK8XT_JrAbs9qimdfSRK2F-0skLcqss.
2. Gould, Jayson "Jay". 2000. Gale Encyclopedia of U.S. Economic History. https://www.encyclopedia.com/history/encyclopedias-almanacs-transcripts-and-maps/gould-jayson-jay.
3. "The Crédit Mobilier Scandal." n.d. *History, Art & Archives—United States House of Representatives.* https://history.house.gov/Historical-Highlights/1851-1900/The-Cr%C3%A9dit-Mobilier-scandal/.
4. U.S. Sutro Tunnel Commission, *op. cit.*, 82.
5. Jay Boyd Crawford. *The Crédit Mobilier of America—Its Origin and History.* Boston: C. W. Calkins & Co., 1880. https://books.google.com/books?id=LgopAAAAYAAJ&pg=PA126#v=onepage&q&f=false.

Chapter 21

1. Helen Hinckley. *Rails from the West ... A Biography of Theodore D. Judah.* San Marino: Golden West Books, 1969.
2. *Loc. cit.*

3. Maury Klein. "Financing the Transcontinental Railroad." n.d. *AP U.S. History Study Guide.* https://ap.gilderlehrman.org/essays/financing-transcontinental-railroad.
4. These four Sacramento merchants eventually dubbed themselves The Big Four and their many-tentacled empire of railroads and freight lines was renamed Southern Pacific Railroad in 1884, although its detractors, especially Adolph Sutro, preferred to call it the Octopus. Each of them later built opulent mansions on San Francisco's Nob Hill. (See http://www.foundsf.org/index.php?title=The_Octopus_and_the_Big_Four.)
5. Hinckley, *op. cit.*
6. Pacific Railway Act." n.d. *Primary Documents in American History.* https://www.loc.gov/rr/program/bib/ourdocs/pacificrail.html.
7. *The First Transcontinental Railroad.* n.d. https://tcrr.com/.
8. Klein, *op. cit.*
9. *First Transcontinental Railroad.* n.d. https://en.wikipedia.org/wiki/First_Transcontinental_Railroad.
10. *The First Transcontinental Railroad.* n.d. https://tcrr.com/.
11. *The First Transcontinental Railroad.* n.d. https://tcrr.com/.
12. Klein, *op. cit.*
13. Alain Plessis. *The history of banks in France.* January 2003. http://www.euro.fbf.fr/en/files/888HK2/History_banks_france_EN.pdf.
14. "Crédit Mobilier of America scandal." n.d. *Wikipedia.* https://en.wikipedia.org/wiki/Cr%C3%A9dit_Mobilier_of_America_scandal.
15. Jay Boyd Crawford. *The Crédit Mobilier of America—Its Origin and History.* Boston: C. W. Calkins & Co., 1880. https://books.google.com/books?id=LgopAAAAYAAJ&pg=PA126#v=onepage&q&f=false.
16. "The Crédit Mobilier Scandal." n.d. *History, Art & Archives—United States House of Representatives.* https://history.house.gov/Historical-Highlights/1851-1900/The-Cr%C3%A9dit-Mobilier-scandal/.
17. Hinckley, *op. cit.*

Chapter 22

1. R.E. Stewart, Jr., and M.F. Stewart. *Adolph Sutro—A Biography.* Berkeley, CA: Howell-North, 1962. 54–55.
2. *Ibid.*, facing page 78.
3. *Ibid.*, 11.
4. *Ibid.*, 110.
5. *Ibid.*, 156–158.
6. Francis West. "History of Sutro 1940–1945." 10 November 2007. *Around Carson.* aroundcarson.com/2007/11/10/884/.
7. The Washoe Zephyr is a seasonal daily wind that blows primarily in the summer from mid-afternoon until late evening from the west to south-

west. As the terrain is generally arid, the Washoe Zephyr typically lifts a considerable quantity of dust into the atmosphere. The Washoe Zephyr first gained notoriety from a passage written by Mark Twain in his 1872 book, *Roughing It*.

Chapter 23

1. Edson S. Bastin. "Bonanza Ores of the Comstock Lode, Virginia City, Nevada." 1922. *Contributions to Economic Geology, Part I*. https://pubs.usgs.gov/bul/0735c/report.pdf.
2. *Science of the Comstock—Environmental*. n.d. Nevada Bureau of Mines and Geology. http://www.nbmg.unr.edu/scienceeducation/ScienceOfTheComstock/Environment-InfluenceOfMining.html.
3. Mark McLaughlin. "Historic water pipeline to Virginia City, Part II." 12 July 2017. *Tahoe Weekly*. https://thetahoeweekly.com/2017/07/historic-water-pipeline-virginia-city-2/.
4. *Ibid*.
5. *Ibid*.
6. Joseph V. Tingley. *Geologic and Natural History Tours in the Reno Area*. Sparks: Bear Printing, 2005. https://books.google.com/books?id=ekf0wBY8LyUC&pg=PA73#v=onepage&q&f=false.
7. *Influence of Mining*. n.d. University of Nevada-Reno. http://www.nbmg.unr.edu/scienceeducation/ScienceOfTheComstock/Environment-InfluenceOfMining.html.

Chapter 24

1. George D. Lyman. *Ralston's Ring*. New York: Charles Scribner's Sons, 1937.
2. Oscar Lewis. *Silver Kings*. New York: Alfred A. Knopf, Inc., 1947.
3. *Ibid*.
4. Eliot Lord. *Comstock Mining and Miners*. Vol. IV. Washington: United States Geological Survey, 1883. https://play.google.com/books/reader?id=jQA0AQAAMAAJ&printsec=frontcover&output=reader&hl=en&pg=GBS.PR3. 311.
5. Lyman, *op. cit*.
6. Bruce C. Cooper. *A Brief Illustrated History of the Palace Hotel of San Francisco*. n.d. http://thepalacehotel.org/.
7. Andrew Carnegie. "Round the World." 1884. Google.com. https://play.google.com/books/reader?id=CQQIAAAAQAAJ&hl=en&pg=GBS.PA11. Carnegie visited the Palace on October 23, 1878.
8. Cooper, *op. cit*.
9. Lyman, *op. cit*.
10. *Ibid*.
11. *San Francisco Bulletin* 11 August 1875: 2.
12. Lyman, *op. cit*.
13. *Ibid*.

Chapter 25

1. Adapted from a line in "To a Mouse" by Robert Burns.
2. R.E. Stewart, Jr., and M.F. Stewart. *Adolph Sutro—A Biography*. Berkeley, CA: Howell-North, 1962.
3. *Ibid*.
4. *Ibid*.
5. A copy of this letter, titled "The California Bank Ring Against the Sutro Tunnel" and dated March 17, 1874, is in the Sutro Library at the San Francisco State University, Box 11, Folder 305.
6. California Senator Aaron Augustus Sargent (1827–1887) served in the U.S. Senate from 1873 to 1879. Sargent was an advocate for the Union Pacific Railroad, women's suffrage, and the Chinese Exclusion Act.
7. Adolph Sutro. "Engineering and Mining Journal." 30 November 1878. google.com/books. https://play.google.com/books/reader?id=8OQ-AQAAMAAJ&printsec=frontcover&output=reader&hl=en&pg=GBS.RA15-PA385. 385.
8. *Loc. cit*.
9. Eliot Lord. *Comstock Mining and Miners*. Vol. IV. Washington: United States Geological Survey, 1883. https://play.google.com/books/reader?id=jQA0AQAAMAAJ&printsec=frontcover&output=reader&hl=en&pg=GBS.PR3.
10. Stewart, *op. cit*.
11. Adolph Sutro. "The Engineering and Mining Journal." 15 November 1879. google.com/books. https://books.google.com/books?id=8sVRAQAAIAAJ&pg=PA387&lpg=PA387&dq=Engineering+and+Mining+Journal+November+15,+1879&source=bl&ots=I890EqByz6&sig=VCtFcg4BinnrkrRyywAXVV289Lc&hl=en&sa=X&ved=0ahUKEwjnn_rZqYPcAhUF3FMKHXySAdgQ6AEITjAE#v=onepage&q=Engineering. 357–358.
12. "Great Fire of 1875." n.d. *Carsonpedia*. http://carsonpedia.com/Great_Fire_of_1875.
13. Lord, *op. cit*., 325–329.
14. *Ibid*.
15. Mark Abbott Stern. *Beyond the Tunnel: The Second Life of Adolph Sutro*. Self-published, 2018.
16. Stewart, *op. cit*.
17. Static electricity was first observed in ancient Greece in about 600 BC. It was rediscovered and studied in 1745 in Germany by Ewald Georg von Kleist.
18. "The Human Battery." *California Farmer and Journal of Useful Sciences* 2 August 1877. https://cdnc.ucr.edu/?a=d&d=CF18770802.2.9&e=-------en--20--1--txt-txIN--------1.
19. Mark Abbott Stern. *Beyond the Tunnel: The Second Life of Adolph Sutro*. Self-published, 2018.
20. George D. Lyman. *Ralston's Ring*. New York: Charles Scribner's Sons, 1937.
21. Lord, *op. cit*.
22. "The Sutro Tunnel united with the Savage

Mine." 9 July 1878. *Virginia Chronicle.* https://www.nevadaappeal.com/news/lahontan-valley/the-sutro-tunnel-united-with-the-savage-mine/.

23. *Ibid.*

24. Stewart, *op. cit.*, 150.

25. "The Sutro Tunnel—The Scene in the Savage Drift When the Connection was Made—Rejoicing Over the Event." *Daily Alta California* 10 July 1878: 4. https://cdnc.ucr.edu/?a=d&d=DAC18780710.2.44&e=-------en--20--1--txt-txIN-------1.

26. Adolph Sutro. "Engineering and Mining Journal." 30 November 1878. google.com/books. https://play.google.com/books/reader?id=8OQAQAAMAAJ&printsec=frontcover&output=reader&hl=en&pg=GBS.RA15-PA385. 387.

Chapter 26

1. R.E. Stewart, Jr., and M.F. Stewart. *Adolph Sutro—A Biography.* Berkeley, CA: Howell-North, 1962. 146.

2. Mark Abbott Stern. *Beyond the Tunnel: The Second Life of Adolph Sutro.* Self-published, 2018.

3. George D. Lyman. *Ralston's Ring.* New York: Charles Scribner's Sons, 1937. 268–269.

4. Adolph Sutro. "The Engineering and Mining Journal." 15 November 1879. google.com/books. https://books.google.com/books?id=8sVRAQAAIAAJ&pg=PA387&lpg=PA387&dq=Engineering+and+Mining+Journal+November+15,+1879&source=bl&ots=I890EqByz6&sig=VCtFcg4BinnrkrRyywAXVV289Lc&hl=en&sa=X&ved=0ahUKEwjnn_rZqYPcAhUF3FMKHXySAdgQ6AEITjAE#v=onepage&q=Engineering. 357.

5. "Completion of the Sutro Tunnel—Rejoicing Over the Event." *Sacramento Daily Union* 1 July 1879. https://cdnc.ucr.edu/?a=d&d=SDU18790701.2.23.11&dliv=none&e=-------en--20--1--txt-txIN--------1.

6. Eliot Lord. *Comstock Mining and Miners.* Vol. IV. Washington: United States Geological Survey, 1883. https://play.google.com/books/reader?id=jQA0AQAAMAAJ&printsec=frontcover&output=reader&hl=en&pg=GBS.PR3. 342.

7. "A Visit to the Sutro Tunnel—The Town of Sutro." *Sacramento Daily Union* 28 April 1879. https://cdnc.ucr.edu/?a=d&d=SDU18790428.2.2.8&dliv=none&e=-------en--20--1--txt-txIN--------1.

8. Sutro, *op. cit.,* 359.

9. Mark Abbott Stern. *Beyond the Tunnel: The Second Life of Adolph Sutro.* Self-published, 2018. 65.

10. Stewart, *op. cit.,* 167–169.

11. "Sutro Tunnel Company—Resignation of Sutro." *Sacramento Daily Union* 2 March 1880. https://cdnc.ucr.edu/?a=d&d=SDU18800302.2.3&e=-------en--20--1--txt-txIN--------1.

12. Stewart, *op. cit.,* 195–196.

13. Theodor Sutro. *Report to the Stockholders of The Sutro Tunnel Company and the Sutro Tunnel.* July 1887. https://archive.org/stream/sutrotunnelcomp00compgoog/sutrotunnelcomp00compgoog_djvu.txt.

Chapter 27

1. R.E. Stewart, Jr., and M.F. Stewart. *Adolph Sutro—A Biography.* Berkeley, CA: Howell-North, 1962.

2. Dr. Emma Sutro Merritt. n.d. https://www.findagrave.com/memorial/76268972/emma-merritt.

3. Stewart, *op. cit.*

4. Dr. Emma Sutro Merritt, *op. cit.*

5. "Rosa Victoria Sutro Morbio." n.d. *Find a Grave.* https://www.findagrave.com/memorial/76280692/rosa-victoria-morbio.

6. "Gustavus Emanuel Sutro." n.d. *Find a Grave.* https://www.findagrave.com/memorial/140585790/gustavus-emanuel-sutro.

7. "Kate Sutro Nussbaum." n.d. *Find a Grave.* https://www.findagrave.com/memorial/140603641/kate-nussbaum.

8. "Charles Walter Sutro." n.d. *Find a Grave.* https://www.findagrave.com/memorial/76330582/charles-walter-sutro.

9. "Edgar Ernest Sutro." n.d. *Find a Grave.* https://www.findagrave.com/memorial/76342691/edgar-ernest-sutro.

10. "Clara Angela de Choiseul-Praslin." n.d. *Geni.* https://www.geni.com/people/Clara-de-Choiseul-Praslin/6000000031513091823.

11. "Adolph Sutro II." n.d. *Find a Grave.* https://www.findagrave.com/memorial/189392979/adolph-sutro,_ii.

12. Frank B. Mercer. "A Few Memories of the Late Adolph Sutro as I Recall Them at this Late Day." Spokane, 8 April 1918.

13. Emma continued her medical studies and, in 1881, was the first female to receive the Doctor of Medicine Degree from the University of California Medical School. See prabook.com/web/emma_laura_sutro.merritt/1111107 and Fred Rosenbaum. *Cosmopolitans—A Social and Cultural History of the Jews of the San Francisco Bay Area.* Berkeley: University of California Press, 2009.

14. Stewart, *op. cit.,* 140–141.

15. Laura Tennant, Jack Folmar. "Images of America—Dayton." 2015. Google.com. Arcadia Publishing. https://books.google.com/books?id=VsD2CQAAQBAJ&pg=PA38&lpg=PA38&dq=a.+Summerfield,+Sutro&source=bl&ots=YaVJT54R7W&sig=vMHEYj0pdbXIhME5txuMKpDxkE&hl=en&sa=X&ved=2ahUKEwiB-u2g0NjcAhWMVt8KHeG5D4EQ6AEwAnoECAgQAQ#v=onepage&q=a.%20Summerfield%2C%20Sutro&f=fals.

16. Stewart, *op. cit.,* 163–164.

17. Grant H. Smith. "The History of the Com-

stock Lode 1850–1920." 1 July 1943. Google.com. University of Nevada. https://books.google.com/books?id=8q_TOO4CmDwC&pg=PA227&lpg=PA227&dq=M.+G.+Gillette,+comstock+lode&source=bl&ots=N5Gcw5xelw&sig=Gzf6CiYIBwR-70IXqgF4ZUteLiU&hl=en&sa=X&ved=2ahUKEwjp2rHQxdjcAhXJuVMKHc2rCiMQ6AEwBHoECAcQAQ#v=onepage&q=M.%20G.%20Gillette%2C%20.

18. Stewart, *op. cit.*, 164.
19. Stewart, *op. cit.*, 158.
20. "Sutro's Bequest." *Leavenworth Times* 14 August 1898: 3.
21. "Sutro's Will Is Read to His Children." *San Francisco Call* 12 August 1898. https://cdnc.ucr.edu/cgi-bin/cdnc?a=d&d=SFC18980812.2.72.
22. "Sutro Saved." *Reno Gazette-Journal* 7 October 1881: 3.
23. "Sutro's Separation." *San Francisco Chronicle* 12 December 1893.
24. *Op. cit.*, 170.
25. Mark Abbott Stern. *Beyond the Tunnel: The Second Life of Adolph Sutro.* Self-published, 2018. 139, 155.
26. Mary Germain Hountalas. *The San Francisco Cliff House.* Berkeley: Ten Speed Press, 2009.

Chapter 28

1. *Hills of San Francisco.* San Francisco: Chronicle Publishing Company, 1959. Cited in Richard Brandi. "Farms, Fire and Forest: Adolph Sutro and Development 'West of Twin Peaks.'" *The Argonaut* Spring 2003.
2. "Map of the City of San Francisco Showing the Lines of the Market Street Railway Company." 1902. *University of Texas Libraries—Perry-Castañeda Library.* https://legacy.lib.utexas.edu/maps/historical/street_railway/1902/txu-oclc-6445490-street_railway-san_francisco-1902.jpg.
3. "Sutro's Rancho San Miguel—1880." 9 August 1880. *Outsidelands.* http://www.outsidelands.org/detail/sutro-rancho-map-1880_big.php.
4. Mark Abbott Stern. *Beyond the Tunnel: The Second Life of Adolph Sutro.* Self-published, 2018.
5. R.E. Stewart, Jr., and M.F. Stewart. Adolph Sutro—A Biography. Berkeley, CA: Howell-North, 1962. 170–172.
6. Mary Germain Hountalas. *The San Francisco Cliff House.* Berkeley: Ten Speed Press, 2009.

Chapter 29

1. Much of the description of Sutro Heights in this chapter is drawn from James Delgado, Denise Bradley, Paul Scolari, Stephen Haller. "The History and Significance of the Adolph Sutro Historic District." 2000. *nps.gov.* https://www.nps.gov/goga/learn/historyculture/upload/sutro_history.pdf.
2. Quoted in Delgado et al., *ibid.* 13.

3. E. J. Jackson. *Autumnal Sunset.* San Francisco: Joseph Winterburn & Co., 1890. https://archive.org/details/autumnalsunset00jack/page/n3.
4. "A New Railroad." *Daily Alta California* 8 May 1885. https://cdnc.ucr.edu/?a=d&d=DAC18850508.2.28&dliv=none&e=-------en--20--1--txt-txIN--------1.
5. Behan, John E., ed. *Real Estate Owned by the City and County of San Francisco.* San Francisco: A. Carlisle & Co., 1909. https://play.google.com/books/reader?id=VfcsAAAAYAAJ&hl=en&pg=GBS.PA117.
6. *Hills of San Francisco.* San Francisco: Chronicle Publishing Company, 1959. Cited in Richard Brandi. "Farms, Fire and Forest: Adolph Sutro and Development 'West of Twin Peaks.'" *The Argonaut* Spring 2003.
7. Jacqueline Proctor. *Adolph Sutro.* n.d. https://mtdavidson.org/adolph-sutro/.
8. Jacqueline Proctor. "The Father of Tree Planting in California." June 2014. *MtDavidson.org.* https://mtdavidson.org/the-father-of-tree-planting-in-california/#sdendnote23sym.
9. Phoebe Cutler. "Eden: Journal of the California Garden & Landscape History Society." Fall 2015. cglhs.com. Ed. Virginia Kean. https://cglhs.org/resources/Documents/Eden-18.4-Fa-2015.pdf.
10. Annalee Newitz. "Mt. Olympus." n.d. *FoundSF.* http://www.foundsf.org/index.php?title=Mt._Olympus.
11. Saperstein, *op. cit.*

Chapter 30

1. "Mrs. Kluge Will Battle for the Sutro Millions." *San Francisco Call* 11 January 1900. https://cdnc.ucr.edu/cgi-bin/cdnc?a=d&d=SFC19000111.2.4&srpos=1&e=--1888---1900--en--20-SFC-1--txt-txIN-Clara+Kluge-ILLUSTRATION------1.
2. *Clara Louisa Kluge Sutro.* n.d. https://www.findagrave.com/memorial/138003454/clara-louisa-sutro.
3. *Adolph Newton Sutro.* n.d. https://www.findagrave.com/memorial/120623771/adolph-newton-sutro.
4. *Adolphina Charlotte Sutro Fullerton.* n.d. https://www.findagrave.com/memorial/137987471/adolphina-charlotte-fullerton.
5. "mrs. Adolph sutro." *San Francisco Call* 20 April 1893. https://cdnc.ucr.edu/cgi-bin/cdnc?a=d&d=SFC18930420.2.52&srpos=1&e=20-04-1893-20-04-1893--en--20-SFC-1--txt-txIN-Sutro-------1.
6. "Death Claims Adolph Sutro, Philanthropist." *San Francisco Call* 9 August 1898. https://cdnc.ucr.edu/cgi-bin/cdnc?a=d&d=SFC18980809.2.141&e=-------en--20--1--txt-txIN--------1.
7. "Mrs Adolph Sutro." *San Francisco Call* 10 December 1893. https://cdnc.ucr.edu/?a=d&d=SFC18931210.2.72&srpos=10&e=-------en--20--1--txt-txIN-%22Mrs.+Adolph+Sutro%22+-------.

8. "Three Funerals—Funeral of Mrs. Sutro." *San Francisco Call* 12 December 1893. https://cdnc.ucr.edu/?a=d&d=SFC18931212.2.118&e=-------en--20--1--txt-txIN--------1.

9. "All to Her Children." *San Francisco Call* 15 December 1893. https://cdnc.ucr.edu/?a=d&d=SFC18931215.2.84&srpos=1&dliv=none&e=--------en--20--1--txt-txIN-Mrs.+Adolph+Sutro+1893-------1.

10. *Leah Harris Sutro.* n.d. https://www.findagrave.com/memorial/8071279/leah-sutro.

11. "Adolph Sutro, II." n.d. *Find a Grave.* https://www.findagrave.com/memorial/189392979/adolph-sutro,_ii.

12. *Gustavus Emanuel Sutro.* n.d. https://www.findagrave.com/memorial/140585790/gustavus-emanuel-sutro.

13. Candi McMahon. "Gustavus Emanuel Sutro." n.d. *Find a Grave.* https://www.findagrave.com/memorial/140585790/gustavus-emanuel-sutro.

14. "Real Estate Transactions." *San Francisco Call* 26 April 1895. https://cdnc.ucr.edu/?a=d&d=SFC18950426.2.152&e=-------en--20--1--txt-txIN--------1.

15. "Real Estate Transactions." *San Francisco Call* 16 May 1895. https://cdnc.ucr.edu/?a=d&d=SFC18950516.2.189&e=-------en--20--1--txt-txIN--------1.

16. "Real Estate Transactions." *San Francisco Call* 2 September 1895. https://cdnc.ucr.edu/cgi-bin/cdnc?a=d&d=SFC18950902.2.152&srpos=12&e=--1888---1900--en--20-SFC-1--txt-txIN-Clara+Kluge-ARTICLE------1.

17. Liv Jenks. "The wedding cake that wasn't." *The New Fillmore* 1 August 2017. http://newfillmore.com/2017/08/01/the-wedding-cake-that-wasnt/.

18. *Ibid.*

19. "Real Estate Transactions." *San Francisco Call* 5 June 1898: 14. https://cdnc.ucr.edu/cgi-bin/cdnc?a=d&d=SFC18980605.2.110.3&srpos=10&e=--1888---1900--en--20-SFC-1--txt-txIN-Clara+Kluge-------1.

Chapter 31

1. Mary Germain Hountalas. *The San Francisco Cliff House.* Berkeley: Ten Speed Press, 2009.

2. *Ibid.*

3. *Ibid.*

4. Mark Twain. "A Trip to the Cliff House." San Francisco *Daily Morning Call* 25 June 1864. http://www.twainquotes.com/18640625.html.

5. Mark Twain. 3 July 1864. *Cliff House Project.* http://www.cliffhouseproject.com/history/clemens/clemens.htm.

6. "Tightrope Walk." 28 September 1865. *Cliff House Project.* Marysville (CA) Daily Appeal. http://www.cliffhouseproject.com/history/cooke/tightrope.htm.

7. Marilyn Blaisdell. *San Francisciana: Photographs of the Cliff House.* 1985.

8. Hountalas, *op. cit.*

9. J.M. Wilkins. "First Cliff House—1863." 6 October 1918. *Cliff House Project.* San Francisco Chronicle. http://www.cliffhouseproject.com/history/1863/1863.htm.

Chapter 32

1. J.M. Wilkins. "First Cliff House—1863." 6 October 1918. *Cliff House Project.* San Francisco Chronicle. http://www.cliffhouseproject.com/history/1863/1863.htm.

2. James R. Smith. *San Francisco's Lost Landmarks.* Fresno: Craven Street Books, 2005.

3. The captain and crew made it to land, where they witnessed the explosion from a safe distance. They eventually returned to the ruined hulk of the *Parallel* to reclaim their belongings, but nothing was left.

4. Compiled from newspaper reports at "Shipwreck of the Parallel." 16 January 1887. *Cliff House Project.* http://www.cliffhouseproject.com/history/parallel/parallel.htm.

5. R.E. Stewart, Jr., and M.F. Stewart. *Adolph Sutro—A Biography.* Berkeley, CA: Howell-North, 1962.

6. "Ashen Heaps." 26 December 1894. *Cliff House Project.* San Francisco Morning Call. http://www.cliffhouseproject.com/history/fire1894/N67902pdfFile%20Dec%2026%201894%20-%20pg%201.pdf.

7. "Christmas Fire." 24 November 1895. *Cliff House Project.* San Francisco Call. http://www.cliffhouseproject.com/history/fire1894/xmasfire.htm.

Chapter 33

1. "Ashen Heaps." 26 December 1894. *Cliff House Project.* San Francisco Morning Call. http://www.cliffhouseproject.com/history/fire1894/N67902pdfFile%20Dec%2026%201894%20-%20pg%201.pdf.

2. "The New Cliff House." 13 April 1895. *Cliff House Project.* San Francisco Chronicle. http://www.cliffhouseproject.com/history/1895/1895.htm.

3. "The New Cliff House." 25 June 1895. *Cliff House Project.* San Francisco Call. http://www.cliffhouseproject.com/history/1895/1895.htm.

4. The New Cliff House." 10 July 1895. *Cliff House Project.* San Francisco Call. http://www.cliffhouseproject.com/history/1895/1895.htm.

5. "Will Face the Ocean." 27 January 1895. *Cliff House Project.* San Francisco Examiner. http://www.cliffhouseproject.com/history/1895/1895.htm.

6. "Cliff House and Baths Dedicated." 2 February 1896. *Cliff House Project.* San Francisco Chronicle. http://www.cliffhouseproject.com/history/1896/1896.htm.

7. "A Conspiracy that Failed." 6 April 1896. *Cliff House Project.* San Francisco Chronicle. http://www.cliffhouseproject.com/history/Vanderbilt/SF%20Chronicle%20-%2006%20Apr%201896%20-%20Vanderbilt%20visit.pdf.

8. James Delgado, Denise Bradley, Paul Scolari, Stephen Haller. "The History and Significance of the Adolph Sutro Historic District." 2000. *nps.gov.* https://www.nps.gov/goga/learn/historyculture/upload/sutro_history.pdf.

9. "Cliff House is Destroyed by Fire." 8 September 1907. *Cliff House Project.* San Francisco Chronicle. http://www.cliffhouseproject.com/history/fire1907/fire.htm.

Chapter 34

1. John A. Martini. *Sutro's Glass Palace.* Bodega Bay: Samuel E. Stokes, Hole in the Head Press, 2014.

2. Settling Pond and Tank capacities from n.d. http://wikimapia.org/#lang=en&lat=37.780143&lon=-122.512949&z=19&m=w.

3. "To Architects." *San Francisco Chronicle* 5 August 1891: 8. Cited in John A. Martini, *Sutro's Glass Palace.* Bodega Bay: Samuel E. Stokes, Hole in the Head Press, 2014.

4. "Baths at the Beach." *San Francisco Chronicle* 5 August 1891: 10. https://www.newspapers.com/image/27468470/?terms=Baths%2Bat%2Bthe%2BBeach&match=2.

5. Taber. *Sutro Baths-Cliff House-Sutro Heights.* San Francisco, 1895.

6. "The Sutro Baths Are Rapidly Nearing Completion." *San Francisco Call* 27 August 1893. https://cdnc.ucr.edu/cgi-bin/cdnc?a=d&d=SFC18930827.2.74&srpos=1&e=27-08-1893-27-08-1893--en--20-SFC-1--txt-txIN-Sutro-------1.

7. Ariel Rubissow. *Cliff House & Lands End—San Francisco's Seaside Retreat.* Golden Gate National Park Association, 1993.

8. "The New Road to the Cliff." *San Francisco Call* 2 February 1896. https://cdnc.ucr.edu/?a=d&d=SFC18960202.2.75&dliv=none&e=-------en--20--1--txt-txIN--------1.

9. "Twenty Thousand." *San Francisco Call* 7 February 1896. https://cdnc.ucr.edu/?a=d&d=SFC18960207.2.146&dliv=none&e=-------en--20--1--txt-txIN--------1.

10. Marilyn and Robert Blaisdell. *San Francisciana Photographs of Sutro Baths.* San Francisco: Marilyn Blaisdell, 1987.

11. "Sterilizers for Bath Houses." *San Francisco Examiner* 19 September 1900: 24. https://www.newspapers.com/image/457703116/?terms=Sterilizers.

12. A.S. Baldwin. *Estate of Adolph Sutro, Deceased.* 1910.

13. John A. Martini. *Sutro's Glass Palace.* Bodega Bay: Samuel E. Stokes, Hole in the Head Press, 2014.

14. "Saltwater Bathing for the People. Grand Opening of a Superb Palace of Water." *San Francisco Evening Bulletin* 7 April 1894.

Chapter 35

1. Edward F. O'Day. "Varied Types: 347—Robert E. Cowan." *Town Talk: The Pacific and Bay Cities Weekly* 8 September 1917.

2. Quoted in Russ Davidson. "Adolph Sutro as Book Collector: A New Look." *California State Library Foundation* 2012.

3. R.E. Stewart, Jr., and M.F. Stewart. *Adolph Sutro—A Biography.* Berkeley, CA: Howell-North, 1962.

4. Gerald Le Grys Norgate. "Spencer, Charles (1674–1722)." *Dictionary of National Biography, 1885–1900* 53 (1885–1900).

5. Richard Dillon. "Adolph Sutro Finds a Librarian." *The Journal of Library History* July 1967: 227.

6. Martin Spahn. "Kulturkampf." 1910. *The Catholic Encyclopedia.* Ed. Kevin Knight. http://www.newadvent.org/cathen/08703b.htm.

7. Incunabula are books, pamphlets, or broadsides printed in Europe before 1501, such as the Gutenberg Bible.

8. "Mrs Sutro's Birthday Celebration." *New York Times* 15 March 1883: 2. https://timesmachine.nytimes.com/timesmachine/1883/03/15/106247648.pdf.

9. William Richard Cutter, ed. *American Biography—A New Cyclopedia.* Vol. V. New York City, 1919. https://play.google.com/books/reader?id=x2UUAAAAYAAJ&hl=en&pg=GBS.PP13.

10. £20 in 1884 corresponds to about $2,600 in 2018.

11. Cited in Davidson, *ibid.*

12. *Op. cit.*

13. *Op. cit.*

14. *Op. cit.*

15. *Op. cit.*

16. Fred Waldeck. "Adolph Sutro's Lost Library." *College and Research Libraries* January 1957.

17. Oscar Lewis, Edgar M. Kahn. *Seven Pioneer San Francisco Libraries.* San Francisco: Literary Licensing, LLC, 2013 (Reprint).

18. "Sutro's Books." *The Morning Call* 15 June 1893. https://cdnc.ucr.edu/cgi-bin/cdnc?a=d&d=SFC18930615.2.102&srpos=3&e=13-06-1893-18-06-1893--en--20-SFC-1--txt-txIN-Sutro-------1.

19. Adolph Sutro. "Letter to the Regents of the University of California and to the Committee of Affiliated Colleges on the Selection of a Site for the Affiliated Colleges." September 5, 1895.

20. "Real Estate Transactions." *San Francisco Call* 10 October 1895: 12. https://cdnc.ucr.edu/?a=d&d=SFC18951010.2.171&e=-------en--20--1--txt-txIN--------1.

21. The Latin phrase is based on Psalm 104:23: "Man goeth forth unto his work and to his labour until the evening" (KJV).

Chapter 36

1. "Adolph Sutro." n.d. *Wikipedia.* https://en.wikipedia.org/wiki/Adolph_Sutro.
2. John Bonner. "Story of Adolph Sutro's Great Successes in Life." *San Francisco Call* 18 February 1898. http://www.cliffhouseproject.com/history/sutroillness/San%20Francisco%20Call%20-%2013%20Feb%201898.pdf.
3. "The New Mayor." *San Francisco Morning Call* 8 November 1894: 3. http://www.cliffhouseproject.com/history/mayor/N68368pdfFile%20-%20Sutro%20Elected.pdf.
4. "Sutro Illness." 8 February 1898. *Cliff House Project.* Los Angeles Herald. http://www.cliffhouseproject.com/history/sutroillness/SutroIllness.htm.
5. "Mr. Sutro's Mob." *San Francisco Call* 26 January 1893: 3. https://cdnc.ucr.edu/?a=d&d=SFC18930126.2.48&dliv=none&e=-------en--20--1--txt-txIN--------1.
6. In 1885, the Central Pacific Railroad was leased by the Southern Pacific Railroad. From that time on, the names became virtually interchangeable. The railroads formally merged in 1959.
7. Stephen E. Ambrose. *Nothing Like It In the World—The Men Who Built the Transcontinental Railroad 1863–1869.* New York: Simon & Schuster, 2000.
8. "Direct Talk." *San Francisco Call* 20 June 1894: 12. https://cdnc.ucr.edu/?a=d&d=SFC18940620.2.173&e=-------en--20--1--txt-txIN--------1.
9. Fred Rosenbaum. *Cosmopolitans—A Social and Cultural History of the Jews of the San Francisco Bay Area.* Berkeley: University of California Press, 2009.
10. "Sutro for Mayor—The People's Party After Him." *San Francisco Call* 23 July 1894. https://cdnc.ucr.edu/?a=d&d=SFC18940723.2.136&dliv=none&e=-------en--20--1--txt-txIN--------1.
11. "Will Accept." *San Francisco Call* 24 July 1894. https://cdnc.ucr.edu/?a=d&d=SFC18940724.2.16&dliv=none&e=-------en--20--1--txt-txIN--------1.
12. Edward W. Townsend. "Adolph Sutro: Mayor-Elect of San Francisco." *The Review of Reviews* December 1894.
13. R.E. Stewart, Jr., and M.F. Stewart. *Adolph Sutro—A Biography.* Berkeley, CA: Howell-North, 1962.
14. Townsend, *op. cit.*
15. Stewart, *op. cit.*
16. "Has Wearied of the Work." *Los Angeles Herald* 16 February 1895. https://cdnc.ucr.edu/?a=d&d=LAH18950216.2.10&e=-------en--20--1--txt-txIN--------1.
17. In 2014, Sutro's descendants donated 1,380 acres of the Arcadia Ranch property, along with a $450,000 endowment for managing the property, to the Land Trust of Napa County. See article by Kevin Courtney, dated June 16, 2014 at https://napavalleyregister.com/news/local/land-trust-acquires-acres-on-atlas-peak/article_206bfa78-b48c-5b4e-9b65-ab598a44bb19.html.
18. "The Retreat of the Mayor of San Francisco." *Industry* September 1895: 515–517.
19. "Who is Mayor of this Town?" *San Francisco Call* 3 July 1896. https://cdnc.ucr.edu/?a=d&d=SFC18960703.2.139&dliv=none&e=-------en--20--1--txt-txIN--------1.
20. *Adolph Sutro (1830–1898).* n.d. http://www.americanjerusalem.com/characters/adolph-sutro-1830-ae-1898/19.
21. Samuel G. Hilborn. "Appendix to the Congressional Record." 9 January 1897. Government Publishing Office. https://www.govinfo.gov/content/pkg/GPO-CRECB-1897-pt3-v29/pdf/GPO-CRECB-1897-pt3-v29-13.pdf.
22. "Markets of the World." *Los Angeles Herald* 12 January 1897. https://cdnc.ucr.edu/cgi-bin/cdnc?a=d&d=LAH18970112.2.25&e=-------en--20--1--txt-txIN--------1.
23. Alfred Henry Lewis. "Black Eye for Collis P." *New York Journal* 12 January 1897. https://www.loc.gov/resource/sn84024350/1897-01-12/ed-1/?sp=1&st=text&r=0.332,0.208,0.396,0.324,0.

Chapter 37

1. Mark Abbott Stern. *Beyond the Tunnel: The Second Life of Adolph Sutro.* Self-published, 2018.
2. "Adolph Sutro Declared Mentally Incompetent." 7 February 1898. *Cliff House Project.* http://www.cliffhouseproject.com/history/sutroillness/SutroIllness.htm.
3. 20 January 1898. *Cliff House Project.* Red Bluff (CA) Daily News. http://www.cliffhouseproject.com/history/sutroillness/SutroIllness.htm.
4. "Adolph Sutro Declared Mentally Incompetent," *op. cit.*
5. "Adolph Sutro Forcibly Taken From His Home." *San Francisco Call* 6 May 1898: 14. http://www.cliffhouseproject.com/history/sutroillness/San%20Francisco%20Call%20-%206%20May%201898.pdf.
6. "Laid at Rest with Little Ceremony." *San Francisco Call* 11 August 1898. https://cdnc.ucr.edu/?a=d&d=SFC18980811.2.154&e=-------en--20--1--txt-txIN--------1.
7. "Magnes collection on Adolph Sutro, 1858–1993." n.d. *The Magnes Collection of Jewish Art and Life.* https://magnes.berkeley.edu/collections/archives/western-jewish-americana/magnes-collection-adolph-sutro-1858–1993.
8. Frances Dinkelspiel. "Resurrecting the dead: the ghosts of past Jewish San Franciscans." 4 November 2014. http://francesdinkelspiel.com/2014/11/resurrecting-the-dead-the-ghosts-of-past-jewish-san-franciscans/.
9. Sutro's Will Is Read to His Children." *San Francisco Call* 12 August 1898. https://cdnc.ucr.edu/cgi-bin/cdnc?a=d&d=SFC18980812.2.72.

10. "Miss Trundle's Fortune." *Topeka State Journal* 19 August 1898.
11. "Sutro's Heir Dead." *Topeka State Journal* 14 September 1898.
12. "Supreme Court Ends Struggle." *San Francisco Call* 14 May 1903.
13. *Reports of Cases Determined in the Supreme Court of the State of California*. 25 November 1901. https://play.google.com/books/reader?id=rV0WAQAAIAAJ&hl=en&pg=GBS.PA580.
14. "Sutro's Will Criticized." *San Francisco Call* 13 August 1898. https://cdnc.ucr.edu/?a=d&d=SFC18980813.2.103&dliv=none&e=-------en--20--1--txt-txIN--------1.
15. "Sutro's Will Is Read to His Children." *San Francisco Call* 12 August 1898. https://cdnc.ucr.edu/cgi-bin/cdnc?a=d&d=SFC18980812.2.72.
16. *Loc. cit.*
17. Is This Woman the Contract Wife of Adolph Sutro?" *San Francisco Chronicle* 10 March 1898. 1.
18. Without a will, thus allowing the state to decide on asset distribution.
19. "Sutro Heirs Win Contest Over Lands." *San Francisco Call* 31 October 1905: 7. https://cdnc.ucr.edu/cgi-bin/cdnc?a=d&d=SFC19051031.2.97&e=-------en--20--1--txt-txIN--------1.
20. "Sutro's Family and His Contested Will." 29 October 1909. *nps.gov*. https://www.nps.gov/goga/learn/historyculture/upload/Sutro_Family_sr_2014.pdf.
21. A.S. Baldwin. *Estate of Adolph Sutro, Deceased*. 1910.
22. "Battle is On for Sutro's Millions." 26 October 1898. *San Francisco Call*. https://cdnc.ucr.edu/cgi-bin/cdnc?a=d&d=SFC18981026.2.113&srpos=3&e=-02-1898---2010--en--50-SFC-1-byDA-txt-txIN-%22Clara+Kluge%22-------1.
23. "Will Soon Contest Adolph Sutro's Will." 16 November 1898. *San Francisco Call*. https://cdnc.ucr.edu/cgi-bin/cdnc?a=d&d=SFC18981116.2.74&srpos=57&e=-02-1898---2010--en--20-SFC-41--txt-txIN-Sutro+will-------1.
24. "Final Assault Now Made on Sutro's Will." 19 January 1900. *San Francisco Call*. https://cdnc.ucr.edu/cgi-bin/cdnc?a=d&d=SFC19000119.2.75.
25. "Real Estate Transactions." *San Francisco Call* July 19, 1902; July 19, 1903; December 21, 1904; January 13, 1905; January 24, 1905; February 4, 1905; February 15, 1905; February 25, 1905; March 2, 1905; June 13, 1905; June 23, 1905; July 26, 1905; February 15, 1906.
26. "Builder's Contracts." *San Francisco Call* 29 November 1904. https://cdnc.ucr.edu/?a=d&d=SFC19041129.2.114&e=-------en--20--1--txt-txIN--------1.
27. "Contests Will Be Dismissed." 21 January 1902. *San Francisco Call*. https://cdnc.ucr.edu/cgi-bin/cdnc?a=d&d=SFC19020121.2.50&srpos=33&e=-02-1898---2010--en--20-SFC-21--txt-txIN-Sutro+will-------1.
28. "Clara Kluge, Also sometimes called Clara Kluge Sutro, to Emma L. Merritt and Charles W. Sutro." DEED. San Francisco, 8 June 1912. Gleeson Library, University of San Francisco.
29. "Aldophine Charlotte Kluge, Also sometimes called Adolphine Charlotte Sutro, to Emma L. Merritt and Charles W. Sutro." DEED. San Francisco, 8 June 1912. Gleeson Library, University of San Francisco.
30. "Recent Sales of City Realty." *San Francisco Call* 18 January 1913. https://cdnc.ucr.edu/cgi-bin/cdnc?a=d&d=SFC19130118.2.184&srpos=28&e=-02-1898---2010--en--50-SFC-1-byDA-txt-txIN-%22Clara+Kluge%22-------1.
31. Adolph Newton Sutro. "Will Erect First Division Monument." June 1920. *California Legion Monthly*. American Legion. https://books.google.com/books?id=sdI3AQAAMAAJ&pg=RA2-PA22&lpg=RA2-PA22&dq=adolph+newton+sutro&source=bl&ots=wBxFFUXJco&sig=rb3Woz9MAZkA-Act50enQ_sx3Ds&hl=en&sa=X&ved=2ahUKEwjTn7Oy3qveAhXlp1kKHQqhCbEQ6AEwDnoECAIQAQ#v=onepage&q=adolph%20newton%20sutro&f=fa.
32. "Adolphine Sutro Fullerton." n.d. askart.com. http://www.askart.com/artist/Adolphine_Sutro_Fullerton/11173983/Adolphine_Sutro_Fullerton.aspx.
33. "Clara Louisa Kluge Sutro." n.d. *Find a Grave*. https://www.findagrave.com/memorial/138003454.
34. "Adolphina Charlotte Sutro Fullerton." n.d. *Find a Grave*. https://www.findagrave.com/memorial/137987471/adolphina-charlotte-fullerton.
35. "Adolph Newton Sutro." n.d. *Find a Grave*. https://www.findagrave.com/memorial/120623771/adolph-newton-sutro.

Chapter 38

1. *Comstock Lode*. n.d. https://westernmininghistory.com/mine_detail/10310576/.
2. Jason Spidell, and Robert R. Kautz. "Historic Properties Treatment Plan for Mitigation of Historic Sites within the Comstock Mining, LLC Right-of-Way Permit, Storey County, Nevada." n.d. *U.S. Bureau of Land Management*. https://eplanning.blm.gov/epl-front-office/projects/nepa/35610/70945/77641/Attachment_3_-_Historic_Properties_Treatment_Plan_-_Historic_Site_Redacted.pdf.
3. Italo Gavazzi. "American Flat: Stepchild of the Comstock Lode-Part I." *Nevada Historical Society Quarterly* Summer 1998: 92–100.
4. *Loc. cit.*
5. Grant H. Smith, and Joseph V. Tingley. *The History of the Comstock Lode, 1850–1997*. Reno: University of Nevada Press, 1998.
6. Susan Juetten. *Residential Mining in Nevada's Historic Comstock*. 13 October 2014. http://www.desertreport.org/?p=1315.
7. "Comstock reports $12.9M loss: Company

continues to reduce costs." *Elko Daily Free Press* 10 March 2017. https://elkodaily.com/mining/comstock-reports-m-loss-company-continues-to-reduce-costs/article_665a059b-b82c-597e-98ed-3dced84c78f2.html.

8. Eliot Lord. *Comstock Mining and Miners*. Vol. IV. Washington: United States Geological Survey, 1883. https://play.google.com/books/reader?id=jQA0AQAAMAAJ&printsec=frontcover&output=reader&hl=en&pg=GBS.PR3. 408.

9. Theodore Sutro. *Report to the Stockholders of The Sutro Tunnel Company and The Sutro Tunnel*. July 1887. https://archive.org/stream/sutrotunnelcomp00compgoog/sutrotunnelcomp00compgoog_djvu.txt.

10. "To Unwater the Comstock." *San Francisco Call* 13 August 1898. https://cdnc.ucr.edu/?a=d&d=SFC18980813.2.83&dliv=none&e=-------en--20--1--txt-txIN--------1.

11. Joe Basco. *Sutro, 1900, Comstock Tunnel Company*. n.d. https://sites.google.com/site/bascojoenv/home/lyon/sutro-1900-comstock-tunnel-company.

12. Laura Tennant. "Sutro Owned 8,000 Acres in Lyon County." *Lyon County Reflections* 1997.

13. *Loc. cit.*

14. R.L. Herrick. "Progress on the Comstock Lode." *Mines and Minerals* November 1908: 150–159. https://books.googleusercontent.com/books/content?req=AKW5QafvMB44-8xGIIcIaYRfw9U75tVnVUHAlRLWVnVSi2-Wro28txNc4snOLJw9aTZW5gZvCKl-IcliuF7yBtS14Ahv0PyugNzisg9wB3N7_Nhg7Od6peutSk715ihlN1I379UuAMjMK5qNv_6fD6RCwAj7GYz_8WowigxdG4psI-fJvTr8XpmrhD9rqnfetEERIhZ7u.

15. *Loc. cit.*

16. *Historical Gold Prices*. n.d. http://onlygold.com/Info/Historical-Gold-Prices.asp.

17. *Goldfield News*. 4 December 1909.

18. Hugh A. Shamberger. *The Story of the Water Supply for the Comstock*. 1972. U.S. Government Printing Office. https://pubs.usgs.gov/pp/0779/report.pdf.

19. Francis West. "History of Sutro 1940–1945." 10 November 2007. *Around Carson*. aroundcarson.com/2007/11/10/884/.

20. *Loc. cit.*

21. Stony and Laura Tennant. Private communication.

Chapter 39

1. Cindy Casey. "Architecture Spotlight: Sutro Heights Park." 26 April 2012. *Untapped Cities*. https://untappedcities.com/2012/04/26/architecture-spotlight-sutro-heights-park/.

2. Courtesy of L. Tom Perry Special Collections, Harold B. Lee Library, Brigham Young University, Provo, UT.

3. Adolph G. Sutro was the son of Adolph's son, Edgar Ernest Sutro and Henrietta Louise Sutro.

4. John A. Martini. *Sutro's Glass Palace*. Bodega Bay: Samuel E. Stokes, Hole in the Head Press, 2014.

5. John Martini. "Re: Sutro Train Questions." 15 September 2103. *OutsideLands.org of the Western Neighborhoods Project*. http://www.outsidelands.org/cgi-bin/mboard/stories2/thread.cgi?2420,1.

6. "Railroad Men Scramble for Sutro's Line." *San Francisco Call* 18 October 1899. https://cdnc.ucr.edu/?a=d&d=SFC18991018.2.146&dliv=none&e=-------en--20--1--txt-txIN--------1.

7. "Cliff House—History and Memories." 13 February 1949. *Facebook*. https://www.facebook.com/groups/SFCliffHouse/?multi_permalinks=1199960803497412&notif_id=1550161723469332&notif_t=group_highlights.

8. "Sutro's Will Is Read to His Children." *San Francisco Call* 12 August 1898. https://cdnc.ucr.edu/cgi-bin/cdnc?a=d&d=SFC18980812.2.72.

9. "Sutro's Will Criticized." *San Francisco Call* 13 August 1898. https://cdnc.ucr.edu/?a=d&d=SFC18980813.2.103&dliv=none&e=-------en--20-1--txt-txIN--------1.

10. "The Great 1906 San Francisco Earthquake." n.d. *USGS*. https://earthquake.usgs.gov/earthquakes/events/1906calif/18april/.

11. Fred Waldeck. "Adolph Sutro's Lost Library." *College and Research Libraries* January 1957.

12. *In the Matter of the Estate of Adolph Sutro, Deceased*, 1913. In the Superior Court of the State of California, In and For the City and County of San Francisco. No. 51. Dept. No. 9 (Probate).

13. Russ Davidson. "Adolph Sutro as Book Collector: A New Look." *California State Library Foundation Bulletin* 2012.

14. Gary E. Strong. "Reflections on the Sutro Library." *California State Library Foundation Bulletin* 2012.

15. Gary F. Kurutz. "The Sutro Library's Long Journey Is Over." *California State Library Foundation Bulletin* 2012.

16. "Sutro Heirs to Rebuild the Famous Cliff House." 10 March 1908. *Cliff House Project*. Los Angeles Herald. http://www.cliffhouseproject.com/history/1908/1908.htm.

17. "Adopt New Plans for Cliff House." 27 September 1908. *Cliff House Project*. San Francisco Call. http://www.cliffhouseproject.com/history/1908/1908.htm.

18. "New Cliff House Contract Filed." 9 October 1908. *Cliff House Project*. San Francisco Chronicle. http://www.cliffhouseproject.com/history/1908/1908.htm.

19. "Reid Brothers, Architects (Partners)." n.d. *PCAD*. http://pcad.lib.washington.edu/firm/284/.

20. "New Cliff House Opens." 4 July 1909. *Cliff House Project*. San Francisco Call. http://www.cliffhouseproject.com/history/1909/1909.htm.

21. *Golden Gate National Recreation Area*. n.d. https://www.nps.gov/goga/planyourvisit/maps.htm.

22. *The Cliff House*. n.d. https://cliffhouse.com/history/.

Bibliography

Aachen. n.d. en.wikipedia.org/wiki/Aachen.

Ad for Steamship to Panama and on to California (1850). 8 October 1850. 10 April 2018. https://ghostsofbaltimore.org/2013/09/24/ad-steamship-panama-california-1850/.

"Adolph Newton Sutro." n.d. *Find a Grave.* https://www.findagrave.com/memorial/120623771/adolph-newton-sutro.

Adolph Sutro. n.d. https://www.findagrave.com/memorial/6639928/adolph-sutro.

"Adolph Sutro." n.d. *Wikipedia.* https://en.wikipedia.org/wiki/Adolph_Sutro.

Adolph Sutro (1830–1898). n.d. http://www.americanjerusalem.com/characters/adolph-sutro-1830-ae-1898/19.

"Adolph Sutro Declared Mentally Incompetent." 7 February 1898. Cliff House Project. http://www.cliffhouseproject.com/history/sutroillness/SutroIllness.htm.

"Adolph Sutro Forcibly Taken from His Home." *San Francisco Call* 6 May 1898: 14. http://www.cliffhouseproject.com/history/sutroillness/San%20Francisco%20Call%20-%206%20May%201898.pdf.

"Adolph Sutro, II." n.d. *Find a Grave.* https://www.findagrave.com/memorial/189392979/adolph-sutro,_ii.

"Adolphina Charlotte Sutro Fullerton." n.d. *Find a Grave.* https://www.findagrave.com/memorial/137987471/adolphina-charlotte-fullerton.

"Adolphine Charlotte Kluge, Also sometimes called Adolphine Charlotte Sutro, to Emma L. Merritt and Charles W. Sutro." *DEED.* San Francisco, 8 June 1912. Gleeson Library, University of San Francisco.

"Adolphine Sutro Fullerton." n.d. askart.com. http://www.askart.com/artist/Adolphine_Sutro_Fullerton/11173983/Adolphine_Sutro_Fullerton.aspx.

"Adopt New Plans for Cliff House." 27 September 1908. Cliff House Project. *San Francisco Call.* http://www.cliffhouseproject.com/history/1908/1908.htm.

Albertson, Dean. "The Discovery of Gold in California as Viewed by New York and London." Winter 1949. *The Virtual Museum of the City of San Francisco.* The Pacific Spectator. http://www.sfmuseum.net/hist5/albertson.html.

"All to Her Children." *San Francisco Call* 15 December 1893. https://cdnc.ucr.edu/?a=d&d=SFC18931215.2.84&srpos=1&dliv=none&e=-------en--20--1--txt-txIN-Mrs.+Adolph+Sutro+1893+-------1.

"Almarin B. Paul." *History of the New California, Its Resources and People.* Ed. Leigh H. Irvine. Vol. 2. The Lewis Publishing Company, 1905. https://oac.cdlib.org/findaid/ark:/13030/c8q244pv/entire_text/.

"Along the Road." n.d. *Virginia and Truckee.* http://www.virginiaandtruckee.com/.

Ambrose, Stephen E. *Nothing Like It in the World—The Men Who Built the Transcontinental Railroad 1863–1869.* New York: Simon & Schuster, 2000.

"The American Cyclopaedia (1879)/Amalgamation." n.d. *Wikisource.* 7 May 2018. https://en.wikisource.org/wiki/The_American_Cyclop%C3%A6dia_(1879)/Amalgamation.

Arehart Greg B., Mark Coolbaugh, Simon Poulson. "Geothermal Resources Council Transactions." 12 October 2003. *Evidence for a Magmatic Source of Heat for the Steamboat Springs Geothermal System Using Trace Elements and Gas Geochemistry.* Great Basin Center for Geothermal Energy, University of Nevada. http://www.atlasgeoinc.com/wp-content/uploads/Arehart_etal_GRC_2003_Magmatic_Steamboat.pdf.

"Ashen Heaps." 26 December 1894. Cliff House Project. *San Francisco Morning Call.* http://www.cliffhouseproject.com/history/fire1894/N67902pdfFile%20Dec%2026%201894%20-%20pg%201.pdf.

"August Helbing (1824–1896)." n.d. *American Jerusalem.* http://www.americanjerusalem.com/characters/august-helbing-1824-ae-1896/22.

Bagley, Will. *Scoundrel's Tale: The Samuel Brannan Papers*. Utah State University Press, 1999.

Bailey, Paul. *Sam Brannan and the California Mormons*. Los Angeles: Westernlore Press, 1943.

Bain, Andrew. *Carson River Mercury Site—Dayton, NV*. n.d. https://cumulis.epa.gov/supercpad/Site Profiles/index.cfm?fuseaction=second.Cleanup&id=0903020#bkground.

Baldwin, A. S. Baldwin. *Estate of Adolph Sutro, Deceased*. 1910.

Basco, Joe. *Sutro, 1900, Comstock Tunnel Company*. n.d. https://sites.google.com/site/bascojoenv/home/lyon/sutro-1900-comstock-tunnel-company.

Bastin, Edson S. "Bonanza Ores of the Comstock Lode, Virginia City, Nevada." 1922. *Contributions to Economic Geology, Part I*. https://pubs.usgs.gov/bul/0735c/report.pdf.

"Baths at the Beach." *San Francisco Chronicle* 5 August 1891: 10. https://www.newspapers.com/image/27468470/?terms=Baths%2Bat%2Bthe%2BBeach&match=2.

"Battle Is On for Sutro's Millions." 26 October 1898. *San Francisco Call*. https://cdnc.ucr.edu/cgi-bin/cdnc?a=d&d=SFC18981026.2.113&srpos=3&e=-02-1898---2010--en-50-SFC-1-byDA-txt-txIN-%22Clara+Kluge%22-------1.

Benko, Ralph J. "President Polk: '...as would scarcely command belief....'" 12 May 2012. *The Gold Standard Now*. http://www.thegoldstandardnow.org/key-blogs-6/1223-the-california-gold-rush-begins.

Berkove, Lawrence I. "Free Silver and the Change in Dan De Quille." n.d. *American Jewish Archives*. http://americanjewisharchives.org/publications/journal/PDF/1989_41_01_00_berkove.pdf.

"Bernard Frankenheimer." n.d. *Find a Grave*. https://www.findagrave.com/memorial/144032434/bernhard-frankenheimer.

Bigler, Henry W. Coloma, 24 January 1848.

Blaisdell, Marilyn, and Robert Blaisdell. *San Francisciana Photographs of Sutro Baths*. San Francisco: Marilyn Blaisdell, 1987.

Blaisdell, Marilyn. *San Francisciana: Photographs of the Cliff House*. 1985.

Bomboy, Scott. "The man who delivered California to the U.S., and was fired for it." 10 March 2017. *National Constitution Center*. https://constitutioncenter.org/blog/the-man-who-delivered-california-to-the-u-s-and-was-fired-for-it.

Bonanza. n.d. https://www.amazon.com/gp/video/detail/B0172XX15I?ref_=atv_dp_season_select.

Bonner, John. "Story of Adolph Sutro's Great Successes in Life." *San Francisco Call* 18 February 1898. http://www.cliffhouseproject.com/history/sutroillness/San%20Francisco%20Call%20-%2013%20Feb%201898.pdf.

Brandi, Richard. "Farms, Fire and Forest: Adolph Sutro and Development 'West of Twin Peaks.'" *The Argonaut* Spring 2003.

Brown, James S. "California Gold: An Authentic History of the First Find with the Names of Those Interested in the Discovery." 24 January 1894. *The Virtual Museum of the City of San Francisco*. http://www.sfmuseum.net/hist6/grush.html.

"Builder's Contracts." *San Francisco Call* 29 November 1904. https://cdnc.ucr.edu/?a=d&d=SFC19041129.2.114&e=-------en--20--1--txt-txIN---------1.

"California Steam Navigation Company." 15 January 2019. *Wikipedia*. https://en.wikipedia.org/wiki/California_Steam_Navigation_Company.

Campbell, Eugene E. "The Apostasy of Samuel Brannan." *Utah Historical Quaterly* 1959.

Carnegie, Andrew. "Round the World." 1884. Google.com. https://play.google.com/books/reader?id=CQQIAAAAQAAJ&hl=en&pg=GBS.PA11.

Casey, Cindy. "Architecture Spotlight: Sutro Heights Park." 26 April 2012. *Untapped Cities*. https://untappedcities.com/2012/04/26/architecture-spotlight-sutro-heights-park/.

"Charlemagne." 19 September 2018. *History*. Ed. History.com editors. https://www.history.com/topics/middle-ages/charlemagne.

"Charlemagne and Aachen." n.d. *Victoria and Albert Museum*. http://www.vam.ac.uk/content/articles/c/charlemagne-and-aachen/.

Charles Morgan (businessman). n.d. 17 April 2018. https://en.wikipedia.org/wiki/Charles_Morgan_(businessman).

Charles Spencer, 3rd Earl of Sunderland. n.d. https://en.wikipedia.org/wiki/Charles_Spencer,_3rd_Earl_of_Sunderland.

"Charles Walter Sutro." n.d. *Find a Grave*. https://www.findagrave.com/memorial/76330582/charles-walter-sutro.

Chastain, James. "March Revolution." 20 October 2004. *Ohio.edu*. https://www.ohio.edu/chastain/ip/marrev.htm.

"Christmas Fire." 24 November 1895. Cliff House Project. *San Francisco Call*. http://www.cliffhouseproject.com/history/fire1894/xmasfire.htm.

Church, John A. "Heat of the Comstock Mines." *American Institute of Mining Engineers* (1878). https://ia800209.us.archive.org/20/items/heatofcomstockmi00churrich/heatofcomstockmi00churrich.pdf.

"Clara Angela de Choiseul-Praslin." n.d. *Geni*. https://www.geni.com/people/Clara-de-Choiseul-Praslin/6000000031513091823.

"Clara Kluge, Also sometimes called Clara Kluge Sutro, to Emma L. Merritt and Charles W. Sutro." DEED. San Francisco, 8 June 1912. Gleeson Library, University of San Francisco.

Clara Louisa Kluge Sutro. n.d. https://www.findagrave.com/memorial/138003454/clara-louisa-sutro.

The Cliff House. n.d. https://cliffhouse.com/history/.

The Cliff House and Sutro Heights. November Fire Recordings. Albany, 2013. DVD.

"Cliff House and Baths Dedicated." 2 February 1896. Cliff House Project. *San Francisco Chronicle*. http://www.cliffhouseproject.com/history/1896/1896.htm.

"Cliff House—History and Memories." 13 February 1949. Facebook. https://www.facebook.com/groups/SFCliffHouse/?multi_permalinks=1199960803497412&notif_id=1550161723469332&notif_t=group_highlights.

"Cliff House is Destroyed by Fire." 8 September 1907. Cliff House Project. *San Francisco Chronicle*. http://www.cliffhouseproject.com/history/fire1907/fire.htm.

Climate Virginia City—Nevada. n.d. https://www.usclimatedata.com/climate/virginia-city/nevada/united-states/usnv0095.

"Completion of the Sutro Tunnel—Rejoicing Over the Event." *Sacramento Daily Union* 1 July 1879. https://cdnc.ucr.edu/?a=d&d=SDU18790701.2.23.11&dliv=none&e=-------en--20--1--txt-txIN--------1.

Comstock Lode. n.d. https://en.wikipedia.org/wiki/Comstock_Lode.

Comstock Lode. n.d. https://westernmininghistory.com/mine_detail/10310576/.

The Comstock Lode and the Mining Frontier. 2016. 8 May 2018. http://www.digitalhistory.uh.edu/disp_textbook_print.cfm?smtid=2&psid=3149.

Comstock Lode—Creating Nevada History. n.d. 18 April 2018. https://www.legendsofamerica.com/nv-comstocklode/.

Comstock Mining District. n.d. 18 April 2018. http://www.onlinenevada.org/articles/comstock-mining-district.

"Comstock reports $12.9M loss: Company continues to reduce costs." *Elko Daily Free Press* 10 March 2017. https://elkodaily.com/mining/comstock-reports-m-loss-company-continues-to-reduce-costs/article_665a059b-b82c-597e-98ed-3dced84c78f2.html.

"A Conspiracy That Failed." 6 April 1896. Cliff House Project. *San Francisco Chronicle*. http://www.cliffhouseproject.com/history/Vanderbilt/SF%20Chronicle%20-%2006%20Apr%201896%20-%20Vanderbilt%20visit.pdf.

"Contests Will Be Dismissed." 21 January 1902. *San Francisco Call*. https://cdnc.ucr.edu/cgi-bin/cdnc?a=d&d=SFC19020121.2.50&srpos=33&e=-02-1898---2010--en--20-SFC-21--txt-txIN-Sutro+will-------1.

Cooper, Bruce C. *A Brief Illustrated History of the Palace Hotel of San Francisco*. n.d. http://thepalacehotel.org/.

Cornelius Vanderbilt. n.d. 16 April 2018. https://legacy.voteview.com/vanderb2.htm.

Craig, C., et al. "Science of the Comstock—Environment—Influence of Mining." 1999. *Nevada Bureau of Mines and Geology*. http://www.nbmg.unr.edu/_images/ScienceEducation/ScienceOfTheComstock/NBMG_SP19_Map_Mills_Flumes_ RR.png.

Crawford, Jay Boyd. *The Credit Mobilier of America—Its Origin and History*. Boston: C. W. Calkins & Co., 1880. https://books.google.com/books?id=LgopAAAAYAAJ&pg=PA126#v=onepage&q&f=false.

Crédit Mobilier. n.d. https://en.wikipedia.org/wiki/Cr%C3%A9dit_Mobilier.

"Crédit Mobilier of America scandal." n.d. *Wikipedia*. https://en.wikipedia.org/wiki/Cr%C3%A9dit_Mobilier_of_America_scandal.

"The Crédit Mobilier Scandal." n.d. *History, Art & Archives—United States House of Representatives*. https://history.house.gov/Historical-Highlights/1851–1900/The-Cr%C3%A9dit-Mobilier-scandal/.

Cutler, Phoebe. "Eden: Journal of the California Garden & Landscape History Society." Fall 2015. cglhs.com. Ed. Virginia Kean. https://cglhs.org/resources/Documents/Eden-18.4-Fa-2015.pdf.

Cutter, William Richard, ed. *American biography*. Vol. 5. American Historical Society, 1919. www.delabrede.com/Windmuller/Sutro.html.

_____. *American Biography-A New Cyclopedia*. Ed. William Richard Cutter. Vol. V. New York City, 1919. https://play.google.com/books/reader?id=x2UUAAAAYAAJ&hl=en&pg=GBS.PP13.

Dangers Below (Comstock Silver Mines). Ed. Robert R. Van Ryzin. n.d. http://numismaster.com/ta/inside_numis.jsp?page=dangers-comstock-silver-mines.

Davidson, Russ. "Adolph Sutro as Book Collector: A New Look." *California State Library Foundation Bulletin* 2012.

"Death Claims Adolph Sutro, Philanthropist." *San Francisco Call* 9 August 1898. https://cdnc.ucr.edu/cgi-bin/cdnc?a=d&d=SFC18980809.2.141&e=-------en--20--1--txt-txIN--------1.

"Death of Sharon." *San Francisco Chronicle* 14 September 1885: 2.

Delgado, James. "The History and Significance of the Adolph Sutro Historic District." 2000. nps.gov. https://www.nps.gov/goga/learn/historyculture/upload/sutro_history.pdf.

DeQuille, Dan. *History of the Big Bonanza*. Las Vegas: Nevada Publications, 1887 (Reprint).

_____. "Philip Deidesheimer." *Territorial Enterprise (draft of article)*. Sutro Library, Box 14, Folder 444, Undated.

"Digging Deeper into the Comstock." 10 October 2009. *Guide for the Earth Science Week Field Trip*. Nevada Bureau of Mines and Geology. http://dwgateway.library.unr.edu/keck/mining/dox/e48.pdf.

Dillon, Richard. "Adolph Sutro Finds a Librarian." *The Journal of Library History* July 1967: 227.

Dinkelspiel, Frances. "Resurrecting the dead: the ghosts of past Jewish San Franciscans." 4 November 2014. http://francesdinkelspiel.com/2014/11/resurrecting-the-dead-the-ghosts-of-past-jewish-san-franciscans/.

"Direct Talk." *San Francisco Call* 20 June 1894: 12.

https://cdnc.ucr.edu/?a=d&d=SFC18940620.2.1 73&e=-------en--20--1--txt-txIN--------1.

Dr Emma Sutro Merritt. n.d. https://www.findagrave.com/memorial/76268972/emma-merritt.

Donner Party. n.d. https://en.wikipedia.org/wiki/Donner_Party#Rescue.

Drabelle, Dennis. *Mile-High Fever: Silver Mines, Boom Towns, and High Living on the Comstock Lode.* New York: St. Martin's Press, 2009.

Duek, Julieta. "Committee of Vigilance of San Francisco." 2013. *FoundSF.* http://www.foundsf.org/index.php?title=Committee_of_Vigilance_of_San_Francisco.

"Edgar Ernest Sutro." n.d. *Find a Grave.* https://www.findagrave.com/memorial/76342691/edgar-ernest-sutro.

Edwards, Julie A. S. *Immigrant Ships Transcribers Guild—Ship Peter Hattrick.* 31 January 2000. 3 April 2018. https://immigrantships.net/v3/1800v3/peterhattrick18500930.html#Sutro.

Elise Sutro Schucking. n.d. https://www.findagrave.com/memorial/98914311/elise-schucking.

Emanuel Sali Sutro. n.d. https://www.findagrave.com/memorial/146723622/emanuel-sali-sutro.

Emil Sutro. n.d. https://www.findagrave.com/memorial/58043145/emil-sutro.

Emma Bertha Sutro. n.d. https://www.findagrave.com/memorial/141124131/emma-bertha-winterberg.

"Eureka Benevolent Society (San Francisco, Calif.) records, 1850–1977." n.d. *The Magnes Collection of Jewish Art and Life.* University of Californis, Berkeley. https://magnes.berkeley.edu/collections/archives/western-jewish-americana/eureka-benevolent-society-san-francisco-calif-records.

"Final Assault Now Made on Sutro's Will." 19 January 1900. *San Francisco Call.* https://cdnc.ucr.edu/cgi-bin/cdnc?a=d&d=SFC19000119.2.75.

1st millionaire dies broke. n.d. http://www.calgoldrush.com/profiles/pro_brannan.html.

First Transcontinental Railroad. n.d. https://en.wikipedia.org/wiki/First_Transcontinental_Railroad.

The First Transcontinental Railroad. n.d. https://tcrr.com/.

"Fraser Canyon Gold Rush." n.d. *Wikipedia.* https://en.wikipedia.org/wiki/Fraser_Canyon_Gold_Rush.

"Fraser River Gold Rush." n.d. *Canadian Encyclopedia.* https://www.thecanadianencyclopedia.ca/en/article/fraser-river-gold-rush/.

Gardner, Richard Lyle. *The Comstock: Economic History of Mining Bonanza.* 2009. http://www.comstockhistory.com/media//DIR_9001/mss1.pdf.

Garner, Richard Lyle. "The Comstock: Economic History of Mining Bonanza 1865–1885." 2009. http://www.comstockhistory.com/media//DIR_9001/mss1.pdf.

Garside, B.W. Purkey, and L.J. *Geologic and Natural History Tours in the Reno Area.* Vol. Special Publication 19. Reno: Nevada Bureau of Mines and Geology, 1995.

Gavazzi, Italo. "American Flat: Stepchild of the Comstock Lode-Part I." *Nevada Historical Society Quarterly* Summer 1998: 92–100.

German revolutions of 1848–1849. n.d. https://en.wikipedia.org/wiki/German_revolutions_of_1848%E2%80%9349.

"The Gold Cure for Depression." 1932.

"The Gold Rush of 1849." 2010. History.com. http://www.history.com/topics/gold-rush-of-1849.

The Gold Rushes of North America (1847–1900); Part III. 1859–1864—The Comstock Lode. n.d. http://www.calliope.org/gold/gold3.html.

Golden Gate National Recreation Area. n.d. https://www.nps.gov/goga/planyourvisit/maps.htm.

Gould, Jayson "Jay." 2000. Gale Encyclopedia of U.S. Economic History. https://www.encyclopedia.com/history/encyclopedias-almanacs-transcripts-and-maps/gould-jayson-jay.

Gray, Tom. "The Treaty of Guadalupe Hidalgo." n.d. *National Archives Educator Resources.* https://www.archives.gov/education/lessons/guadalupe-hidalgo.

"Great Fire of 1875." n.d. *Carsonpedia.* http://carsonpedia.com/Great_Fire_of_1875.

"The Great 1906 San Francisco Earthquake." n.d. *USGS.* https://earthquake.usgs.gov/earthquakes/events/1906calif/18april/.

"Gustavus Emanuel Sutro." n.d. *Find a Grave.* https://www.findagrave.com/memorial/140585790/gustavus-emanuel-sutro.

Hamblin, Joan. "Voyage of the 'Brooklyn.'" July 1997. *The Church of Jesus Christ of Latter Day Saints.* https://www.lds.org/ensign/1997/07/voyage-of-the-brooklyn?lang=eng.

Hardesty, Donald. *Mining Technology in the Nineteenth Century.* 10 December 2010. http://www.onlinenevada.org/articles/mining-technology-nineteenth-century.

"Has Wearied of the Work." *Los Angeles Herald* 16 February 1895. https://cdnc.ucr.edu/?a=d&d=LAH18950216.2.10&e=-------en--20--1--txt-txIN--------1.

Hermann Schussler. n.d. https://en.wikipedia.org/wiki/Hermann_Schussler.

Hermann Schussler: A water-systems engineer and architect of Bay Area dams. 8 June 2009. *San Mateo Daily Journal.* http://www.watereducation.org/aquafornia-news/hermann-schussler-water-systems-engineer-and-architect-bay-area-dams.

Herrick, R. L. "Progress on the Comstock Lode." *Mines and Minerals* November 1908: 150–159. https://books.googleusercontent.com/books/content?req=AKW5QafvMB44-8xGIIcIaYRfw9U75tVnVUHAlRLWVnVSi2-Wro28txNc4snOLJw9aTZW5gZvCKl-IcliuF7yBtS14Ahv0PyugNzisg9wB3N7_Nhg7Od6peutSk715ihlN1I379

UuAMjMK5qNv_6fD6RCwAj7GYz_8Wowigxd G4psI-fJvTr8XpmrhD9rqnfetEERIhZ7u.

Hilborn, Samuel G. "Appendix to the Congressional Record." 9 January 1897. Government Publishing Office. https://www.govinfo.gov/content/pkg/GPO-CRECB-1897-pt3-v29/pdf/GPO-CRECB-1897-pt3-v29-13.pdf.

Hills of San Francisco. San Francisco: Chronicle Publishing Company, 1959.

Hinckley, Helen. *Rails from the West ... A Biography of Theodore D. Judah.* San Marino: Golden West Books, 1969.

Historical Gold Prices. n.d. http://onlygold.com/Info/Historical-Gold-Prices.asp.

History of the Panama Railroad. n.d. 16 April 2018. http://www.panamarailroad.org/history1.html.

Hittell, Theodore. "The Gold Discovery." 1897. *The Virtual Museum of the City of San Francisco.* http://www.sfmuseum.net/hist6/impact.html.

Hountalas, Mary Germain. *The San Francisco Cliff House.* Berkeley: Ten Speed Press, 2009.

Hugo Aron Sutro. n.d. https://www.findagrave.com/memorial/140641977/hugo-aron-sutro.

"The Human Battery." *California Farmer and Journal of Useful Sciences* 2 August 1877. https://cdnc.ucr.edu/?a=d&d=CF18770802.2.9&e=-------en--20--1--txt-txIN--------1.

In the Matter of the Estate of Adolph Sutro, Deceased. No. 51, Dept. No. 9 Probate. Superior Court of the State of California, in and for the City and County of San Francisco. December 1913.

Influence of Mining. n.d. University of Nevada–Reno. http://www.nbmg.unr.edu/scienceeducation/ScienceOfTheComstock/Environment-InfluenceOfMining.html.

"Is This Woman the Contract Wife of Adolph Sutro?" *San Francisco Chronicle* 10 March 1898.

Jackson, Donald Dale. "Sutro Baths: the greatest show on water." *Smithsonian* February 1993: 120.

Jackson, E. J. *Autumnal Sunset.* San Francisco: Joseph Winterburn & Co., 1890. https://archive.org/details/autumnalsunset00jack/page/n3.

Jackson, W. Turrentine. "Lewis Richard Price, British Mining Entrepreneur and Traveler in California." *Pacific Historical Review* November 1960: 331–348. http://phr.ucpress.edu/content/29/4/331.

James, Ronald. "Milling Technology in the Nineteenth Century." 15 July 2011. *Online Nevada Encyclopedia.* http://www.onlinenevada.org/articles/milling-technology-nineteenth-century.

Jenks, Liv. "The wedding cake that wasn't." *The New Fillmore* 1 August 2017. http://newfillmore.com/2017/08/01/the-wedding-cake-that-wasnt/.

"John Augustus Sutter." 2001. *New Perspectives on the West.* PBS. http://www.pbs.org/weta/thewest/people/s_z/sutter.htm.

John Sutter. n.d. en.wikipedia.org/wiki/John_Sutter.

Juetten, Susan. *Residential Mining in Nevada's Historic Comstock.* 13 October 2014. http://www.desertreport.org/?p=1315.

Juliana Sutro Jordan. n.d. https://www.findagrave.com/memorial/25644103/juliana-jordan.

"Kate Sutro Nussbaum." n.d. *Find a Grave.* https://www.findagrave.com/memorial/140603641/kate-nussbaum.

Klein, Maury. "Financing the Transcontinental Railroad." n.d. *AP US History Study Guide.* https://ap.gilderlehrman.org/essays/financing-transcontinental-railroad.

Kuepper, Justin. "3 Of The Most Lucrative Land Deals In History." 23 August 2017. *Investopedia.* https://www.investopedia.com/financial-edge/1012/3-of-the-most-lucrative-land-deals-in-history.aspx.

Kurutz, Gary F. "The Sutro Library's Long Journey Is Over." *California State Library Foundation Bulletin* 2012.

"Laid at Rest with Little Ceremony." *San Francisco Call* 11 August 1898. https://cdnc.ucr.edu/?a=d&d=SFC18980811.2.154&e=-------en--20--1--txt-txIN--------1.

L'Amour, Louis. *Comstock Lode.* New York: Bantam Books, 1981.

Laura Sutro Drost. n.d. https://www.findagrave.com/memorial/178542254/laura-drost.

"law of parsimony." n.d. Dictionary.com. https://www.dictionary.com/browse/law-of-parsimony.

Lawliss, Chuck. *Ghost Towns, Gamblers & Gold.* New York: Gallery Books, A division of W.H. Smith Publishers, Inc., 1985.

Leah Harris Sutro. n.d. https://www.findagrave.com/memorial/8071279/leah-sutro.

Leibman, Jack. *Adolph Sutro Arrives in SF (Part 4).* n.d. 3 April 2018. http://www.sfcityguides.org/public_guidelines.html?article=378&submitted=TRUE&srch_text=sutro&submitted2=TRUE&topic=.

———. *Adolph Sutro in Panama (Part 2).* n.d. SF City Guides. 28 February 2018. http://www.sfcityguides.org/public_guidelines.html?article=320&submitted=TRUE&srch_text=sutro&submitted2=TRUE&topic=.

———. *Adolph Sutro Slogs Through Panama (Part 3).* n.d. 3 April 2018. http://www.sfcityguides.org/public_guidelines.html?article=351&submitted=TRUE&srch_text=sutro&submitted2=TRUE&topic=.

———. *Adolph Sutro Travels to California (Part 1).* n.d. SF City Guides. 6 April 2018. http://www.sfcityguides.org/public_guidelines.html?article=247&submitted=TRUE&srch_text=sutro&submitted2=TRUE&topic=.

Lewis, Alfred Henry. "Black Eye for Collis P." *New York Journal* 12 January 1897. https://www.loc.gov/resource/sn84024350/1897-01-12/ed-1/?sp=1&st=text&r=0.332,0.208,0.396,0.324,0.

Lewis, Oscar. *Silver Kings.* New York: Alfred A. Knopf, Inc., 1947.

Lewis, Oscar, and Edgar M. Kahn. *Seven Pioneer*

San Francisco Libraries. San Francisco: Literary Licensing, LLC, 2013 (Reprint).

Life of John Augustus Sutter 1803–1880. n.d. http://score.rims.k12.ca.us/activity/suttersfort/pages/sutter.html.

Locke, Augustus. "The Abnormal Temperatures on the Comstock Lode." *Economic Geology* 1912: 583–587.

Lord, Eliot. *Comstock Mining and Miners*. Vol. IV. Washington: United States Geological Survey, 1883. https://play.google.com/books/reader?id=jQA0AQAAMAAJ&printsec=frontcover&output=reader&hl=en&pg=GBS.PR3.

Ludwig Sutro. n.d. https://www.findagrave.com/memorial/12604421/ludwig-sutro.

Lyman, George D. *Ralston's Ring*. New York: Charles Scribner's Sons, 1937.

_____. *The Saga of the Comstock Lode—Boom Days in Virginia City*. New York: Ballantine Books, 1934.

Lyons, David M., et al. "Mercury contamination in the Carson River, Nevada: A preliminary study of the impact of mining wastes." December 1996. *Springer Link*. https://link.springer.com/article/10.1007/BF00283569.

"Magnes collection on Adolph Sutro, 1858–1993." n.d. *The Magnes Collection of Jewish Art and Life*. https://magnes.berkeley.edu/collections/archives/western-jewish-americana/magnes-collection-adolph-sutro-1858–1993.

Magovern, Betty. "SUTRO—A Family Tree." San Francisco, 1992.

Makley, Michael J. *The Infamous King of the Comstock: William Sharon and the Gilded Age in the West*. Ed. Michael Green. 1. Reno: University of Nevada Press, 2006.

"Map of Mexico." n.d. https://www.youtube.com/watch?v=ft3bIpOVoow.

"Map of the City of San Francisco Showing the Lines of the Market Street Railway Company." 1902. *University of Texas Libraries—Perry-Castañeda Library*. https://legacy.lib.utexas.edu/maps/historical/street_railway/1902/txu-oclc-6445490-street_railway-san_francisco-1902.jpg.

"Maps, Museums, Monuments and Markers." n.d. *Mormon Battalion Association*. http://www.mormonbattalion.com/Museums_Monuments_Maps_and_Trails.

"Markets of the World." *Los Angeles Herald* 12 January 1897. https://cdnc.ucr.edu/cgi-bin/cdnc?a=d&d=LAH18970112.2.25&e=-------en--20--1--txt-txIN--------1.

Marshall, Daniel P. "Fraser River Gold Rush." 30 May 2014. *The Canadian Encyclopedia*. https://www.thecanadianencyclopedia.ca/en/article/fraser-river-gold-rush.

Martini, John. "Re: Sutro Train Questions." 15 September 2103. *OutsideLands.org of the Western Neighborhoods Project*. http://www.outsidelands.org/cgi-bin/mboard/stories2/thread.cgi?2420,1.

Martini, John A. *Sutro's Glass Palace*. Bodega Bay: Samuel E. Stokes, Hole in the Head Press, 2014.

Mason, Richard Barnes. "Official Report on the Gold Mines." 17 August 1848. *The Virtual Museum of the City of San Francisco*. http://www.sfmuseum.net/hist6/masonrpt.html.

May, Meredith. "Sydney Ducks and vigilante justice in SF, 1851." 9 December 2012. *SFGate*. https://www.sfgate.com/entertainment/article/Sydney-Ducks-and-vigilante-justice-in-SF-1851-4097306.php.

McGlashan, C.F. "History of the Donner Party." 1922. *Books-About-California*. A. Carlisle & Co. http://www.books-about-california.com/Pages/History_of_Donner_Party/Donner_Party_chapter_21.html.

McLaughlin, Mark. "Historic water pipeline to Virginia City, Part II." 12 July 2017. *Tahoe Weekly*. https://thetahoeweekly.com/2017/07/historic-water-pipeline-virginia-city-2/.

McMahon, Candi. "Gustavus Emanuel Sutro." n.d. *Find a Grave*. https://www.findagrave.com/memorial/140585790/gustavus-emanuel-sutro.

Mercer, Frank B. "A Few Memories of the Late Adolph Sutro as I Recall Them at this Late Day." Spokane, 8 April 1918.

Metcalf, Brandon J. "Four Things to Know about the Journey of the Mormon Battalion." 24 January 2018. *Church History*. https://history.lds.org/article/historic-sites/journey-of-the-mormon-battalion?lang=eng.

"Miss Trundle's Fortune." *The Topeka State Journal* 19 August 1898.

"Mr. Sutro's Mob." *San Francisco Call* 26 January 1893. https://cdnc.ucr.edu/?a=d&d=SFC18930126.2.48&dliv=none&e=-------en--20--1--txt-txIN--------1.

Mormon Battalion. n.d. https://en.wikipedia.org/wiki/Mormon_Battalion.

Morrison, John Harrison. *History of American Steam Navigation*. New York: W.F. Sametz & Co., Inc., 1903.

"Mrs Adolph Sutro." *San Francisco Call* 10 December 1893. https://cdnc.ucr.edu/?a=d&d=SFC18931210.2.72&srpos=10&e=-------en--20--1--txt-txIN-%22Mrs.+Adolph+Sutro%22+-------.

"Mrs Adolph Sutro." *San Francisco Call* 20 April 1893. https://cdnc.ucr.edu/cgi-bin/cdnc?a=d&d=SFC18930420.2.52&srpos=1&e=20-04-1893-20-04-1893--en--20-SFC-1--txt-txIN-Sutro-------1.

"Mrs Kluge Will Battle for the Sutro Millions." *San Francisco Call* 11 January 1900. https://cdnc.ucr.edu/cgi-bin/cdnc?a=d&d=SFC19000111.2.4&srpos=1&e=--1888---1900--en--20-SFC-1--txt-txIN-Clara+Kluge-ILLUSTRATION------1.

"Mrs Sutro's Birthday Celebration." *New York Times* 15 March 1883: 2. https://timesmachine.nytimes.com/timesmachine/1883/03/15/106247648.pdf.

"The New Cliff House." 10 July 1895. *Cliff House Project*. *San Francisco Call*. http://www.cliffhouseproject.com/history/1895/1895.htm.

"The New Cliff House." 25 June 1895. Cliff House Project. *San Francisco Call*. http://www.cliffhouseproject.com/history/1895/1895.htm.

"The New Cliff House." 13 April 1895. Cliff House Project. *San Francisco Chronicle*. http://www.cliffhouseproject.com/history/1895/1895.htm.

"New Cliff House Contract Filed." 9 October 1908. Cliff House Project. *San Francisco Chronicle*. http://www.cliffhouseproject.com/history/1908/1908.htm.

"New Cliff House Opens." 4 July 1909. Cliff House Project. *San Francisco Call*. http://www.cliffhouseproject.com/history/1909/1909.htm.

"The New Mayor." *San Francisco Morning Call* 8 November 1894: 3. http://www.cliffhouseproject.com/history/mayor/N68368pdfFile%20-%20Sutro%20Elected.pdf.

"A New Railroad." *Daily Alta California* 8 May 1885. https://cdnc.ucr.edu/?a=d&d=DAC18850508.2.28&dliv=none&e=-------en--20--1--txt-txIN--------1.

"The New Road to the Cliff." *San Francisco Call* 2 February 1896. https://cdnc.ucr.edu/?a=d&d=SFC18960202.2.75&dliv=none&e=-------en--20--1--txt-txIN--------1.

Newitz, Annalee. "Mt. Olympus." n.d. *FoundSF*. http://www.foundsf.org/index.php?title=Mt._Olympus.

1906 San Francisco Earthquake. n.d. https://en.wikipedia.org/wiki/1906_San_Francisco_earthquake#Damage.

Norgate, Gerald le Grys. "Spencer, Charles (1674–1722)." *Dictionary of National Biography, 1885–1900* 53 (1885–1900).

Occam's razor. n.d. https://en.wikipedia.org/wiki/Occam%27s_razor.

O'Day, Edward F. "Varied Types: 347—Robert E. Cowan." *Town Talk: The Pacific and Bay Cities Weekly* 8 September 1917.

Otto Sutro. n.d. https://www.findagrave.com/memorial/178508916/otto-sutro.

"Pacific Railway Act." n.d. *Primary Documents in American History*. https://www.loc.gov/rr/program/bib/ourdocs/pacificrail.html.

"Pacific Railway Act (1862)." n.d. *OurDocuments.gov*. https://www.ourdocuments.gov/doc.php?flash=true&doc=32.

Palace Hotel, San Francisco. n.d. https://en.wikipedia.org/wiki/Palace_Hotel,_San_Francisco.

Pan Amalgamation. n.d. https://en.wikipedia.org/wiki/Pan_amalgamation#Washoe_process.

Pan amalgamation-Washoe process. n.d. https://en.wikipedia.org/wiki/Pan_amalgamation.

"Panama Railroad." n.d. M Kalano. 16 April 2018. http://www.dickholt.net/images/605_originalline.jpg.

"Passenger Lists: San Francisco 1800s." n.d. *The Maritime Heritage Project—San Francisco 1846–1899*. http://www.maritimeheritage.org/passengers/SS-California-21November1850.html.

Perry, Victor Elmo. "Pass Bearer Through Lines." 18 April 1956. *Virtual Museum of the City of San Francisco*. http://www.sfmuseum.org/hist3/perry.html.

Philip Deidesheimer. n.d. https://en.wikipedia.org/wiki/Philip_Deidesheimer.

"Philip Deidesheimer: Jewish Mine Support Engineer of the Comstock Lode, Virginia City, Nevada." 5 September 2014. *Jewish Museum of the American West*. http://www.jmaw.org/deidesheimer-jewish-nevada/.

Photographs of W.C. Ralston and His Mansion in Belmont, Calif., 1872–1874. n.d. 17 April 2018. http://www.oac.cdlib.org/findaid/ark:/13030/tf3t1nb6b1/entire_text/.

Plessis, Alain. *The history of banks in France*. January 2003. http://www.euro.fbf.fr/en/files/888HK2/History_banks_france_EN.pdf.

Polk, James K. "Fourth Annual Message." n.d. *The American Presidency Project*. Ed. Gerhard Peters and John T. Woolley. http://www.presidency.ucsb.edu/ws/index.php?pid=29489.

Pony Express. n.d. https://en.wikipedia.org/wiki/Pony_Express#Eastbound.

Pony Express debuts. n.d. https://www.history.com/this-day-in-history/pony-express-debuts.

Proctor, Jacqueline. *Adolph Sutro*. n.d. https://mtdavidson.org/adolph-sutro/.

Proctor, Jacqueline. "The Father of Tree Planting in California." June 2014. *MtDavidson.org*. https://mtdavidson.org/the-father-of-tree-planting-in-california/#sdendnote23sym.

Purkey, B. W., and L. J. Garside. *Geologic and Natural History Tours in the Reno Area*. Vol. SP19. Reno: Nevada Bureau of Mines and Geology, 1995.

"Railroad Men Scramble for Sutro's Line." *San Francisco Call* 18 October 1899. https://cdnc.ucr.edu/?a=d&d=SFC18991018.2.146&dliv=none&e=-------en--20--1--txt-txIN--------1.

Raymond, R. W. *Report to Congress*. Annual. Washington, D.C., 1868.

"Real Estate Transactions." *San Francisco Call* 26 April 1895. https://cdnc.ucr.edu/?a=d&d=SFC18950426.2.152&e=-------en--20--1--txt-txIN--------1.

"Real Estate Transactions." *San Francisco Call* 16 May 1895. https://cdnc.ucr.edu/?a=d&d=SFC18950516.2.189&e=-------en--20--1--txt-txIN--------1.

"Real Estate Transactions." *San Francisco Call* 2 September 1895. https://cdnc.ucr.edu/cgi-bin/cdnc?a=d&d=SFC18950902.2.152&srpos=12&e=--1888---1900--en--20-SFC-1--txt-txIN-Clara+Kluge-ARTICLE------1.

"Real Estate Transactions." *San Francisco Call* 10 October 1895: 12. https://cdnc.ucr.edu/?a=d&d=SFC18951010.2.171&e=-------en--20--1--txt-txIN--------1.

"Real Estate Transactions." *San Francisco Call* 5 June 1898: 14. https://cdnc.ucr.edu/cgi-bin/cdnc?a=d&d=SFC18980605.2.110.3&srpos=10&e=--

1888---1900--en--20-SFC-1--txt-txIN-Clara+Kluge-------1.

"Real Estate Transactions." *San Francisco Call* July 19, 1902; July 19, 1903; December 21, 1904; January 13, 1905; January 24, 1905; February 4, 1905; February 15, 1905; February 25, 1905; March 2, 1905; June 13, 1905; June 23, 1905; July 26, 1905; February 15, 1906.

"Recent Sales of City Realty." *San Francisco Call* 18 January 1913. https://cdnc.ucr.edu/cgi-bin/cdnc?a=d&d=SFC19130118.2.184&srpos=28&e=-02-1898---2010--en--50-SFC-1-byDA-txt-txIN-%22Clara+Kluge%22-------1.

"Reid & Reid." n.d. *Wikipedia.* https://en.wikipedia.org/wiki/Reid_%26_Reid.

"Reid Brothers, Architects (Partners)." n.d. *PCAD.* http://pcad.lib.washington.edu/firm/284/.

Report of the Commissioners and Evidence in Regard to The Sutro Tunnel and Report of the Committee. Washington: Government Printing Office, 1872.

Reports of Cases Determined in the Supreme Court of the State of California. 25 November 1901. https://play.google.com/books/reader?id=rV0WAQAAIAAJ&hl=en&pg=GBS.PA580.

"The Retreat of the Mayor of San Francisco." *Industry* September 1895: 515–517.

Rising Tide. n.d. Smithsonian Institution. 10 April 2018. https://postalmuseum.si.edu/makingway/p3.html.

"Rosa Victoria Sutro Morbio." n.d. *Find a Grave.* https://www.findagrave.com/memorial/76280692/rosa-victoria-morbio.

Rosenbaum, Fred. *Cosmopolitans—A Social and Cultural History of the Jews of the San Francisco Bay Area.* Berkeley: University of California Press, 2009.

Roth, Arnold. "Stockton's Jewish Community and Temple Israel." n.d. *Temple Israel Stockton.* http://www.templeisraelstockton.com/about-us/our-history?tmpl=component&type=raw.

Routes to the Rush! n.d. http://questgarden.com/147/47/9/120826095515/process.htm.

Rubissow, Ariel. *Cliff House & Lands End—San Francisco's Seaside Retreat.* Golden Gate National Park Association, 1993.

Sachar, Howard. "German Jewish Immigrants." n.d. *My Jewish Learning.* https://www.myjewishlearning.com/article/german-jewish-immigrants/.

"Saltwater Bathing for the People. Grand Opening of a Superb Palace of Water." *San Francisco Evening Bulletin* 7 April 1894.

Samuel Brannan. n.d. https://en.wikipedia.org/wiki/Samuel_Brannan.

San Francisco Committee of Vigilance. n.d. 18 April 2018. https://en.wikipedia.org/wiki/San_Francisco_Committee_of_Vigilance.

"San Francisco Gold Rush Chronology—1846–1849." n.d. *The Virtual Museum of the City of San Francisco.* http://www.sfmuseum.net/hist/chron1.html#TOP.

San Francisco—Its Builders Past and Present. Chicago: S. J. Clarke Publishing Co., 1913. http://www.ebooksread.com/Authors-eng/sj-clarke-publishing-company/san-francisco—its-builders-past-and-present—pictorial-and-biographical-vol-fna/1-san-francisco—its-builders-past-and-present—pictorial-and-biographical-vol-fna.shtml.

Saperstein, Susan. "Sutro's Triumph of Light Statue." n.d. *SFCityGuides.* http://www.sfcityguides.org/public_guidelines.html?article=1214&submitted=TRUE&srch_text=&submitted2=&topic=B#.

"Science of the Comstock—Chemistry." n.d. Nevada Bureau of Mines and Geology. http://www.nbmg.unr.edu/scienceeducation/ScienceOfTheComstock/Chemistry-Ore.html.

Science of the Comstock—Environmental. n.d. Nevada Bureau of Mines and Geology. http://www.nbmg.unr.edu/scienceeducation/ScienceOfTheComstock/Environment-InfluenceOfMining.html.

Scott, Reva. *Samuel Brannan and The Golden Fleece: A Biography.* Kessinger Publishing, LLC, 2010.

"The Seal Rocks." *The San Francisco Call* 12 September 1903: 6. http://www.cliffhouseproject.com/environs/sealrocks/The%20San%20Francisco%20Call%20-%20Sept%2012,%20190303.pdf.

Shaffer, Marc. *American Jerusalem—Jews and the Making of San Francisco.* Ed. Stephanie Mechura. Prod. Jackie Krentzman. San Francisco: Afterimage Public Media, 2013. DVD.

Shamberger, Hugh A. *The Story of the Water Supply for the Comstock.* 1972. US Government Printing Office. https://pubs.usgs.gov/pp/0779/report.pdf.

"Ship Passengers—Sea Captains." n.d. *The Maritime Heritage Project.* https://www.maritimeheritage.org/passengers/br073146.htm.

"Shipwreck of the Parallel." 16 January 1887. *Cliff House Project.* http://www.cliffhouseproject.com/history/parallel/parallel.htm.

Smith, Grant H. "The History of the Comstock Lode 1850–1920." 1 July 1943. Google.com. University of Nevada. https://books.google.com/books?id=8q_TOO4CmDwC&pg=PA227&lpg=PA227&dq=M.+G.+Gillette,+comstock+lode&source=bl&ots=N5Gcw5xelw&sig=Gzf6CiYIBwR-70IXqgF4ZUteLiU&hl=en&sa=X&ved=2ahUKEwjp2rHQxdjcAhXJuVMKHc2rCiMQ6AEwBHoECAcQAQ#v=onepage&q=M.%20G.%20Gillette%2C%20.

Smith, Grant H., and Joseph V. Tingley. *The History of the Comstock Lode, 1850–1997.* Reno: University of Nevada Press, 1998.

Smith, James R. *San Francisco's Lost Landmarks.* Fresno: Craven Street Books, 2005.

Spahn, Martin. "Kulturkampf." 1910. *The Catholic Encyclopedia.* Ed. Kevin Knight. http://www.newadvent.org/cathen/08703b.htm.

Spidell, Jason, and Robert R. Kautz. "Historic Properties Treatment Plan for Mitigation of Historic Sites within the Comstock Mining, LLC Right-of-Way Permit, Storey County, Nevada." n.d. *U.S. Bureau of Land Management.* https://eplanning.blm.gov/epl-front-office/projects/nepa/35610/70945/77641/Attachment_3_-_Historic_Properties_Treatment_Plan_-_Historic_Site_Redacted.pdf.

SS Yankee Blade. n.d. Maritime Heritage.org. 16 April 2018. http://www.maritimeheritage.org/captains/SS-Yankee-Blade-30September1854.html.

Steamships on the Panama Route—Both Atlantic and Pacific. n.d. 6 April 2018. http://www.theshipslist.com/ships/descriptions/panamafleet.shtml.

"Sterilizers for Bath Houses." *San Francisco Examiner* 19 September 1900: 24. https://www.newspapers.com/image/457703116/?terms=Sterilizers.

Stern, Mark Abbott. *Beyond the Tunnel: The Second Life of Adolph Sutro.* Self-published, 2018.

Stewart, R.E. *Adolph Sutro—A Biography.* Berkeley, CA: Howell-North, 1962.

Strong, Gary E. "Reflections on the Sutro Library." *California State Library Foundation Bulletin* 2012.

"Supreme Court Ends Struggle." *San Francisco Call* 14 May 1903.

"Sutro." 1919. *American biography: A New Cyclopedia, Volume 5.* Ed. William Richard Cutter. The American Historical Society. http://www.delabrede.com/Windmuller/Sutro.html.

Sutro, Adolph. *The Advantages and Necessity of a Deep Drain Tunnel for the Great Comstock Ledge.* San Francisco, 1865. https://ia800306.us.archive.org/30/items/advantagesnecess00sutrrich/advantagesnecess00sutrrich.pdf.

_____. *Closing Argument of Adolph Sutro on the Bill Before Congress to Aid The Sutro Tunnel.* Washington: House of Representatives, 1872. file:///D:/Word/Book%20Publication/Adolph%20Sutro/09%20Mr%20Sutro%20Goes%20to%20Washoe--1859--1860/Closing_Argument_on%20the%20Sutor%20Tunnel.pdf.

_____. *1851: Samuel Whittaker and Robert McKenzie Lynched in San Francisco.* n.d. 18 April 2018. http://www.executedtoday.com/2015/08/24/1851-samuel-whittaker-and-robert-mckenzie-lynched-in-san-francisco/.

_____. "The Engineering and Mining Journal." 15 November 1879. google.com/books. https://books.google.com/books?id=8sVRAQAAIAAJ-&pg=PA387&lpg=PA387&dq=Engineering+and+Mining+Journal+November+15,+1879&source=bl&ots=I890EqByz6&sig=VCtFcg4Bin nrkrRyywAXVV289Lc&hl=en&sa=X&ved=0ah UKEwjnn_rZqYPcAhUF3FMKHXySAdg Q6AEITjAE#v=onepage&q=Engineering.

_____. "Engineering and Mining Journal." 30 November 1878. google.com/books. https://play.google.com/books/reader?id=8OQ-AQAA MAAJ&printsec=frontcover&output=reader& hl=en&pg=GBS.RA15-PA385.

_____. "Lecture on Mines and Mining." *The Daily Independent—Supplement* 31 October 1874.

_____. "Letter to his brother, Sali." 1 December 1850.

_____. "Letter to his family." Stockton, 29 August 1851.

_____. "Letter to his mother." Memel, Fall 1849.

_____. "Letter to Mr. D. Bethel." San Francisco, 12 November 1869.

_____. "Letter to the Regents of the University of California and to the Committee of Affiliated Colleges on the Selection of a Site for the Affiliated Colleges." September 5, 1895.

_____. "A Trip to Washoe." *Daily Alta California* 11 April 1860. https://cdnc.ucr.edu/cgi-bin/cdnc?a=d&d=DAC18600411.2.13&e=-------en--20--1--txt-txIN--------1.

_____. "A Trip to Washoe." *Daily Alta California.* 13 April 1860. https://cdnc.ucr.edu/cgi-bin/cdnc?a=d&d=DAC18600413.2.18&e=-------en--20--1--txt-txIN--------1.

_____. "A Trip to Washoe." *Daily Alta California* 14 April 1860. https://cdnc.ucr.edu/cgi-bin/cdnc?a=d&d=DAC18600414&e=-------en--20--1--txt-txIN--------1.

Sutro, Adolph Newton. "Will Erect First Division Monument." June 1920. *California Legion Monthly.* American Legion. https://books.google.com/books?id=sdI3AQAAMAAJ&pg=RA2-PA 22&lpg=RA2-PA22& dq=adolph+newton+sutro &source=bl&ots=wBxFFUXJco&sig=rb3Woz 9MAZkA-Act50enQ_sx3Ds&hl=en&sa=X&ved =2ahUKEwjTn7Oy 3qveAhXlp1kKHQqhCbEQ 6AEwDnoECAI QAQ#v=onepage&q=adolph% 20newton%20sutro&f=fa.

Sutro, Leah. "The Last Will and Testament of Leah Sutro." 24 August 2001. *Mayor Adolph Sutro— various newly-released documents.* http://www.ststlocations.com/Archives/Genealogy/Sutro/.

Sutro, Theodore. *Report to the Stockholders of The Sutro Tunnel Company and The Sutro Tunnel.* July 1887. https://archive.org/stream/sutrotunnel comp00compgoog/sutrotunnelcomp00comp-goog_djvu.txt.

Sutro Baths. n.d. http://www.cliffhouseproject.com/environs/sutrobaths/sutro_baths.htm.

"The Sutro Baths Are Rapidly Nearing Completion." *San Francisco Call* 27 August 1893. https://cdnc.ucr.edu/cgi-bin/cdnc?a=d&d=SFC1893 0827.2.74&srpos=1&e=-27-08-1893-27-08-1893--en--20-SFC-1--txt-txIN-Sutro-------1.

"Sutro for Mayor—The People's Party After Him." *San Francisco Call* 23 July 1894. https://cdnc.ucr.edu/?a=d&d=SFC18940723.2.136&dliv=none &e=-------en--20--1--txt-txIN--------1.

"Sutro Heirs Ask Shares of Estate." 6 August 1908. *San Francisco Call.* https://cdnc.ucr.edu/cgi-bin/cdnc?a=d&d=SFC19080806.2.70&srpos=41 &e=-02-1898---2010--en--20-SFC-41--txt-tx IN-Sutro+will-------1.

"Sutro Heirs to Rebuild the Famous Cliff House." 10 March 1908. Cliff House Project. *Los Angeles Herald.* http://www.cliffhouseproject.com/history/1908/Los%20Angeles%20Herald%20-%2010%20March%201908.pdf.

"Sutro Heirs Win Contest Over Lands." *San Francisco Call* 31 October 1905: 7. https://cdnc.ucr.edu/cgi-bin/cdnc?a=d&d=SFC19051031.2.97&e=-------en--20--1--txt-txIN--------1.

"Sutro Illness." 8 February 1898. Cliff House Project. *Los Angeles Herald.* http://www.cliffhouseproject.com/history/sutroillness/SutroIllness.htm.

"Sutro Saved." *Reno Gazette-Journal* 7 October 1881: 3.

"The Sutro Tunnel." *Engineering and Mining Journal* November 1878: 380–384. 7 May 2018. https://books.google.com/books?id=FpggAQAAMAAJ&pg=PA386-IA8&lpg=PA384&focus=viewport&dq=adolph+sutro+antwerp+to+new+york&output=text.

"The Sutro Tunnel and Its Projector." *The Engineering and Mining Journal* 30 November 1878: 384. https://play.google.com/books/reader?id=8OQ-AQAAMAAJ&printsec=frontcover&output=reader&hl=en&pg=GBS.RA15-PA384.

Sutro Tunnel Co. n.d. https://www.manta.com/c/mmz7lhq/sutro-tunnel-co.

"Sutro Tunnel Company—Resignation of Sutro." *Sacramento Daily Union* 2 March 1880. https://cdnc.ucr.edu/?a=d&d=SDU18800302.2.3&e=------en--20--1--txt-txIN--------1.

"The Sutro Tunnel—The Scene in the Savage Drift When the Connection was Made—Rejoicing Over the Event." *Daily Alta California* 10 July 1878: 4. https://cdnc.ucr.edu/?a=d&d=DAC18780710.2.44&e=-------en--20--1--txt-txIN--------1.

"The Sutro Tunnel united with the Savage Mine." 9 July 1878. *Virginia Chronicle.* https://www.nevadaappeal.com/news/lahontan-valley/the-sutro-tunnel-united-with-the-savage-mine/.

"Sutro's Bequest." *Leavenworth Times* 14 August 1898: 3.

"Sutro's Books." *The Morning Call* 15 June 1893. https://cdnc.ucr.edu/cgi-bin/cdnc?a=d&d=SFC18930615.2.102&srpos=3&e=13-06-1893-18-06-1893--en--20-SFC-1--txt-txIN-Sutro-------1.

"Sutro's Family and His Contested Will." 29 October 1909. *nps.gov.* https://www.nps.gov/goga/learn/historyculture/upload/Sutro_Family_sr_2014.pdf.

"Sutro's Heir Dead." *The Topeka State Journal* 14 September 1898.

"Sutro's Rancho San Miguel—1880." 9 August 1880. *Outsidelands.* http://www.outsidelands.org/detail/sutro-rancho-map-1880_big.php.

"Sutro's Separation." *San Francisco Chronicle* 12 December 1893.

"Sutro's Will Criticized." *San Francisco Call* 13 August 1898. https://cdnc.ucr.edu/?a=d&d=SFC18980813.2.103&dliv=none&e=-------en--20--1--txt-txIN--------1.

"Sutro's Will Is Read to His Children." *San Francisco Call* 12 August 1898. https://cdnc.ucr.edu/cgi-bin/cdnc?a=d&d=SFC18980812.2.72.

Sutter Hock Farm. n.d. 3 May 2018. en.wikipedia.org/wiki/Sutter_Hock_Farm.

Sutter, General John A. "The Discovery of Gold in California." November 1857. Virtual Museum of the City of San Francisco. *Hutchings' California Magazine.* http://www.sfmuseum.net/hist2/gold.html.

Sutter, John. "Capt. Sutter's account of the first discovery of the Gold." 1854. Virtual Museum of the City of San Francisco. Britton & Rey. http://www.sfmuseum.net/hist2/gold2.html.

Sydney Ducks. n.d. 18 April 2018. https://en.wikipedia.org/wiki/Sydney_Ducks.

Taber. *Sutro Baths-Cliff House-Sutro Heights.* San Francisco, 1895.

Tennant, Laura. "Sutro Owned 8,000 Acres in Lyon County." *Lyon County Reflections* 1997.

_____ and Jack Folmar. "Images of America—Dayton." 2015. Google.com. Arcadia Publishing. https://books.google.com/books?id=VsD2CQAAQBAJ&pg=PA38&lpg=PA38&dq=a.+Summerfield,+Sutro&source=bl&ots=YaVJT54R7W&sig=vMHEYj0pdbXIhME5txuMKpDxkE&hl=en&sa=X&ved=2ahUKEwiB-u2g0NjcAhWMVt8KHeG5D4EQ6AEwAnoECAgQAQ#v=onepage&q=a.%20Summerfield%2C%20Sutro&f=fals.

"Theodore Dehone Judah." n.d. *Who Made America?* http://www.pbs.org/wgbh/theymadeamerica/whomade/judah_hi.html.

Theodore Sutro. n.d. https://www.findagrave.com/memorial/126500043/theodore-sutro.

"Thirty-Ninth Congress." 25 July 1866. *Statutes-At-Large.* Congress of the United States. https://www.loc.gov/law/help/statutes-at-large/39th-congress/session-1/c39s1ch244.pdf.

"Thomas Bard McFarland." n.d. *Wikipedia.* https://en.wikipedia.org/wiki/Thomas_Bard_McFarland.

"Three Funerals—Funeral of Mrs. Sutro." *San Francisco Call* 12 December 1893. https://cdnc.ucr.edu/?a=d&d=SFC18931212.2.118&e=-------en--20--1--txt-txIN--------1.

The Tide Turns. n.d. Smithsonian Institution. 11 April 2018. https://postalmuseum.si.edu/makingway/p4.html.

"Tightrope Walk." 28 September 1865. Cliff House Project. Marysville (CA) Daily Appeal. http://www.cliffhouseproject.com/history/cooke/tightrope.htm.

Tingley, Joseph V. *Geologic and Natural History Tours in the Reno Area.* Sparks: Bear Printing, 2005. https://books.google.com/books?id=ekf0wBY8LyUC&pg=PA73#v=onepage&q&f=false.

"To Architects." *San Francisco Chronicle* 5 August 1891: 8.

"To Unwater the Comstock." *San Francisco Call* 13 August 1898. https://cdnc.ucr.edu/?a=d&d=SFC18980813.2.83&dliv=none&e=-------en--20--1--txt-txIN--------1.

Townsend, Edward W. "Adolph Sutro: Mayor-Elect of San Francisco." *The Review of Reviews* December 1894.

Twain, Mark. 3 July 1864. Cliff House Project. http://www.cliffhouseproject.com/history/clemens/clemens.htm.

———. "Frightful Accident to Dan De Quille." 20 April 1864. *Virginia City Territorial Enterprise 1862–1868*. http://www.twainquotes.com/18640420t.html.

———. "Mark Twain's Letters, Volume 4: 1870–1871." 1995. books.google.com. Ed. Michael B. Frank Victor Fischer. University of California Press. https://books.google.com/books?id=wDiDCnOP6lIC&pg=PA447&lpg=PA447&dq=Twain+and+Sutro&source=bl&ots=m4qVx5UDaT&sig=CRGwVJKz7jDbquF4Kq7_sOqxTmk&hl=en&sa=X&ved=0ahUKEwj30eLvuMzbAhVyp1kKHQnGBF4Q6AEIYzAI#v=onepage&q=Sutro&f=false.

———. *Roughing It*. Hartford: American Publishing Company, 1872. https://www.gutenberg.org/files/3177/3177-h/3177-h.htm.

———. "A Trip to the Cliff House." *Daily Morning Call* 25 June 1864. http://www.twainquotes.com/18640625.html.

"Twenty Thousand." *San Francisco Call* 7 February 1896. https://cdnc.ucr.edu/?a=d&d=SFC18960207.2.146&dliv=none&e=-------en--20--1--txt-txIN--------1.

U.S. Sutro Tunnel Commission. *report of the Commissioners and Evidence Taken at the Committee on Mines and Mining of the House of Representatives of the United States, in Regard to the Sutro Tunnel, Together with the Arguments*. Washington, 1872. https://books.googleusercontent.com/books/content?req=AKW5QaeJPn3wa63cIMYOH8JRPIgm8_y1wEGdYi3CVvPXTXb6yT2LideNlpIr39RRPPU68Cj_7OsDmkjc5tEX5vTOtuqkSKzvfFz0ADzNCt48IPKiPugVPYUhgyyMkvQWDRdLEcBACu-rXmAxg7OOc5umQdsWh271wkZ1N4vQcBK8XT_JrAbs9qimdfSRK2F-0skLcqss.

Virginia and Truckee Railroad. n.d. https://en.wikipedia.org/wiki/Virginia_and_Truckee_Railroad.

"A Visit to the Sutro Tunnel—The Town of Sutro." *Sacramento Daily Union* 28 April 1879. https://cdnc.ucr.edu/?a=d&d=SDU18790428.2.2.8&dliv=none&e=-------en--20--1--txt-txIN--------1.

Waldeck, Fred. "Adolph Sutro's Lost Library." *College and Research Libraries* January 1957.

Weiser, Kathy. "John A. Sutter—Boom & Bust in California." May 2017. *Legends of America*. https://www.legendsofamerica.com/ca-john sutter/.

West, Francis. "History of Sutro 1940–1945." 10 November 2007. *Around Carson*. aroundcarson.com/2007/11/10/884/.

"Who is Mayor of this Town?" *San Francisco Call* 3 July 1896. https://cdnc.ucr.edu/?a=d&d=SFC18960703.2.139&dliv=none&e=-------en--20--1--txt-txIN--------1.

Wilkins, J. M. "First Cliff House—1863." 6 October 1918. Cliff House Project. *San Francisco Chronicle*. http://www.cliffhouseproject.com/history/1863/1863.htm.

"Will Accept." *San Francisco Call* 24 July 1894. https://cdnc.ucr.edu/?a=d&d=SFC18940724.2.16&dliv=none&e=-------en--20--1--txt-txIN--------1.

"Will Face the Ocean." 27 January 1895. Cliff House Project. San Francisco Examiner. http://www.cliffhouseproject.com/history/1895/1895.htm.

"Will Soon Contest Adolph Sutro's Will." 16 November 1898. *San Francisco Call*. https://cdnc.ucr.edu/cgi-bin/cdnc?a=d&d=SFC18981116.2.74&srpos=57&e=-02-1898---2010--en--20-SFC-41--txt-txIN-Sutro+will-------1.

William Walker and the Transit Company in Nicaragua. n.d. 16 April 2018. https://nicatips.com/news/william-walker-transit-company-nicaragua/.

William Wright, aka Dan De Quille. n.d. http://www.onlinenevada.org/articles/william-wright-aka-dan-de-quille.

Wright, John Wilfrid, and John Lyman. "Surveying." n.d. *Encyclopædia Britannica*. https://www.britannica.com/technology/surveying.

Wyrsch, Tom. *Sutro's The Palace at Lands End*. November Fire Recordings. Albany, 2011. DVD.

Young, Bob. *Empire builder: Sam Brannan*. J. Messner, 1967.

Young, Otis E., Jr. *Western Mining: An Informal Account of Precious-Metals Prospecting*. Norman: University of Oklahoma Press, 1970. https://books.google.com/books?id=EQedpB0bxVAC&printsec=frontcover&source=gbs_atb#v=onepage&q&f=false.

Zollman, Joellyn. "Jewish Immigration to America: Three Waves." n.d. *My Jewish Learning*. https://www.myjewishlearning.com/article/jewish-immigration-to-america-three-waves/.

Index

Aachen, Prussia 13–15, 39, 133, 176, 206
Abbot-Downing Company 45–46
Acapulco 35
Adams, Edward 158
Ainsworth, J.C. 68
Alameda County 165
Allen, Mrs. George 12, 162, 218; *see also* Trundle, Hattie
Alta California 6, 16, 23
Alvarado, Juan Bautista 16
American Flat cyanide mill 223
American Hotel, Panama City 34
American River 17–19, 21, 24–26, 66, 179
Ames, Oakes 130
Antwerp 15, 169
aquarium 186, 196–198, 241
Arbor Day 173–174
Arcadia Ranch 214
Arizona 23
Arizona Comstock Company 223
Aron, Joseph 90, 111, 124–125, 148, 164
Arrington, N.O. 74–76
As You Like It 170
Aspinwall, Panama 69
Aspinwall, William H. 31, 69–70
assessment 104, 106, 138, 140, 148
Atlantic (ship) 186
Atwood, Melville 43
Auction Lunch Saloon 139
Austria 15, 28

Babcock, W.F. 58
Baldwin, A.S. 219
Baldwin Hotel 160, 164
Baltic Sea 14
Baltimore (city) 15, 30, 37–38, 51, 92, 160
Baltimore Sun (newspaper) 32
Bank of California 67–68, 72–78, 83–85, 88–93, 98, 105, 113, 118, 120–124, 131, 138, 140, 142–145, 164, 225
"Bank Ring" 90, 98, 138, 140, 142, 146, 149, 164, 196; *see also* Ralston's Ring

Banks, Mr. 119–120
Barbary Coast 165, 183
Batterman, C.C. 121–122, 124
Battery Street (San Francisco) 39, 164, 209, 242
Beal, Charles L. 177
Belcher, Edward A. 216
Belcher mine 63, 66, 80, 93, 104, 156
Belgium 13, 169, 207
Bella Union Music Hall 165, 182
Belmont Estate 143
Ben Butler (sea lion) 173, 201
Ben-Simon, Zev 241
Bennett, James Gordon 86
Bernhardt, Sarah 194
Best & Belcher mine 93, 149, 224–225
Bethel, John D. 110–112
Bickle, George 94
Bickle, Richard 94
Bierce, Ambrose 55
Big Bonanza (book) 55, 95
Big Bonanza (silver strike) 140–143, 149
Big Brother and the Holding Company 232
Bigler, Henry 18
Billy the Kid mine 224
Birmingham, Alabama 14
Black, Jeremiah 149
Blackburn, Abner 41
Blaisdell, Marilyn 201
Blaisdell, Richard 201
Board of Supervisors (San Francisco) 143, 175, 214
Bonanza (TV program) 59
Bonanza Kings 8, 140–142, 146, 149, 156–157, 161, 194
Brannan, Sam 25–26, 38, 179
British Columbia 40–41, 159
Broderick, David 66
Brooklyn (city) 32
Brooklyn (ship) 25
Brother Jonathan (ship) 71
Browne, Ross E. 131–132
Bryan, William Jennings 170

Index

Buchanan, James 23
Buckley, John P. 179
Budd, Lieutenant 35
Bull, Alpheus 88–89
Bullion mine 93, 104
Bullion Ravine 137
Burleigh drill 149, 153, 157
Butler, Charles 165, 179, 183
Buxheim Library 207
Byfield Tract 165

California (ship) 28, 34–35, 40, 42, 50
California mine 66, 141, 156
California Star (newspaper) 24–26
California Street (San Francisco) 38–39, 50, 144, 164
California Supreme Court 218–220
Californian (newspaper) 24, 26
camera obscura 191
Campbell & Pettus 191
Cape Hatteras 32
Cape Horn 30–31, 35, 169
Carnegie, Andrew 142, 170
Carson City 8, 46–47, 49, 54–55, 98, 100–101
Carson River 48, 50, 52–53, 79–80, 99–101, 105, 107, 121–122, 133
Carthusian Monastery 207
Cass, Lewis 26–27
Catten, Panama 33
Celeste, Rosa 181
Central Pacific Railroad 86, 102, 127–129, 212
Chagres, Panama 31–33, 35
Charlemagne 13
Chauncey, Henry M. 70
Cherokee (ship) 32, 35
Chollar-Hale mine 58–59, 224
Chollar-Potosi mine 93, 121, 156
Church, John A. 59–60
Civil War 7, 54, 77, 93–94, 127
Clay Street (San Francisco) 39, 219–220
Clemens, Henry 54
Clemens, Orion 54–55
Clemens, Samuel 54–56; *see also* Twain, Mark
Clementine (ship) 16
Cliff House 5, 7, 165–166, 168, 170, 172–173, 179–195, 200–203, 205, 211–212. 216, 235, 238–239, 241, 245–247
Cliff House and Ferries Railroad 172, 200, 241–242
Coffey, Judge James V. 219, 245
Coleridge, Samuel Taylor 136
Colfax, Schuyler 130
Colley, Charles 191, 199
Colma, California 177
Coloma, California 17
Colorado 23
Columbia (ship) 16
Columbia River 126
Columbia University 158
Committee on Mines and Mining 79, 93, 114, 118, 124–125, 131, 149, 156

Comstock, Henry Tompkins Paige "Old Pancake" 42–43, 103
Comstock Foundation for History and Culture 228
Comstock Lode 1, 5, 7–8, 42–44, 47, 49–50, 52, 54, 56, 58, 60–61, 64, 73, 79, 85–86, 88, 92, 103, 113–116, 122, 138, 148–149, 151, 157, 161, 181, 212, 223
Comstock Mining Inc. 224
Comstock Pumping Association 226–227
Concord Coach 45–46
Congregation Sherith Israel 217
Consolidated Virginia mine 66, 104, 140–143, 152–153, 156, 161
Constitution (ship) 68
Contract and Finance Company 129
Convoy (ship) 68
Cooke, James 180–181
Cornell University 113, 209–210
Coulter, George T. 112–114
Council Bluffs 7, 17, 30, 128
Cowan, Robert E. 206
Crédit Mobilier 112, 124–126, 129–130, 146
Crocker, Charles 127, 179
Crown Point mine 60, 63, 66, 88–89, 93–97, 101, 104–105, 113, 149, 224, 227
Cruces, Panama 32–34
Crystal Springs Reservoir 107
Curie, Marie 247

Daily Alta California (newspaper) 45, 47, 184
Daily Appeal (newspaper) 180
Daily News (newspaper) 101, 216
Daily Tribune (newspaper) 170
Davis, Jefferson 126
Day, Captain 119
Dayton, Nevada 41, 160, 162, 226, 228, 230
Degrand, P.P.F. 28
Deidesheimer, Philip 58–59, 79, 99, 142
Delaney, John 150
Delgado, James 217
Democrat 26–27
Depew, Chauncey 194
DeQuille, Dan 55, 59, 95, 102, 110, 141; *see also* Wright, William
diamond drill 61
Diana statue 235
dividend 66, 87, 104, 138, 140
Dolce far Niente Balcony 169, 172
Dominion (ship) 68
Don Quixote 90, 164
Donner Party 17
Donohoe, Joseph 72–73
Donohoe, Ralston & Co. 72–73
Dubeld, Anna 16, 22
Durant, Thomas 128–130

Eggesteyn Bible 242
El Dorado 29
Emanu-El Mausoleum 177
EPA Superfund site 53

Erie Railroad 124
Eureka Benevolent Society 37, 90
Europa (ship) 28
Europe 13, 57, 92–93, 98, 110, 116, 122, 146, 159, 163, 169, 173, 206–207, 209
Exchange Street (Virginia City) 47

Fair, James Graham 8, 136, 139–141, 157–158, 161, 167, 194
Fillmore, Millard 26
Fillmore Street (San Francisco) 163, 176
Finney, James Fennimore "Old Virginny" 42–43
Flag Rock 184
Flood, James G. 8, 139–141, 194
Flowery Peak 47
Flowery Range 107
Folsom, California 44–45, 49, 126
Foreman, Henry L. 153
Forest Hill 174, 247
Fort Point 172
Fort Sumter 127
Fort Vancouver, Oregon Territory 16
Foster, John G. 113, 118–121, 124
Foster, Junius 179, 182, 184
Franco-Prussian War 94, 112
Frankenheimer, Bernard 37, 39
Frasier, Robert 239, 241, 246
Free Soil Party 26–27
Frémont, John C. 32, 35, 40
French Revolution 28
Fretz, Ralph S. 68–69
Froebel, Friedrich 213
Front Street (San Francisco) 47
Fry, John D. 66–67, 74–75, 142
Fullerton, Adolphine Charlotte 222; *see also* Kluge, Adolphine Charlotte; Sutro, Adolphine Charlotte
Fullerton, N.N. 222
Funding Bill 212, 214–215

Garfield, James A. 130
Garrison, Cornelius K. 68–69, 71–72
Garrison, Fretz & Co. 69, 71
Garrison, Morgan, Fretz and Ralston 71
Geary, John 66
Geary Boulevard (San Francisco) 200
Geefs, Willem 169
General Sutter Inn 22
Geneva Bible 242
Genoa 46
Gillette, M.G. 154, 161
Gleeson Library 243
Gold Canyon 41, 77
Gold Hill 47, 80, 86–87, 89–90, 95–98, 101, 131, 136–137, 139, 162, 223–224
Golden Gate 35, 172, 184, 186, 189–190
Golden Gate National Recreation Area (GGNRA) 169, 205, 217, 234, 240–241, 246
Golden Gate Park 165, 172–174, 181, 241
Goodman, Joseph 54
Goodwin, Charles Carroll 77

Gould, Jay 3, 124
Gould and Curry 50, 66, 80, 104, 140–141
Government House 50
Grant, Ulysses S. 93, 112, 130, 161–163, 194
Great Flowery lode 116
Greeley, Horace 30, 158
Grey Eagle (ship) 28
Greytown, Nicaragua 71
Grosh, Ethan Allen 42, 43
Grosh, Hosea Ballou 42, 43

H & N mine 138–140
Haiti 32
Hale & Norcross mine 58–59, 138–140, 156–157, 223–224
Hannibal, Missouri 54
Harper's Weekly (magazine) 144, 161
Harris, Leah (wife) 40, 159; *see also* Sutro, Leah
Harris, Stephen R. 28
Harrison, Benjamin 170–171
Harte, Bret 55, 194
Hawaii 16, 25
Hayes, Rutherford B. 194
Hearst, George 75
Hearst, William Randolph 75, 179
Helbing, August 37–39, 90
Hess, Greg 228
Heydenfeldt, Solomon 213
Hibernia Savings 188
Hilborn, Samuel 214
Historical Society of Dayton Valley 1, 108, 133, 135, 147–148, 150, 154, 226
Hock Farm 21–22
Hofstätder, E. 208
Holden, Edward S. 209
Holman, William 149
Home of Peace Cemetery 177
Honolulu 16
Hoosac Tunnel 149–150
Hopkins, Mark 127, 167
Hountalas, Dan and Mary 246
House Main Committee on Railroads 127
House of Representatives 79, 93, 112, 118, 124–126, 130, 214–215, 218
Houston Oil and Minerals Company 228
H.R. 2966 125, 130
Hungary 28
Huntington, Collis P. 86, 127–128, 194, 201, 212, 214

Imperial Empire mine 66
incunabula 207, 209, 242
Independence, Missouri 30
insider trading 124, 138
International Hotel 162

J. Paul Leonard Library 243–244
Jackson, E.J. 170
James, Isaac E. 99–101
Jefferson, Thomas 23

Johnson, Andrew 93–94
Jones, John Percival 93, 95, 149, 211
Jones, R. 20
Joplin, Janis 232
Judah, Anna Pierce 45, 127
Judah, Theodore 45, 126–128, 130, 212
Julia mine 156
Justis Mining Company 122

Kaapche, O.G. 14–15, 47
Kandern, Germany 16
Kelly, Eugene 72–73
Kelly, Nicholas 41
Kendall, C.W. 147–148
Kentuck mine 66, 93–97, 104, 139
Kern County, California 143
Ki, Ah 77
Kimball, George P. 142
King, A.J. 40
Kinkead, J.H. 161
Kirk, Jen 184, 189
KISS 61
Kluge, Adolph Newton 176, 219; *see also* Sutro, Adolph Newton
Kluge, Adolphine Charlotte 176, 219; *see also* Fullerton, Adolphine Charlotte; Sutro, Adolphine Charlotte
Kluge, Clara Louisa 176–178, 214, 218–221, 276

Laguna Honda Reservoir 173
Lake County 165
Lake Nicaragua 71
Lake Tahoe (Bigler) 46, 136
Landers, John 226
Lands End 8, 165, 172, 179, 196, 198, 241, 247
Lane Medical Library 243
Larkin, Thomas O. 28
Larrson, Robin 232
Last Chance, California 42
lateral tunnels 85, 157–158, 226
Lavelle, Millie 181
Law, George 31
Law of Parsimony 61
Lee, Robert E. 77
Leese and Waller 91
Leipzig, Germany 176
Leman, Walter 208
Lemme, Emil 191, 199
Leonard, Franklin, Jr. 227
Leonard, Franklin, Sr. 226–227
Leonard, Sarah Lee 226
Levy, Samuel 213
Lewis, William 185–186
Lexington (ship) 28
Librería Abadiano bookstore 208
Lincoln, Abraham 54, 77, 127
"The Line" 108
Lititz, Pennsylvania 21–22
Liverpool, England 92
Locke, Augustus 61
Loma Prieta earthquake 243, 246

London, England 28, 40, 56, 85, 92, 98, 112, 114, 146–148, 150, 160, 164, 170, 207–208
London Times 28
Lord, Eliot 63, 94, 99–101, 104, 117, 140, 141, 153
Loring Cut 223
Los Angeles 17, 26, 222
Low, George 138–139
Lucerne mine 224
Lucerne Vulcan Iron Works 107, 137
Luckhardt, C.A. 122–124
Lyon County 100

Mackay, John 8, 35, 93, 136, 139–141, 161, 194
Madonna (ship) 69
Marin County 186
Marin Headlands 165, 172
Market Street (San Francisco) 142, 164
Market Street Railway Company 165, 201, 242
Marlett Lake 137
Marshall, James W. 17–20
Martini, John 198
Mason, Richard Barnes 20, 28, 45
matrikel 9
Mayer, Carl Friedrich 207–208
mayor of San Francisco 5, 11, 28, 45, 66, 166, 178, 194, 200–201, 210–216, 219
Mazatlan, Mexico 35
McCalmont, Hugh 112, 146
McCalmont, Robert 112, 114, 131, 146–147, 150, 164
McCalmont Brothers 112–113, 146–147, 153, 158
McDougall, John 38
McKenzie, Robert 38–39
McKinley, William 194
McLaughlin, Patrick 42
McMahan, Candi 177
Memel, East Prussia 14–15, 32, 47, 196
Memphis (ship) 68
Memphis, Tennessee 54, 68–69
Mercer, Frank 160
mercury 50, 52–53
Merritt, Emma Sutro (daughter) 11, 205, 217, 220, 234–235, 242; *see also* Sutro, Emma Laura
Merritt, George 160, 207, 234
Mexican-American War 6, 17, 23, 25–26
Mexican mine 63, 80
Mexico 16, 21, 23–24, 26–27, 50, 208
Meyer, Helbing, Strauss & Co. 37
Miller, Captain 186
Mills, Darius Ogden (D.O.) 73, 78, 85, 145
Mining and Scientific Press 137
Mississippi River 54, 68–69
Montana 7, 43
Monte Christo lode 116
Monterey, Alta California 16, 36
Montgomery Street (San Francisco) 38–40, 67, 139, 209, 242–243
Monumental Fire Company 38

Index

Moore, Elliott, J. 177
Morbio, Albert 160, 177
Morgan, Charles 72
Morgan Mill 106
Mormon 18, 25, 38, 41, 46, 128, 179
Mormon Battalion 17
Morrow, R.F. 241
Morse code 109
Moss, George 209, 242
Mount Davidson 47, 103, 111, 174, 233, 247
Mount Olympus 175
Mount Sutro (Mount Parnassus) 174, 209–210, 242, 244, 247
Mount Tamalpais 165
mules 31, 32, 34, 44, 46, 49, 57, 99, 102, 151–154, 156, 226
Murphy, John 94
Musee Mecanique 5

Napa County 165, 188, 214
National Historic Landmark District 226, 228
National Park Service 167, 198, 234–235, 241, 246
National Register of Historic Places 226, 228
Negley, James S. 120, 149
Neptune Beach House 145
Nevada Bureau of Mines and Geology (NBMG) 61, 104, 106
Nevada Legislature 79, 87, 90, 100
New Archangel 16
New Granada (Panama) 70
New Helvetia 16–22, 25–26
New Mexico 16, 23
New Montgomery Street Real Estate Company 142
New Orleans (city) 69
New Orleans (ship) 69
New York Central Railroad 194
New York City 16, 25, 32, 35, 130, 181, 207
New York Herald (newspaper) 28, 86, 108
Newland, Wesley 113
Neylan, Patrick 1, 133, 226
Niagara Gorge Railroad 45
Nicaragua 45, 71
Nicaragua Transit Company 71
Nieto, Joseph 217
Nixon, Richard M. 227
Norcross-Savage mine 58–59, 224
North America mine 66–67, 122
North Beach 143, 145
Nye, James W. 54, 92–93

O'Brien, William S. 8, 139–141
Occam's Razor 61
"Octopus" 200–201, 211, 213
Odd Fellows Cemetery 11, 217
Ohio State University 59–60
Ophir mine 42–43, 58–59, 63, 67, 74, 80, 119–120, 122, 139–140, 143, 147–148, 152
Oriental Bank 85, 92
O'Riley, Peter 42

Ormsby County 100
"Outside Lands" 164–165, 174, 181
Overman mine 63, 66

Pacific Mail Steamship Company 28, 31, 35, 69–70, 127
Pacific Ocean 3, 5, 69, 71, 165–166, 168, 172, 197, 216, 235, 243, 246
Pacific Railroad Act 128
Pacific Woolen Mills Company 142
Palace Hotel 142–143, 145
Panama 30–35, 37, 40, 45, 51, 68–71, 90, 112, 127, 130, 179, 212
Panama (ship) 28
Panama Canal 30, 70
Panama Railroad 31, 70
Parallel (ship) 186–188
Parapet 168–169, 172, 193, 234–235
Parterre gardens 167
patio process 50, 52
Paul, Almarin 51–52
Peckman, E.P. 67
Penrod, Manny 42
Perkins, Fredric 209, 242
Perrin's 49
Peter Hattrick (ship) 15, 30
Pier 39 246
Pierce, Franklin 126
Pine Street (San Francisco) 39
Piper's Opera House 97
Plantin of Antwerp Polyglot 242
Playland at the Beach 203, 238, 246
Point Arguello 71
Point Bonita Lighthouse 186
Point Lobos 177, 179, 181, 239, 241
poker 76–77
Polk, James K. 23–24, 26–28
Ponderosa Ranch 59
Ponderosa Saloon 225
Pony Express 7, 49
Populist Party 200, 213
Potosi mine 80, 93, 113, 121, 156
Powell Street Railroad 172, 200, 241
Price, Lewis Richard 112–113
Prohibition 246
Promontory Point, Utah 128, 130
Prouse, William 41
Prussia 7, 9, 13–15, 29, 32, 37–39, 47, 92, 94, 112, 114, 172, 196, 206–207
Pyrrhic Victory 164

Ralston, James 77
Ralston, William Chapman "Billy" 8, 43, 68–69, 71–78, 82–85, 90–93, 99, 105, 124, 138–140, 142–145, 152, 164, 167
Ralston's Ring 143; *see also* Bank Ring
Rancho San Miguel Tract 165
Randall, Henry 71
Randohr, John 50
Rastede, Germany 107
Raymond, R.W. 103–104, 122, 124

Red Bluff, California, *Daily News* (newspaper) 216
Red Dog Saloon 232
Reese, Michael 143
Reid & Reid 245
Rensselaer Institute 45
Requa, Isaac L. 93, 113, 121–122, 124, 156
Richards, Samuel 150
Richthofen, Baron Ferdinand 79–82, 157
Rio Grande 23
Risdon Iron and Locomotive Works 137
Rockwell, John 15
Rocky Mountains 128
Rohrer, Ron 203
Romberg, Paul 243
Roosevelt, Theodore 194
Roughing It 56
Royal State Library (Bavaria) 207
Russia (ship) 92

Sacramento 7, 17–18, 26, 39, 44–45, 49, 50, 66, 126–128, 187, 212, 242
Sacramento River 17, 26, 44, 66
Sacramento Street (San Francisco) 39, 71, 211, 243
Sacramento Union (newspaper) 195
Sacramento Valley Railroad (SVRR) 45, 126
St. Francis Woods 175, 247
St. Joseph, Missouri 30, 54
St. Louis 16, 54, 66, 68
Salt Lake 18, 25, 170
Salvation Army 188, 211
San Andreas (lake, valley) 107
San Diego 17, 26, 36
San Francisco Bay 28, 35, 69, 143, 145, 172, 186
San Francisco Bulletin (newspaper) 143
San Francisco Call (newspaper) 143, 177, 188, 201, 209, 211, 214, 217, 220, 245
San Francisco Chronicle (newspaper) 162, 185, 194, 199
San Francisco Earthquake 107, 194, 242
San Francisco Examiner (newspaper) 205
San Francisco Mining Exchange 139
San Francisco Municipal Railroad (MUNI) 241–242
San Francisco Public Library 8, 175, 243
San Francisco State University (SFSU) 243–244
San Francisco Stock and Exchange Board 65–67
San Francisco Stock Exchange 144
San Joaquin River 37
San Jose 187, 242
San Juan del Norte 71
San Juan del Sur 71
San Mateo County 165
Sanchez Street School 175
Sansome Street (San Francisco) 37, 50, 145
Santa Barbara 36
Santa Fe 16
Santa Rosa 242
Sargent, Aaron Augustus 148–149

Savage mine 87–89, 91, 93, 107–108, 154–158, 161, 230
Schryver, Jim 227–228
Schussler, Hermann 107–108, 136–137
Scotland 137, 208
sea lion 165, 172–173, 179–180, 182, 201, 216, 246
Seal Rock House 179, 187
Seal Rocks 165, 172–173, 186, 201, 217, 246
Seligman, Isaac 147, 150
Senate Bill 16 148–149
Senate Committee on Pacific Railroads 127
Senate Judiciary Committee 149
Sharon, G.H. 76
Sharon, William 8, 43, 66–67, 74–78, 90, 93, 99–102, 105–106, 121, 123–124, 136, 138–143, 145, 211, 225
Sherman, William Tecumseh 20, 28
Sherwood Forest 174
Sierra Buttes 112–113
Sierra Nevada 17, 26, 45, 50, 96, 126, 128, 136–137, 157
Silver City 47, 162
Sitka, Alaska 16
Sky Tram 239
Smith, Henry 186–187
South Carolina 127
Southern Pacific Railroad (SPRR) 194, 200–201, 212–215, 241
Spencer, Charles 207
Spring Valley Water Company 107, 143
Sproule, Adam 69
"square sets" 58–59, 79, 99, 142
stamp 50–51, 102, 231
Stanford, Leland 127, 179
Stanford University 209, 243
State Library in Sacramento 242
State University of California 243
Stateler, J.W. 74–76
Steamboat Springs, Nevada 61
Steamer Alta California (newspaper) 39
Stephens, John L. 70
Stewart, William 84, 86, 93, 211
Stockton, California 37, 39, 212
Stockton Street (San Francisco) 67, 71
Stonehill, E.B. 162
Stoner, Harold G. 238
stope 58–59, 114
Storey County 100
Strait of Magellan 30
Strawberry Valley 45–46, 49
Strong, Gary 243
Stroufe, John 185–186
Stuart, James 38
Sully (ship) 16
Summerfield, Alexander 162
Sunderland, Thomas 118, 121, 124
Sunderland Library 207
Sutro (new town) 228–230, 233
Sutro (town) 86, 131–135, 157–158, 228–233
Sutro, Adolph, II (son) 159, 177

Index

Sutro, Adolph G. (grandson) 236
Sutro, Adolph Newton Kluge (son) 220–222; see also Kluge, Adolph Newton
Sutro, Adolphine Charlotte 220–221; see also Fullerton, Adolphine Charlotte; Kluge, Adolphine Charlotte
Sutro, Charles (cousin) 40
Sutro, Charles Walter (son) 154, 159–160, 176, 177, 216, 220, 246
Sutro, Clara Angela (daughter) 91, 159–160, 176, 177, 216, 245
Sutro, Edgar Ernest (son) 154, 159–160, 176, 177, 220, 245
Sutro, Elise (sister) 14
Sutro, Emanuel (father) 13–14
Sutro, Emanuel "Sali" (brother) 13–15, 30, 37–38
Sutro, Emil (brother) 13, 15, 38
Sutro, Emma Bertha (sister) 14
Sutro, Emma Laura (daughter) 40, 159–160, 165, 176, 177, 179, 207, 210, 218–219, 236, 245; see also Merritt, Emma Sutro
Sutro, Gustav (cousin) 40–41, 172, 200
Sutro, Gustavus Emanuel (son) 50, 159–160, 177
Sutro, Hugo Aron (brother) 13, 38, 51
Sutro, Juliana (sister) 13
Sutro, Kate (daughter) 154, 159–160, 177, 245
Sutro, Laura (sister) 13
Sutro, Leah (wife) 1, 11, 40–41, 50, 90–91, 159–160, 162–164, 176–177, 218; see also Harris, Leah
Sutro, Ludwig (brother) 13, 38
Sutro, Otto (brother) 13, 15, 38
Sutro, Rosa (mother) 13–15, 30, 207
Sutro, Rosa Victoria (daughter) 41, 154, 159–160, 177
Sutro, Simon (uncle) 13
Sutro, Theodore (brother) 14, 158, 207, 218–219, 226
Sutro Bar 232
Sutro Baths 3–7, 166, 173, 188, 194, 196–205, 216, 236–241, 246
Sutro Depot 241
Sutro Electric Railway 166, 194, 200–201, 212, 241–242
Sutro Heights 3, 7, 11, 166–177, 188, 190–191, 193, 199–200, 206, 209–214, 216–217, 220, 234, 241, 246
Sutro House 50
Sutro Library 6, 8, 41, 203, 206–210, 213, 218, 242–244
Sutro Mansion 133–134, 159–160, 162–163, 166, 226, 231–233
Sutro Metallurgical Works 50–51, 53, 105, 246
Sutro Tunnel and Drainage Company 231
Sutro Tunnel Coalition 224
Sutro Tunnel Commission 112–117
Sutro Tunnel Company (California) 111–112, 114, 125, 134, 148–149, 153, 158, 217, 223, 226
Sutro Tunnel Company (Nevada) 84–86, 88–89, 91, 93

Sutro Tunnel Company and the Sutro Tunnel 226–227
Sutro's (at the Cliff House) 246
Sutter, John 16–22, 24, 26
Sutter's Fort 17–18, 20–21, 25–26, 38
Sutter's Mill 15
Swansea mill 77
Switzerland 16, 22
Sydney Ducks 38

Taft, William Howard 194
Tait, John 245
Taylor, Zachary 26–27
Tennant, Laura 133, 229
Tennant, Stony 232
Territorial Enterprise (newspaper) 54–55, 59, 62, 63, 97, 98, 110, 137, 141
Tetlow, Samuel 165–167, 182–183
Texas 23, 128
theodolite 108
Thomas, C.C. 226
Tibbey, Edney S. 75–76
Toland Medical School 210
transcontinental railroad 7, 30, 112, 126, 130, 212
Treaty of Guadalupe Hidalgo 23–24
Trist, Nicholas Phillip 23–24
Triumph of Entropy 175
Triumph of Light 174–175
Tropic Beach 237–238
Tropic of Cancer 32
Troutt, Judge James M. 219–220
Troy, New York 45
Trundle, Hattie 12, 162, 217–218; see also Allen, Mrs. George
Tunnel Act (1866) 86, 112, 131, 148–149, 156
Twain, Mark 8, 55–57, 65, 92–93, 179, 180, 194, 198; see also Clemens, Samuel
Twin Peaks 173
$2 per ton 85–90, 112, 114, 146, 148, 149, 152, 156
Tyler, Sam 68

Uncle Sam (ship) 71
Uncle Sam mine 66, 80
Union Club 143
Union Mill and Mining Company 78, 106, 121, 140
Union Pacific Railroad 124, 128–130
United Comstock Silver Mines 223
United Railroads 242
U.S. Army 113
U.S. Mail Steamship Company 31
University of California 170, 209–210, 219, 242–243, 247
University of San Francisco 4, 243
Utah 7, 23, 25–26, 42, 128, 130

Vacaville 187
Van Buren, Martin 26–27
Vanderbilt, Commodore Cornelius 45, 71, 194

Vassar College 11, 159, 218
Veale, Thomas 58
Victoria, British Columbia 41, 159
Victorian Cliff House 7, 193, 195, 201, 205, 216, 247
Vigilance Committee 38–39, 51, 72
Virginia and Gold Hill Water Company 136
Virginia and Truckee Railroad 48, 89, 100–102, 105
Virginia City 1, 7, 8, 12, 35, 43, 44–45, 47–50, 54, 59, 61, 74–79, 86–87, 90, 92, 95–101, 103, 107–110, 113, 120, 124, 131, 136–139, 141, 146, 152, 158–159, 162, 177, 180, 185, 217–218, 223–226, 228, 232
von Dalberg, Wolfgang Heribert 207
Voorsanger, Rabbi Jacob 176
Vulcan Iron Works (San Francisco) 64

Wakelee, Charles 74–75
Waldron, Mr. 119–120
War Production Board 224
Warendorff, Helena (aunt) 13
Warendorff, Rosa (mother) 13
Warner, Robert 208
Washington, D.C. 12, 20, 22, 86, 126, 156, 218, 220
Washington Street (San Francisco) 39, 50, 139
Washoe (mountains, region) 41, 43–53, 80, 81, 102, 105, 124, 126, 136, 159
Washoe Pan Process 51–52, 105
Watkins, T.H. 58
Weaver, Ella 242
Webb, William H. 35
Wells Fargo 75

West, Albert 230
West, Francis 231–232
West, Lyla 230
Westport, Oregon Territory 16
Westwood Highlands 174
Westwood Park 174
Whig Party 26–27
White, Andrew Dickson 209
Whitney, Asa 126
Whitney, George 238–239, 246
Whitney Brothers 246
Whittaker, Samuel 38–39
Wiertz, Antoine 174–175
Wilde, Oscar 170
Wilkins, James M. 184–186, 188, 195
Wilson, John 186–187
Wilson, Woodrow 246
Woodfords 46
Woodward, Robert 208
Works Progress Administration (WPA) 234
Wright, H.G. 113, 118
Wright, William 55, 102; *see also* DeQuille, Dan

Yale, New Caledonia 40
Yankee Blade 71
yellow fever 30, 33, 70, 130
Yellow Jacket mine 63, 66, 80, 93, 94–97. 102, 106, 224
Yerba Buena 6, 16, 17, 25
Yerrington, H.M. 101, 107
Young, Brigham 25, 128
Young America mine 59

Zurich 107

www.ingramcontent.com/pod-product-compliance
Lightning Source LLC
Chambersburg PA
CBHW060337010526
44117CB00017B/2859